MW00800014

75 SAVE-AN-EYE GAMES

PLAYING SO OTHERS MAY SEE

Erie, Pennsylvania 2013

Address all correspondence to:
Linda Hackshaw, CEO
The Sight Center of Northwest Pennsylvania
2545 West 26th Street
Erie, Pennsylvania 16506

Cover Design by Bensur Creative Marketing Group

Copyright © 2013 by the Erie Lions Club. All rights reserved. No part of this publication may be reproduced or transmitted in any form by any means, electronic or mechanical, including photocopy, recording, or any information storage or retrieval system, without prior written permission of the Erie Lions Club.

Many newspaper clippings are reprinted with permission from the Times Publishing Company, Erie, PA. Copyright © 2013

Printed in the United States of America

ISBN No. 978-0-9895049-0-4

Contents

Dedications

Since its inception in 1939, more than 4,500 young men have competed in the Erie Lions Club Save-An-Eye All-Star Games. But it takes more than players to stage a successful football game. Coaches, parents, referees, ticket sellers, concession workers, announcers, media and others make this annual event something that people look forward to. The Erie Lions Club coordinates this monumental effort with the goal of providing an entertaining sporting event that raises funds to aid those who have difficulty with their eyesight. To all the people, who for the past 74 years have contributed to the game in any way, we dedicate this book.

– The Save-An-Eye Book Committee

I dedicate the time I spent in helping produce this book to my late father, Bill Camp. He played football and basketball (the only two sports offered) at Oil City St. Joseph High School in the 1930s. (I was a member of the school's final graduating class in 1962.) Dad was a true sports fan and gave me my first taste of athletics. Those early experiences likely played a role in my becoming a sports writer and editor. I remain in awe of Dad's amazing work ethic and resolve in raising a family of 10 children in a small home in Oil City. One of his favorite sayings was, "If something is worth doing, it's worth doing right." I attempted to follow that adage in working on this book. Hopefully that effort shows in the finished product.

– Jim Camp

It is with great affection that I dedicate my efforts on this book to two special men; first, to Tyco Swick for hiring me many years ago and allowing me the flexibility I needed to work, to raise my family and to explore my own interests . . . like writing. As the Save-An-Eye Game manager for more than four decades, Tyco taught me to appreciate the players, their families and coaches and the Lions who sponsor this fine event. He also shared his social servant's heart in the thoughtful dispensation of the proceeds of the Game to help those less fortunate; and second, to Bill Vorsheck for sharing his Save-An-Eye story with me with such conviction that it inspired the compilation of this book. I learned to love the Game from both of them.

– Linda Hackshaw

My work on this book is in memory of my father-in-law, Frank Ropelewski. He was an outstanding running back for Academy, but he never played in the Save-An-Eye Game. He graduated one year before the game was inaugurated. That did not stop him from coming back to Veterans Stadium as a referee for the games during four different decades.

– Joe Mattis

My connection with this book reflects my many years as a High School Athletic

$\mathcal{M}$y connection with this book reflects my many years as a High School Athletic Director and my involvement with District 10, Pennsylvania State Athletic Directors Association and the PIAA. My dedication is to a man — Bill Vorsheck — who was very involved with athletics at a variety of schools and who was instrumental in the development of this book.

– John Post

$\mathcal{I}$ would like to dedicate my contribution to this book to my late father, Louis "Rip" Ruzzi, who lost his battle with cancer 12 years ago. He was the ultimate sports fan with a tremendous passion for athletics and competing. He would have enjoyed watching this Save-An-Eye Football Game.

– Mike Ruzzi

$\mathcal{O}$ver the years that I have been associated with the Save-An-Eye Game I have had the privilege of working with great coaching legends and with journeymen coaches still building their careers. But to a man, they have all committed themselves to the game when their "turn" came. Football coaches are a unique breed, especially at the high school level. They are teachers, role models, even father-figures in many instances. They reach young men in ways that other forms of teaching can never duplicate. I dedicate this book to the coaches who have helped make the Save-An-Eye Game a sports and charitable institution in Erie County.

– Tyco V. Swick

$\mathcal{I}$ would like to dedicate this book to all the players who were chosen to play in the 75 years of "Save-an-Eye City and County All-Star Games," in recognition of the time and dedication these athletes and their families gave from their childhood through graduation. All the work, practices, successes and disappointments on the field contributed to their skills as athletes; experiences they would build upon in their later life to become men. To their parents who encouraged and supported their sons' commitment and effort. To the coaches who were teachers on the field of athletic endeavor. To the officials who volunteered year after year to make the game possible. To all the players who will be chosen to play in years to come. And finally to Linda Hackshaw, Tyco Swick, Mike Ruzzi, John Post, Joe Mattis, Jim Camp and Gene Ware for their time, experience and dedication to making this book possible.

– Bill Vorsheck

$\mathcal{I}$ dedicate my efforts on this project to the many children and adults who have been helped at The Sight Center of Northwest Pennsylvania (formerly Erie Center for the Blind) through their administration of the Save-An-Eye fund. More than $3 million in eye care has been provided to those less fortunate in this community because of the efforts of the Erie Lions Club through the Save-An-Eye Game. It is the people that we help that have inspired me to participate on the board of the Sight Center for more than 40 years and to assist with this book.

– Gene Ware

Foreword

After ending a 40-year newspaper career in 2004, I had visions of easing into a new lifestyle. Meeting deadlines, writing columns and getting paid to watch sporting events would eventually fade in the rearview mirror as the road to retirement beckoned. That was the plan. But, like many plans, this one drifted in direction.

Tyco Swick of the Erie Lions Club ignited the change in my thoughts about how to spend my first months as a non-member of the working class. After I addressed a Lions Club meeting, Tyco told me about plans to upgrade the organization's website. "We would like to expand our history of the Save-An-Eye Game," he said. I told him I would be willing to help. That was the answer the longtime game manager was seeking. He had dangled the bait and I was hooked.

I knew some of the background of the game after covering the event for many years for the Times Publishing Company. I likely used the familiar phrase "the second oldest all-star game of its kind in the country" dozens of times in stories through the years. I had known and interviewed many of the coaches and players who made the game a yearly must-see on the Erie sports scene.

What I didn't know about were the huge gaps that dotted the recorded Save-An-Eye history. There was no complete listing of the thousands of players who had competed, nor did a summary of the games exist. This was the job I stepped into, not realizing the challenge that came with the undertaking.

One trip to the microfilm room at the Blasco Memorial Library was all it took to convince me of the struggle I faced. My first spool of microfilm provided a cloudy look at the early days of the Save-An-Eye. However, in those days attention to detail was obviously not a high priority. For instance, many of the players were listed by last name only. Some had just an initial instead of a first name. And it was anyone's guess where many of the players went to school. There was no complete roster for the reader (or the researcher).

My goal was to secure a list of all participating players, including first and last names and their respective schools. I also intended to compose a capsule summary of each game. This daunting task was finally accomplished months later after many hours squinting at the microfilm. I joked several times that I spent so much time at the library that some patrons thought I worked there. I started my retirement by logging more hours than I had while working at the newspaper.

But, even after viewing dozens of microfilm reels, I was still lacking key information to complete my task. Next came numerous phone calls. I sought assistance from former coaches and players and contacted relatives of those who had participated in the game. I also talked to several high school librarians. Most everyone was more than gracious with their time. My research took more than six months, but eventually yielded a list of over 4,000 names, plus a short wrap-up of each game.

The time spent was labor intensive, but also brought much satisfaction. I enjoyed reading about the Save-An-Eye games through the years. Many of the stories were familiar. Several even carried my byline. Scanning articles from the newspaper long before I joined the staff in 1966 was informative. I learned a great deal about Erie's football history and the Lions Club game in particular.

I finished the first part of my work shortly before the 2005 game and turned the rosters and game summaries over to the Lions Club. Since then, I have submitted each year's game rosters and write-up for inclusion on the club's website. The upcoming 75th anniversary game set in motion the plans to publish this book. I quickly agreed when asked to assist with that undertaking.

I haven't been back to the microfilm room for quite some time. But I must credit the Blasco Library and the cooperative staff members there for helping to make this book possible. There are many more people who made contributions. I will not attempt to name each of them, but I am extremely grateful for their assistance with my research. Suffice to say it was a group effort. Without each of them this book could not have become a reality.

Hopefully many people will recall past games as they scan these pages. The Erie Lions Club has done a marvelous job of promoting this annual event for three-quarters of a century. Charity remains the real winner as thousands of Erie County residents have benefitted in the form of glasses and eye examinations. With the celebration of the diamond jubilee comes the hope that the Save-An-Eye Game will sparkle for years to come.

– Jim Camp

Don Krahe of Tech played for the East team in the 1941 Save-An-Eye Game. Don's brother, Jack of Cathedral Prep, was the quarterback on the 1948 West team, and Don's grandson, Mike of Cathedral Prep, was a lineman on the 2000 City team. The Krahes are just one of numerous families who had multiple members play in Save-An-Eye games since the first game in 1939.

Acknowledgements

This book would not have been possible without the contributions of many individuals. To ignore them would be errant. Each donation, whether it be a photo, story, or just a recollection of their part of the history of the Erie Lions Club Save-An-Eye All-Star Football Games, was valuable. Here are those to whom we are especially thankful.

- Members of the Erie Lions Club, which provides valuable funding to the Erie Sight Center from the game each year, for continuing to sponsor a quality football game each year from its inception to the present.

- Players, coaches, referees, family, or friends of past participants in the Save-An-Eye Games who allowed us to copy clippings and photos and other historical information.

- The Times Publishing Company, which opened its story and photo files, many of which have been reproduced. They are reprinted with permission from the Times Publishing Company, Erie, PA. Copyright 2013.

- Members of the media, especially Mike Ruzzi, Sports Director of WICU TV, and Jeff Kirik, Sports Editor of the Erie Times-News, who provided publicity for the book project.

- The staff of The Sight Center of Northwest Pennsylvania for hosting our committee meetings, for their efforts to greet and interview all those who contributed to this effort and for keeping the ship afloat while the CEO worked on the project.

- The employees at the Heritage Room at the Blasco Library where Jim Camp spent may hours spooling microfilm. Their assistance in the project was invaluable.

- Larson Texts, who guided us through the layout process and put together an extremely attractive book.

- Erie County Judge Daniel J. Brabender Jr., who lent his extensive Save-An-Eye files to the committee.

- Alyson Sandrock of Bensur Creative Marketing Group, for the cover design.

- John Huegel and Christine Erin Shewfelt for their quality photography.

- Bill and Betsy Vorsheck of the Vorsheck Family Foundation, who provided the financial support to get the book project started.

- And any others who may have been inadvertently overlooked, who added to the valuable information included in this book.

Introduction & History

$\mathcal{T}$he Erie Lions Club is part of the largest organization of service clubs in the world, Lions International. It is one of the oldest member clubs, receiving its charter in 1922 and becoming the first Lions Club in Erie County, Pennsylvania.

In its early years as a service club, the Erie Lions provided a wide variety of support to the Erie community, but in 1938 the annual Save-An-Eye All-Star football game, with its mission of funding services for blindness prevention and support to those with visual impairment, was established. We're told the idea was born around a lunch table at the Boston Store by a handful of men with a vision for great things: Gus Pulakos, Samuel P. Black, Sr., Dr. Donald H. Smith and perhaps others whose names are not recorded. The Save-An-Eye quickly became the hallmark of the Erie Lions Club and is now the second oldest high school all-star football game in the nation.

In 1957, a separate not-for-profit corporation was established to formalize the Club's focus on vision-related concerns. "The Erie Lions Club, Save-An-Eye Fund, Inc." was incorporated on September 18th with the stated purposes of "... sight conservation, correction of defective vision ..., and in general to assist persons having impaired vision." Its initial emphasis was to provide eye care to needy children since there were no government or insurance programs to provide eye exams, glasses, patching and the like at the time. Since the beginning of the Save-an-Eye, over 14,000 Erie County children have received the private-care equivalent of $3,000,000 in eye care services.

In 1965, the Lion member who coordinated the eye care program for children retired, leaving a void in the provision of services. Since the missions of the Save-An-Eye and the Sight Center (then called Erie Center for the Blind) had substantial overlap, the Center assumed administration of the eye care program and the symbiotic relationship between the Erie Lions Club and the agency began. The fund has since been expanded to provide eye care to needy adults as well as children.

It was, and is, a mutually beneficial relationship: The Sight Center provides the staff time and professional expertise needed to effectively manage the eye care program, and the Erie Lions Club provides funding, thus enabling each organization to better achieve their common missions.

Since the inception of the Center in 1939, it has been customary for its Executive Director to belong to the Erie Lions Club. Lion Tyco Swick gave that relationship added depth when he became – and continues to be – Game Manager more than four decades ago. The relationship between the organizations was a hallmark of Tyco's 45-year tenure as Executive Director and continues today in his retirement. In his words:

> 66 *When I became a member of the Erie Lions Club I confess that I had never even heard of the Save-An-Eye Game, much less comprehended its importance to those who played in it or to this community. After a period of relative inactivity in the Club, I was asked to be the County Team Representative; thus began my fledgling involvement with the Save-An-Eye Game. I agreed to perform that task because the game supported eye care services, not because I had any real appreciation of the game itself.*

One night at a County practice, a player from North East, Rodney Stage, now deceased, approached me and confided: 'Mr. Swick, you may not believe this, but through high school, every block I threw, every tackle I ever made, I had only one goal in mind – to play in the Save-An-Eye Game.' I was impressed with his sincerity, though at the time I still only vaguely comprehended the intensity of his enthusiasm to play in the game. But the seed was planted in my mind by him, and as my tenure with the game lengthened, I inevitably came to the same profound appreciation as Rodney Stage had shared. Since then I have encountered many other players and coaches as well, like Rodney, who mirrored these feelings.

The charity the game supports is crucial to its mission, but the game itself has its own existence. It is an esteemed local sports institution that most local football players aspire to play in. Yes, the game primarily exists to raise funds for charity, but players enthusiastically participate because it is an honor to be selected to play and an experience most do not forget. As we interviewed many past players in preparation for this book, their game memories were vivid in detail and reverently reported.

The experience of working on this book truly has again reinforced what Rodney Stage confided to me many years ago – 'It is an honor and privilege to be associated with this great game.' **99**

The compilation of this book has been a labor of love for many. I thank the members of the committee, the Erie Lions and all of those who contributed their time and expertise.

Enjoy!

Linda Hackshaw, Book Committee Chair
CEO, The Sight Center of NWPA

Lion Tyco Swick, game manager for more than four decades, in his element.

The 2013 Erie Lions Club

Front row (left to right): Linda Hackshaw, Tyco Swick, Catherine Valerio, Christopher King, and Douglas White. Middle row: Thomas Valerio, Robert Laird, David Schillinger, Dale DeMarco, Ronald Brown, Harjinder Sabherwal, and Timothy Baird. Top row: Richard Romeo Sr., Chris Shewfelt, Frank Riley Jr., Brett Hammel, Edward DiMattio, Stephen Squeglia, and Clarence "Carney" Metzgar.

Not present: Johathan Chase, Duane "Skip" Christenson, Gregory Deemer, Patrick Filutze, Robert Fisher, Harry Johnson, Timothy Mahoney, August "Gus" Picardo, W. James Scott, Robert Sensor, John Vogel, and Ernest Wright.

The Book Committee

The original idea of this book came from Mike Ruzzi, the Sports Director of WICU TV. When talking with Bill Vorsheck about the upcoming 75th Save-An-Eye Game, Ruzzi remarked, "Someone should write a book about it." And thus the book project was conceived.

The Save-An-Eye Book Committee conducted its initial meeting on January 17, 2013. A unique group encompassing multiple talents, the members decided to publish a book outlining the first 74 years of the Erie Lions Club Save-An-Eye All-Star Games. This was an ambitious undertaking considering they would put together a coffee-table style book in about five months and have it printed in time for the 75th game on July 26.

The backbone of the book came from Jim Camp. He had spent many months researching the past games and had compiled rosters and summaries of the previous 74 games. He came out of retirement to add his quality writing talents to the project.

Joe Mattis, who had worked for Camp as a Sports Reporter for the Erie Morning News and Erie Times-News before retiring, also began using his multiple writing, statistical and intuitive skills in putting the book together.

Gene Ware, who had already written and published several books, put a book outline together and added his publishing expertise to the group.

John Post bent over backward to be a rock solid presence by lending support to each of the committee members when they needed it most.

Tyco Swick, who had spent many, many years as the Save-An-Eye Game Manager, provided valuable insight with his inside knowledge of past games.

Mike Ruzzi added significant ideas about how to gather information for the book and other insights that added to the quality of the project.

Bill Vorsheck was a steadying influence on the committee, and he provided the financial support of the Vorsheck Family Foundation to get the project moving.

Linda Hackshaw imparted her proficiency as the chair of the committee and pulled everything together to get the book to the publisher.

It has been a tedious process, but with all members adding their pieces to the puzzle it became the quality product you now have in your hands.

The Book Committee

Front row (left to right): Eugene H. Ware, author and retired financial planner; Linda Hackshaw, CEO, The Sight Center of Northwest PA; and Tyco Swick, former Executive Director, The Sight Center of Northwest PA. Back row: Joe Mattis, retired Sports Reporter, Erie Times-News; John Post, retired teacher, coach and sports administrator, Iroquois High School; and Bill Vorsheck, director of the Vorsheck Family Foundation and retired teacher and coach. Inset (left): Mike Ruzzi, Sports Director, WICU TV. Inset (right): Jim Camp, retired Sports Editor, Erie Morning News and Erie Times-News columnist.

Chapter 1

In announcing plans for the first Save-An-Eye Game, the Erie Lions Club also established a unique way to cap the Erie high school football season. While abandoning their customary tag day, Lions members hoped to use funds from the contest to provide eye examinations and glasses for Erie County students in need. Cost of tickets for the December 2, 1939 attraction remained the same as for other high school games at the Stadium: 25¢ for students, 50¢ for adults and $1 for box seats.

1939: Save-An-Eye Kickoff

Coaches from throughout Erie County decided that the rosters would include 35 players each and the starting lineups must feature at least one player from each school. The East team included players from Tech, East, Wesleyville, Lawrence Park, Harbor Creek, North East, Wattsburg and Union City. The West roster had seniors from Academy, Strong Vincent, Cathedral Prep, Millcreek, Fairview, Girard, Albion, McKean, Waterford and Edinboro. Lowell Drake of Academy was selected as West coach, Jim Hyde of East directed the East team.

Unfortunately the game was played in several inches of mud after steady rainfall that weekend. The East scored first, but the West responded with a flurry in the third quarter for a convincing 18-6 win. Two of the West touchdowns were set up courtesy of blocked punts by Ralph Erven of Fairview and Bob Orlando of Strong Vincent. Erven's effort preceded a 1-yard run by Dick DiTullio of Vincent. Orlando scored himself after blocking the punt of Clark Tysinski of East. Tysinski and Vic Fuller of Edinboro staged a punting duel in the first half, broken only when Tysinski passed to Jim Flanigan of East for a 21-yard touchdown, the first in game history. Despite the rainy conditions, the Lions Club netted $1,600 for its charity from the initial Save-An-Eye venture.

East

Ray Alexander	Union City
Fred Alois	Tech
Charles Bendig	Harbor Creek
Art Chimenti	Tech
Travis Cox	Union City
Robert Ebisch	East
Joe Emington	Lawrence Park
John Emington	Lawrence Park
Leonard Fetzner	Tech
Ernest Finke	Harbor Creek
Jim Flanigan	East
Chester Gasconi	North East
Henry Hart	East
Robert Hayes	Lawrence Park
William Heath	Wesleyville
George Heath	Wesleyville
John Hunter	Waterford
Clarence Hutchinson	North East
Ray Justka	East
Milton Konieczko	Tech
William Law	Wesleyville
Al Lubowicki	Tech
George McQuiston	Union City
Louis Nardo	Wesleyville
George O'Neil	Lawrence Park
Mike Pfister	Tech
William Regelman	Tech
Art Romecki	Wesleyville
Robert Shepard	Union City
Walter Swanson	East
Charles Thomas	East
Clark Tysinski	East
Frank Voytek	East

West

Bob Barclay	Strong Vincent
Ken Beatty	Girard
Frank Bell	Academy
Henry Benczkowski	Academy
Bob Christensen	Strong Vincent
James Coursey	Millcreek
Richard DiTullio	Strong Vincent
Ralph Erven	Fairview
Mike Evanoff	McKean
Bob Formaini	Cathedral Prep
Vic Fuller	Edinboro
John Goodill	Cathedral Prep
Paul Graham	Albion
Andy Holup	Edinboro
Richard Knepper	Academy
Floyd Lawson	Academy
Wilfred Lohse	Cathedral Prep
George Luninger	Fairview
Ron McCoy	Girard
John McMahon	Cathedral Prep
Charles Miller	Strong Vincent
Wayne Norris	McKean
Paul Oberacker	Strong Vincent
Ed Onachilla	Albion
Bob Orlando	Strong Vincent
Harold Pfister	Cathedral Prep
Gabriel Popp	Cathedral Prep
Matt Rausch	Albion
Bill Rickard	Albion
John Roehl	Academy
Max Rosenberg	Fairview
Dom Sementelli	Strong Vincent
Jerome Seth	Cathedral Prep
Bob Shollenberger	Girard
Roger Soth	Academy
Charles Zimmerman	Strong Vincent

Head coach: Jim Hyde of East
Assistants: Eddie Abramoski of Tech, Hienie Anderson of Lawrence Park, Jim Manafo of Wesleyville, Bill Cummins of Harbor Creek, Ralph Van Stone of North East, Fred Pusch of Union City, J.J. McGahen of Waterford

Head coach: Lowell Drake of Academy
Assistants: Sam Kramer of Strong Vincent, Jim Foti of Cathedral Prep, Gus Anderson of Millcreek, Bob Arrowsmith of Fairview, Al Harper of McKean, George Mooney of Edinboro, Joe Leson of Girard, Ken Westlake of Albion

WEST 18 - EAST 6

*T*he inaugural East-West football game was played Saturday, December 2, 1939, at Erie Stadium. The field was ankle-deep in mud after 24 hours of rain. East's Clark Tysinski threw a 21-yard pass to Jim Flanigan of East for the first touchdown in game history. Dick DiTullio of Strong Vincent had a 1-yard touchdown run. Bob Orlando of Strong Vincent scored on a 3-yard fumble recovery for the West. Hank Benczkowski of Academy scored on a 28-yard run. Winning coach Lowell Drake selected Roger Soth of Academy, Ralph Erven of Fairview, Orlando, Dick DiTullio of Strong Vincent, Max Rosenberg of Fairview and Jerry Seth of Cathedral Prep as outstanding players. East coach Jim Hyde tabbed Tysinski, Flanigan, Fred Alois of Tech and Louie Nardo of Wesleyville for individual honors.

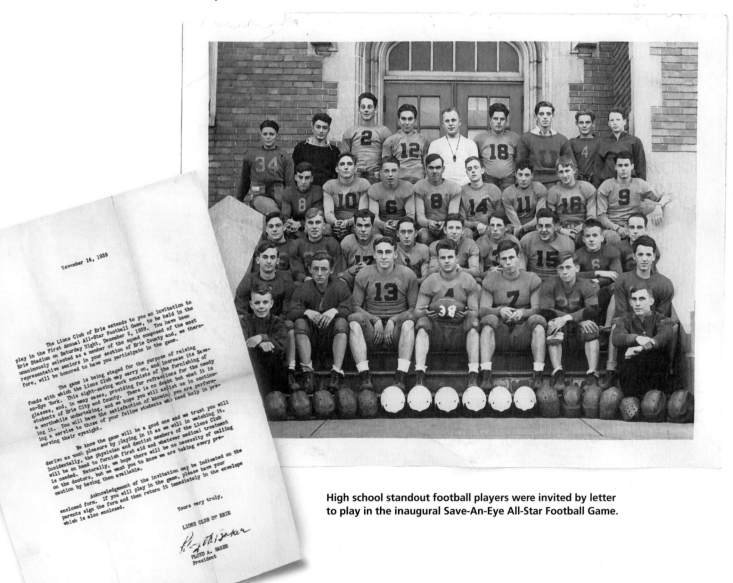

High school standout football players were invited by letter to play in the inaugural Save-An-Eye All-Star Football Game.

Recalled by daughter Ann McCoy Pompeani

66 He didn't talk much about the Save-An-Eye Game. He always called it the City-County All-Star Game. He said he played in the first game. He didn't talk much about himself, but he made sure we had the jersey.

Ron "Bud" McCoy – 1939

He lettered in 1938 and 1939 for Rice Avenue Union High School in Girard.
He coached at McDowell for Joe Moore until he had a heart attack in 1969 when he was 47. He died in 1991 when he was 69. Joe (Moore) got sidelined one time. He punched out Chubby Kuhl, the referee. Bud wound up taking over the head coach's position. 99

SATURDAY, DECEMBER 2, 1939.

EAST-WEST ALL STARS MEET IN STADIUM TONIG

GREET KICK-OFF IN 'SAVE-AN-EYE' F

Fans Show Interest In East, West Game

Coaches Commend Lions Club For Its Undertaking And Promise Full Cooperation; Merchants Lend Hand

By RAY PEEBLES
Dispatch-Herald Sports Editor

THAT loud roar you may have heard emanating from around 8th and State Sts. shortly after noon Tuesday originated in the Boston Store dining room, where members of the Erie Lions Club formally opened the ticket sale for their all-star football game to be played in the Stadium on Saturday, Dec. 2.

The roar from the Lions signalized the start of a campaign that is expected to pack the Stadium when two all-star teams from the city and county high schools lock horns for the benefit of the Lions Club's "Save An Eye" campaign.

The Kiwanis Club, meeting in the same building, got a sample of the Lions' enthusiasm when a couple of opportunists among the Lions donned the special jerseys to be worn by the all-stars and invaded the Kiwanis meeting.

Coaches Attend

Providing a real football background for the meeting was the appearance of Lowell C. Drake, Academy High athletic director, and Jim Hyde, East High athletic boss. Drake will serve as head coach of the West All-Stars, while Hyde will head the coaching staff of the East All-Stars in the charity game, the first of its kind to be played here.

Both coaches commented on the widespread interest being displayed in the game throughout the city and county, commended the Lions

in their newspaper advertising.

In addition window cards and automobile bumper cards are being distributed throughout the county.

Letters inviting the players selected by the coaches to participate in the All-Star game are being prepared and will be sent out in the near future.

In the meantime the Lions are going at the ticket sale like a jungle lion goes after his prey.

IT'S NEWS these days when PRICES

Albion School Band Will Play

Starting lineups for the East and West All-Star football teams ... the benefit of the "Save-... the West ...

left to right, are Matthew Rausch of Albi... Girard; Vic Fuller of Edinboro, and M... the East line, from left to ...

WEST WINS OVER EAST, 18 TO 6

Highlights Of East Vs. West Charity Gridiron Battle In Local Stadium

" I went to Albion High School then. It's Northwestern now. It was me and two other guys from Albion (Paul Graham and Matt Rausch) who came in for the game. I was a halfback.

My best memory of the game was just playing in it. It was a great honor. I felt really good about being chosen for it. As I recall, there wasn't a real big crowd. It didn't get worked up, being the first game. I think there were 3,000 fans there.

I was trying to wrack my memory to remember if the game was on Thanksgiving Day or on Thanksgiving weekend, but I just can't remember. But it was in that Thanksgiving time. After that many years, I don't remember who won. But it was a close game. We ran the double-wing.

(Rickard's West team beat the East, 18-6.)

Our coach (at Albion) was Ken Westlake. They had a couple of other coaches from different schools help him.

It's unbelievable the kind of uniforms and equipment these kids get nowadays. We had to supply our own shoulder pads.

Billie Rickard – 1939

When I got out of school that was the end of my football playing. I went in the Marines for 42 months. I was a fly boy. I flew on a torpedo bomber in the South Pacific. I was a radio gunner. I lost the end of my finger. When we were landing, I took my seat belt off. You weren't supposed to do that. We were going down the runway pretty fast and when he started hitting the brakes, the one on the left locked and we slammed into another plane. I didn't even know what hit me. I woke up in the hospital and the only thing wrong with me was they had to take my pinky finger off.

After that, I went to work on the railroad. I could have gone to college but I stayed right here working on the railroad for 41 years. I still live in Albion.

Now I do a lot of woodworking in my garage. **"**

One of Erie Lions Club members that helped start the Save-An-Eye All-Star Football Game in 1939, recalled by son Donald H. Smith

66 I went to my first (high school) game when I was 7 years old in 1934. Then I started going to football practices after school. I went to Jefferson School and I lived about four blocks from the school. I was allowed – even at 8 years old – to stay after school and not arrive home right after school was let out.

The players were huge people. I was desirous of when I got there to play football. I played for five years for Academy High School.

My dad (Dr. James R. Smith) and I used to go to the games in the Stadium. He graduated from West Point and he retired as a lieutenant colonel in the National Guard.

Because of his closeness from where he worked at City Hall to the Boston Store Building, he would get on the elevator and go up to have lunch with the Lions Club people. He joined immediately.

Dr. James R. Smith

His close friend, who was a spark plug with my father to get the game started, was Gus Pulakos.

I'm sure there were other people involved to get it done. My father was a very quiet man, and very unassuming. If he were here today (he died in 1957) he would not take any credit for this happening.

(It was the original group of Erie Lions Club members and others who started what would become the Sight Center in 1938 and the Save-An-Eye Game in 1939.)

I played football in seventh, eighth, ninth, tenth and eleventh grades. I never played my senior year. In tenth grade, I was captain of the Academy football team. I hoped to be in that capacity when I was a senior. I played for Lowell Drake. I played at the end of his dynasty which was 1944 when I was in eleventh grade.

The number one disappointment in my life was that I didn't get to play football my senior year in high school. I had pneumonia in 1933. I had my tonsils removed at Thanksgiving and came down with the classic pneumonia before Christmas. Dr. Norbert Gannon saved my life. I missed six months of school but I accelerated my subjects and caught back up and graduated on time. 99

Lions' "Save-an-Eye" Welfare

ALL-STAR FOOTBALL GAME

December 2nd, 1939

8:00 P. M.   Stadium

The Lions Club of Erie takes this opportunity to thank you for your support in making this game possible. In purchasing your tickets for this game you directly contributed to the Lions' "Save-an-Eye" welfare work.

Do you know that over 1400 pairs of glasses have been purchased for Erie school children? . . . that 150 repairs, 3 glass eyes and 3 cataract operations have been made possible? . . . that 30 white canes have been furnished to blind persons?

Through the support of folks like you, the work has been extended to practically all public and parochial schools in Erie City and County.

We, the Lions Club are sure that when you get an idea of the help you have made possible among the needy of Erie City and County schools, you will feel well repaid for your interest and co-operation.

THE LIONS CLUB of ERIE

Chapter 2

The East owned a 6-4 advantage in the decade, with close games the norm. The exception was in 1943 when the East rang up a 25-0 victory. That fifth Save-An-Eye game featured players from Coach Lowell Drake's powerhouse championship Academy team. Drake used an all-Academy lineup during the second half in rolling to the win.

The 1943 game was switched to the Saturday after Thanksgiving to allow Strong Vincent players to participate. Vincent played a game at Watertown, N.Y., on Thanksgiving. The 1940s also saw several games played under horrible weather conditions.

The 1940s

Besides the Academy domination in 1943, several individuals gave outstanding performances. Ted Morasky of Cathedral Prep, one of the smallest players on the field at 150 pounds, completed all six of his passes for 119 yards in 1941. Don Fabian of Strong Vincent threw for the only two touchdowns in 1942. This game had a tie breaker in effect. After several ties during the regular season, the coaches and Lions Club members decided the Save-An-Eye would have a winner. If the teams were tied after regulation time, each club would get four plays from the 50-yard line. The team gaining the greater amount of yards would be declared the winner. The tie-breaker was not needed thanks to the two touchdown passes by Fabian. Eddie Pasky of Academy scored all the points for the winners in 1944.

Ray Hedderick of Millcreek tallied the only touchdown on a 58-yard interception return in 1945. Chuck Brasington of East blocked a punt in the fourth quarter and went 24 yards for the only score in 1946. A crowd estimated at over 14,000 fans watched the West dominate in 1947, limiting the East to a single first down. The final game of the decade featured a switch in format, with the County players squaring off in the first and third quarters, City players battling in the second and fourth quarters.

East

Walter Bailey	Lawrence Park
Ed Bernik	Tech
Bud Bloom	Wesleyville
Carm Bonito	Wesleyville
Ed Clark	Union City
Clarence Cray	Tech
Bill Crotty	East
John Davis	East
Orvid Erickson	Wesleyville
Stan Flowers	Tech
Neil French	Lawrence Park
Fred Gartner	North East
Vince Gigleimo	East
John Grabowski	North East
Larry Hanlin	Union City
Ralph Hogan	Tech
Harold Hutchinson	North East
Carl Langer	Harbor Creek
Walter Lundstrom	East
David Lyons	Waterford
Jim Mahon	East
Steve Maxumczyk	East
Walter Morrow	Harbor Creek
Louis Newara	North East
John Pearson	Lawrence Park
Howard Proctor	Waterford
Mike Roszkowski	Tech
Art Thomas	East
Nick Triana	North East
Ben Winslow	Harbor Creek
Ray "Jambers" Wisniewski	Tech

Head coach: Eddie Abramoski of East
Assistants: Hienie Anderson of Lawrence Park, Jim Manafo of Wesleyville, Bill Cummins of Harbor Creek, Stan Ralston of North East, Fred Pusch of Union City, J.J. McGahen of Waterford

West

Jerry Baskin	Fairview
Bill Beatman	Academy
Pete Bricker	Millcreek
Walter Conn	Strong Vincent
Jack Erb	Cathedral Prep
Mike Evanoff	McKean
Russ Fratto	Millcreek
Bob Gay	Millcreek
Jack Hines	Strong Vincent
Bill Kramer	Academy
Pete Krivonak	Academy
Willie Krivonak	Academy
Jack Lally	Cathedral Prep
Roger Lamb	Cathedral Prep
Norm Manross	Academy
Joe McCafferty	Cathedral Prep
Jim McCarthy	Strong Vincent
Marvin Millspaw	Edinboro
Cyril Papson	Fairview
Jim Phillips	Strong Vincent
George Pulakos	Millcreek
Harry Ramsey	Academy
Jack Roach	Strong Vincent
Jim Roesch	Strong Vincent
Ernie Salzer	Millcreek
Roy Sedler	Girard
Mendel Sisley	Girard
Bill Stebinski	Albion
Jack Summerville	Albion
Walter Traut	Academy
Dick Weidler	Girard
Dick Weigle	Fairview

Head coach: Lowell Drake of Academy
Assistants: Sam Kramer of Strong Vincent, Jim Foti of Cathedral Prep, Gus Anderson of Millcreek, Bernard Harkins of Fairview, Al Harper of McKean, George Mooney of Edinboro, Joe Leson of Girard, Ken Westlake of Albion

EAST 12 - WEST 7

$\mathcal{M}$iserable weather conditions marred the second renewal of the Save-An-Eye Game. The Stadium turf was covered with ice, several inches thick in some spots, which made running treacherous. Many players switched from cleats to sneakers at halftime in an attempt to gain better footing. Walter Lundstrom of East scored on a 46-yard interception return in the third quarter for the winning touchdown. Clarence Cray of Tech threw a huge block on the play. Bob Gay of Millcreek tossed a 9-yard touchdown pass to Jack Lally of Prep in the first quarter. The score came after a 9-yard punt into the howling wind. Gay ran 21 yards to the 11 and three plays later, Gay and Lally teamed for the touchdown. Ray (Jambers) Wisniewski of Tech scored on a 5-yard run in the second quarter after Walter Bailey of Lawrence Park recovered a blocked punt on the 10. Wisniewski needed three cracks to bull into the end zone. The conditions limited the crowd to 1,200. Some young fans tried to keep warm at halftime by building a small bonfire in the stands. The police quickly forced them to extinguish the blaze. Bales of straw were given to each team. Players buried their feet in it to keep warm on the sidelines.

ERIE DISPATCH-HERALD: SATURDAY, DECEMBER 7,

EAST BEATS WEST, 12-7,

Lundstrom Runs 46 Yards On Int

FRANK SERFOZO

LIONS "SAVE-AN-EYE" WELFARE
FOR ERIE CITY AND COUNTY

All-Star Football Game

DEC. 6, 1940   8:00 P.M.   STADIUM

The Lions Club of Erie takes this opportunity to thank you for your support in making this game possible. In purchasing your tickets for this game you contributed directly to the Lions' "Save-An-Eye" welfare work.

Do you know that over 1700 pairs of glasses have been purchased for Erie school children since the club started this work? . . . that 200 repairs, 3 glass eyes and 3 cataract operations have been made possible? . . . that last year 120 pairs of glasses were purchased for students in 21 schools throughout the county? . . . that 195 pairs were provided for needy cases in 35 schools in the city? . . . that 35 white canes have been furnished to folks like you, the work has been extended to practically all public and parochial schools in Erie City and County.

Through the support of folks like you, the work has been extended to practically all public and parochial schools in Erie City and County.

We feel that this aid to the needy will be a source of satisfaction to all who have contributed, and that the gratitude of those benefited will amply repay you for your cooperation.

THE LIONS CLUB OF ERIE

Coach Eddie Abramoski is a local boy who made good in his home town. A native Eastsider, he starred in football, track and basketball at East High and matriculated at St. Lawrence University, Canton, N.Y. He was appointed athletic director at Technical High when the institution was opened in 1931 and has been there ever since, doing a remarkable job in basketball and track as well as football. His teams are always well coached and never fail to give a good account of themselves. On the road Coach Abramoski's teams are colorful drawing cards. He likes to see his teams win as well as any other coach, but he doesn't take defeats too seriously. Eddie's aim is to see that his boys get something out of athletics. This year Coach Abramoski succeeded Jim Hyde as coach of the East all-stars. He will be assisted by Heinie Anderson of Lawrence Park, Jimmy Manafo of Wesleyville, Bill Cummins of Harborcreek, Stan Ralston of North East, Fred Pusch of Union City and J. J. McGahen of Waterford.

Coach Eddie Abramoski

ALL-STAR LINE-UP FOR EAST TEAM

NUMBER	PLAYER	POSITION	SCHOOL
	N. Triano	Quarter Back	North East
14	S. Maxumczyk	Quarter Back	East
20	N. French	Half Back	Lawrence Park
21	C. Langer	Half Back	Harborcreek
26	C. Bonito	Half Back	Wesleyville
18	Crotty	Full Back	East
27	R. Wisniewski	Full Back	Tech
8	Gingliano	Full Back	East
7	W. Lundstrom	End	Lawrence Park
1	W. Bailey	End	North East
11	F. Gartner	End	Harborcreek
24	B. Winslow	End	Wesleyville
10	B. Bloom	End	Tech
16	S. Flowers	End	East
33	J. Mahon	Center	North East
31	L. Newars	Center	Waterford
6	Proctor	Center	East
28	A. Thomas	Guard	Lawrence Park
17	H. Pearson	Guard	North East
3	H. Hutchinson	Guard	Harborcreek
30	W. Morrow	Guard	Wesleyville
12	O. Erickson	Guard	Union City
15	Hanlin	Guard	Tech
32	R. Hogan	Guard	Tech
19	C. Cray	Tackle	East
4	J. Davis	Tackle	North East
2	J. Grabowski	Tackle	Waterford
23	Lyons	Tackle	Union City
9	E. Clark	Tackle	Tech
29	E. Bernik	Tackle	Tech
25	M. Rozkkowski		
22			

FOR WEST TEAM

POSITION	SCHOOL
Quarterback	Academy
Quarterback	Fairview
Quarterback	Girard
Half Back	Millcreek
Half Back	Millcreek
Half Back	Academy
Back	Prep
Back	Albion
Back	Vincent
Back	Academy
Back	Vincent
Back	Prep
Back	McKean
	Prep
	Prep
	Girard
	Academy
	Fairview
	Millcreek
	Academy
	Academy
	Vincent
	Vincent
	Albion
	Millcreek
	Edinboro
	Vincent
	Vincent
	Fairview
Guard	Girard
Tackle	Millcreek
Tackle	
Tackle	
Tackle	

J. Rocach
C. Papson
R. Sedler
C. Fratto

Game 3 – November 27, 1941

East

Swede Anderson	Wesleyville
Dave Brockelbank	Wesleyville
Joe Canella	North East
Frank Chimera	North East
Bill Coyne	East
John Dougherty	East
Jesse Hammerman	East
Art Hannah	Lawrence Park
Grant Hare	Union City
Mehnert Henry	Harbor Creek
Carl Henry	Union City
Art Johnson	Lawrence Park
Pete Kapetan	North East
Don Krahe	Tech
Ed Kubiak	Tech
Dick Langer	Harbor Creek
Bill Marinelli	Lawrence Park
Lynn McLean	Harbor Creek
Ron Nece	Harbor Creek
Harry Nye	Waterford
Harry Parker	Lawrence Park
Joe Patalita	Tech
Ray Pomorski	East
Walt Razanauskas	Tech
Bull Romecki	Wesleyville
Stan Salen	North East
Joe Shannon	East
Ronnie Shields	Waterford
Jerry Smith	Tech
Mike Varchola	East
Ed Yezzi	Tech

Coach: Eddie Abramoski of East

West

George Brece	Albion
Buff Burnett	Albion
Byron Clapper	McKean
David Crawford	Academy
Jack Cugnin	Academy
Bill Fabian	Strong Vincent
Joe Finney	Edinboro
Gale Fobes	Albion
Tom Franzkowski	Academy
Bill Getz	Fairview
Bill Grant	Cathedral Prep
Phil Haendler	Academy
Curtis Hinkle	Fairview
Al Holland	Fairview
Joe Holowich	Edinboro
Tom Lee	Strong Vincent
Bill Lossie	Millcreek
Calvin Love	Millcreek
Bill McCamey	Millcreek
Bud McClain	Cathedral Prep
Bill McManus	Strong Vincent
Press Mead	Strong Vincent
Ted Morasky	Cathedral Prep
Geno Posterti	Academy
Jack Quinn	Cathedral Prep
Len Rastatter	Academy
Joe Robasky	Academy
Bill Rusch	Strong Vincent
Jack Sadler	Strong Vincent
Chuck Skelton	Edinboro
Curly Stearns	Girard
Ed Strucheon	Girard
Lud Ulrich	Academy
Howie Weaver	McKean
Ed Zimmer	McKean

Coach: Lowell Drake of Academy

WEST 14 - EAST 0

$\mathcal{T}$ed Morasky of Prep directed a wide-open West offense orchestrated by coach Lowell Drake of Academy. Morasky connected on all six of his passes for 119 yards. The diminutive 150-pounder fired 17 yards to Bill Fabian of Strong Vincent and 35 yards to Phil Haendler of Academy on the first scoring drive. Haendler fumbled on the play, but the ball was recovered by Tom Franzkowski of Academy on the two. Morasky blasted into the end zone for the touchdown and threw a pass to Haendler for the extra point. Joe Robasky of Academy intercepted a pass and ran 47 yards for the second West touchdown. Robasky kicked the extra point. East High running backs Joe Shannon and Ray Pomorski and Jerry Smith of Tech starred in a losing cause. Bill Marinelli of Lawrence Park, determined to play in the game, drove in from Albany, N.Y. where his family was on vacation.

As recalled by his wife Mary and daughters Kathy and Randee

66 Bill graduated from McDowell High School in 1941 and studied one semester at Penn State University before he went off to the war with the United States Navy.

Bill McCamey – 1941

He talked about two things a lot — the Navy and the Save-An-Eye Game. They were both really important to him. He always went to the games and wore his player cap. His long-time friend and teammate, Cal Love, took him to the games for years when they were getting older.

I guess when we were kids we didn't think too much about it, but mom met some of his friends from high school at a reunion and we were all so shocked when they talked about dad as a 'football hero!'

To us, he was just a great dad and husband. He was as sweet and kind as he looks in that picture. 99

Game 4 – November 26, 1942

East

John Benson	Wesleyville
Roy Bernardini	Tech
Dave Bock	Lawrence Park
Harley Briggs	North East
Homer Bury	Wesleyville
Glen Crawford	Harbor Creek
Bernard Daugherty	Tech
Jerry Delinski	East
Bob Dishinger	Tech
Don Geraci	North East
Albert Johnson	Lawrence Park
Bob Kelleher	East
Ed Klimow	East
Pete Kosterman	Harbor Creek
Frank Lichtenwalter	Tech
John Lutz	Wesleyville
Bob Mahon	East
Bob McClean	Harbor Creek
Elmer McKay	Lawrence Park
Joe Newara	North East
Les Patmore	Lawrence Park
Ray Proctor	Waterford
Tom Rizzo	North East
Don Sangston	Wesleyville
Al Sarti	East
Chester Smogorzewski	Tech
Bill Stephenson	Harbor Creek
John Swanseger	East
Rich Wisinski	Tech

Coach: Eddie Abramoski of East

West

Eugene Bambauer	Strong Vincent
Seymour Baskin	Fairview
Don Bevilacqua	Strong Vincent
Lowell Blake	Academy
Bill Connors	Albion
Don Daggett	Girard
Bob Davern	Girard
John DeLiva	Strong Vincent
Dick East	Fairview
Don Fabian	Strong Vincent
John Flanigan	Cathedral Prep
Harry Fornalczyk	Academy
Bob Fuhrman	Strong Vincent
Gus Gladd	Albion
Mert Hinkle	Fairview
Bob Hopkins	Girard
Paul Kelly	Academy
Rich Ketchel	Academy
Walter King	Edinboro
Jim McVay	Academy
Andy Mukina	Edinboro
Chet Nyberg	Strong Vincent
Bud Sedler	Girard
Ben Skelton	Edinboro
Walter Taylor	Millcreek
Norman Tousey	Millcreek
Jim Vincent	Strong Vincent
Eugene Weidler	Albion
Joe Weschler	Cathedral Prep
John Wiley	Academy
Ray Winslow	Millcreek
Frank Wood	Albion

Coach: Lowell Drake of Academy

WEST 13 - EAST 0

*D*on Fabian of Strong Vincent accounted for both touchdowns, throwing passes of 27 and 21 yards for scores to Bud Sedler of Girard and Ray Winslow of Millcreek. Don Bevilacqua of Strong Vincent kicked the conversion. A 72-yard drive in the first quarter was capped by the Fabian-to-Sedler scoring toss. Sedler, converted from tackle to end for the game, took the pass on the 18 and broke two tackles on the way to the end zone. In the second quarter a blocked punt was recovered by the West on the East 20. After a penalty and a 4-yard gain by Fabian, the Vincent quarterback hit Winslow for the 21-yard score. Bevilacqua added the final point on his placement kick. The West threatened a final time on the last play of the game. Jim McVay and John Wiley, both Academy athletes, teamed on a 51-yard pass that ended with Wiley tackled on the East 17-yard line as the game ended. Les Patmore of Lawrence Park was a standout in defeat for the East with his running, passing, and kicking.

Overtime Play to Be Used If Necessary

BY RAY PEEBLES
Dispatch-Herald Sports Editor

WHEN East meets West in the fourth annual Lions Club "Save An Eye" football game at the Stadium Thanksgiving Day, the outcome will not be a tie.

That situation was taken care of Tuesday evening when city and county coaches, meeting with Lions Club officials at the East Erie Turners, decided that in the event the teams are deadlocked at the end of the regulation playing time an experiment will be conducted with a new form of "extra period" to break the tie and bring about a definite decision.

If a tie results, the ball will be placed on the 50-yard line and each team given possession of it for four downs. The team gaining the greater amount of yardage in four attempts will be declared the winner of the game.

A tie score has not cropped up in the brief history of the annual "Save-An-Eye" games, but with so many deadlocks appearing in city series competition this season the coaches agreed last night to take steps to prevent an unsatisfactory ending to the postseason game this year.

It was also announced at the meeting last night that Erie's first show since the beginning will be staged between

SPORTS ROUNDUP
By Hugh S. Fullerton, Jr.

NEW YORK, Nov. 18. (AP)—Football isn't all fun dept.: A few weeks ago you may have read that when he Woodward, Iowa, high school ball coach answered Uncle Sam's own par- r his

Game 5 – November 27, 1943

East

Player	School
Sandy Adams	North East
Warren Aikens	Harbor Creek
Art Amendola	East
Charles Anderson	North East
Ray Baer	Academy
Frank Baranowski	East
Paul Barone	Wesleyville
Tony Benito	Wesleyville
Eugene Brown	Academy
John Cadwallader	Union City
Roy Cline	East
James Coyne	Academy
Fred Ferraro	Harbor Creek
Pete Fischer	Academy
Robert Fitzgerald	Union City
Tom Gill	Lawrence Park
George Hausman	Academy
Vincent Jaworek	Academy
Al Kline	Academy
Edward Lavange	Harbor Creek
James Meehl	North East
Ed Metzger	Wesleyville
Fred Moorehead	Harbor Creek
Carl Nemenz	Academy
Jack Schrecengost	Academy
Arthur "Deco" Schwindt	Academy
Francis Skeabeck	East
Louis Smith	North East
George Stanley	Harbor Creek
Louis Truitt	Academy
Ronnie Whipple	Lawrence Park
Bill White	Lawrence Park
Blaine Wilcox	Waterford
Bud Wright	Waterford
Glen Yosten	Lawrence Park
Charles Yunker	Waterford

Coach: Lowell Drake of Academy

West

Player	School
Walter Dean	Tech
Sam Donato	Strong Vincent
Harold Dowler	Edinboro
Dick Ernfeldt	Fairview
Howard Godfrey	Millcreek
Leo Goetz	Fairview
Bob Gossman	Girard
Jack Grieshober	Strong Vincent
Merrill Grubbs	Fairview
Bill Hellyer	Albion
Jack Hill	Albion
Jim Hillman	Millcreek
George Holowach	Edinboro
William Jones	Albion
Dick Jones	Edinboro
John Kanuk	Girard
Jack Kirsh	Cathedral Prep
Robert Kubiak	Cathedral Prep
William McIntyre	Strong Vincent
Carl Onda	Cathedral Prep
Joe Osiecki	Tech
William Pellow	Girard
Emmett Phillips	Millcreek
Bernard Postewka	Tech
Chet Schmelter	Girard
Ronald Schultz	Tech
Edward Schwarz	Strong Vincent
Joe Shugart	Strong Vincent
Paul Siever	Tech
Russell Silverthorn	Millcreek
Charles Sult	Strong Vincent
William Walker	Fairview
Arthur Weaver	Strong Vincent
Fred Wolchik	Albion
William Wood	Albion
Lane Wroth	Strong Vincent

Coach: Sam Kramer of Strong Vincent

EAST 25 - WEST 0

*A*fter a scoreless first half, the East took control when coach Lowell Drake used an offensive unit with all 11 members from his championship Academy team. Two Lions teamed up for the first touchdown when "Deco" Schwindt threw a 16-yard pass to George Hausman in the third quarter. The East dominated the final quarter, including a touchdown run by another Academy grad, fullback Vince Jaworek. That score was set up following an interception by Francis Skeabeck of East. Paul Barone of Wesleyville returned an interception 40 yards for another East score. Among the Lions who were stars in the game were Schwindt, Lou Truitt, Al Kline, Jaworek, Jim Coyne, Eugene Brown, Ray Baer, Carl Nemenz and Jack Schrecengost. The East also featured Paul Barone of Wesleyville, Roy Cline and Art Amendola of East.

Lions Club
Save-An-Eye

Saturday, November 27, 1943
Stadium - Erie, Penna.

The Lion's Tale

THAT YOU MAY KNOW

It is "Save-An-Eye" time in Erie and the Lions Club takes this opportunity to thank you for your support in making this game possible. In purchasing tickets for this game, you have contributed directly to the "Save-An-Eye" welfare work.

Starting with a tag day and then, six years ago, changing the All-Star Game, the Lions Club has directed the purchase and paid for 2,100 pairs of glasses for the school children of City and County of Erie.

Two years ago, we conceived the idea of an eye clinic and groundwork has already been laid for such an undertaking. Eye specialists of Erie are asking us to delay this temporarily, until the proper equipment can be se...now, this particular equipment is not obt...of our doctors and nurses are i...But, in the meantime, th..."Save-An-Eye" service t...n the Armed Forc...

East All-Stars Beat West

Seahawks Top
Eleven

ERIE DISPATCH-HERALD
FOURTH SECTION

Win by 25 to 0
in 'Save an Eye'
Football Game

East

James Akin	North East
Ralph Albert	Waterford
Jack Anderson	Lawrence Park
Donald Betts	Corry
Richard Bretz	Harbor Creek
Bob Detzel	East
Jack Donihi	Academy
Donald Faller	Harbor Creek
Donald George	East
Chuck Hagmann	Academy
Charles Hazen	Lawrence Park
Ralph Hooven	Lawrence Park
Cecil Hull	Waterford
Joseph Kimmel	Wesleyville
Lewis Klus	Union City
Robert Kramer	Wesleyville
Gunther Martena	Waterford
George Martin	Wesleyville
Robert Miniger	East
Ed Pasky	Academy
Joe Pomorski	East
Robert Reinwald	Academy
Bill Roach	Academy
Vincent Shioleno	North East
William Suminski	East
Donald Triana	North East
Howard Wilkinson	Harbor Creek
Francis Wontenay	Union City

Coach: Lowell Drake of Academy

West

Art Arkelian	Strong Vincent
Bill Brabender	Strong Vincent
Don Buseck	Fairview
Joe Cerami	Strong Vincent
Paul Crossman	Girard
Ray Dombrowski	Tech
Ronald Doucette	Edinboro
Norman Kleckner	Millcreek
Edward Konkol	Tech
Frank Landi	Strong Vincent
Robert Lawrence	Albion
Jim Mahoney	Cathedral Prep
Carl Marthaler	Cathedral Prep
Paul Morabito	Tech
Anthony Mucciarone	Strong Vincent
Ray Oldach	Cathedral Prep
Paul Onachila	Albion
Robert Pollok	Girard
Bill Rausch	Girard
James Ritchie	Fairview
Thomas Rodak	Edinboro
Dick Scheffner	Cathedral Prep
James Seth	Cathedral Prep
James Sheridan	Millcreek
Eugene Smith	Tech
Charles Taylor	Fairview
George Vadmer	Edinboro
Thomas Wells	Millcreek
Richard Wisniewski	Tech
Donald Wolfe	Albion

Coach: Sam Kramer of Strong Vincent

EAST 13 - WEST 6

*A*cademy quarterback Eddie Pasky scored all the points for the winners. He had a pair of 1-yard quarterback sneaks and kicked an extra point. Pasky also had an interception on the 1-yard line in the final minute to preserve the East win. Bill Roach of Academy had an interception to set up the winning touchdown. Joe Cerami of Strong Vincent passed 10 yards to Ray Dombrowski of Tech for the only West touchdown. The PAT kick by Art Arkelian of Strong Vincent was blocked. East standouts included Ralph Hooven of Lawrence Park, who played every minute; Don Faller of Harbor Creek, Chuck Hagmann of Academy, Bob Reinwald of Academy and Roach. West stars were Jim Mahoney of Prep, Bill Rausch of Girard, Tom Wells of Millcreek, Ray Oldach of Prep, Dombrowski, Cerami and Bill Brabender of Vincent.

Then-mayor, Charlie R. Barber, declared Friday, November 24, 1944 "Save-An-Eye Day" in Erie and urged citizens to purchase tickets for the all-star football game to be staged at the Stadium that night by the Lions Club with all profits going to the club's "Save-An-Eye" Fund.

"Save-An-Eye Day"

Pointing out that "since the Lions Club has undertaken this project, more than 2,200 pairs of glasses have been distributed without cost to worthy children . . ." Mayor Barber called upon Erie citizens "to purchase tickets and attend this game to the end that many more needy children who have defective eyesight may be helped through this project."

– Reprinted from the Erie Times-News, November, 1944

Art Arkelian will celebrate two milestones in 2014. The longtime Erie promoter is already making plans for the 50th Erie County Sports Banquet. The February event has attracted dozens of celebrities to town over the years.

In addition, 2014 will mark the 70th anniversary of Arkelian's appearance in the Save-An-Eye Game. The well-known businessman represented Strong Vincent in the game. He still has fond memories of the experience.

Art Arkelian – 1944

"It meant an awful lot to be selected to play in the Save-An-Eye Game," he recalled. "My high school coach Sam Kramer coached our West team and even though we lost the game, it still brings back wonderful memories."

The team practiced for "about a week" under Kramer before the game. For Arkelian, those drills included renewing relationships with some of his teammates while also meeting many players.

"I knew some of the guys from both teams going in, but made many new friendships," he noted. Among those new faces was a running back from Fairview.

"I met Don Buseck, who played the other halfback position for the West team," Arkelian said. "And his son Dr. Mark Buseck put in a new hip for me a few years back."

Another familiar face on game night was from Lawrence Park. "One of my best friends was Ralph Hooven," Art said. "He ran a punt back for a touchdown in the game."

Two other close friends also participated in the 1944 contest, Chuck Hagmann of Academy and Jim Mahoney of Prep. "The three of us all made All-State that year," Arkelian said. "I kept in touch with them through the years, but unfortunately they're both gone now."

Even though decades have passed since the East-West battle, Arkelian recalls the game with a smile. "I really enjoyed the Save-An-Eye Game and am still friends with some of those guys nearly 70 years later," he commented.

"It's wonderful when you can play football against guys, try to beat them and then sit down afterwards and make friendships that last a lifetime."

– Jim Camp

East Team

LOWELL C. DRAKE

Lowell Drake, head coach of the East Team in the game, is the dean of Erie football coaches.

Coming to Erie from Ashtabula, O., in 1923, Dra... in the development of scholastic football here. His long have been noted as smart, well coached eleven... become known as a keen student of football and first order.

It was Drake who introduced intersectional f... his Academy eleven to Atlanta several years ag... intersectional games up to the beginning of the

He introduced, too, the football training c... gridders out of the city for a week or two o... each year.

Drake has served as head coach of o... since the Lions Club inaugurated the "Sav... with him this year are Coaches Jim Hyde... Union City; Jack Tinson, Corry; T. R. ... Yost, Lawrence Park; Harry Massing, F... Wesleyville; and Stan Ralston, North F...

9

West Team

HAROLD I. (Sam) KRAMER

Thwarted in his first attempt as coach of the West All-Stars to produce a victory last year, Harold I. (Sam) Kramer hopes with no little amount of confidence to turn the trick tonight. But the task at hand is not easy for the Strong Vincent mentor and his corps of capable aides.

Kramer is a disciple of hard football, learning his lessons first at Old Central High and later at Grove City College. In recent years, Kramer has tempered his style with a little razzle-dazzle but depends on straight football for his points.

The Westside football chieftain has just completed his 20th year as a football coach, a tenure of duty which started at Ellwood City in 1925, then shifted to Beaver Falls, Braddock, Central and Strong Vincent.

Coming back to his Alma Mater in 1929, Kramer coached at Central for one year then was transferred with the faculty and student body to Strong Vincent in 1930. He has been head mentor there since. He has produced two city football champions—the teams of 1934 and 1938. His team tied for the crown in 1942.

Commenting on tonight's game, Kramer said: "We have some fine football talent in the West All-Stars. It will take a very good East team to nick us this time."

11

East	
Pete Bechtos	East
Fred Behnken	North East
Dick Bullock	Cambridge Springs
Terry Burgess	Academy
Joe Buto	Academy
Howard Davis	Union City
Bill Dolinsky	Cambridge Springs
Dick Foster	Corry
Al Fracassi	Academy
Don Harrington	East
Howard Henning	Academy
Harry Johnson	East
John Kaminski	Harbor Creek
Bob Lawton	Lawrence Park
Joe Lohse	Wesleyville
Frank Maille	Wesleyville
Sam Martina	North East
Winfield McGahen	Waterford
Fred Mitchell	Corry
Bob Morgan	Academy
Al Reidel	East
Vincent Salmon	Waterford
Andy Samsel	Lawrence Park
Bob Swanson	East
Dave Witherow	Harbor Creek
Marshall Young	Union City

Coach: Jim Hyde of East

West	
Art Anderson	Tech
Allan Benson	Strong Vincent
Chuck Colvin	Cathedral Prep
Dewey Davis	Millcreek
John Dohanic	Girard
Len Ekimoff	Tech
George Hagle	Cathedral Prep
Judd Harrington	Albion
Ray Hedderick	Millcreek
Simon Holowack	Edinboro
Homer Hutchison	Edinboro
Bill LeFevre	Strong Vincent
John Mancini	Cathedral Prep
Don Marinelli	Tech
Jim Minton	Cathedral Prep
Bill Passerotti	Strong Vincent
Art Sementelli	Tech
Jim Smith	Conneautville
Don Snodgrass	Strong Vincent
Frank Sobieski	Conneautville
John Strucher	Strong Vincent
Ray Sullivan	Cathedral Prep
Don Swanson	Millcreek
Gerald Teed	Albion
Dick Walker	Fairview
Ed Yarrington	Fairview
Joe Zuravleff	Tech

Coach: Eddie Abramoski of Tech

WEST 11 - EAST 0

*T*his game was played in miserable weather conditions, with the temperature at zero. Ray Hedderick of McDowell returned an interception 54 yards for the game's only touchdown. Joe Zuravleff of Tech caught the PAT pass. The West also recorded two safeties when Joe Lohse of Wesleyville and Al Reidel of East recovered fumbles in the end zone. The East was limited to minus 4 yards rushing. West stars included Hedderick, Zuravleff and Jack Strucher of Strong Vincent. Bob Morgan of Academy and Bob Swanson of East were East standouts. This game was the first in the series in which Lowell Drake did not participate as a coach. He had been on the sidelines for the six previous Save-An-Eye Games.

SATURDAY, NOVEMBER 24, 1945

...efeats East All-Stars, 11-0

Hedderick Skates 54 Yards for Score

An unscheduled ice extravaganza was put on between halves of the Lions Club Save-An-Eye football game at the Stadium Friday, November 3, 1945 as silken-clad, bare-legged baton twirlers and drum majorettes defied snow and wintry winds to go through with an entertaining program.

1945 – Ice Carnival

More than a score of girls from Academy High, wearing white silk skirts and silk blouses tinted every color of the rainbow made the spectators shiver – and applaud – as they went through a dance number to the accompaniment of the Academy band.

Previous to the appearance of the Academy entertainers, the Corry High band and majorettes took over the field. The band spelled out a big H-E-L-L-O in the center of the field as the majorettes and cheerleaders went through their paces.

– Reprinted from the Erie Times-News, November 24, 1945

Game 8 – November 23, 1946

East

Leo Beill	East
Robert Bender	East
Chuck Brasington	East
Bob Bretz	Harbor Creek
Wilbur Brezee	Lawrence Park
Herb Burns	Union City
Joe Concilla	North East
Don Edwards	Wesleyville
Dick Grieb	Lawrence Park
Jack Hammond	Academy
Richard Kestle	Waterford
Ronald Krape	Academy
John Langer	Harbor Creek
William Lawrence	East
Eugene Mahon	East
Paul Nenman	North East
Bill Pavkov	Waterford
Cosimo Pellican	Academy
Joe San Pietro	Academy
Howard Schirmer	Cambridge Springs
Norm Sherrod	Union City
Louie Sherwood	Corry
Don Soliday	Wesleyville
Dick Thomas	Cambridge Springs
Bob Wachter	Academy
John Walter	Academy
Jack Wilson	North East

Coach: Ed "Pee Wee" Thomas of Academy

West

John Arkelian	Strong Vincent
Dick Carlson	Tech
Martin Chulick	Girard
Adam Gorski	Cathedral Prep
Wilbur Grubbs	Fairview
Harry Harabedian	Cathedral Prep
Don Hostettler	Edinboro
John Januleski	Cathedral Prep
Pete Karuba	Tech
Ray Kazebee	Conneautville
Len Kubiak	Tech
Jim Lytle	Millcreek
Jim Mullard	Strong Vincent
Kenneth Nye	Albion
John Offner	Edinboro
Gary Orr	Cathedral Prep
Ed Palkovic	Tech
Pete Panetta	Strong Vincent
Art Patterson	Millcreek
Larry Pennica	Girard
Fred Schroeck	Cathedral Prep
Scott Sherretts	Albion
Chuck Sorger	Strong Vincent
Frank Stepchnek	Conneautville
William Weislogel	Fairview
Dick Wronek	Strong Vincent

Coach: Ted Sowle of Cathedral Prep

EAST 6 - WEST 0

*C*huck Brasington of East returned a blocked punt 24 yards for the game's only score. Brasington blocked the punt of Len Kubiak of Tech in the fourth quarter. The West dominated the stats, but not the scoreboard. The West rushed for 122 yards while limiting the East to 29.

The staunch East defense featured East's Burly B's, Brasington, Bob Bender and Leo Beill. Jack Wilson of Corry was also a star for the winners. In the fourth quarter he punted out of bounds at the 13-yard line. He then intercepted a pass and followed with a punt out of bounds at the West 10.

Wilson iced the win with an interception in the final minute. Kubiak, Johnny Arkelian and Pete Panetta of Strong Vincent, Adam Gorski, Gary Orr and Fred Schroeck of Prep were standouts for the West.

Blocked Kick, 24-Yard Run Wins Game

Jack Wilson's Punting Outstanding For East

By Peg Parsons

CHUCK BRASINGTON rounded out four years of brilliant scholastic footballing last night with a sterling performance in the eighth annual Lions Club "Save-An-Eye" game by blocking a punt and carrying the ball over for a touchdown as the East All-Stars registered a startling 6-0 upset over the star-studded West All-Stars in the stadium.

Upwards of 11,000 fans—the largest crowd ever to see a "Save-An-Eye" battle—saw Brasington break up a closely fought game with a 24-yard touchdown run in the fourth quarter's early moments.

STYMIED ON EVERY scoring effort by a valiantly-battling underdog East All-Star squad, the Wests found themselves shoved back to their own 30 by Jack Wilson's out-of-bounds punt early in the fourth quarter.

Fred Schroeck picked up two yards, but that was more than nullified by a five-yard penalty. Then Leonard Kubiak, keyman in the West's offense, rammed in for four, taking the ball back to the 31.

On third down, Kubiak dropped back to the 20 for a punt. Brasington charged in from his left guard position, blocked the kick and scooped up the pigskin on the 24.

LIKE A FLASH, Brasington, who served one of his four years of footballing for East in the backfield, was off for the goal line. He juggled the pigskin in his arms, finally gaining permanent possession as he hit the five, then stepped over the line for the game's *nlav away.*

As it turned out, it was unimportant that Wilson's' attempt for point from placement went awry.

East's All-Stars, coached by Ed (Peewee) Thomas, Academy mentor, had enough points to win.

THE VAUNTED WEST Stars, favored to win by *fr* to four touchdowns, rolled *first downs as compared to* the winners, but never *se* threatened to score.

Flanked by such stars *a* Johnny Arkelian, Fred Schroe* Pete Panetta and Gary Orr, *k* biak engineered his team to *a* net gain of 162 yards.

But Kubiak's passing, figured *t* be a thorn in the East All-Star *sides*, failed to click with *onl* three of 18 aerials hitting the mark for 40 yards.

SLOPPY BALL-HANDLING by both teams marred the battle in *t*he opening quarter, 11 fumbles *b*eing charged to the two. Both *t*bs had touchdown-aimed drives *ha*lted by fumbles in the first period, but later in the game it was *t*ight defensive play that stop*ped* the hard-running West squad.

*A*nd figuring in that defensive *play* were the pass interceptions *K*ubiak's aerials by Wilson, a *half*back from Corry, who took *sp*otlight away from his bet-*ter k*own rivals.

*Wilso*n's punting was the stand-*out* feature of the game as he, time *an*d *aga*in, rocked the Wests far *back* on their heels by booming *out* *of* bounds.

WITH THEIR backs *to the* wall, West was con*fronted by* a steel-like wall *man*ned by Brasington, Leo *Beill,* Walters, Joe San *Pietro,* Bender, Ronnie Krape *and Bo*b, the latter of Law-*rence with* frequent re-*inforcements fr*om city and county *team members who pl*ay away.

THE GAME WAS highlighted by a colorful spectacle before the contest and between the halves as city and county school bands and majorettes combined to add a "big league" touch. The halftime performance offered a colorful panorama without equal in the history of Erie football. Summary:

E. All-Stars (6)		W. All-Stars (0)	
Bretz	LE		Grubbs
Beill	LT		Karuba
Brasington	LG		Kabazee
Sherrod	C		Lytle
Thomas	RG		Offner
Sherwood	RT		Nye
Grieb	RE		Sorger
Concilla	QB		Kubiak
Edwards	LH		Arkelian
Pellican	RH		Chulick
Hammond	FB		Orr

Scoring

	Scoring Play	East	West
Time	FIRST QUARTER	0	0
	None		
	SECOND QUARTER	0	0
	None		
	THIRD QUARTER	0	0
	None		
	FOURTH QUARTER		
2:15	Brasington (Run with blocked punt)	6	0

Substitutes — East: Pavkov, Kestle, Mahon, Bresee, Schirmer, Thomas, Lawrence, San Pietro, Walters, Neuman, Langer, Krape, Burns, Bender, Wanchter. West: Pennica, Sherretts, Harabedian, Stenchuck, Patterson, Januleski, Hostetler, Schroeck, Gorski, Morosky, Wroneck, Mullard, Panetta, Weislogel, CCarlson, Palkovic.

Officials: Referee — Cochran; Umpire—Komora; Head Linesman—Bradford; Field Judge—Nason. Time of periods—12 minutes.

Game 9 – November 21, 1947

East

William Alcorn	Waterford
Art Anderson	Lawrence Park
Bob Arndt	Academy
Ed Bielec	East
Robert Carrick	East
Doug Eades	Harbor Creek
Jack Flick	Cambridge Springs
Bill Freeman	Academy
Edward Garnow	North East
Charles Gurtson	Corry
Richard Gurtson	Corry
Jack Hanley	Union City
Alex Kapetan	North East
Richard Kehl	Academy
Robert Martin	Harbor Creek
Bill Morrow	Wesleyville
Charles Oldach	East
Jack Overocker	Wesleyville
Lewis Penna	East
Max Randall	Lawrence Park
Robert Shields	Academy
Steve Simon	East
Joe Smollek	Union City
Eugene Sunberg	Academy
Harley Tau	Cambridge Springs
William Yunker	Waterford

Head coach: Jim Hyde of East
Assistants: Ed "Pee Wee" Thomas of Academy, James Hall of Cambridge Springs, Robert Lytle of Corry, Joe Sivak of Harbor Creek, Russell Yost of Lawrence Park, Hienie Anderson of North East, Ed Poly of Union City, Frank Dennison of Waterford, Jim Manafo of Wesleyville

West

Richard Abbey	Conneautville
Dana Arneman	Millcreek
Ray Barczak	Tech
Arnold Bentley	Albion
Jack Campbell	Strong Vincent
Chris Filipowski	Cathedral Prep
Culver Hall	Tech
Ardell Hayes	Edinboro
Herman Hedderick	Millcreek
Ted Hutchison	Edinboro
Vincent Jenco	Cathedral Prep
Chaney Johnson	Strong Vincent
Vitus Kaiser	Cathedral Prep
Edward Kranz	Cathedral Prep
Gerald McCray	Fairview
Norbert Miazga	Tech
Bill Podoll	Albion
Tony Pol	Tech
John Porreca	Tech
Maynard Sanders	Girard
Butch Silverthorne	Girard
Stanley Sowry	Conneautville
Robert Steinmetz	Strong Vincent
John Walker	Fairview
Tony Zambroski	Cathedral Prep
Henry Zimmerman	Strong Vincent
Don Zonna	Strong Vincent

Head coach: Cy James of Cathedral Prep
Assistants: Joe Lisek of Albion, Paul Gibson of Conneautville, Ed Gumbert of Edinboro, J.B. "Joe" Timmons of Fairview, Alex Rohde of Girard, Gus Anderson of Millcreek, Sam Kramer of Strong Vincent, Eddie Abramoski of Tech

WEST 21 - EAST 7

*T*he score would have been wider, but the West fumbled eight times and lost six. The West piled up 381 total yards, including 245 yards rushing while limiting the East to three yards rushing and eight yards on one pass completion. Jack Campbell of Strong Vincent scored on runs of 1 and 3 yards. Vitus Kaiser of Prep threw a 45-yard touchdown pass to Chaney Johnson of Strong Vincent. Lou Penna of East scored on a 7-yard run. Receivers Johnson, Herm Hedderick of Millcreek, Butch Silverthorne of Girard and Ray Barczak of Tech were West stars. The game, watched by a large crowd of 14,000 fans, was tied 7-7 after three quarters.

West captains Tony Pol and Tony Zambroski

Game 10 – November 26, 1948

East

Richard Bargielski .... Tech
Don Barney .... Academy
Julius "Whitey" Borkowski .... Academy
John Danowski .... Academy
Bill Demyanovich .... East
Richard Farren .... Wesleyville
Merlin Hawley .... Waterford
William House .... North East
Richard Landis .... Union City
Pat Leighton .... East
Robert Long .... Corry
John Malinowski .... Tech
Louis Matosian .... Lawrence Park
Raymond Musser .... Lawrence Park
Nels Nelson .... Harbor Creek
Dom Nicolia .... Academy
Jim Ruggiero .... Tech
Ralph Schneider .... Academy
William Shay .... Wesleyville
Albert Shields .... Waterford
Arnold Simmons .... Harbor Creek
Tony Starocci .... Tech
Joe Suminski .... Tech
Matt Wisniewski .... East
David Young .... Union City
Dan Young .... North East

Coach: Jim Hyde of East

West

Sam Alward .... Strong Vincent
Junior Baker .... Cambridge Springs
Gilbert Brown .... Millcreek
Sam Cianflocco .... Strong Vincent
Don Fessler .... Cathedral Prep
Robert Fogle .... Strong Vincent
Lawrence Frey .... Girard
George Geiger .... Cathedral Prep
Richard Hasbee .... Cambridge Springs
Rob Heidt .... Millcreek
Robert Heldreth .... Conneautville
John Hinkle .... Fairview
Kenneth Johnson .... Fairview
Charles Kibler .... Girard
Jack Krahe .... Cathedral Prep
Angelo LaFuria .... Strong Vincent
Frank Liebert .... Cathedral Prep
Paul Madden .... Albion
Frank Mukina .... Edinboro
Sam Pizzo .... Strong Vincent
Ronald Powell .... Cambridge Springs
Dick Rogers, ... Kanty Prep
Stan Rosikowski .... Kanty Prep
Fred Skelton .... Edinboro
Richard Thayer .... Conneautville
Lewis Weaver .... Albion
Jerry Widmann .... Cathedral Prep
Richard Winslow .... Millcreek

Coach: Walt Strosser of Cathedral Prep

EAST 13 - WEST 0

A crowd of 9,000 on hand for the opening kickoff dwindled to less than 1,000 after halftime due to a driving rainstorm. The horrible conditions, which turned the Stadium turf into a slippery mess, produced 11 fumbles. Julius "Whitey" Borkowski of Academy returned a punt 77 yards for a touchdown. Tony Starocci of Tech had a 38-yard touchdown run. Dave Young of Union City kicked the game's only extra point. The West had just one first down.

East All-Stars Strike Early,

Muddy Field Results In 'Slow' Game

By Peg Parsons

STRIKING WITH lightning-like fury for two first-quarter touchdowns, the East All-Stars last night defeated the West All-Stars, 13 to 0, in the 10th annual Lions club "Save-an-Eye" game and evened the series at five games all.

Ed Borkowski, triple-threat Academy product, engineered the game-winning score with an 80-yard return of a West punt, and Tech's Tony Starocci galloped 38 yards with the "insurance" score. Dave Young of Union City scored the extra point on a plunge following Borkowski's brilliant run.

MORE THAN 8,000 persons watched the kickoff and remained through the first quarter, but all except a possible 1,000 hearties were driven from the stadium by a heavy rain which started a half-hour before the game.

That rain, developing into a near deluge, turned the well-worn stadium turf into a muddy quagmire and the players did little more than slip and slide after the two touchdowns were recorded.

Lineups For Tonight

WEST ALL-STARS

NO.	WEST ALL-STARS	POS.	EAST ALL-STARS	NO.
	Lawrence Frey (G)	LE	Bill Demyanovich (Ea)	5
	Sam Cianflocco (SV)	LT	Raymond Musser (LP)	53
	Frank Mukina (Ed)	LG	Dan Youngs (NE)	25
	Frank Liebert (CP)	C	Richard Farren (WE)	29
	Bob Heldt (M)	RG	Matt Wisniewski (Ea)	49
	Richard Kasbee (CS)	RT	Nels Nelson (H)	27
	Albert Brown (M)	RE	John Malinowski (T)	21
	Jack Rogers (KP)	QB	Edward Borkowski (Ac)	33
	Bill Madden (Al)	LH	Albert Shields (Wa)	11
	Jim Hinkle (F)	RH	Robert Long (C)	7
	Bert Heldreth (Co)	FB	David Young (UC)	39

SUBSTITUTIONS

WEST ALL-STARS—Junior Baker (CS) 2, Angelo LaFuria (SV) 6, Robert (SV) 8, Fred Skelton (Ed) 12, Kenneth Johnson (F) 14, Stan Rogers (KP) 16, Richard Thayer (Co) 18, Sam Alward (SV) 30, Lewis (Co) 32, Ronald Powell (CS) 38, Richard Winslow (M) 40, Jerry Pizzo (SV) 58, Jack Krahe (CP) 48, Don Fessler (CP) 50, George Geiger (G) 60.

EAST ALL-STARS—Tony Starocci (T) 3, Merlin Hawley (Wa) 13, Arnold Ruggiero (T) 17, Joe Suminski (T) 19, William Rouse Schneider (Ac) 31, John Danowski (Ac) 35, Dom Nicolia Landis (UC) 41, Louis Matosian (LP) 43, Pat Leighton (Ea) (Ac) 55, William Shay (We) 57, Richard Bargielski (T) 59.

Howard Kelly (referee), John Bradford (umpire), John Grasman), Fred Nason (field judge).

KICKOFF—8:15 p.m.

Game 11 – November 24, 1949

East

Alan Baker	Wattsburg
Richard Barber	Tech
Joe Concilla	North East
James Diffenbacher	Wesleyville
Peter DiNicola	Harbor Creek
Frank Engel	Academy
Ross Etter	East
Joe Fracassi	Academy
Tom Freeman	Tech
Gene Garn	Wesleyville
Robert Gibbs	North East
Paul Henry	Union City
Rex Ireland	Corry
Zigmund Jasinski	Tech
Gordon Kidder	Wesleyville
George Knight	Lawrence Park
Jim Kujan	East
Merle Lindsay	Academy
Richard May	Academy
Marshall McCall	Wattsburg
Joe McLaren	Lawrence Park
Joseph Musiek	Union City
Richard Paterniti	East
Ed Peck	Tech
Joe Pettinato	Tech
Art Pitts	Corry
William Rees	East
Tom Rogers	Academy
Wirt Ross	Harbor Creek
Tom Weltzel	Union City

Coach: Ted Robb of Tech

West

Frank Anthony	Cathedral Prep
Robert Baker	Cambridge Springs
Robert Bierig	Strong Vincent
David Blackman	Cathedral Prep
John Bryan	Albion
Thomas Buck	Strong Vincent
William Byham	Girard
Jack Dalton	Cathedral Prep
Robert Fox	Fairview
John Fuller	Conneautville
Bud Gnadge	Cambridge Springs
William Goodwin	Girard
Don Guerrin	Cathedral Prep
Charles Haise	Strong Vincent
Charles Haller	Cathedral Prep
Ed Janek	Kanty Prep
Jack Konkol	Cathedral Prep
Robert Lewis	Albion
Jack McNulty	Cathedral Prep
Kenan O'Brien	Edinboro
Ben Pizzo	Strong Vincent
Pat Ricart	Strong Vincent
Norman Rogers	Fairview
Gene Rumsey	Conneautville
Larry Schirmer	Edinboro
Robert Shaw	Strong Vincent
Tom Solvedt	Strong Vincent
David Spate	Millcreek
Ron Starkey	Kanty Prep
Don Virosko	Millcreek

Coach: Walt Strosser of Cathedral Prep

EAST 20 - WEST 6

A format change saw the East and West teams use County players in the first and third quarters and City players in the second and fourth quarters. Joe Concilla of North East scored on a 6-yard run, Art Pitts of Corry had a 1-yard touchdown run and Ziggy Jasinski of Tech scored a 1-yard touchdown. Bob Bierig of Strong Vincent netted the West touchdown on a 1-yard run. Gene Garn of Wesleyville was an offensive ace for the East. The East was also stopped three times inside the 10-yard line in the first half.

East, West Meet In 'Rubber Tilt' Of Grid Series

11th Lions' Club Fray Is Listed For Stadium

BY TOM MACQUIRE

A "rubber game" in the highly successful history of the Lions' Club Club Save-an-Eye All-Star series is scheduled in the Stadium Thursday night with the 11th worthy charity classic. Game time is 8:10 o'clock.

A good holiday turnout is expected to witness the struggle between the Eastern All-Stars and Western All-Stars to snatch the lead in the series. In 10 previous games each team has scored five triumphs.

. . . . .

ACTUALLY, there will be two games played tonight. County school representatives will

Chapter 3

The 1950s saw the implementation of the current City-County format for the Save-An-Eye. After using different methods of showcasing the first 13 games in the series, the Lions Club unveiled the City-County rivalry in 1952. The East-West format remained in place for the 1950 and 1951 games before the switch to the City-County setup which remains in place today. After the West breezed to 19-0 and 25-0 shutouts in the first two games of the decade, the City began its domination, reeling off seven straight wins.

The 1950s

It took until 1959 when the County broke through for a 19-12 win. Jack Humphreys of Lawrence Park starred in that game, accounting for all three touchdowns. Humphreys scored on a punt return of 83 yards, a pass to Ben Pratt of McDowell and a 9-yard run. Grove Blanchard of Academy scored both touchdowns for the City. Caesar Montevecchio ran for one touchdown and threw to former Prep teammate Len Tomczak for another in 1952.

The City relied on strong defense to post close wins the next two years. Jim Lynch of Cathedral Prep rushed for 140 yards in 1953. Pete Alex of Tech passed to Dana Tomczak of Prep and Tim Holland of Prep scored from 13 yards out in 1954. The 1955 game saw a thrilling finish when the Cathedral Prep duo of Tom Corapi and Johnny Torrelli teamed on a 19-yard half-back-to-quarterback touchdown pass with 35 seconds left.

The City rolled up a 33-12 win in 1956 using a strong running attack. Future college standouts Art Baker of Academy and Ron Costello of Cathedral Prep led the City in 1957. The City bagged a 13-6 win in 1958, holding off a late County rally. Large crowds were the norm during the decade, with attendance at several games well over 10,000.

Game 12 – December 2, 1950

East

City Roster

Ed Abramoski	East
Roy Andrews	Academy
Chuck Bemmus	Academy
Bob Buzzard	Academy
Augie Cocarelli	Tech
Tommy Gibbons	Academy
John Gorski	Tech
Fred Morris	East
Dick Passerotti	East
Dick Pohl	East
Buddy Rowell	Academy
Len Rzepecki	Tech
George Sachrison	East
Paul Schrock	Tech
Joe Sinecki	Tech

County Roster

Henry Abbott	Waterford
Joe Bonito	Wesleyville
Vance Burdick	Waterford
Bill Chircuzzio	Corry
Bill Collins	Wesleyville
Bob Conley	Lawrence Park
Neil Henderson	North East
Bob Koegal	Union City
Mickey Maloney	Harbor Creek
Dick Marr	Wesleyville
Pat Miller	Corry
Gus Pede	Harbor Creek
Dick Pulling	North East
Bill Simmons	Harbor Creek
Don Spears	Lawrence Park

Coach: Jim Hyde of East

West

City Roster

Frank Angelotti	Strong Vincent
Carmen Bianco	Strong Vincent
Alex Clemente	Strong Vincent
Len Cyterski	Cathedral Prep
Dick Deeds	Cathedral Prep
Jerry Donatucci	Cathedral Prep
Jim Green	Strong Vincent
Al Guilianelli	Strong Vincent
Bob Obert	Cathedral Prep
George Palmer	Cathedral Prep
Larry Raymond	Strong Vincent
Lee Schlecht	Cathedral Prep
Jim Schneider	Strong Vincent
Mike Torrelli	Cathedral Prep

County Roster

Stan Albro	Kanty Prep
Andy Bartfai	Albion
Joe Brink	Cambridge Springs
John Conley	Conneautville
Harold Hicks	Fairview
Roa Jones	Cambridge Springs
Russ Lasher	Albion
Ted Lesko	Girard
Edwin Magzai	Kanty Prep
Royce Mallory	Edinboro
Ron Meigaard	Millcreek
Gene Puingley	Edinboro
Don Sedler	Girard
Dean Smock	Conneautville
Norm Veith	Fairview
Rich Vommero	Millcreek

Coach: Sam Kramer of Strong Vincent

WEST 19 - EAST 0

This game was postponed twice, once due to a snowstorm, then because of basketball games and the East prom. A heavy rain limited the crowd to 1,500 fans after 5,000 advance tickets were sold. Stan Albro of Kanty Prep scored on a 10-yard run, Gene Puingley of Edinboro scored from 1 yard out and Mike Torrelli of Cathedral Prep scored a 3-yard touchdown and added the PAT run.

Roa Jones of Cambridge Springs was another offensive star for the winners on the slick field. Buddy Powell and Tommy Gibbons of Academy were East standouts. Larry Raymond of Strong Vincent intercepted a pass to end the East's deepest threat, to the West 27-yard line in the fourth quarter.

> 66 I wasn't in on the kickoff and then went in on the next play. I played all but the last two minutes of the game. (Coach Sam) Kramer said anyone who had a clean jersey after two plays was coming out.

Russ Lasher – 1950

I was the right guard. The County made two touchdowns. One was made right behind me into the end zone, and the other I pulled and we went around end for a touchdown. Mike Torrelli took a punt and ran it back for a touchdown and we won 19-0. (Torrelli actually ran 3 yards for the touchdown.)

We were supposed to play Thanksgiving Day but they had a bad storm. They moved it to a week later and the field was covered with ice. They spread sand all over the field. We just wore ankle socks so your knees got all chewed up. It was a cold game.

My one grandson (Jeffrey Strait) played in 1994. He was an all-around back. My other grandson (J.C. Strait), played in 1995. He was the quarterback. 99

Game 13 – November 16, 1951

East

City Roster

Henry Baltine .... Tech
Larry Berdis .... Tech
Lee Cabeloff..................................... East
Harry Campbell .... Tech
Bill Caryl .... Academy
Bob Cubbison .... Academy
Tony DiPaolo .... East
Tom Hodges .... Academy
Jim Johnson..................................... East
Dick Lewis .... East
Kevin Quinn .... East
Bob Spinelli .... Academy
James Trott .... Academy
John Wasiliewski .... East
Steve Yurkiewicz .... Tech
Dan Yurkovic .... Tech

County Roster

Don Bendig....................Lawrence Park
Dick Eaglen ....Harbor Creek
Frank Frith ....Wesleyville
Bill Gay ....Harbor Creek
Ervin Goodwill .... Corry
Bud Harris............................ Union City
Bud Hoffman.........................Wesleyville
Tom Hollaran ....Harbor Creek
Ron McCall ....Waterford
Skip Moore .... Corry
Frank Papparazzo....................North East
Bruce Pieper........................ Union City
Norm Rushton ....Lawrence Park
Bill Schmid ....Wesleyville
Bill Sherwood.........................Waterford
Jim Villa.............................North East

Coaches: Duke Detzel of East,
Jim Manafo of Wesleyville

West

City Roster

Gus Anderson......................Strong Vincent
Dave Dahlkemper...............Cathedral Prep
Tom Dudenhoefer ....Cathedral Prep
Don Herbe........................Strong Vincent
Bob Kierzek ....Cathedral Prep
Caesar Montevecchio.........Cathedral Prep
Joe Peplinski ....Cathedral Prep
Dick Quadri......................Cathedral Prep
Dick Reusch......................Cathedral Prep
Marlowe Tolbert ....Strong Vincent
Len Tomczak ....Cathedral Prep
Bob Wall.........................Strong Vincent
Paul Wilson ....Strong Vincent
Don Wolf ....Cathedral Prep
Carl Zimmerman ....Strong Vincent
Norm Zymslinski ....Cathedral Prep

County Roster

Don Bertram .... Cambridge Springs
Bob Davenport................ Conneaut Valley
Paul Davis...........................Millcreek
Dick Dundon ....Edinboro
Richard Johnson .... Conneaut Valley
John Lowery .... Albion
Richard Meeder................................Girard
Floyd Patterson .... Albion
Jack Rust...................... Cambridge Springs
Jim Snyder ....Edinboro
Vic Sokolowski.........................Kanty Prep
Frank Storacci............................Millcreek
Anthony Topolski.....................Kanty Prep
George Traut ....Fairview
Jack Van Honk ....Millcreek
Jon Van Cise.............................Girard

Coaches: Walt Strosser of Cathedral
Prep, Paul Goll of McDowell

WEST 25 - EAST 0

*T*he East County faced the West County in the first and third quarters. The East and West City teams battled in the second and fourth quarters. Norm Zymslinski of Prep scored off a 22-yard punt return and on a 21-yard run. Len Tomczak of Prep had a 32-yard run for a touchdown. Vic Sokolowski of Kanty Prep passed 14 yards to John Van Cise of Girard for the third score. That touchdown was set up by a fumble recovery by Jack Rust of Cambridge Springs.

Strong Vincent players Paul Wilson, Bob Wall and Gus Anderson starred. Dick Quadri, Prep tackle, opened huge holes to spark the rushing game. Caesar Montevecchio of Prep kicked the game's only extra point. West County defensive linemen Jim Snyder of Edinboro, Jack Van Honk of Millcreek and Bob Davenport of Conneaut Valley were other standouts. Due to a scheduling change, playing the game before the next season rather than after the current season, some players from the 1951 game also played in the 1952 contest.

When the Save-An-Eye Game was instituted in 1939, NCAA sanction was necessary. This was because the NCAA regarded the post-high school all-stars as college eligible and therefore under its purview. In the 1950s, due to a proliferation of all-star games around the country that produced scant net revenue for their related charities, the NCAA required financial records from each game to be submitted for review.

Sanctioned – 1951

Robert Munson and another unidentified member of the Erie Lions Club were summoned to Chicago to present the financial information regarding the Save-An-Eye Game to the NCAA. Upon completion of the review, Munson happily reported back to the Erie Club that the NCAA described the Save-An-Eye Game as a model for conducting an all-star game. Low operating costs and a high percentage of game revenues supporting the charitable goal of the game were cited by the NCAA as the reason the game continued to be sanctioned. NCAA sanction continued until the late 1960s when the NCAA turned oversight of all-star games to the various state athletic organizations.

Bill Caryl has vivid memories of his appearances in the Save-An-Eye Game. That is appearances, as in multiple games. Playing in two of the charity contests is a feat the former Academy lineman shares with 31 other players.

Due to a shift in the scheduling, some athletes got the chance to enjoy the Save-An-Eye experience in both 1951 and 1952.

Bill Caryl – 1951 and 1952

The first of those games was played following the 1951 regular season, on November 16. The Erie Lions Club decided to move the contest to an earlier date on the 1952 calendar, staging the Save-An-Eye on September 1. That change enabled 19 City players and 13 County athletes to compete twice. Caryl was the only Academy representative to play in both games.

Players in the '50s received a gold charm to commemorate their Save-An-Eye experience.

Now living in Wellesley, Mass., the 79-year-old recalls his first Save-An-Eye experience. "We practiced at East High because Duke Detzel was our coach," he said in a phone interview. "We didn't have a lot of practices because everybody had been playing all season and we were all in shape." Detzel kept it simple, according to Caryl. "Everybody ran mostly the same plays, off tackle runs and basic passes, nothing too sophisticated," he said. "He just threw the guys together, had a couple scrimmages and we played the game." Caryl was familiar with many of his Save-An-Eye teammates. "You knew a lot of the guys from playing against them," he said.

The Penn State grad played at tackle in those days. He was one of the bigger players at 175 pounds. "Very few guys weighed over 200 pounds," he related. Caryl was actually more of a guard. "I played inside tackle on Academy's single wing," he said. "We would start in the T-formation, then shift to the single wing, with two tackles on one side of the ball. I did all the pulling and leading the play, something a guard would normally do," Caryl said. "Whenever I blocked somebody and went down I knew Willie Baker would be running right up my back."

Willie was the oldest of the Baker brothers, Caryl said. Charlie and Art followed him in the Academy backfield. Art Baker later went to Syracuse. "He ran interference for Ernie Davis when Davis won the Heisman Trophy," Caryl said.

The 1951 Save-An-Eye game featured an unusual format. The East County battled the West County in the first and third quarters. The East and West City teams played in the second and fourth periods. Caryl was on the East City team that had a roster of just 16 players. "Harry Campbell of Tech and I were the only tackles, so we played the entire game," he said. Even an early injury failed to cut into his playing time. "I got hurt on the opening kickoff, but I didn't even leave the field," he said. "I got up out of the mud, shook it off and kept playing." All four teams were on the sidelines for the entire game, he said. "We all stayed there while the County played, then we all went up to the locker room at halftime."

The weather was miserable for the 1951 game. "It was very muddy and we were all soaking wet," he said. "It took my mother six washings to get the mud out of my jersey." That uniform carried the number 28. Caryl wore 9 on his City uniform in his other Save-An-Eye game. "Numbers didn't make a difference in the 1950s," he said.

The 1952 game saw the switch to the City-County format which is still in effect. Ted Robb and Sam Kramer were the City coaches in 1952. Many of the players from the previous year had other obligations and could not play for a second time.

"Some of the guys had gone in the army and some had gone away to start practice for college," Caryl said. "Guys had jobs and some were already married."

The City earned a 19-6 win in 1952 with Cathedral Prep grads Caesar Montevecchio and Len Tomczak leading the way. That game drew a capacity crowd, not unusual in those times. "Businesses would buy a bunch of tickets and give them out so many people came for free," Caryl said. "There were limited sports on television and the high school games always drew big crowds." Three former teammates joined Caryl for the 1952 game. "Tony Masi was a guard, Ron Price played center and Gene Graney was one of our ends," he said. "Price and Masi were two of my best friends along with Ron Palombi. I went to school with Palmobi for 12 years at McKinley, Wilson and then Academy."

After spending a year at Behrend Center following his 1952 Academy graduation, Caryl gave some thought to giving football a shot at Penn State. Those ideas were quickly squelched. "The first guy I met when I walked on the Penn State campus was Rosie Greer," he said. "He was about 6'5" and 255 pounds. That was pretty much when I decided I couldn't play there."

Caryl, who had also competed in wrestling at Academy, went back to the mats at University Park. "I got into intramural wrestling and got to the finals one year," he said. "That was it for my sports career at Penn State." He did get one more chance to play football while serving with the U.S. Army in Germany. "They put out a call for football players and I signed up," he said. "Two hours later a guy from Tennessee and I were in a jeep headed to join the football team." Caryl spent five months with the Army football team. "We only lost one game playing in Europe," he said. After returning home following his Army stint, Caryl was hired by Erie Resistor (later Erie Technological Products). He was assigned to a Resistor sales office in Massachusetts in 1961. The father of four and his wife have lived in the same house in Wellesley for 50 years. Caryl is also an avid sports memorabilia collector and frequents auctions.

He returns to Erie occasionally and was back for his 60th Academy reunion in 2012. "We had 325 in our class and we had a pretty good turnout for the reunion," he said. "But many of the guys have died unfortunately." Caryl has not seen many Save-An-Eye games since playing in the two contests over 60 years ago. "I was back for one of the games at General McLane (1995)," he said. "Unfortunately I haven't been able to see others." Regardless, Caryl is one of just 32 players who can lay claim to being a member of two all-star teams. The group shares a unique spot in Save-An-Eye history.

– Jim Camp

City

Gus Anderson.........................Strong Vincent
Henry Baltine .... Tech
Lee Cabeloff .... East
Harry Campbell .... Tech
Bill Caryl .... Academy
Tom Damico .... East
Gene Graney .... Academy
Don Herbe ....Strong Vincent
Jim Johnson .... East
Tony Masi .... Academy
Jake Mitchell ....Strong Vincent
Caesar Montevecchio.........Cathedral Prep
Bob Oatman .... East
Joe Peplinski ....Cathedral Prep
Dick Platz .... East
Ron Price .... Academy
Dick Quadri......................Cathedral Prep
Kevin Quinn .... East
Gene Rachocki .... East
Dick Reusch......................Cathedral Prep
Len Strong... Tech
Len Tomczak ....Cathedral Prep
Phil Trejchel .... Tech
Bob Wall ....Strong Vincent
Paul Wilson ....Strong Vincent
Don Wolf ....Cathedral Prep
Steve Yurkiewicz .... Tech
Dan Yurkovic..................................... Tech
Carl Zimmerman ....Strong Vincent

Coaches: Ted Robb of Tech, Sam Kramer of Strong Vincent

County

Paul Bacik.......................................Fairview
Don Bendig.........................Lawrence Park
Don Bertram .... Cambridge Springs
Bob Davenport.......................Waterford
Paul Davis.............................Millcreek
Chuck Freeman ....Millcreek
Joe Gido......................................Girard
Jerry Holland ....Fairview
Tom Holloran......................Harbor Creek
Bernard Maynard ....Wesleyville
Ron Mayott.......................... Union City
Ron McCall ....Waterford
Jack Meeder ....Millcreek
Don Murray .... North East
Frank Papparazzo......................North East
Dick Peterman.......................Harbor Creek
Bruce Pieper....................... Union City
Bill Sherwood ....Waterford
Jim Snyder ....Edinboro
Vic Sokoloski..............................Kanty Prep
John Styborski............. Cambridge Springs
Anthony Topolski......................Kanty Prep
Dan Tuschak..Girard
Jack Van Honk ....Millcreek
Jim Villa.......................................North East
Oliver Whaley.......................Harbor Creek
John Yatzor ....Edinboro

Coaches: Paul Goll of McDowell, Joe Setcavage of North East

CITY 19 - COUNTY 6

A capacity crowd watched the first City-County game in the series. The City, featuring Caesar Montevecchio of Prep, passed for 226 yards. A fake punt accounted for the first touchdown. Jimmy Johnson of East threw to Montevecchio, who caught the ball on the County 49, got several key blocks and went the distance for the score. Montevecchio then passed 40 yards to Len Tomczak of Prep for a touchdown with 10 seconds left in the first half. Tomczak made a great catch on the 5-yard line and went into the end zone untouched. Montevecchio kicked the only extra point.

Don Wolf of Prep had a 7-yard run for the final City score. Bruce Pieper of Union City intercepted a pass to set up the County score. Jim Villa of North East had a 26-yard run to spark the march, going the final 5 yards for the touchdown. Jim Peplinski of Prep recovered a fumble to stop the only other County threat. This was the first game played in September following the senior players' graduation rather than immediately after the fall season ended. That allowed many players from the 1951 game to also play in this game.

Thirty-two players share a singular place in Save-An-Eye Game history. They are the only athletes who played in two charity games. That distinction came about due to a quirk in the scheduling. The 1951 game was held following that season on November 16. Then the 1952 game was staged prior to the start of the regular season on September 1.

The 1951 game also had a different format, with the East and West County players facing off in the first and third quarters, the East and West City squads battling in the second and fourth quarters. The Lions Club switched to the present City-County format beginning in 1952.

Here is a list of the 32 players who participated in both the 1951 and 1952 games:

City		County	
Gus Anderson	Strong Vincent	Don Bendig	Lawrence Park
Henry Baltine	Tech	Don Bertram	Cambridge Springs
Lee Cabeloff	East	Paul Davis	Millcreek
Harry Campbell	Tech	Tom Holloran	Harbor Creek
Bill Caryl	Academy	Ron McCall	Waterford
Don Herbe	Strong Vincent	Frank Papparazzo	North East
Jim Johnson	East	Bruce Pieper	Union City
Caesar Montevecchio	Cathedral Prep	Bill Sherwood	Waterford
Joe Peplinski	Cathedral Prep	Jim Snyder	Edinboro
Dick Quadri	Cathedral Prep	Vic Sokoloski	Kanty Prep
Kevin Quinn	East	Anthony Topolski	Kanty Prep
Dick Reusch	Cathedral Prep	Jack Van Honk	Millcreek
Len Tomczak	Cathedral Prep	Jim Villa	North East
Bob Wall	Strong Vincent		
Paul Wilson	Strong Vincent		
Don Wolf	Cathedral Prep		
Steve Yurkiewicz	Tech		
Dan Yurkovic	Tech		
Carl Zimmerman	Strong Vincent		

– Jim Camp

Phil Trejchel achieved a remarkable turnaround in two seasons of varsity football at Tech. As a Tech junior in 1951 he failed to see a minute of playing time for coach Ted Robb. "I never got off the bench the entire season," he recalled.

However, that all changed the following year.

Phil Trejchel – 1952

"I played on both the offensive and defensive lines and never left the field," Trejchel said. His steady performance earned a coveted selection to the Save-An-Eye Game. "I often wondered how I improved so much in one year from not playing to being chosen for the Save-An-Eye Game," he cracked. The selection meant a lot to the gritty 155-pounder. "It was a big deal to be picked," he said. "To get to play in the all-star game was great. I never expected that to happen." Now 78 years old, Trejchel admitted he remembered little about the actual game. "I remember playing on the kickoffs," he said. "I was a special teams guy."

The 1952 game was noteworthy in Save-An-Eye history. It marked the first City-County format that continues to the present. The City pounded out a 19-6 win in the game behind Cathedral Prep quarterback Caesar Montevecchio. The Rambler quarterback threw for one touchdown, caught a pass for a second and kicked an extra point. Montevecchio was one of the players Trejchel met during the week of practice preceding the game. "I only knew the guys from Tech," he said. "Everybody else was new." Centaur teammates who joined Trejchel on the City team included Harry Campbell, Henry Baltine, Steve Yurkiewicz, Len Strong and Dan Yurkovic.

One Tech player who did not participate in the Save-An-Eye was Don "Dapper" Polagyi. He had already left town to join the University of Cincinnati football team. Polagyi's absence cost the Save-An-Eye a real attraction, according to Trejchel. "Dapper was the best all-around athlete I ever saw," he said. "He made it look easy . . . football, basketball, baseball. He was a terrific talent."

The 1952 Save-An-Eye marked Trejchel's last game. "It was the highlight of my football career and my final game," he said. But it was not his last time in uniform. Trejchel and his twin brother Al entered the Navy in February, 1953. Phil spent four years in the service and then took a job as a police officer in Washington, D.C. He retired after 20 years, returned to Erie and worked as a clerk for the Pennsylvania Liquor Control Board for 18 years.

Trejchel also spent 24 years in the Coast Guard Reserves, including six months on active duty in Saudi Arabia during Desert Storm at 56 years of age. He retired as a Chief Petty Officer. Among his mementoes are a card presented to each Save-An-Eye player by the Erie Lions Club and a gold football charm with a 1952 engraving.

– Jim Camp

This Certifies that

PHIL TREJCHL

rendered a valuable service to the Lions Club of Erie and to the citizens
of Erie by participating in the 1952 Lions Club football game as a

FOOTBALL PLAYER

General Chairman

LIONS CLUB OF ERIE, PENNSYLVANIA

Top right: Phil Trejchel
Bottom: Twins Phil (left) and Al Trejchel (right) with Coach Ted Robb

Game 15 – September 7, 1953

City

Tony Anthony ....Cathedral Prep
Tony Baranowski .... Tech
Dom Bianco.........................Strong Vincent
Marlow Burt ....Strong Vincent
Dick Clark ....Strong Vincent
Bob Craig.. Tech
John Dittrich ....Cathedral Prep
Carl Feick .... East
Bob Ford.............................Strong Vincent
Joe Franz .... Academy
Ron Giacomelli .... Tech
Al Gunner .... Academy
Jim Hill .... East
Don Kimmelman................Strong Vincent
Ted Loader .... East
Jim Lynch ....Cathedral Prep
Ron Malek .... Tech
Joe Pontoriero.....................Cathedral Prep
Ron Potocki ....Cathedral Prep
John Preister .... East
Mike Rocco..................................... Academy
Ron Rogers .... Tech
George Schneider .... Academy
Gordy Shay .... Academy
Dick Speros........................Strong Vincent
Jerry Szorek .... East
Tom Valahovic.................................. Tech
Bob Walker .... Academy
Phil Wedzik .... East
Dan Wisniewski................................. East

Coach: Jack Komora of Academy

County

Red Adelhart .... Millcreek
Dick Alcorn ....Edinboro
Bill Angelotti ....Millcreek
Roger Brady ....Wesleyville
Carl Bretz ....Harbor Creek
Bob Brown .... Cambridge Springs
Marc Brunner ....Wesleyville
Ben Budzowski.........................Edinboro
Jim Cross ....Millcreek
Ed Dalglish ....Lawrence Park
Jack Debold............................Millcreek
George Donachy........ Cambridge Springs
Karl Griffith.............................. Union City
Bob Habel ....Fairview
Hal Hart ....Wesleyville
Don Heald .... Conneaut Valley
Ernie Lamphere................................. Corry
John Minnich .... Conneaut Valley
Les Owens....................................Waterford
Tim Platz ....Fairview
Gerald Roberts...........................Waterford
Don Schlindwein.................Harbor Creek
George Scieford .... North East
Karl Sedmina........................ Union City
Joe Timmons ....Fairview
Bill Vorsheck.......................Lawrence Park
Don Whipple ....Lawrence Park
Ed Wise .... Albion
Steve Woitovich ....Girard

Coaches: J.B "Joe" Timmons of Fairview,
Carm Bonito of Waterford

CITY 12 - COUNTY 6

A staunch City defense, which stopped four County drives inside the 30-yard line, was decisive. Mike Rocco of Academy passed 7 yards to Phil Wedzik of East for the first City score. Jim Lynch of Prep ran 37 yards for the other touchdown. Lynch had 15 carries for 140 yards in the game. Bill Vorsheck of Lawrence Park blocked a punt in the fourth quarter to set up the County touchdown. Vorsheck then caught two passes for 19 yards before Steve Woitovich of Girard ran 13 yards for the touchdown. Vorsheck caught five passes for 105 yards.

The County had a first-and-goal at the 2-yard line in the closing minutes, but was stopped by the City defense. Three runs resulted in losses back to the 24-yard line. A fourth-down pass netted seven yards, but proved meaningless. The City had a 208-27 advantage in rushing yardage.

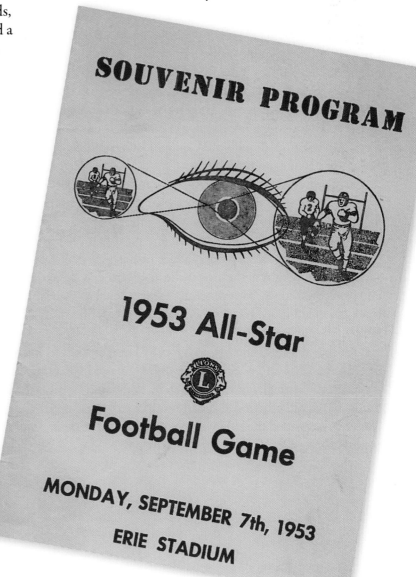

SOUVENIR PROGRAM

1953 All-Star

Football Game

MONDAY, SEPTEMBER 7th, 1953

ERIE STADIUM

For some, the Save-An-Eye is just another high school football game, for those who play in it, it can be the event of a lifetime. For Bill Vorsheck, it was a life changing event—twice!

It was 1953 and at eighteen, Bill Vorsheck thought he knew exactly what he wanted in life – a high school diploma, marriage to his neighborhood sweetheart and a job in a local plant. Several colleges offered the young football star scholarships, but he wasn't interested. He didn't realize, however, how much he would miss football after graduation, and he soon learned that high school grads didn't get the area's dream jobs. Just two months after graduation, Bill faced what seemed like a long and dismal future.

Bill Vorsheck

Then came the invitation to play in the 15th annual Erie Lion's Club Save-An-Eye Football Game. Bill knew it was a chance of a lifetime to play his beloved game one last time in the prestigious event in front of 10,000 local fans, and played his heart out. According to The Erie Dispatch, "Vorsheck, easily the County's outstanding performer, set up his team's fourth-period (and only) score when he deflected a punt by Mike Rocco deep in City territory." And from The Erie Times-News, "Bill Vorsheck, Lawrence Park's sensational end, was the big guy individually for the County . . . Vorsheck hauled down two straight passes in the fourth quarter for 19 yards and made 105 yards on the receiving end of five aerials as Ed Dalglish and Roger Brady pooled their talents for 111 yards through the air." Although the County lost as predicted, Bill was named the game's Most Valuable Player for his outstanding efforts.

Exhilarated and ears still ringing from the thunder of the crowd, Bill entered the locker room after the game and found five college scouts awaiting his return with scholarship offers in hand. Life changed in a moment of team defeat but personal glory.

One week later Bill was enrolled and playing football for Youngstown State University on a full football scholarship. After graduating with his Bachelor of Science in Education, Bill held several teaching jobs in the area including Ripley, N.Y., where he was a teacher and head football and basketball coach. He eventually settled down as a social studies teacher and head football and track coach at Girard High School. By the 1960s life was steady and good for Bill and his young family.

Known as a solid and inspired football coach, Bill was invited to lead the County all-stars in both the 1965 and 1967 Save-An-Eye Games. He was thrilled at the chance to experience the game again; especially in 1967 which he felt would be his last game. As he had played his heart out in 1953, Bill coached his heart out in 1967. Against all odds and every prediction, the County "Suburbans" wiped the field with the City "Slickers" in an unprecedented 25-0 win in front of a record-setting crowd of 16,000 hometown fans.

Once again according to The Erie Times, "The hepped up charges of Coaches Bill Vorsheck of Girard and Joe Moore of McDowell did a better clean-up job than the Ajax White Knight as they white-washed the City, 25 to 0." The September 5, 1967 article goes on to say, "It was a clean, well-played game...The City's biggest mistake was showing up. The Slickers were in the game for most of the first half, but as play progressed it was obvious that the County was in better physical condition and had come to play." They described Vorsheck's style as similar to the "old style of Coach Jack Landry" and praised his outstanding job.

Two other fans of Vorsheck's style were his 1967 co-coach, Joe Moore, and local physician, Dr. Daniel Snow. Bill credits the Save-An-Eye with bringing into his life these two men, who became his life-long friends and mentors. As a result, his career took another dramatic turn and he followed his heart into the realm of psychotherapy and medical hypnosis. He and Dr. Snow founded and operated The Erie Institute of Hypnosis from the 1970s until Bill retired and passed the business on to his son, Bill Jr. When asked what was the best thing to come of his second change in life-course, he doesn't hesitate to answer, "It's how I met my wife, Betsy, when she interned for us!"

For some, the Save-An-Eye is a last chance to play football in front of their hometown crowd; for others it's the beginning of life-long friendships; and for still others, like Bill, The Save-An-Eye Game is all that and more . . . it's a life-changing event!

– Linda Hackshaw

(Erie Dispatch Photos)

COUNTY LINEMEN - Bill Vorsheck, Bill Angelotti, Tim Platz, Ernie Lamphere, Marc Brunner, Don Whipple, Hal Hart

All-Stars

The Times

Night

the biggest give-away in
k for adults and fifty
An-Eye All-Star football
will be the cheapest
ver presented at the

such material been
Never before have
so much enthusiasm
efore have the kids
hape for the All-Star
he heat been so ter-
to tip-top condition
wo teams been so
before has there
rofits derived from

you to come out to
is!
ate ad. The All-
ll. It will put the
the boys are on a
You will see great

will be the closest
so aptly put it, "A
of bad bounces could

en break, this game
s all the ingredients.
hdown because of tre-
he County could make

—Steve Woitovich—
in this area in years.
his boy, who is a mite

W

He can stop on
change directions
also can pass,
he big City line
m. Once he's by

let us turn the
trate a point,
eived football

Cincinnati
Penn State
rn Reserve
ery Rock
Brown U.
W & J
State
Pitt
e City

1953
ht's

m on
show to
Youngs-
s will be

ille, Bill
my, Bob
iew, will

e most
have
hould
uch-

City

City Schools Play On Weekend

ERIE'S 1953 football season
will be ushered in Labor Day
evening at the Stadium with the
City and County tangling in the
15th annual Lions Club 'Save-An-
Eye' encounter.

The regular scholastic season
gets off to a flying start Friday
night with East and Millcreek renewing their rivalry at the Stadium. Prep entertains powerful
Aliquippa here Saturday evening, while Tech, Strong Vincent
and Academy see action on the
road against formidable opposition Friday night.

With a full week of pre-game
preparation, both Lions club
squads are rarin' to go in the
charity affair which should draw
a near-capacity crowd to the upper State St. bowl.

Coaches Jack Komora and Bob
Arrowsmith have assembled a
City All-Star team that is favored to make it two in a row over
the County since the old East-
West system of matching oppon-
ents was abandoned a year ago.

Jim Lynch and Joe Pontoriero
of Prep's championship 1952
eleven; Willie Baker, Dick
Speros and Dan Wisniewski of
Academy, Vincent and East, re-
spectively, are the leading runners.

The City has a fine aerial
weapon also with such throwers
as Tech's Tony Baranowski and
an Academy twosome of Gordon
Shay and Mike Rocco.

At the ends are such fine pass
receivers as Phil Wedzik and
John Priesler of East and George
Schneider of Academy. Komora
and Arrowsmith can call on John
Ditrich of Prep, and Carl Feick
and Jerry Szorek of East for
plenty of weight at the tackles,
while outstanding guards are
Tony Anthony of Prep, Joe
Franz of Academy and Dom
Bianco of Vincent.

Ron Potocki of Prep leads the
centers, but Ted Loader of East,
Marlow Burt of Vincent and
Alan Gunner of Academy are
also tough boys at the snapper-
back position.

The County, coached by Tom
Timmons, former Fairview mentor, and Carmen Bonito of
Waterford, hopes to throw a few
surprises into the City camp.

The County will give up a lo
of poundage but hopes to make
up for that in speed, deception
and fight.

There are several outstanding
backs on the County roster,
namely, Roger Brady of Wesleyville; Ed Dalglish of Millcreek
Park; Jack Debold of Fairview;
Bob Habel of Fairview; Girard's
Steve Woitovich who is headed
for Pitt; and Ed Wise of Albion.
Bill Vorsheck of Lawrence
Park, Hal Hart of Wesleyville
and Ben Budzowski of Edinboro
are the cream of the ends.
Don Schlindwine of Harborcreek; Bill Angelotti of Millcreek
Lawrence Park's Don Whip-
weight at

ERIE LIONS' CLUB

ALL-STAR FOOTBALL GAME

SEPTEMBER 7, 1953

udent:

The ANNUAL ERIE LIONS' CLUB ALL-STAR FOOTBALL GAME
led to be played on Labor Day, September 7, 1953.

Once again we are asking members of the City and
ol bands, and also the twirlers, to participate in
halves program. Mr. Schliken and Mr. Porsch will be
the combined bands while Mr. Swahn and Miss Spaths
the twirlers.

he between halves performance this year is to be
an historical pageant. It will be an exception-
and should prove to be a wonderful experience
cipating.

tice sessions for both band members and the
uled for the following dates: August 24,
tember 2, and 4th. Time; 7 to 8:30 p.m.
ld appreciate your attending all of the
nd, I am sure, the instructors mentioned
than grateful for your participation.
e session participants will receive
uniforms and equipment.

ET THE FIRST PRACTICE SESSION

VENING - AUGUST 24, 1953

UM - 26th & STATE STREETS

Thanks A Lot,

W. W. Openlander
Chairman Entertainment Committee

u cannot take part in this years'
ciate your letting us know by
ommerce Building, Erie, Pa.

Strong County Backfield Poses Threat For City

COUNTY COACHES Joe Timmons and Carmen Bonito short on bench strength for their coming encounter with crew next Monday night in the annual Lions Club "Save game, but with the fine array of backs at their com Countians could make things rough.

This was shown at last night's drill at East where the pitching of Roger Brady and Ed Dalglish and the catching of Ends Tiny Hart and Bill Vorshcek stood out like a beacon light.

Along with a glittering passing exhibition, the County lads had some good running from backs Chuck Woitovich, Bob Habel, Hank DeBold and Jack Cross

Tonight the County squad will get a chance to mix it up a little during a s scrimmage in an effort chance to

"But w formance the way summed work.

On Jack smith throu at F pec bo th

12   THE ERIE DISPATCH
Tuesday, Sept. 8, 1953

Linemen Lead City All-Stars To 12-6 Triumph

37-Yarder By Lynch Decides

STATISTICS

	City	Co.
First Downs	15	8
Rushing yardage	208	27
Passing yardage	70	111
Passes attempted	14	14
Passes completed	4	6
average	2	4
	31	31

UNABLE TO do a thing in first half, the ... Again the 11 in the flock of red thrown b ugh. The victim fensive Steve Woitovich County finally moved forward on hailed on the 24. The its final play when Dalglish pass ed to Woitovich on the 17.

But it was much too little and much too late. The City took over and ran out the clock in four plays.

Despite some fine runing, particularly by Lynch who gained 140 of his teams 208 yards on the ground, the City didnt' score until the closing minutes of the first half. Earlier drives sputtered on the nine, 12 and 21-yard stripes.

The City got a break when it turned into a 15-yard advance on a clipping penalty that put the winners in business on the County 40. Lynch ripped off 18 yards to the 22 and Gordon Shay hit Dan Wisniewski with the seven. Mike Rocco with a touchdown strike

---

STATISTICS

	City	Co.
First Downs	15	8
Rushing yardage	208	27
Passing yardage	70	111
Passes attempted	14	14
Passes completed	4	6
Punts	2	4
Punting average	31	31
Fumbles lost	0	1
Yards penalized	45	35

By TOM MACGUIRE

The "experts" were predicting last week that the City All-Stars would beat the County All-Stars by a touchdown in the Lions Club Save-an-Eye game and that the difference would be the city's fine line.

For once the "experts" were right, almost to the smallest detail, the City beat the County, 12-6, in the 15th running of the spectacle at the Stadium last night. And the difference was the City's magnificent line—with a generous assist from Halfback Jimmy Lynch.

* * *

THE CITY'S forwards spent the entire night building up an impressive set of defensive statistics—the County made only 27 yards rushing and 138 all told. But the boys saved their major ort until there was a scant two tes left in the

---

UNABLE TO do a thing in the first half, the County moved to the 11 in the third period but was thrown back by the city's fine defensive platoon. The City took possession on the 20 and whipped up an 80-yard march for its second touchdown. Wisniewski and Lynch picked up the major gains before Jimmy traveled the last 37 for the score.

Vorscheck, easily the County's outstanding performer, set up his team's fourth-period score when he deflected a punt by Rocco deep in City territory. The effort enabled the County to start from the City 32 and hit paydirt in four plays. Vorscheck caught two straight passes for the first 19 and Steve Woitovich dashed the last 13 through a yawning hole in the left side of the line.

Passing was the County's strong point with Vorscheck catching five tosses for 105 yards. Dalglisch and Brady were about even on the throwing end.

The City made 70 yards off the arms of Shay and Rocco ... The crowd of 10,000 was good

... achy, Adel... Lamphere, Sedmina, Grit... Wise, Alcorn, Bretzm Dal... Cross, Timmons.

City

Pete Alex	Tech
Bob Alo	Tech
Ron Biletnikoff	Academy
Don Burger	Academy
Joe Cuzzola	Cathedral Prep
John Daniels	East
Paul Demyanovich	East
Rich Dickey	Strong Vincent
Ed DiNicola	Tech
Phil DiNicola	Strong Vincent
Rich Doyle	Strong Vincent
George Foor	East
Ed Hokaj	Cathedral Prep
Tim Holland	Cathedral Prep
Jack Laraway	Academy
Mel Laskoff	East
Ken Legenzoff	East
Jim Letcher	Academy
Dick McCrillis	Academy
Rich Pasquale	Tech
Gus Patsy	Academy
Joe Romeo	Strong Vincent
Jim Ross	East
Jim Schumacker	Cathedral Prep
Dana Tomczak	Cathedral Prep
Bob Vomero	East
Walt Watral	East
John Zuck	Tech

Coaches: Ted Robb of Tech, Joe Robie of Cathedral Prep

County

Doug Barnes	Union City
Dick Bischoff	Millcreek
Bruce Boyle	Harbor Creek
John Buffington	North East
John Corklin	Cambridge Springs
Ted Elchynski	Corry
Harold Fiddler	Millcreek
Chuck Fleming	Corry
Jack Frey	Girard
Rich Fuller	Edinboro
Ron Gates	Corry
Don Gourley	Lawrence Park
Phil Hazen	Waterford
Don Johnson	Conneaut Valley
Joe Kardosh	Conneaut Valley
Bob Manners	Edinboro
Tom Mitchell	Millcreek
Wes Nicklas	Waterford
Mel Oakes	Wesleyville
Dave Pfeil	Girard
Walt Ptaskiewicz	Wesleyville
Glen Rust	Cambridge Springs
Dell Shields	Waterford
Jim Smith	North East
Jack Strubel	Fairview
Stan Styborski	Cambridge Springs
Don Swartwood	Harbor Creek
Ken Traut	Fairview
Norm Troyer	Union City
Ken Weed	Millcreek
Jack Yount	Lawrence Park

Coaches: Ed Poly of Lawrence Park, Terry Darcangelo of Cambridge Springs

CITY 14 - COUNTY 0

Fumble recoveries set up both City touchdowns. Ken Legenzoff of East covered a loose ball on the 4-yard line with 50 seconds left in the first half. The recovery ended a long County march which featured Jack Yount of Lawrence Park, Norm Troyer of Union City and Dell Shields of Waterford.

The City went the distance in three plays. Tim Holland of Cathedral Prep ran for 46 yards. Mel Laskoff of East passed 27 yards to Dana Tomczak of Prep. Pete Alex of Tech then hit Tomczak for a 23-yard touchdown pass. Tomczak made a leaping catch in the corner of the end zone as the half ended. Don Burger of Academy recovered a fumble to set up Holland's 13-yard run for a touchdown on the first play of the fourth quarter. Laskoff kicked both extra points. The City had a 127-18 edge in passing.

16TH SAVE-AN-EYE CLASSIC
City Eleven Rated Slim All-Star Choice
with a tricky spread format!

Tim Holland vividly remembers two things about the 1954 Save-An-Eye Game. "It was a beautiful night, and it was a big thrill to play in the game," Holland said. Oh, he also recalls quite a few other things about the game. One of those things was a 46-yard run that helped set up a City touchdown just before the first half ended. The other was his 13-yard touchdown run in the fourth quarter of a 14-0 City win. "That first run helped us get going," Holland said, who had played for Cathedral Prep. "Pete Alex—he was the MVP—had a great game. He threw a touchdown pass to Dana Tomczak."

The touchdown pass that Holland remembered covered 23 yards.

Tim Holland – 1954

Holland said the City coaches, Ted Robb of Tech and Joe Robie of Cathedral Prep, had the team run a Tandem-T offense. "Sometimes the snap went directly to the quarterback and sometimes the snap went straight back to the tailback." Holland's touchdown run came on a quarterback sneak. "The defense had a six-man line and it opened right up."

Holland later became a coach and twice coached the City team in Save-An-Eye games. Once was in 1994, 40 years after he played in the game. He was the head City coach and Joe Tarasovitch, his assistant coach at Central, was on his staff. The other game he coached was when he assisted Tarasovitch, then the Fort LeBoeuf head coach, for the County team.

– Joe Mattis

Game 17 – September 5, 1955

City		County	
Richard Anderson	Tech	Don Brandon	Fairview
Charles Augustine	Cathedral Prep	Ron Brecious	McDowell
Ed Bednarowicz	Tech	Sherman Clark	Harbor Creek
Erwin Bloxdorf	Academy	Jim Concilla	North East
Fred Bongiorno	Strong Vincent	Richard Cross	McDowell
Bill Bujnoski	Cathedral Prep	Clyde Eaton	Fairview
Tom Corapi	Cathedral Prep	John Gage	Albion
Ed DeLuca	East	Kay Garn	Wesleyville
Dan Desser	Cathedral Prep	Bruce Goetz	Girard
Dick Dill	Cathedral Prep	Frank Hlifka	Girard
William Dodge	East	Jack Johnson	Lawrence Park
Ernest Dunn	Academy	Ron Jones	Waterford
James Graham	Academy	Walter Kreide	Wesleyville
Frank Haraczy	Cathedral Prep	Howard Markham	Waterford
Ron Haugsdahl	Strong Vincent	Tom Mowery	Fairview
Gordon Ketchel	Tech	Bob O'Leary	St. Gregory
Bernard Kowalski	Tech	Bob Pavolko	Albion
George Mangol	Cathedral Prep	Carl Pekala	Lawrence Park
Graham Parsons	Academy	David Riggs	Union City
Walter Pelkowski	Strong Vincent	Walter Sanders	Corry
Jim Schaaf	Cathedral Prep	Carl Schlipf	Wesleyville
Paul Shopene	East	Richard Schmeider	Wesleyville
George Smith	East	Harold Seifert	Harbor Creek
Ken Sullivan	Academy	James Shaver	Corry
Ron Thomas	Strong Vincent	Dick Sorenson	Corry
Tom Tomb	Strong Vincent	James Tobin	Cambridge Springs
John Torrelli	Academy	Dick Triana	St. Gregory
Fred Trott	Academy	Nick Triana	North East
Jerry Winters	Academy	Mike Wander	McDowell
Angelo Zonno	Strong Vincent	Ted Woitovich	Girard

Coaches: Walt Strosser of Cathedral Prep, Mike Ferrare of Academy

Coaches: Lou Hanna of Corry, Russell Brant of Union City

CITY 19 - COUNTY 13

 $\mathcal{M}$ ore than 13,000 fans saw quarterback Johnny Torrelli of Cathedral Prep score on a 19-yard halfback pass from Tom Corapi of Prep with 35 seconds left to decide the game. Torrelli also had a 90-yard kickoff runback for a touchdown. Chuck Augustine of Prep ran 9 yards for a touchdown and a 6-0 City halftime lead. John Gage of Albion went 30 yards with a fumble recovery for a score and Jack Johnson of Lawrence Park added the conversion.

Dick Sorenson of Corry scored on a 1-yard plunge for the County. The County had a 13-12 lead until the final dramatic City touchdown. The County comeback featured Tom Mowery of Fairview and Jim Concilla of North East. Mowery and Torrelli won MVP awards.

All-Star Grid Teams Battle In Stadiums

Football, All-Star variety, makes its annual Erie appearance Monday night with the 17th Lions Club Save-An-Eye charity game.

Supplying the bill-of-fare in the 8 p. m. Stadium tilt are a total of 60 star gladiators representing the City and County.

THESE ATHLETES will exhibit their respective talents while carrying out assignments grasped in one week from Walt Strosser and Mike Ferrare of the City and Lou Hanna and Russ Brandt of the County.

Enlivening the glasses-for-the-needy program will be a halftime ceremony replete with marching bands, twirlers, and majorettes.

Successful since the switch to City-County from East-West status in 1952, the "city boys" will attempt to annex their fourth straight victory at the expense of their "country cousins."

The County, naturally, will be bent on stopping the City march by combining the wizardry or Corry's Hanna with a maze of moleskin talent that features a versatile and speedy backfield.

ROMPING IN THE COUNTY secondary will be such area renowns as Fairview's Dangerous Duo, Tom Mowry and Don Brandon; Girard's durable Ted Woitovich; Harborcreek's slippery Sherm Clark; triple threat Jim Concilla, North East; pile-driving Dick Sorenson, Corry; and Wesleyville's one-two combination of Carl Schlipf and Kay Garn.

Hanna, who masterminded Corry to two Section II championships in four seasons, will stick to his single wing attack -- the same style offensive that helped Corry to a 20-game winning streak extending through three campaigns.

County lines in the past have shown considerable aggressiveness, attested to the three previous scores. The County has never permitted more than three touchdowns, losing 19-6, 12-6 and 14-0 last year.

THIS YEAR'S COUNTY line hopes to continue the tradition of its predecessors. The '55 line has the ingredients with such prize package tackles as Don Gage, Albion 200-pounder and co-captain with Wesleyville guard Walt Kreide; Clyde Eaton, Fairview 210-pounder; Bruce Getz, Girard 205-pounder; and Jack Johnson, 203-pounder from Lawrence Park.

Against this array, Strosser and Ferrare will retaliate with a T formation offensive and a slightly smaller but aggressive line. Forming the nucleus of the T pattern are Cathedral Prep's Johnny Augustine and Academy All-City Johnny

Torrelli. Augustine knows the T blindfolded under Strosser. Torrelli runs and passes with almost equal dexterity.

Running with Augustine and Torrelli, who will alternate at quarterback, are Fred Bongiorno, Strong Vincent; Graham Parsons, Academy; Gordy Ketchel and Ed Bednarowicz of Tech; Ed DeLuca and George Smith, East; and George Mangol of Prep.

PREP HIGH SCHOOL All-American Jim Schaaf and Vincent's Walt Pelkowski are the only City linemen over the 200-pound mark. Both are tackles.

But Strosser and Ferrare can call upon the experienced services of slightly lighter All-City campaigners Ernie Dunn, Erwin Riesdorf, and Jerry Winter, Academy; Dick ___ and Paul Shopene, East.

Nats' Last Hope: T...

Erie T...

In 1955 Jim Concilla came within 35 seconds of walking off the Veterans Stadium field with the satisfaction of playing on a winning team. But quarterback Johnny Torrelli spoiled the dreams of North East's Concilla and his County teammates. Torrelli's late touchdown run lifted the City to a 19-13 victory.

Jim Concilla – 1955

One of the positive things that came out of that game was a lifelong friendship with Academy's Fred Trott, even though he played for the City team. "We became good friends and roommates at Edinboro," said Concilla, who visited with Trott in Florida this past winter. Concilla had a great career with North East as both a player and coach. In his senior season, quarterback Concilla trailed only senior Tom Mowery of Fairview and junior Grapepicker teammate Tony Sanfilippo in scoring as North East won the Erie County League championship.

After graduating from Edinboro, Concilla was coaching at Silver Creek in New York when he got a call from the North East superintendent of schools. "He wanted me to coach and teach math," Concilla said. After some negotiations, the super had his man. "I played under Bob Thurbon at North East," Concilla said.

"He taught me the fundamentals, but he was a tough coach. When I began coaching, I was tough, too. I had about 11 seniors on the North East team, and in a week I had only four left."

Before the next season, a young Jim Camp of the Erie Morning News came to a preseason practice to talk to Concilla about the North East team. "He asked me how our team would be," Concilla said. "I told him, 'We're gonna go undefeated.'" Concilla could not have called it better as the Grapepickers finished the 1968 season without a loss.

– Joe Mattis

Your Support of this Save-An-Eye Game....

has during the past year provided medical eye care, examinations, and glasses to over 480 individuals for whom 425 pair of glasses where provided. This work costing nearly $5,500 covered medical fees for eye examinations, lenses, frames, repairs to old glasses, and 19 pair of special safety glasses for the machine shop classes of Technical High School. Since the Lions Club program was initiated in 1935, over 6,000 pairs of glasses have been provided to those in need throughout Erie County. This you have done through your support of the Erie Lions Club.

1955
Erie Lions Save-an-Eye
ALL-STAR
FOOTBALL GAME

COUNTY SCHOOLS
LAWRENCE PARK
ALBION
McDOWELL - CAMBRIDGE SPRINGS
NORTH EAST - HARBORCREEK
WESLEYVILLE
CORRY - UNION CITY
GIRARD - WATERFORD
ST. GREGORY   FAIRVIEW

CITY SCHOOLS
ERIE EAST   ERIE TECH
STRONG VINCENT
CATHEDRAL
ERIE ACA

Your Support of this Save-An-Eye Game....

made it possible for the Erie Lions Club to lend substantial financial assistance to a New Erie Center for the Blind at East 21st St. when it was established this past year. The Erie Lions contribution of $3,000 assisted in the leasing, re-pairing, and equipping a building providing general offices, recreation rooms, training room, kitchen, and workshop. These facilities has made it possible to pro-vide for the blind and visu-ally impaired; a workshop employing ten blind men and women, cooking classes for blind hoome-makers, re-creation for 75 blind per-sons, talking book machines for 103 blind people, radios for 30 indigent blind, counseling to 150 blind persons, and prevention of blindness care to over 200. Your support of the Erie Lions Club has made this possible.

ERIE'S CENTER FOR THE BLIND
ERIE COUNTY BRANCH
PENNSYLVANIA ASSOCIATION FOR THE BLIND, INC.

Game 18 – September 3, 1956

City

Dave Blake	Academy
Fran Brady	Tech
Tim Bujnowski	East
Tom Cahill	Strong Vincent
Don Chludzinski	Tech
Paul DeRaimo	Tech
Pete Donatucci	Cathedral Prep
Bob Federoff	East
George Fessler	Cathedral Prep
Tom Freebourn	Strong Vincent
John Fries	Cathedral Prep
John Gorney	Cathedral Prep
Mike Gregory	Academy
Ron Hahn	Strong Vincent
Dave Hilbert	Academy
Paul Hilbert	East
Allyn Lesko	Strong Vincent
John Mahon	East
John Miller	East
Ray Nicolia	Cathedral Prep
Tony Nunes	Tech
Ernie Riley	Academy
Pedro Sampani	Tech
John Scheffner	Academy
Joe Schlossle	Cathedral Prep
Tim Skarupski	Tech
David Squeglia	Cathedral Prep
Ron Williams	Academy
Dick Wood	East
Dick Wright	Strong Vincent
Bart Zurn	Strong Vincent

Coaches: Al Calabrese of Tech, Chubby Kuhl of East

County

Tom Allen	Harbor Creek
Phil Almendinger	Millcreek
Jack Delavern	Millcreek
Art DiRienzo	Millcreek
Ken Eaton	Fairview
George Gido	Girard
Jim Goodman	Lawrence Park
Vern Graham	Fort LeBoeuf
Bob Gumbert	Edinboro
Tom Hilinski	Harbor Creek
Jack Hrinda	Girard
John Klomp	Wesleyville
Bill Lewis	North East
Al Nicastro	St. Gregory
Ron Rickards	Albion
Tony Sanfilippo	North East
Dick Scott	Harbor Creek
Jim Smith	Wesleyville
Lyman Sornberger	Fairview
Merle Spacht	North East
Roland Thomas	Union City
Dick Vidic	Wesleyville
Roy Wilkinson	Corry

Coaches: John Fails of Harbor Creek, Joe Setcavage of North East.

CITY 33 - COUNTY 12

The City dominated in front of 14,000 fans. A balanced attack helped the City roll up a 234-36 edge in rushing. Tony Nunes of Tech had 57 yards on the ground. Paul DeRaimo of Tech also had 57 yards. Tom Freebourn of Strong Vincent had 35 yards rushing and Ray Nicolia of Prep added 30 yards. Nicolia scored on a 55-yard interception return and kicked three extra points. Dave Blake of Academy scored on a 74-yard pass from Nunes. Nunes, DeRaimo and Mike Gregory of Academy also scored on 1-yard runs for the winners.

Tony Sanfilippo of North East plunged 1 yard and Jack Delavern of Millcreek caught a 65-yard pass from Tom Hilinski of Harbor Creek for County touchdowns. Sanfilippo accounted for 55 yards rushing, 27 yards receiving and 21 yards passing.

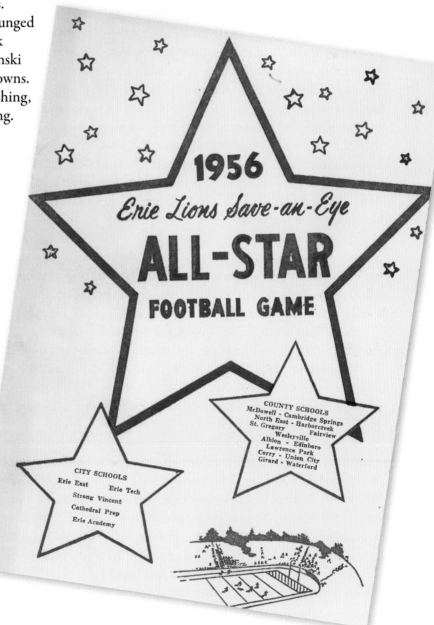

1956
Erie Lions Save-an-Eye
ALL-STAR
FOOTBALL GAME

COUNTY SCHOOLS
McDowell - Cambridge Springs
North East - Harborcreek
St. Gregory   Fairview
Wesleyville
Albion - Edinboro
Lawrence Park
Corry - Union City
Girard - Waterford

CITY SCHOOLS
Erie East   Erie Tech
Strong Vincent
Cathedral Prep
Erie Academy

Frank "Butch" Perino had a good reason for his summer workouts at North East's A.C. Field with his close friend, Tony Sanfilippo, in 1956. Perino was an offensive guard and defensive end at North East St. Gregory High School, a small Catholic school that eventually closed in 1968.

Sanfilippo was one of the outstanding running backs in Erie County at North East High School. Both had been selected to play for the County Team in the Save-An-Eye Game on Labor Day and they wanted to be in top shape.

Frank "Butch" Perino – 1956

Player Medal 1956

"It was going to be my last high school game," recalled Perino, called Butch by his grandmother as a child and still known by that nickname today. "I was just 5'10" and 170 pounds – we had a small school and no big players — but we were fast. And in my senior year we were 7-1, and six of those wins were shutouts." One afternoon in August, Perino had a pain in his abdomen. "I tried to walk it off, but that didn't work," he said. "Then at 2 a.m., I passed out in the bathroom." He was taken to the hospital for what was thought to be a bowel obstruction. In reality, the symptoms were from his appendix, which was surgically removed. "I woke up with a bandage on the left side of my abdomen," Perino said. "The doctor asked me, 'Were you going to play in a football game?' That's all you talked about before we took you into surgery."

Perino's dream of playing against many of the City players that he grew up with near Strong Vincent before moving to North East was dashed. Still, he was on the sideline and he carried a water bucket to the County players on the field during time outs in a game won by the City, 33-12. Even though he is not listed as a player, Perino received a commemorative medal awarded to all players selected on the City and County squads. He still cherishes that medal today.

Perino did get to see his son Jeff play and coach in the Save-An-Eye Game. Jeff, who was a lineman at North East and later at Bethany College, played in the 1980 Save-An-Eye Game and was an assistant County coach in 1982 and 1983 while a college student. "I was home for the summer and working out. My high school coach, Rip Simmons, was coaching the County team. He asked me to help in those games," said Jeff Perino, who now teaches theater at Dr. Phillips High School in Orlando, Florida.

Two months after the 1956 Save-An-Eye Game, Butch Perino began working at Penelec. That was the beginning of a career with the utility company that lasted until he retired in 1994. Would things have been different in his life if Perino had played in that 1956 game? Maybe. "Back then, college coaches came to scout the players in the Save-An-Eye Game, and some would offer scholarships to players based on how they played," Perino said. "We had beaten North East in a scrimmage and Bob Thurbon, an assistant North East coach, said if I did well maybe he could get me some help going to a school." Obviously, that never happened.

"I still have some disappointment that I could not play, "Perino said. "I always wonder where my life would have gone if maybe I went to college. But I still had a good life and have no regrets."

– Joe Mattis

The Save-An-Eye Game was renowned
for its halftime entertainment.

'Save-An-Eye' Game To Feature Spectacular Half - Time Show

"Glorifying the American Girl" will be the theme for the spectacular gridiron show, being presented between halves of the Lions Club of Erie All-Star "Save-An-Eye" football game being played in the Erie Stadium Labor Day, Sept. 3. Game time is 8 p. m. and the half-time show is scheduled to get under way at 9:15 p. m. Highlight of the performance will be the appearance of "Miss Erie," Carolyn Morgan, in the grand finale.

In charge of this year's spectacle are Carl Peterson, co-ordinator of music in the Erie schools, Al Cerutti and William King, musical directors for Harborcreek and Albion schools, directing the musical portion of the show. Also Clarence Swahn, Academy High, assisted by the Misses Carolyn Fulton, Nadine Field, Carol Kensill and Dianne Linsey, is responsible for the intricate drills and marching formations of the twirlers. The instructors have adopted some new and novel ideas for this year's performance and predict the precision wok of the girls will really be something to witness.

great half-time show, are to be commended for their community spirit. These youngsters devote at least two weeks of their vacation

period rehearsing for this show and are deserving of a great deal of credit for their part in assisting the Lions Club of Erie in this an-

nual project to raise funds in order to carry on the "Save-An-Eye" work for another year," A Lions Club officer said.

Many people look forward to seeing this outstanding portion of the [...] event each year and [...]d Openlander, chairman [...]time show, assures the [...]is year's per-[...] and better [...] fifty

August 8, 1956

Dear Friend:

It is time to announce the rehearsal schedule for band and twirlers for the big SAVE-AN-EYE game on Labor Day.

Here it is:

    August 20 - 22 - 24

    August 27 - 29 - 31

    GAME - Labor Day - September 3rd.

Rehearsals will begin at 7:00 P.M. sharp, at the Stadium in Erie. Please plan to arrive 15 minutes early. In case of rain, rehearsals will be held the following evening.

This year's show should be terrific! We have a potential band of 150 and 150 majorettes, if everyone comes through. The show will be called "Glorifying the American Girl" and we have some attractive music and formation work to prepare. Directors are Al Cerutti of Harborcreek, William King of Albion, Carl Peterson and Clarence Swahn from Erie.

Because of the size and scope of the show we must insist on almost perfect attendance. All participants must be present for 5 of the 6 rehearsals. No excuses can be accepted for the final rehearsal on August 31st.

We know you will want to help with this fine charity venture.

See you EARLY on AUGUST 20th.

        Sincerely,

        Willard Openlander,
        Music Chairman
        LIONS' CLUB SAVE-AN-EYE GAME

Frank "Butch" Perino 1956

Game 19 – September 2, 1957

City

Art Baker	Academy
William Carey	Cathedral Prep
Bob Cenfetelli	Tech
Ron Costello	Cathedral Prep
Ed Davis	Cathedral Prep
Richard Donikowski	Tech
Richard Doolittle	Strong Vincent
Felix Emeideo	Tech
James Jaycox	Tech
Art Jensen	Academy
Ron Kujawinski	Cathedral Prep
Bob Lugo	Cathedral Prep
Alan Marthesen	Academy
John Murphy	Cathedral Prep
Ron Pasarelli	Strong Vincent
Richard Perfetto	Strong Vincent
Harold Redinger	Strong Vincent
Carl Rundquist	Tech
Richard Sementilli	Strong Vincent
Richard Sins	Academy
Don Sokoloff	East
Dale Sorensen	East
Ray Stahon	Academy
Eugene Tomczak	Cathedral Prep
Tom Yacobizzi	Strong Vincent
John Zolikoff	East

Coaches: John Krkoska of Strong Vincent, Ray Dombrowski of Tech

County

John Austin	Edinboro
Carl Benden	North East
Elvin Brown	Cambridge Springs
Robert Burick	Lawrence Park
Herb Carr	Millcreek
Norb Cross	Waterford
Connie French	Corry
Jim Getsinger	Conneautville
Bert Hackenberg	Harbor Creek
Steve Holowach	Cambridge Springs
Laverne Hurlburt	Union City
Myron Latimer	Millcreek
Ken Leuschen	Millcreek
George Logan	Conneautville
Dave Mackowski	Millcreek
Jack Magee	Union City
Ralph McKay	Girard
Ted Miller	Edinboro
William Mitchell	Corry
William Morley	Cranesville
Bob Morosky	Wesleyville
Ralph Niebauer	Fairview
Richard Pavolko	Albion
John Puzarowski	Harbor Creek
Robert Ross	Wesleyville
Joe Sosnowski	North East
Chuck Villa	North East
Jim Wagner	Harbor Creek
Vic Waisley	Fairview
Dan Woitovich	Girard

Coaches: John Rimmy of Fairview, Paul Goll of Millcreek

CITY 12 - COUNTY 2

*T*he start of the game was delayed 15 minutes due to rain. Despite the weather, 12,000 fans attended. Ron Costello of Cathedral Prep and Art Baker of Academy starred for the City. The County owned an early 2-0 lead when Connie French of Corry tackled Costello in the end zone on attempted pass.

Costello passed 6 yards to Hal Redinger of Strong Vincent for the first touchdown. Baker led a drive for the second City touchdown. His 17-yard run on fourth-and-8 was the key play. Baker went the final 5 yards on the next play. Dan Woitovich of Girard hit 5 of 12 passes for 50 yards for the County. Bob Lugo of Prep and Gene Tomczak of Prep aided the City ground game. Costello, headed for Xavier, hit 6 of 10 passes for 80 yards. Baker, a Syracuse signee, picked up 49 yards on 10 carries.

Ron Costello, shown running the ball for Cathedral Prep, was the quarterback for the 1957 City team.

BANDS

Football wouldn't be football without the spirited blare of trumpets and the invigorating lift of a lively band marching in forceful cadence across the green! Viewers of the 1957 Save-an-Eye game have a real treat in store for them. Not just one school band, but a 100 piece band, assembled from the star musicians of NINETEEN city and county schools will play for you! Don Ricart and Al Cerutti, musical directors of East High and Harborcreek, have really exceeded themselves this year—creating a musical show for your enjoyment around selections all of which discuss various phases of the WEATHER. These stars make no touchdowns, but we feel sure they will make a hit with you.

GIRLS! GIRLS

It has always seemed to the writer
pleasant job of all the teachers at Aca
other duties, he instructs the girl twi
Surrounded, hour after hour, by be
From the cream of the crop in the
built a pageant like nothing you hav
own costume for the show, so their
ical theme - the WEATHER. A s
Girls!

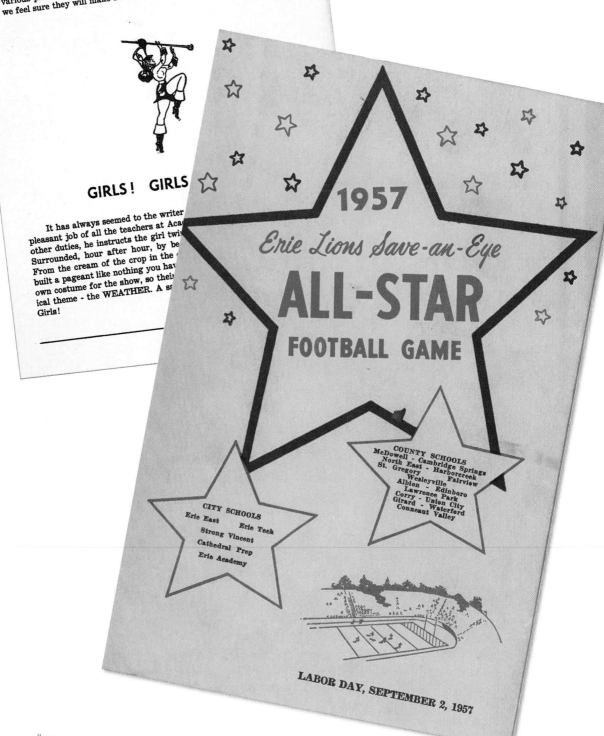

1957
Erie Lions Save-an-Eye
ALL-STAR
FOOTBALL GAME

COUNTY SCHOOLS
McDowell - Cambridge Springs
North East - Harborcreek
St. Gregory - Fairview
Wesleyville
Albion - Edinboro
Lawrence Park
Corry - Union City
Girard - Waterford
Conneaut Valley

CITY SCHOOLS
Erie East   Erie Tech
Strong Vincent
Cathedral Prep
Erie Academy

LABOR DAY, SEPTEMBER 2, 1957

SAVE-AN-EYE FACTS

The Erie Lions Club's first Save-an-Eye venture was a "tag day" which netted $211.39.

The first Save-an-Eye football game was held in 1939. It earned $1400.00.

This is the NINETEENTH annual Save-an-Eye game.

During the past year, the Save-an-Eye fund spent over $8000.00 for glasses and eye examinations ALONE.

The Erie Lions Club Orthoptic Clinic at St. Vincent's Hospital will be 11 years old in October 1957. The Save-an-Eye Fund pays the entire operating deficit of the clinic.

The football used in tonight's game was one of six used in the famous Rose Bowl game last New Year's Day. It must be returned to the Wilson Sporting Goods Co. Museum when we are through with it.

Famous football coaches are in the stadium tonight, to scout the talents of the boys who play that others might see.

One of the Game Managers is a former Save-an-Eye star. When in high school, Chuck Hagmann believed in Save-an-Eye. As a man he still works for it, heart and soul.

John Bradford has been Field Judge in all 19 Save-an-Eye games.

Vision defects outnumber all others disclosed by school physical exams.

The Erie Lions Club Save-an-Eye Fund, Inc. is a non-profit corporation, no part of whose funds can benefit any member or officer. Contributions to it are fully deductible for tax purposes.

Page 13

Save-An-Eye trivia from the program

Game 20 – September 1, 1958

City

Dick Baniszewski	Cathedral Prep
Joe Berarducci	Strong Vincent
John Bobango	East
Dave Carter	Academy
Don Delo	East
Bill Eberlein	Cathedral Prep
Larry Frame	Academy
Jim Freeman	Cathedral Prep
Bill Hathaway	Academy
Ed King	Academy
Walt Litz	Tech
Gabe Morretini	Tech
Dennis Murphy	Tech
John Nelson	Cathedral Prep
Ed Onorato	Tech
Leon Ott	Academy
Dave Parmeter	Tech
Byron Smith	Tech
Gary Valerio	Strong Vincent
Tom Walkiewicz	Cathedral Prep
George Wurst	Academy
John Zack	Cathedral Prep

County

Walter Baldauf	Fairview
Norm Beemis	North East
Gary Besonson	Union City
Greg Besonson	Union City
Steve Bretz	Harbor Creek
Tony Burgett	Edinboro
Andy Connor	Millcreek
Dick Feidler	Millcreek
Gary Garn	Wesleyville
Ben Greer	Albion
Harry Harbaugh	Girard
Chuck James	North East
Dave Kibler	Girard
Robert Kidon	Fairview
Dick Kierstan	North East
John McClellan	Waterford
Steve Moorhead	Harbor Creek
Vince Moran	Millcreek
Bob Nichols	Corry
Jerry Olson	Lawrence Park
Pat Podoll	Albion
Allan Repine	Lawrence Park
Barney Rutkowski	Wesleyville
Mike Saccamozzone	St. Gregory
Duane Taylor	Albion
Don Trohoske	Millcreek
Dave Vannoy	Corry
Lee Williams	Corry
Carl Wolfrom	Waterford

Coaches: Duke Detzel of East,
Tony Zambroski of Cathedral Prep

Coaches: Carm Bonito of Waterford,
Darwin Cook of Albion

CITY 13 - COUNTY 6

*G*ary Valerio of Strong Vincent blocked a punt and returned it 42 yards to set up the first City touchdown. Leon Ott of Academy scored on a double reverse. Walt Litz of Tech kicked the extra point. John Zack of Prep recovered a fumble on the County 9-yard line. One play later Litz passed 6 yards to Tom Walkiewicz of Prep for the touchdown.

Dick Feidler of Millcreek recovered a fumble on the City 11-yard line to set up the County's only touchdown. Lee Williams of Corry scored on a 3-yard run. Walkiewicz broke up two pass plays midway through the fourth quarter to end a County threat. Barney Rutkowski of Wesleyville completed two passes in the final minute before time elapsed, ending the final County threat. 12,000 attended the game.

> 66 I played offensive and defensive end. In those days, we played both ways. I played fairly well on defense and I scored one touchdown that helped the City beat the County.

Tom Walkiewicz – 1958

> (Cathedral Prep teammate) John Nelson and I attended Xavier University after that. I got through college on a football scholarship. John and I were roommates for three years. He now lives in Florida. He turned out to be one the best players Xavier had. He got drafted by the Chicago Bears. He didn't make it with the Bears though. He got hurt. That was my problem, two artificial knees later. 99

TRIBUTE TO TERMINAL
Tom Walkiewicz (center) accepts trophy as outstanding city player in recent Save-An-Eye All-Star football game. Presenting award to rangy end is Kennard Koons, game consultant, while Lions Club President M. E. Colby looks on.

ERIE, PENNSYLVANIA

Dear Lou,

You have been selected to play in the Lions Club Save-an-Eye Football Game which is to be played Labor Day evening at the Erie Stadium.

It is very important that we know if you can play in this game, so please let us know immediately in the following manner. If you can play, have your parents sign the parent permission card and return it in the enclosed envelope. This will indicate to us that you [will play].

[If you] can not play, indicate at the top of the parent [permissio]n card that you can't play and return it to us in [the enclos]ed envelope without your parent's signiture.

[Call] Ken Koons at 23-261 or myself at 25-604 or [me if] anything turns up between now and Labor Day that [makes it im]possible for you to play in the game. This is [as] important as we will have to get someone to take your place.

Sincerely yours,

Chuck Hagmann

Chuck Hagmann
Game Chairman

Walkiewicz Starred

TOM WALKIEWICZ, Prep's big end, was the top man for the City in pass catching and also as a defensive bulwark. Tom was in on half the tackles and scored the second City TD.

WALT LITZ also shares the top glory spot for the City. The little Tech field general ran his team to perfection.

EVERYONE was waiting for Leon Ott to explode. The Lions' halfback did just that on a 28-yard double-reverse for the first City TD. Ott had plenty of help on his jaunt, especially from Walkiewicz who blasted a County defender on the ten to open the door for the speedy ball carrier.

GABE MORRETINI also lent a helping hand on occasion. Twice Gabe set up a City first down with a neat bit of running.

AS WE SAID earlier, the game was an all-around success.

The Save-An-Eye Game is not all about players, coaches and referees. At one time it included girls. Gretchen Prozan, then know by her maiden name of Theobald, remembers the opportunity to be a part of the annual charity game. That was back in the late 1950s when she was a student at East High and a twirler at halftime. "I really enjoyed it," she said as she approached her 70th birthday earlier this year. "I was pretty excited. I really liked being in front of all of those people," she said of performing in front of a crowd of 12,000 in 1958.

Back in those days, the twirlers had to do other things besides perform at the game. "We made our own uniforms, so to speak," she said. "They were very simple. It was a Bolero over a white blouse with a shorter skirt."

Gretchen (Theobald) Prozan – 1958

The twirlers were a group made up of girls from all the schools that competed in the game. Because of that, there was not an opportunity to have many practices. "It must have been a pretty simple routine," Prozan recalled. "We practiced, but I'm not sure how many times."

Prozan said she began twirling while in seventh grade. When there was a chance to twirl for the Save-An-Eye Game, she went with friends to the tryout. "I was one of the youngest," she said. "It was very important to me at the time. My sister was also a twirler." Even though she is sure she performed at halftime of the 1958 game, Gretchen knows that was not her only Save-An-Eye Game. "That was quite some time ago. I think I might have twirled at the games in either 1957 or 1959, but I am sure I twirled more than once." Even though that part of her experience is not so clear in her mind today, there is one thing she will never forget. "It was an adrenaline rush," Prozan said.

– Joe Mattis

Game 21 – September 7, 1959

City

Stan Baginski	East
Richard Benz	Academy
Grove Blanchard	Academy
Dick Connors	Academy
Chris Cooney	Cathedral Prep
Gary Damico	Academy
Joe DeSanti	Tech
Don Detisch	Academy
Charles Grebielski	Academy
Bill Habersack	Cathedral Prep
Sam Hester	Strong Vincent
Bill Keller	East
Bob Morosky	East
Chuck Myers	Academy
Terry Pfeffer	Strong Vincent
Dave Quadri	Cathedral Prep
Tom Raleigh	Academy
Ron Rzepecki	East
Bob Rzepecki	East
Ted Skarupski	Tech
Terry St. John	Academy
Vince Teed	Cathedral Prep
Rich Valahovic	Tech
Rich Walach	East
Bill Whitford	Cathedral Prep

Coaches: Dick Detzel of Cathedral Prep, Jack Komora of Academy

County

Nick Alfieri	Harbor Creek
Bob Bailey	Corry
Larry Beard	Harbor Creek
Fred Bennett	Union City
Duane Black	McDowell
Robin Burrows	Lawrence Park
Ron Davis	Cambridge Springs
John Dingfelder	McDowell
Duane Farrell	Union City
Bob Glasgow	Lawrence Park
David Henry	Harbor Creek
Jack Humphreys	Lawrence Park
Bill Klenz	North East
Tom Klomp	Wesleyville
Jim Lamb	Lawrence Park
John Leech	Fort LeBoeuf
Tom Leopold	Fairview
George Naylor	Girard
David Pifer	Union City
Don Potter	Lawrence Park
Ben Pratt	McDowell
Wilbur Shenk	Fairview
Harry Thomas	Fort LeBoeuf
Don VanKeuren	Corry

Coaches: Ed Poly of Lawrence Park, Jim Manafo of Wesleyville

COUNTY 19 - CITY 12

*T*he County earned its first win under the current format behind Jack Humphreys of Lawrence Park. With 13,500 watching, he accounted for all three touchdowns on an 83-yard punt return, a 37-yard pass to Ben Pratt of McDowell and a 9-yard run. Humphreys also returned an interception 50 yards. Humphreys opened the scoring on a 9-yard run. Pratt kicked the extra point. Humphreys also made a touchdown-saving tackle. Stan Baginski of East, who ran 33 yards to the County 40 on the previous play, again broke loose, but Humphreys brought him down.

Grove Blanchard of Academy accounted for both City touchdowns. He ran 87 yards for one touchdown and scored another on a 31-yard pass from Chuck Myers of Academy with seven seconds left in the game.

County Out To Wreck City's Unbeaten Mark

By JACK POLANCY

The Erie County All-Star football team, boasting "their biggest line ever," will attempt to smash a string of seven straight City All-Star victories tonight in the Stadium.

Kickoff time, in this 21st renewal of the Lions Club "Save-An-Eye" grid classic is set for 8:00 p. m.

The All-Star Game, which originally began as an East versus West affair, was switched to a City-County duel in 1952. Since that time the County lads have ended on the short end of the final score.

Some 12,000 fans sat in on last year's tussel and witnessed the City kids take full advantage of two first half breaks for a 13-6 victory.

This year the County hopes hinge on three points; (1) A line which boasts a pair of Times-News All-County selections in Ft. LeBoeuf's 220-pound Dave Pifer and Edinboro's rugged Denny Russin, plus added weight in the form of the Bisons' John Leech who tips the scales at 240; (2) A set of fast backs featuring Fairview's Wilbur Shenk who scored 102 points last season, and Lawrence Park's J a c k

Humphreys, one of the best backs the County has seen in a few seasons; (3) Wesleyville's Jim Manafo and Lawrence Park's Ed Poly as the Couty coaches. Both are considered as the best in the area.

Of course the City isn't with-out its heroes.

The backfield is lightning fast with Academy's Dick Conner supplying most of the speed. The East High trio of Dick Walach, Stan Baginski and Bill Keller is the same trio that sparked the Warriors to the City title last year.

Along with these four will use such Vincent'

Chapter 4

$\mathcal{D}$efensive domination helped the City grind out eight wins in these ten games. Four of those victories came via shutouts. The County held the City scoreless in posting its two wins in the 1960s. The Save-An-Eye soared in popularity during this decade with huge crowds, including an estimated 16,000 in 1967. Cathedral Prep products Dave Tullio and Pat Tomczak combined for two touchdown passes in the 1960 game. The County, led by Wally Mahle of Fort LeBoeuf, walked off with a 14-0 win the next year. Mahle (Syracuse) and Rich Arrington (Notre Dame) of East were standouts.

The 1960s

The City piled up the most points of the decade with a 31-6 romp in 1962, spiced by a ground game led by East grads Tom Carpenter and Art Miller. An opportunistic City team took advantage of a blocked punt, a poor County kick and a fumble recovery to set up all its points in the 18-0 verdict in 1963. Tippy Pohl of East threw for 102 yards. One of the rare ties in the series came the next year when Mina George of East threw a 7-yard touchdown pass to Pat Lupo of Cathedral Prep with one second left.

The City, with Dave Wenrick of Prep at the helm, cruised to a 21-0 win in 1965. Wenrick, Jim Fries of Prep and Mel Cooper of East posted touchdowns. A late County drive was stopped at the City 5-yard line in 1966, preserving a 12-7 victory. Bob Woods of East caught a 4-yard pass from Barry Masterson of Prep for the deciding touchdown.

The County's 25-0 romp in 1967 had Tony Major of Iroquois catch five passes for 208 yards and two touchdowns. Denny Satyshur of East and Jerry Mifsud of Prep each scored two touchdowns in a 26-0 verdict in 1968. Closing out the decade, the threesome of Ron Nietupski of Tech, Don Aleksiewicz of East and Pat Steenberge of Prep paced a 12-0 win.

City

Harold Arrowsmith............Strong Vincent
Tom Biel ....Strong Vincent
Chuck Buerger .... East
Hubert Cioccio .... East
Craig Conboy....................Strong Vincent
Bill Cook ....Strong Vincent
Jim D'Andrea ....Strong Vincent
Bruce Decker .... Academy
Dick Dilimone .... Tech
Chuck Evanoff....................... Academy
Ron Evanoff .... Academy
Frank Huber .... Academy
Marty Kelly........................... Tech
Don Kwiatkowski .... East
Mike LeCorchick..............Cathedral Prep
Jim Miller .... Academy
Jack Moore ....Strong Vincent
Jim Nunes............................ Tech
Joe Ott ....Cathedral Prep
Doug Palmer .... Tech
Ted Peggy .... Tech
Tom Rehberg....................Cathedral Prep
Rich Scolio.....................Cathedral Prep
Joe Scully.....................Cathedral Prep
Dan Shade ....Cathedral Prep
Ted Skarupski .... Tech
Pat Tomczak ....Cathedral Prep
Dave Tullio ....Cathedral Prep
Ron Vomero....................Cathedral Prep
Elmer Woodard........................ Academy
Bill Ziegler .... Academy

Coaches: Lou Tullio of Academy,
Carney Metzgar of East

County

Joe Allesie ....Wesleyville
Larry Amenta ....St. Gregory
Jim Carter.....................General McLane
Floyd Chandler ....McDowell
Doug Elwell ....McDowell
Dennis Fiscus..........................North East
Gerry Fuller ....General McLane
Don Hayes ....Edinboro
Tom Heasley ....Edinboro
Sam Heller ....Wesleyville
Dave Horanic ....McDowell
John Kohut .... Albion
Bob McCammon ....Harbor Creek
Milt Phenneger ....Fairview
John Reagan.......................... Albion
Al Renshaw ....Lawrence Park
Steve Samol........................McDowell
Ron Shilling........................Girard
Arlyn Snyder....................Lawrence Park
Bob Terrill ....Fort LeBoeuf
Dick Vogt........................Fort LeBoeuf
Tom Woodring............ Cambridge Springs

Coaches: Paul Wilson of Girard, Bob
Jamison of General McLane

CITY 13 - COUNTY 6

*C*athedral Prep grads Dave Tullio and Pat Tomczak teamed for touchdown passes of 5 and 7 yards for the two City scores. With 10,147 fans on hand, Tullio set up the first City touchdown with a 23-yard run. After the Tullio-to-Tomczak touchdown connection, Joe Ott of Prep kicked the PAT. Joe Allessie of Wesleyville hit Ron Shilling of Girard for a 7-yard touchdown pass for the County. Elmer Woodard of Academy ran 20 yards on the City's other scoring drive. Tullio threw 17 yards to Doug Palmer of Tech, then hit Tomczak for 7 yards and the touchdown.

The County drove to the City 23-yard line midway in the fourth quarter before Don Kwiatkowski of East recovered a fumble. A Shilling interception and a fumble recovery by Gerry Fuller of General McLane gave the County two more chances, but both drives stalled.

Tullio, Tomczak Spark City

Short Passes Spoil
...nty Upset Plans

It's All-Star Football Time

Game 23 – September 4, 1961

City

John Alacce	East
Chuck Allen	Academy
Frank Antalek	Cathedral Prep
Rich Arrington	East
Tom Baginski	East
Frank Bizzarro	Academy
Chet Chrzanowski	Cathedral Prep
Fred Delfino	Academy
Larry Dibler	Academy
Bill Difenbach	Cathedral Prep
Mike Hakel	Tech
Ed James	Academy
Ken Kowalski	Academy
Jim Kubaney	Cathedral Prep
Gerald Legenzoff	Academy
Amos Mitchell	East
Dave Paris	Cathedral Prep
Ernie Pascarella	East
William Roznek	Tech
Tom Rys	Cathedral Prep
Joe St.George	Cathedral Prep
Marty Stepnoski	Tech
Fred Stover	East
Bill Swift	Academy
Bill Ziemer	Academy

Coaches: Tom Duff of Cathedral Prep, Jim Mahoney of Cathedral Prep

County

Don Baumgardner	McDowell
Dave Crotty	Lawrence Park
Bill Gaber	Fort LeBoeuf
Jim Grumblatt	Fort LeBoeuf
John Gustafson	Fairview
Sam Hazen	Fort LeBoeuf
Dick Heiden	North East
Hal Hunter	Union City
Tom Irish	Harbor Creek
George Kostrubanic	Fairview
Mike Lewis	Cambridge Springs
Walley Mahle	Fort LeBoeuf
Bob McKay	Girard
Dave Nishnick	Fort LeBoeuf
Dick Payne	Girard
Doug Payne	Fairview
Steve Rebro	Harbor Creek
Dick Schau	McDowell
Doug Seus	McDowell
Bob Smock	Cambridge Springs
Anthony Spada	North East
Don Stefano	Lawrence Park
Larry Thompson	Northwestern
Larry Valentine	Northwestern
Ron Zuck	Harbor Creek

Coaches: Paul Goll of McDowell, Arnold "Rip" Simmons of North East

COUNTY 14 - CITY 0

$\mathcal{W}$alley Mahle of Fort LeBoeuf led the County, with 11,000 fans watching. Mahle, who later played at Syracuse, scored on a 20-yard run. Sam Hazen of Fort LeBoeuf had a safety for the winners, tackling Tom Baginski of East in the end zone. An interception by George Kostrubanic of Fairview set up the other County touchdown in the fourth quarter. Kostrubanic returned the ball 31 yards to the County 34. Dick Schau of McDowell ran 34 yards with 15 seconds left for the touchdown. Rick Seus of McDowell had 31 yards on 10 carries. Dick Heiden of North East aided the County ground game. Mahle had nine carries for 54 yards. Bill Gabor of Fort LeBoeuf, Dave Crotty of Lawrence Park and Don Stefano of Lawrence Park were outstanding on defense. Rich Arrington of East, who went on to play at Notre Dame, was a standout in a losing cause for the City.

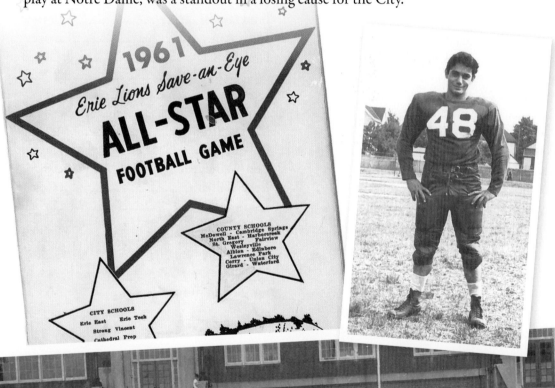

"We had so much fun playing we didn't care who won or lost. We just enjoyed being with each other and playing football."
John Alacce 1961

City Team

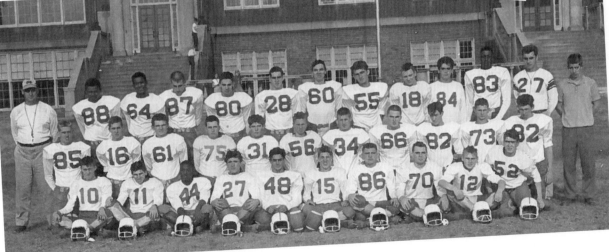

Game 24 – September 3, 1962

City

Ed Arrington	East
Ike Battles	East
Robert Brei	Tech
Jay Buchanan	Strong Vincent
Brian Carlson	Strong Vincent
Tom Carpenter	East
James Cermak	Academy
Ron Chimenti	Cathedral Prep
Ed Goodrich	Strong Vincent
Ron Gorney	Cathedral Prep
James Hedderick	Academy
Bill Horihan	Tech
Tom Irwin	Academy
Bob Kaczenski	Cathedral Prep
Robert Kowalewski	East
Eugene Kurt	Cathedral Prep
Al Lubiejewski	Cathedral Prep
Dennis Markham	Academy
Dale Massing	Strong Vincent
Art Miller	East
Richard Nikolishen	Tech
Vincent Rapp	Strong Vincent
Edwin Reid	Academy
Dick Scheppner	Cathedral Prep
Gil Stoddard	Academy
Joseph Wasiulewski	Tech
Dan Wenrick	Tech

Coaches: Tony Verga of Academy, Ralph Calabrese of Strong Vincent

County

Jim Bucklin	Wattsburg
Doug Burch	North East
Bud Carter	General McLane
Michael Chriest	St. Gregory
Dennis Curry	Fairview
Jim Dale	Fairview
Terry Darada	Fort LeBoeuf
Whitey Eiser	Harbor Creek
Bernie Erwin	Wesleyville
Chuck Faulkner	McDowell
Ken Faulkner	McDowell
Pat Finnucan	Conneaut Valley
Mike George	Fairview
Frank Haibach	Fort LeBoeuf
Jim Hamike	Fairview
Vic Kalicky	Fairview
Dick McClure	Girard
Jim Moorehead	Lawrence Park
John Nowak	Conneaut Valley
Tim Reid	Lawrence Park
Martin Schuller	General McLane
Bill Simon	McDowell
Bob Williams	Lawrence Park
Jerry Williams	Corry
Doug Zirkle	McDowell

Coaches: Dick Sabo of Northwestern, Jim Bowen of Fairview

CITY 31 - COUNTY 6

A punishing City ground game featuring East products Tom Carpenter and Art Miller was the difference in front of 12,000 fans. Carpenter rushed 11 times for 99 yards. Carpenter scored on runs of 3 and 11 yards. Miller carried nine times for 94 yards, including a 56-yard touchdown. Ron Chimenti of Prep hit 4 of 15 passing for 98 yards, including a 16-yard strike to Al Lubiejewski of Prep for a touchdown. Rich Scheppner of Cathedral Prep scored on a 30-yard interception return. Miller accounted for the only PAT in the game with a kick. The City led 25-0 at halftime. The County lost four of its seven fumbles. A brawl erupted with two minutes left, emptying both benches. Order was restored and the game finished.

By his own admission, Ron Chimenti "didn't have my best game" during the City's 31-6 win. The County limited the Cathedral Prep quarterback to four completions in 15 attempts even though his successful passes covered almost 100 yards. But Chimenti had a good feeling about one of his passes. That was a 16-yard strike to former Prep teammate Al Lubiejewski for a touchdown in the first quarter. "The redeeming factor was the pass to Alois," Chimenti said from his home in Fort Myers, Florida. "Alois was the right end. I rolled to the right. Alois ran toward the goal post, cut to the corner and I hit him for the touchdown."

Ever since he was in fifth grade at St. Johns, Chimenti was a regular in the stands at Veterans Stadium when Cathedral Prep played there. "Dave Tullio, the Prep quarterback, was my hero back then," he said. Chimenti also watched Save-An-Eye games every year with a thought in his mind. "I dreamed about some day playing for Prep and playing in the Save-An-Eye Game," he said.

Ron Chimenti – 1962

The 5'10", 160-pounder had a great career at Prep. He became a starter after several games as a junior and continued in that role until he graduated. "We had only one loss in the games I started," he said. "Youngstown Ursuline beat us 28-8 in my senior (1961) season." Chimenti went on to Xavier University and was a roommate of Prep teammate Rick Scheppner, who returned an interception 30 yards for a touchdown for the City. "I was the second string quarterback at Xavier and holder for the extra points and field goals," Chimenti said.

Thinking back on the Save-An-Eye game, Chimenti said, "I was honored and excited to play in the game. I have fond, fond memories of it."

– Joe Mattis

Game 25 – September 2, 1963

City

Rich Borkowski	Tech
Bill Campbell	Strong Vincent
Shad Connelly	Strong Vincent
Sam Copeland	East
John Cutter	Tech
Jerry Dahlkemper	Cathedral Prep
Lou DiPlacido	Cathedral Prep
Ed Giglio	Tech
Bob Goodwill	Cathedral Prep
Claude Haraway	Tech
John Hedberg	East
Jim Holland	Academy
Bill Johnson	Strong Vincent
Leonard Jones	Academy
Willie Kinnard	Tech
Jim Koch	Cathedral Prep
Dave Kozlowski	Tech
Lee Larson	Academy
Don MacGregor	Strong Vincent
Jim Marnella	Cathedral Prep
Jake Pikiewicz	Cathedral Prep
Tippy Pohl	East
Richard Quinn	Academy
Ed Robasky	Cathedral Prep
Bill Roberts	Tech
Dave Ruggerio	Strong Vincent
Tom Schneider	Cathedral Prep
Ara Simonian	Strong Vincent
Rich Skinner	Academy
Herman Woodard	East

Coaches: Walt Strosser of Cathedral Prep, Tony Zambroski of Cathedral Prep

County

Jerry Allison	Union City
Jerry Cass	Harbor Creek
Bill Cauley	General McLane
Rich Conover	McDowell
Bill DeDionisio	Harbor Creek
Dan Grey	Fort LeBoeuf
Jerry Hadley	McDowell
Mike Hanna	Corry
Jack Heller	Wesleyville
Chuck Hutchinson	Lawrence Park
Jim Kline	Fort LeBoeuf
Wayne Lawrence	Fairview
Fred Lewis	Northwestern
Jerry Mahle	Fort LeBoeuf
Terry McIntosh	North East
Dennis McNally	Girard
Terry Miller	Fairview
Craig Mitchell	Fort LeBoeuf
Dave Pawlukovich	Wattsburg
Phil Pawlukovich	Wattsburg
Emil Plalet	Harbor Creek
Bill Salchak	Fort LeBoeuf
Chet Shorts	Fort LeBoeuf
Dick Soudan	Lawrence Park
Ron Tomlin	Harbor Creek
Don Turberson	Wesleyville
Mickey Walker	General McLane
Bill Wentling	McDowell
Joe Williams	Lawrence Park

Coaches: Carm Bonito of Fort LeBeouf, Bill Young of Wattsburg

CITY 18 - COUNTY 0

Three breaks — a blocked punt, a poor kick and a recovered fumble — set up the City scores as 12,000 watched. Bill Roberts of Tech blocked the punt before Jack Pikiewicz of Prep went 1 yard for the first touchdown. A rush by Rich Skinner of Academy caused a County punt that resulted in a 2-yard loss. Len Jones of Academy then scored on a 3-yard run. Rich Borkowski of Tech recovered a fumble on the County 39-yard line in the fourth quarter. Lou DiPlacido of Prep scored on a 6-yard run. Tippy Pohl of East directed the offense, hitting 10 of 14 passing for 102 yards. Willie Kinnard of Tech and Jim Holland of Academy were other City standouts.

Jobie Williams of Lawrence Park and Mike Hanna of Corry led the County. Ken Semple of Wesleyville was awarded the game ball. The halfback would have started for the County, but was injured in an industrial accident and still hospitalized on game day.

Jim Marnella was an outstanding lineman for Cathedral Prep. He played center in the 1963 game and has a vivid memory of his final play. "I don't remember who the (County) nose guard was, but I was having a good game against him," Marnella said.

"Then, on my last play, I got hit in the mouth. My tooth went through my lip and I still have a scar on the outside from it."

Jim Marnella – 1963

That wasn't the only time Marnella had a hard time because of the Save-An-Eye Game. He said it happened almost every day while preparing for the game.

"Jim Koch was my teammate at Prep," Marnella said. "He was a huge lineman at 6'3" and 270 pounds. I was only 190. Koch had broken his arm and had a cast up to his elbow. He played nose guard in practice and beat the heck out of me with his cast every day in practice."

Marnella also remembers Tom Schneider, another Prep lineman and teammate who was injured. "In practice Tom was run over by Academy fullback Jim Holland, a real bruiser," Marnella recalled. "Tom injured his knee and was not able to play in the game." Marnella, who went on to play basketball and baseball at Slippery Rock, later coached in several Save-An-Eye Games.

– Joe Mattis

Game 26 – September 7, 1964

City

Bob Alex	Cathedral Prep
Joe Anthony	Academy
Bob Barnett	East
Steve Benson	Cathedral Prep
Ed Bielak	Tech
Jim Burrows	Tech
Dan Butler	East
Russ Crowner	East
Dennis Edmonds	Academy
Don Gehrlein	Cathedral Prep
Mina George	East
Barry Grossman	Strong Vincent
Bill Hertel	Cathedral Prep
Phil Hilbert	East
Ron Jones	Cathedral Prep
Howard Kelley	East
Brad Kingston	Strong Vincent
John Loeb	Strong Vincent
Pat Lupo	Cathedral Prep
Ted Maleski	East
Tom Niland	Cathedral Prep
Larry Ozimek	Cathedral Prep
Dennis Patora	Tech
Bob Rudd	East
Elmer Smith	Strong Vincent
Ray Tomb	Academy
Paul Tomlin	East
Don Waskiewicz	Tech
Cliff Williams	East

Coaches: Duke Detzel of East,
Bill Brabender of East

County

Quinton Boroi	Harbor Creek
Dennis Boyuzick	General McLane
Dave Brandell	Fairview
Al Bryon	Wesleyville
Dan Chase	Fairview
Bob Culbertson	Corry
Tom Doyle	St. Gregory
Larry Fitzgerald	Wesleyville
Ron Fuhrer	Fort LeBoeuf
Art Hotchkiss	Corry
Joe Kobylinski	Harbor Creek
John Luchs	North East
Larry Marlett	Corry
John Mikovich	Girard
Jim Mosher	McDowell
Frank Musiek	Union City
Steve Nishnick	Fort LeBoeuf
Dave Phenneger	Fairview
Harry Pier	Girard
Al Post	Wattsburg
John Rice	Union City
Jerry Rife	McDowell
Jim Sauers	Fort LeBoeuf
Alton Skelly	Fairview
Bill Thaler	General McLane
Paul Weldon	Northwestern
Orrin Woods	Fairview

Coaches: Ed Poly of Lawrence Park,
John Smilo of Wesleyville

CITY 6 - COUNTY 6

$\mathcal{M}$ina George of East threw a 7-yard touchdown pass to Pat Lupo of Prep with 1 second left to produce the tie. The late touchdown was set up by a fumble recovery by Bob Barnett of East on the County 42. An 18-yard George pass to Barry Grossman of Strong Vincent aided the drive. Barnett picked up a first down on fourth-and-1 at the 6-yard line. Then after each side was penalized, George hit Lupo for the tying score. George's PAT pass was batted down.

Dan Chase of Fairview passed 14 yards to Larry Fitzgerald of Wesleyville for the County touchdown in the second quarter. The PAT kick went wide. The City had the ball for 18 minutes during the second half, but failed to score until the final play. Quint Boroi of Harbor Creek, John Mikovich of Girard and Chip Rife of McDowell starred for the County. Retiring East coach Duke Detzel and new Warrior coach Bill Brabender led the City.

the trophy to Club President Stanley.   Coach Carl Simon.

LUTHER MEMORIAL IS 1944 SEASON CHAMPIONS.

City, County All-Stars Set For Save-an-Eye Struggle

There will be talent galore at the disposal of Lion's Club Save-... ...tball coaches when ... game is ... ... the ...

Brabender of the City and Ed Poly and John Smilo of the County can call on All-Star ... plenty from last year's ...Scholastic ...

City and 28 from the County—will open drills on Aug. 31 for this big game.

All proceeds from this struggle go into the Lion's Club Save-an-Eye fund for needy children. Players selected for this game for the County are: ends Jerry ...k, Girard ...

Dowell; Jim Mosher, McDowell; Dave Phenneger, Fairview. Fullbacks Quinton Borol, Harborcreek; John Luchs, North East; Bill Thaler, General Mc-Lane.

City squad: Ends Clifford Wli liams, East; Dan Wasklewicz, ... Patora, Tech; Pat ... Smith, Vin ...

...amy;

City

Craig Allen	Tech
Rich Andrews	Strong Vincent
Sam Biletnikoff	Strong Vincent
George Blinn	East
Dave Bobango	East
Charles Brewton	Tech
Larry Campbell	Academy
John Chrzanowski	East
Melvin Cooper	East
Jim Fries	Cathedral Prep
Bob Gerbracht	Strong Vincent
Ed Grode	Academy
Dan Haley	Cathedral Prep
Tim Hart	East
Jack Jensen	Academy
Jerry Karsznia	Academy
Jim Lorigo	Tech
Bob Mikolajczyk	Cathedral Prep
Bill Nemenz	Tech
Mike Nuara	Strong Vincent
Jim Olszewski	Cathedral Prep
Gene Sanner	Academy
Nick Sansone	Strong Vincent
Joe Schweigert	Academy
Jim Skindell	Strong Vincent
Jerry Trocha	Tech
Dennis Weigle	Academy
Dave Wenrick	Cathedral Prep

Coaches: Dick Detzel of Strong Vincent, Ray Dombrowski of Tech

County

Jack Aaronson	Wesleyville
Bob Amon	Fort LeBoeuf
Ron Andrews	Fairview
Tom Bidwell	Union City
Cleve Blunt	Lawrence Park
Bill Bonnett	Girard
Dennis Brandyberry	Girard
Tom Dawson	General McLane
Sam Hawley	Fairview
John Hendrickson	Wesleyville
Len Izbicki	Fairview
Pete Jazenski	Lawrence Park
Paul Johnson	Fairview
Jim Langley	Wesleyville
Norm Lasher	Union City
Joe Lisek	Northwestern
Dennis Musolf	Fort LeBoeuf
Don Ploss	General McLane
George Popa	McDowell
Bob Potocki	Corry
Paul Reed	Fort LeBoeuf
Doug Rettman	Wesleyville
Jim Smith	Lawrence Park
Dennis Taylor	Fort LeBoeuf
Greg Weislogel	Fairview
Ron Wetmore	Union City
Forest Wheeler	Wesleyville
Dave Wierzchowski	Wesleyville
Albert Wood	Wattsburg

Coaches: Bob Jamison of General McLane, Bill Vorsheck of Girard

CITY 21 - COUNTY 0

Dave Wenrick of Prep, Jim Fries of Prep and Mel Cooper of East scored touchdowns. Wenrick directed the attack. Fries gained 112 yards on 15 carries and had a 42-yard kickoff return. Cooper gained 77 yards on 14 rushes.

A crowd of 14,000 saw Wenrick plunge 1 yard for the first score. Mike Nuara of Strong Vincent kicked the first of his three extra points. The City drove to the County 4-yard line featuring Wenrick's 22-yard rollout before Denny Taylor of Fort LeBoeuf ended the threat with an interception. Jerry Trocha of Tech returned an interception to the City 40. Fries gained 35 yards on two carries and Denny (Tank) Weigle of Academy gained 13 more. Fries went the final yard for the score. Jack Jensen of Academy had an interception to set up Cooper's 16-yard touchdown run in the final minute. The City finished with 268 yards rushing to 96 for the County.

Game 28 – September 5, 1966

City

Tom Adams........................Strong Vincent
Pat Atkins........................Strong Vincent
Jim Bebko.. Tech
Pat Brady .... Tech
Joe Bufalino ....Cathedral Prep
Jim Caldwell .... East
John Coffey....................Strong Vincent
Everett Eddy .... East
Gary Gaber .... Academy
Art Gamble .... Tech
Bill Glecos .... Academy
Andre Heuer......................Cathedral Prep
Bill Hintz ....Cathedral Prep
Jim Jaruszewicz....................Cathedral Prep
Steve Kalista........................Cathedral Prep
Mike Kowalski.......................... Academy
Dennis Lantzy ....Strong Vincent
Gary Lillis ....Cathedral Prep
Bob Martin .... Academy
Barry Masterson................. Cathedral Prep
Mike McCoy.......................Cathedral Prep
Dan Mellow .... Academy
Phil Orlando.. Tech
Ed Pasko .... Tech
Doug Porath .... East
Ed Ranowiecki .... Academy
Larry Ross ....Strong Vincent
Larry Sekula.. East
Tony Truitt.. East
Bob Woods .... East

Coaches: Don Zonno of Academy,
Carney Metzgar of East

County

Dick Bonniger ....Iroquois
Lynn Campbell................. General McLane
Larry Fenton .... North East
Bob Fox ....McDowell
Jack Gentile .... Fort LeBoeuf
Jim Greider ....Iroquois
Vincent Hinkle.............................Fairview
Jeff Ives ....Fairview
Brian Johnson ....Harbor Creek
Jerry Kelly........................... Fort LeBoeuf
John Kutz .... General McLane
Joel Magee ....Harbor Creek
Ken McChesney................................. Corry
Gerry Mikovich................................Girard
Lou Nagy..McDowell
Tracy Passerotti ....Harbor Creek
Rick Pire ....McDowell
Chuck Pituch .... Union City
Doug Porte.....................................McDowell
Norm Ralph........................Harbor Creek
Gary Renaud ....McDowell
Dave Rossell........................... Fort LeBoeuf
Jeff Schweitzer ....Harbor Creek
Denny Shafer .... General McLane
Harvey Smith .... Fort LeBoeuf
Dale Sparber ....Girard
Ken Walker .... General McLane
Norm West...................... General McLane
Denny York ....Iroquois
Jerry Zimmer ....Iroquois

Coaches: Frank Dennis of Harbor Creek,
Vern Hurlburt of Wattsburg

CITY 12 - COUNTY 7

𝒜 4-yard touchdown pass from Barry Masterson of Prep to Bob Woods of East with 5 minutes left decided the game in front of 12,000 fans. The PAT kick was low. The County responded with a drive to the City 5-yard line, but the march stalled with 40 seconds left and the City ran out the clock. Everett Eddy of East scored on a 5-yard run on the opening drive. The PAT kick was wide. Denny York of Iroquois recovered a fumble on the City 7-yard line.

Joel Magee of Harbor Creek then ran 6 yards for the touchdown. Gary Renaud of McDowell ran the PAT for a 7-6 County lead. Joe Bufalino of Prep gained 50 yards on ten carries. Eddy had 46 yards on 14 rushes. Renaud had 46 yards on 11 attempts. Bob Fox of McDowell ran nine times for 40 yards. Gary Mikovich of Girard was outstanding on defense. Mike McCoy of Cathedral Prep played in the game. He went on to star at Notre Dame and in the NFL.

CITY ALL-STARS

The City team, with one of its biggest squads in history, will take on the rugged All-County team in the Lions' Club Save-an-Eye All-Star game at the Stadium tonight. Members of the team, from left to right, first row, Steve Kalista, Joe Bufalino, Gary Lillis, Dennis Lantzy, Barry Masterson, Pat Atkins, Bill Glecos, Larry Sekula, Danny Mellow; second row, Bill Hintz, Pat Brady, Mike Kowalski, Gary Gaber, Jim Caldwell, John Valley, Doug Gorski, Jim Jaruszewicz, Phil Orlando, Ed Ranowicz; third row, Coach Carney Metzgar, Jim Bebko, Mike McCoy, Tony Truitt, Bob Martin, Andre Heuer, Bob Woods. Ed Pasko, Art Gamble and Coach Don Zonno. Missing when picture was taken were Tom Adams, Everett Eddy and Larry Ross.

City, County Renew Lions' Club Rivalry

The annual pre-season football spectacular which drew 14,000 fans a year ago, unfolds for the 28th time Monday at 8:15 under the Stadium arcs.

Another sizable turnout is anticiapted as the City thumps pads against the County in the latest Lions Club Save-An-Eye charity gridiron joust.

The City, a 21-0 winner last year, sports an 11-2-1 record in the current series and is a slight favorite to make the County yell uncle once again.

Loaded with weight up front and studded with fast-moving backs, the City expects to use the ground route to another success. Guiding the squad are Academy's Don Zonno and Carney Metzgar of East.

... with Harbor

And in case of wild pitches, the County can sock away with shippery Norm West of General McLane and the hard running McDowell duo of Gary Renaud and Bob Fox. McLane's Ken Walker is an adept placekicker. Up front, Dennis and Hurl burt will call upon the likes of Trojans Rick Pire and Lou Nagy, Corry's Chuck McChesney and Lancer Bill Kutz.

Linebackers deluxe are Harborcreek's spirited Norm and Girard pep...

Jaruszewicz. The latter is a other 200-pounder.

Lions Bob Martin and Mike Kowalksi bolster the defensive alignment, the former at a linebacking spot, the latter at end.

Passers Barry Masterson of Prep and Colonel John Colfe have excellent receivers in junior Bob Woods Brady...

Dodgers

City	
Joe Abal	Tech
Carl Anderson	Strong Vincent
Jim Anderson	Cathedral Prep
Bob Barney	Academy
Dan Betcher	Cathedral Prep
Ed Carr	East
Harry Fried	Strong Vincent
Ron Fritts	Tech
Tony Genis	Academy
Bob Glecos	Academy
Don Gunter	Cathedral Prep
Steve Hathaway	East
Jim Hayes	Strong Vincent
Ken Jones	Cathedral Prep
Larry Kielak	Tech
Mark Kirkland	Cathedral Prep
Joe Kloos	Strong Vincent
Steve Konieczki	Tech
Greg Myers	Academy
George Orbanek	Cathedral Prep
Tom Robie	Strong Vincent
Chuck Serafini	Strong Vincent
Jim Servidio	Strong Vincent
Bob Shreve	Cathedral Prep
Wain Smith	Strong Vincent
Kevin Sullivan	Cathedral Prep
Joe Tinko	Strong Vincent
Jim Yamma	Tech
Jim Zoldach	Cathedral Prep

Coaches: Duke Detzel of East,
Jack Laraway of Academy,
Gus Thomas of Cathedral Prep

County	
John Anderson	Girard
Paul Burkell	McDowell
Don Crannell	Iroquois
Chuck Dengel	Iroquois
Tom Dougan	Harbor Creek
Jim Dunda	Northwestern
Bob Ellwood	Harbor Creek
Moe Elwell	McDowell
Bill Erickson	McDowell
Tom George	Fairview
John Gillette	Northwestern
Rex Hanlin	Union City
Carl Hillstrom	Corry
John Kosiorek	Wattsburg
Daryl Leopold	Fairview
Tony Major	Iroquois
Gene McChesney	Corry
Jim Michaels	McDowell
John Miles	Fairview
Pat Millspaw	General McLane
Dan Reese	North East
Tom Schoenfeld	Iroquois
Dan Sipple	Wattsburg
Butch Smith	Girard
Butch Unger	Fort LeBoeuf
Jim Vogt	Fort LeBoeuf
Gene Vogt	Wattsburg
Clancy Walsh	Corry
Randy Weislogel	Fairview
Paul Yoculan	Iroquois

Coaches: Joe Moore of McDowell,
Bill Vorsheck of Girard

COUNTY 25 - CITY 0

*T*he largest crowd in Save-An-Eye Game history, more than 16,000, watched the county team under coaches Joe Moore and Bill Vorsheck, crush the City. Tony Major of Iroquois racked up 208 yards in pass receptions. Major had five catches and scored two touchdowns. Chuck Dengel of Iroquois sparked the ground game with 88 yards on 13 carries. Moe Elwell of McDowell hit Major with a 51-yard pass on the first play from scrimmage. Major scored on passes of 76 and 28 yards, both from John Anderson of Girard. Anderson ran 8 yards for a score and Daryl Leopold of Fairview had a 2-yard touchdown run.

Jim Michaels of McDowell ran for the only extra point. After the first Major touchdown Chuck Serafini of Strong Vincent returned the ensuing kickoff 50 yards before being run out of bounds by John Gillette of Northwestern. The City's deepest threat reached the County 11-yard line behind the passing of Jim Servidio of Strong Vincent.

County Team

Erie's Koehler Brewing Company supported the Save-An-Eye and promised "the good life" if you drank their product.

Live the good life
...with the good taste of Koehler beer.

KOEHLER

Erie Brewing Co., Erie, Pa.

Paul Yoculan remembers heading to Veterans Stadium to watch high school football games. But when his family moved to Wesleyville when he was 16 years old, he transferred from Strong Vincent to Wesleyville. That shattered a dream he had held for many years. Erie County League teams did not play games on the premier football field in Northwest Pennsylvania. "It broke my heart," Yoculan said. "I wanted to play in the Stadium."

Paul Yoculan – 1967

After three years as a starter for first Wesleyville and then the newly consolidated Iroquois, he had hoped to get his chance in the Save-An-Eye Game. But there was a problem. The seniors voted to the all-ECL first team were selected to play in the game. Yoculan, an undersized offensive and defensive lineman for the Braves, fell a few votes short. So when County coach Bill Vorsheck of Girard called Yoculan and asked him to play, Yoculan was miffed. "I don't think I should," Yoculan defiantly said. "Why didn't the coaches vote for me?"

"Coach Vorsheck challenged me," Yoculan recalled. "He told me to prove I should have been on the first team and earn that position in practice." First, Yoculan had to get approval to participate in the game. He was headed for Yankton College in South Dakota to play for the Greyhounds (where he was a teammate of future NFL great Lyle Alzedo.) Yankton's coach gave him the OK for the Save-An-Eye Game.

The practices under Vorsheck were not easy. "He worked the snot out of us," Yoculan said. But those hard practices paid off. The County won 25-0 in front of 16,000 fans at Veterans Stadium. That was the most lopsided County victory in Save-An-Eye history. Finally, Yoculan had lived his dream. "It was one of the most important things in my life," he said.

– Joe Mattis

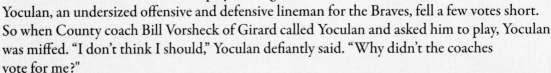

STUN CITY BEFORE RECORD SAVE-AN-EYE THRONG

County Stars Strike By Air, 25-0

BY JACK POLANCY
News Sports Editor

The Minute Men had a plan to tell the countryside just where the British were going to attack back in 1776. It was "one if by land . . . two if by sea."

They didn't have a signal if the attack should come through the air.

And neither did the City All-Stars Monday night.

The County All-Stars . . . striking via the right arms of Moe Elwell and John Anderson—and the great pass-grabbing talents of Iroquois High's Tony Major . . . turned the 29th Annual Lions Club Save-An-Eye All-Star Football game into a rout as they ripped the City secondary apart for a 25-0 victory.

The largest Labor Day crowd in history—estimated at over 16,000—sat in on the show that saw Major—who should really be a general by anyone's standards—latch on to five aerials to total up 59 yards and two touchdowns.

And when Major wasn't driving the City Stars looney—an Iroquois teammate, Chuck Dengel, more than did his share by ripping apart the vaunted City line as he piled up 59 yards in 13 carries to show that the County also had a running game.

The win was only the third in the 16-year history of the current standings for the County . . . and its first since 1961.

It was a complete triumph.

—The closest the City came to putting a figure on the scoreboard was late in the fourth period when the Iroquois line earned the losers a first down on the County 11.

This drive—and the City's last gasp—ended when Tom Schoenfeld, a tackle from Iroquois, ripped through the City line

and blasted Bob Shreve for a 12-yard loss back to the 23. There was 8:00 left on the clock at this time . . . and that was the end for the City All-Stars.

The County, showing off the coaching talents of Girard's Bill Vorsheck and McDowell's Joe Moore, wasted little time in giving the City a hint of what was to happen.

Dengel took the opening kickoff for 18 yards and reached the County 37.

The first play from scrimmage found McDowell's Elwell hitting Major on the City 40 . . . and the big terminal ripped his way to the 12 before Harry Fried got him. The maneuver was good for 51 yards.

Three plays later Anderson skirted left end and dove into the end zone with only 119 seconds gone in the game. Dengel's PAT drive was good, but an offside penalty nullified the one-pointer. A second shot failed and the County led 6-0.

With the big City line opening big holes the hometown kids moved from their 37—following the ensuing kickoff—to the County 30.

At this point Northwestern's John Gillette tossed Servidio for a ten-yard loss and Wattsburg's Dan Sipple followed suit by stopping the Vincent quarterback for a nine-yard loss on the next play.

The All-Stars exchanged punts and neither could go very far in either direction for the next 16 minutes.

With 2:13 left in the half the County received a Steve Konieczki punt on its own five.

Then—the blitz hit again.

Butch Smith was held for no gain, but McDowell's Ji——

chaels ripped off six yards and Dengel added another 13 to gain the 24.

On the next play Anderson faded back . . . saw Major heading South . . . and fired. Major grabbed the ball over the head of two City defenders on the City 40—and was never touched as he ripped his way into touchdown land.

The clock showed 45 seconds—and a 12-0 County lead—when Michaels' PAT run was halted.

Vincent's Chuck Serafini almost got things a bit closer when he took the following kickoff and rambled 50 yards to the County 40 before John Gillette ran him out.

The City, with Shreve passing to Serafini, managed to reach the County 16 before time ran out at the half.

Early in the third heat the County found itself back on its four following a Ron Fritts punt.

Smith's two yard smash and Dengel's 25-yarder brought the ball to the 37. Michaels added in nine and Elwell—on a keeper—chalked up ten to reach the 44 of the City.

Two plays later it was Major again . . . this time making a spectacular grab on the City 28.

Two line shots earned four yards . . . .

. . . his way for 30 to reach the four . . . . . . of Fairview carried it in f . . . third chapter.

The City, . . . into the . . . kil . . .

Anderson, Dengel and Corry's Clancy Walsh combined to bring the ball from their 23 to the City 46.

Major was the target again—and this time he grabbed one good for 22 yards to the 24. Two plays later Major had a TD . . .but an offside penalty pulled it back and put the ball on the 28.

This didn't stop the County.

On the next play Anderson found Major in the corner of the end zone and the Iroquois' end made another spectacular catch for his second TD of the night and the winners' 24th point.

Jim Michaels rammed in the PAT for a 25-0 bulge with 2:55 remaining in the game.

That was all they wrote.

It was enough.

STATISTICS
	CITY	COUNTY
First Downs	11	13
Yards Rushing	90	159
Passes Attempted	127	221
Passes Completed	19	5
Passes Intercepted By	17	5
Yards Lost Att. Pass		
Total Yards Gained		

SHOCK CITY, 25-0, BEFORE RECORD CROWD

County Stars Score 'Major Upset'

By GENE CUNEO

It was bound to come! In the past year the Yankees finished in the American League cellar . . . Catholics started eating

STATISTICS

	CITY	COUNTY
First Downs	11	13
Yards Rushing	90	159
Yards Passing	127	221
Passes Attempted	19	9
Passes Completed	10	53
Passes Intercepted By	3	144
Yards Lost Att. Pass	6	2
Total Yards Gained	217	375
Fumbles	1	4
Fumbles Lost	0	1
Punts	38.5	2
Punting Average	17	26
KO & Punt Returns	135	30
Yards Returned	19	27
Yards Returned	57	

. . . on Friday and Tommy . . . didn't get married . . . stage was set for the . . . . set the City in the . . . Annual Save-

an-Eye All-Star football game. And when they got on this stage, they didn't do a mere walk-on. They hammered up their roles, but good, and stomped the City to bits before an awed sell-out crowd of over 16,000 fans at the Stadium Monday.

The h e p p e d - u p charges of Coaches Bill Vorscheck of Girard and Joe Moore of McDowell did a better clean-up job than the Ajax White Knight as they white-washed the City, 25 to 0.

This was no fluke. It was pure brutality as this band of County youngsters seemed to take out all the frustrations of the many previous County losers on this s p u n k y, but outclassed City crew.

The National Collegiate Athletic Association does not permit

game officials to hand out most valuable player trophies any more, but there's little doubt that all 16,000 plus fans on hand would have voted for Iroquois' Tony Major.

This sure-handed, fleet-footed end put on a pass-catching performance in the Stadium which hasn't been seen since the likes of Jack Konkol, Bernie Flowers, Len Cyterski and Freddy Biletnikoff were writing history.

Major did the impossible — and more. He was just unstoppable. There is no other word to describe his performance.

He scored two touchdowns and set up two o t h e r s. In all he gained over 200 yards with breath-taking catches. And this does not include a 22-yard touchdown pass catch which was nullified by a penalty.

The County, of course, did not live by Major alone. He had on-target passes from Girard's Johnny Anderson and McDowell's Moe Elwell. And brilliant running by his former Iroquois teammate — Chuck Dengel — enabled the pass plays to go.

De . . . . burned out . . . them on

Strong Vincent's Chuck Serafini was the chief and almost only City offensive weapon. He carried for 49 yards in eight tries in the first half, but was used sparingly in the final two periods.

The County used the old style of Coach Tom Landry of the Dallas Cowboys when he alternated Quarterbacks Eddie LeBaron and Don Meredith. Elwell handled much of the running action and some passing, but Anderson unloaded the bombs and also chipped in with a keeper for the first touchdown on a seven yard run.

The statistics, although obviously County, were not as one-sided as the game. The County had 13 first downs to the City's 11. The victors made 159 yards on the ground to the Slickers' 90 and had a wide margin in the air — 221 yards to 127 for the County.

It was a relatively clean, well-played game with no interceptions and only one lost fumble.

The City's biggest mistake was showing up. The Slickers were in the game for most of the first half, but as play progressed it was obvious th . . . County

and had come to play.

On the line, the County had heroes galore — young men like Fairview's Randy Weislogel and John Miles, McDowell's Paul Burkell and Bill Ericckson, Wattsburg's Dan Sipple and Iroquois' John Kosiorek and Iroquois' Don Crannell.

The County put on a "Major" first-half performance. Iroquois' Major was lightning in . . . . twice as the County . . . . 12-0 half-time edge . . . . . . Elwell hit him . . . . . . 51-yard pass play . . . . opened the game . . . . . . to the County . . . . . . caught the Cit . . . . . .

only a desperation tackle caught the County into one hole only to see a roughing-the-kicker penal . . . get them out of danger.

Girard's Butch Smith hit the line for one and McDowell's Jim Michaels ground out four more. The Johnny Anderson of Girard went back to pass, I n s t e a d went around left end on a keeper, going seven yards for the touchdown. He was hit just as he dove into the corner for the score. The County missed the . . . . try on a pass after a penal . . . . . . d it back to the sev . . . . with less

his receiver on the City 12.

Serafini led one drive to the County 33, but his old Vincent teammate Jimmy Servidio was nailed twice for big losses and that drive went awry.

The City later gambled on fourth down and three and Serafini came through again for a first down on the County 45. The Slickers drove to the 24, but there Burkell came up with a fumble and the County took over.

. . . . er a tremendous kick by . . . . Konieczki put the . . . . . h spot. His . . . . . .

kick landed on the four and dug a divot — ala Arnold Palmer — and stopped on the five. There were only two minutes to play and it figured that the County would just try to hold on for a 6-0 intermission lead.

If the City defense thought this, it was the biggest mistake since Hitler opened up a second front in Russia. The County had no intentions of running out the clock. First Smith tried right end for a half yard. Then Dengel went off tackle for a first down on the 20. There were 50 seconds left to play . . . . and the County could have relaxed. In . . . . ad, the area kids electrified . . . . day.

MAJOR EFFORT

. . . the County reaches far for this pass but it's . . . ertips this time. Major, however, hauled . . . sses from John Andersen as one of the . . . . 25-0 victory over the City in the Save-

GOING DOWN

The County defense pours in to wrap up City quarterback Jim Servidio (33) for a loss in the Save-An-Eye game Monday. As two . . . . players send Servidio to earth. John Gillette (51) and Tom George (28) rush in to make sure. The County spent the evening smothering the City in a 25-0 victory. (Times photo by Vince Moskalczyk)

Game 30 – September 2, 1968

City

Dave Baker	Academy
Sid Booker	East
Otto Borgia	Cathedral Prep
Bob Brown	Strong Vincent
Bob Buzzanco	Strong Vincent
Steve Chludzinski	Tech
Chip Christensen	Academy
Rich Fetzner	Cathedral Prep
Dave Fetzner	Tech
Mark Karuba	East
Scott LaVange	Academy
Len LoCastro	Academy
Frank Macko	Academy
Jerry Marzka	Tech
Chic Matthews	Academy
Barry McNerney	Tech
Jerry Mifsud	Cathedral Prep
Tom Morgan	East
John Noonan	Tech
Al Rafalowski	Tech
Tom Ratkowski	Academy
Denny Satyshur	East
Jeff Thomas	Tech
Jeff Trombacco	Cathedral Prep
Jerry Verga	Cathedral Prep
Frank Wingerter	Cathedral Prep

County

Dave Bertges	Wattsburg
Jeff Blakeslee	North East
Phil Brady	Harbor Creek
Jim Detzel	North East
Tom Eaton	North East
John Fuhrer	Fort LeBoeuf
Larry Giewont	Wattsburg
Andy Hanisek	Girard
Dan Keil	Iroquois
Bill Korell	General McLane
Joe Kozik	Wattsburg
Joe Kula	Fort LeBoeuf
Russ LaFuria	North East
Mike Lerch	Wattsburg
Jerry Liebel	Harbor Creek
Greg McGill	North East
Dave Meehl	North East
Tom Miller	Iroquois
Randy Nanni	Iroquois
Rollie Peterson	Wattsburg
Ray Reade	McDowell
Joe Robson	McDowell
Rod Sargent	Fort LeBoeuf
Dave Soltis	Northwestern
Dave Spada	North East
Ron Taylor	Fort LeBoeuf
Dave Vogt	Fort LeBo
Harry White	Northwestern
Rich Widdowson	Wattsburg
Larry Yost	Harbor Creek

Coaches: Tony Zambroski of Cathedral Prep, Glenn Barthelson of Strong Vincent

Coaches: Jim Concilla of North East, Jerry Mathis of Northwestern

CITY 26 - COUNTY 0

*T*wo of the City's most versatile athletes, Jerry Mifsud of Cathedral Prep and Denny Satyshur of East, each scored two touchdowns. With 13,000 fans on hand, Satyshur had a 27-yard touchdown run and scored on a 40-yard pass from Mifsud. Two 4-yard runs accounted for Mifsud's touchdowns. Satyshur also had two extra-point kicks. Otto Borgia of Prep was solid in the City ground game. The City piled up 423 yards offense while holding the County to 57. A 96-yard Satyshur screen pass to Mifsud for an apparent touchdown was called back due to penalty. Satyshur, Mifsud, Borgia and Sid Booker of East sparkled in the City secondary. Academy grads Tom Ratkowski and Chip Christensen were outstanding on the defensive line. Rich Widdowson of Wattsburg starred on the County line. Mifsud was a two-sport star at Edinboro and later played minor league baseball. Satyshur was a quarterback at Duke, then became a golf professional.

Barry McNerney did not want to spend the rest of his life wondering, "What if?" So, in the summer of 1967 with his senior year at Tech Memorial approaching, he decided to try out for the Centaur football team. It was a decision he would never regret. "I went out because of my older brother (Mark). I didn't want to regret not playing football in high school," McNerney recalled.

It was a season with few highs and many lows. Tech, coached by Tom Parry, did not win a game during the 1967 season. "Our biggest brag was that we covered seven onside kicks that year," said McNerney, who played as an offensive guard and linebacker.

When the players for the 1968 Save-An-Eye Game were set, McNerney was not among them. However, when Tech teammate Tom Matson dislocated his shoulder, McNerney asked City coach Tony Zambroski if he could take Matson's place on the roster and got an okay from the Cathedral Prep coach. That decision led to the finest moments on the gridiron for McNerney. "We had a great team with some terrific athletes," McNerney said. "Jerry Mifsud (Prep) and Denny Satyshur (East) were great players. Otto Borgia (Prep) was an unsung hero and Sid Booker (East) also played an outstanding game."

Barry McNerney – 1968

In the City's 26-0 win in front of a reported crowd of 13,000, Mifsud and Satyshur each scored two touchdowns. Borgia helped the City gain 423 yards on offense, and he teamed with Mifsud and Booker to form a solid defensive backfield. "We went out with a bang," McNerney said.

"It was so nice to be involved with winners." McNerney said the City's coaching staff, headed by Zambroski and Strong Vincent's Glenn Barthelson, dealt with the players much differently than what he experienced at Tech. "They didn't treat us like we were still in high school. They treated us like men. We all felt like big guys," McNerney said. And what was it like for McNerney to go out on a winning team, something that did not happen when he played at Tech? "It was such a great experience. It was a terrific feeling that I still remember today."

– Joe Mattis

City

Don Aleksiewicz .... East
John Anderson .... Strong Vincent
Dean Bagnoni .... Tech
Carmen Berarducci .... Tech
Bob Brabender .... Strong Vincent
Bob Brockmyer .... Strong Vincent
Mike Dubowski .... Tech
John Elliott .... Strong Vincent
Bill Essigmann .... East
Rusty Felix .... Cathedral Prep
Mike Ferrare .... Strong Vincent
Ed Hammer .... Academy
John Harkins .... Academy
Tom Jones .... Cathedral Prep
Wayne Jones .... Academy
Jim Kamandulis .... Cathedral Prep
Bob Kwiatkowski .... East
Ron Nietupski .... Tech
Doug Norton .... Tech
Dan Nowacinski .... Tech
Tim Nunes .... Academy
Jim Piekanski .... Strong Vincent
Pat Steenberge .... Cathedral Prep
Lou Strelecki .... Strong Vincent
Jim Szymanowski .... East
Bob Thomas .... Tech
Tom Torok .... Academy
Bruce Trojan .... East
Mark Zimmer .... Cathedral Prep
Harry Zmijewski .... Academy

Coaches: Ron Costello of Tech,
Bob Morgan of Academy

County

Earl Anderson .... McDowell
Arron Ankeny .... General McLane
Larry Bayle .... McDowell
Steve Blackman .... McDowell
Charles Bondurant .... North East
Fred Butler .... Iroquois
Nick Cancilla .... Iroquois
Alan Carroll .... Fort LeBoeuf
Jim Cash .... Fairview
Dan Corbett .... Corry
Jim Daniels .... Fort LeBoeuf
Gary Duris .... Northwestern
Bill Engel .... McDowell
Dennis Harrison .... Corry
Bob Heiden .... North East
Steve Johnson .... Iroquois
LeRoy Kreider .... Northwestern
Gary Lindberg .... Fort LeBoeuf
Rick McCauley .... General McLane
Greg McCreary .... General McLane
Bob Murosky .... Iroquois
Larry Nagelson .... North East
Mac Neil North .... East
Dennis Petrunger .... General McLane
Rick Randolph .... Harbor Creek
Keith Reynolds .... Harbor Creek
Mike Rodeno .... Fairview
John Sauers .... General McLane

Coaches: Dave Hannah of Harbor Creek,
Bob Jamison of General McLane

CITY 12 - COUNTY 0

*T*he trio of Pat Steenberge of Prep, Don Aleksiewicz of East and Ron Nietupski of Tech proved too much for the County to handle in front of a crowd of 15,000. Steenberge hit on 13 of 21 passes for 101 yards and carried 13 times for 69 yards. Aleksiewicz carried 11 times for 43 yards and had six receptions for 52 yards. Nietupski rushed six times for 18 yards and had two receptions for 20 yards. Three Steenberge-to-Aleksiewicz passes sparked a 72-yard drive in the second quarter. Steenberge went the final yard for the touchdown. Late in the half the City had a fourth-and-6 at the County 19. Steenberge hit Rusty Felix of Prep for a 12-yard gain. After a loss, Steenberge hit Aleksiewicz for a 10-yard touchdown.

Gary Lindberg of Fort LeBoeuf had 22 yards on five carries. Keith Reynolds of Harbor Creek added 21 yards on six attempts. Bob Heiden of North East had 19 yards on six rushes. A unique note to this game came when the City had a fourth down and 56 yards to go.

WINNERS AND LOSERS HONORED

City and County All-Star Game players and coaches were honored at a banquet last night at the Shrine Club. Flanked by Lions Club officials John Brosnan and Don Sawer are County co-coaches Bob Jamison and Dave Hannah (left) and City mentors Ron Costello and Bob Morgan (right). The City won the annual Stadium affair, 12-0.

Chapter 5

$\mathscr{T}$he County reeled off three straight wins to start this decade, the longest such streak in Save-An-Eye history. The run of victories spotlighted quarterbacks Randy Whittelsey of Fort LeBoeuf, Mike Sequite of McDowell and Scott Millhouse of McDowell. Whittelsey threw for a touchdown and a two-point conversion in the 14-0 win in 1970. Dan Taylor of Corry rushed for 101 yards. Sequite directed two second-half marches the next year as the County rallied from a halftime deficit. Those drives featured the running-receiving duo of Chuck Britton of McDowell and Jim Dohanic of Girard. Millhouse fired touchdown passes of 20 and 39 yards to Blaine Kibler of Girard in 1972. A punt return by Dave Ciacchini of McDowell set up the first score. Ciacchini also ran for the two-point conversion that decided the 14-12 game.

The 1970s

After the string of County wins, the City closed out the decade by winning six of seven games. The other contest, in 1977, resulted in an 8-8 tie. After 1972, the County would not win again until 1983. Punishing ground attacks helped the City start a 4-year streak in 1973. Tibor Solymosi of Prep piled up 151 yards in a 22-6 win. Gerry DiGello of Tech went for 130 to lead a 22-8 victory.

Russ Madonia of Prep had an even 100 yards as the City prevailed 16-10 in 1975. Steve Barney of Academy scored both touchdowns on runs in the 1976 13-12 win that came on a clutch PAT kick by Jeff Dolak of Tech. The tie in 1977 was played in a driving rainstorm.

The City won again in 1978 at McDowell's Gus Anderson Field, the game shifted to Millcreek due to work at Veterans Stadium. Takeaways decided the 14-0 game in 1979. Kevin Litz of Tech ran an interception back and Mike Easterling of Strong Vincent went 55 yards with a fumble recovery.

City

Nate Beard .... East
Ed Borgia..Prep
Frank Campbell .... Strong Vincent
Bob Crawford.. Tech
Don Evans.. East
Rich Figaski ....Cathedral Prep
Jim Gallegos .... East
Randy Garrity......................Strong Vincent
Gary Gasper........................Strong Vincent
Luther Gibbs... Tech
Tom Hansen ....Cathedral Prep
Jim Kozlowski...................................... Tech
Tom Locke .... Academy
John Matts.. Tech
Dave Michaels .... Academy
Mike Nestor...................................... Tech
Paul Onorato ....Strong Vincent
John Palkovic.....................Cathedral Prep
Dave Petak .... East
Bob Powell.........................Strong Vincent
Bob Spearman .... Academy
Tom Staszewski .... Academy
James E. Szympruch .... Tech
John Tabaka .... Tech
Rusty Tracy ....Cathedral Prep
Tony Verga ....Strong Vincent
Fred Williams..................................... East
Eddie Woodard................................... East
Jim Woodard ....Strong Vincent
Bob Wright .... Tech

Coaches: Joe Kleiner of Strong Vincent,
Don Zonno of Academy

County

Ken Antalek....................................Iroquois
Bill Bechdel.....................................Iroquois
Eric Bucheit ....McDowell
Ernie Chandler......................Northwestern
Dick Coursey.............................McDowell
Bill Dimon ....Northwestern
Terry Dodd ....Fort LeBoeuf
Gary Faulkner.................................Girard
Tait Feisler.................................McDowell
Randy Harris ....McDowell
Paul Jazenski ....Iroquois
Lloyd Kendrick ....General McLane
Dale King ....Northwestern
Jim Leopold ....Fairview
Paul Lobaugh....................................Iroquois
Jerry Nowakowski.................Harbor Creek
Jeff Oleson............................Fort LeBoeuf
Dave Ostrum .... Wattsburg
Dave Penman...........................McDowell
Chuck Peterson.......................... Wattsburg
Rich Przybylski.......................... Wattsburg
Larry Rausch...................................Girard
Wes Smeltzer ....McDowell
Dan Taylor ....Corry
Steve Triana...............................North East
Dan Weaver.......................................Corry
Randy Whittelsey.................Fort LeBoeuf

Coaches: Ed Poly of Iroquois,
Dave Hannah of Harbor Creek

COUNTY 14 - CITY 0

*R*andy Whittelsey of Fort LeBoeuf and Dan Taylor of Corry starred for the County. Whittelsey threw a 20-yard touchdown pass to Dick Coursey of McDowell and hit Dave Ostrum of Wattsburg with a conversion pass. Taylor carried 26 times for 101 yards, including a 1-yard touchdown run that capped a 73-yard march in the fourth quarter. Paul Jazenski of Iroquois, Jim Leopold of Fairview, Ken Antalek of Iroquois and Jerry Nowakowski of Harbor Creek were other standouts for the winners. The County squelched three other scoring opportunities, fumbling on the City 12-yard line and failing to capitalize after recovering two fumbles deep in City territory.

Eddie Woodard of East carried 11 times for 58 yards to lead the way. Bob Powell of Strong Vincent aided the City ground game. The City fumbled six times and lost three. The crowd was 13,000.

COUNTY SQUAD

1st Row — Larry Rausch, Dave Penman, Jerry Nowakowski, Ken Antalek, Ernie Chandler, Lloyd Kendrick, Dave Ostrum, Rick Przybylski, Dick Coursey.
2nd Row — Steve Triana, Dan Weaver, Jim Leopold, Bill Bechdel Paul Jazenski, Paul Lobaugh, Wes Smeltzer, Tait Feisler, Dale King.
3rd Row — Dan Weaver, Gary Faulkner, Eric Bucheit, Randy Harris, Bill Dimon, Jeff Oleson, Randy Whittelsey, Terry Dodd.

Randy Whittelsey had two dreams as a youngster in Waterford. One was to play in the Save-An-Eye Game. The other was to become a rock star.

The Fort LeBoeuf quarterback got his chance to participate in the charity game in 1970. He made the most of it, leading the County to a 14-0 victory. The night before the game, Whittelsey and his band Cardboard Balloon had played at Grapeland in New York state.

"It was a late night and probably not a good idea, but we had fun and made some money," he recalled. Then, turning his attention from keyboard to scoreboard, he fulfilled a longtime quest. "I had looked forward to playing in the all-star game since I was a little kid," Whittelsey said. "I started going to the games with my dad when I was about six."

Randy Whittelsey – 1970

The Whittelseys visited various stadiums around Erie County during the regular season. "In those days you could stand in the end zone at most County fields," he recalled. But father and son made just one trip a year to see a game in Erie. "The only time I went to the Erie Stadium was for the Save-An-Eye Game. The Stadium field was like the mecca for us," Whittelsey said. "That was when there was still a cinder track around the field." Ironically, Whittelsey believes that track played a role in the County's Save-An-Eye win. "Early in the third quarter Paul Jazenski (Iroquois) and Jerry Nowakowski (Harbor Creek) tackled Eddie Woodard (East) onto the track," the LeBoeuf ace recalled. "He was cut up, bleeding on both arms from the cinders. He came up and you could just see in his eyes the game was over."

Whittelsey said one of the keys to the County's game plan was to slow the elusive Woodard. "We knew going into the game we had to stop him," he said. "He was the big guy for the City." Woodard, limited to 58 yards in 11 carries that night, went on to a fine career at Kent State.

The County scored touchdowns on a 20-yard pass from Whittelsey to Dick Coursey of McDowell and a 1-yard run by Dan Taylor of Corry. Whittelsey also hit Dave Ostrum of Wattsburg with a two-point conversion throw. Strong line play also helped the winners, Whittelsey stressed. "We had guys up front like Eric Bucheit, Tait Feisler and Dave "Itchy" Penman of McDowell and Chuck Peterson of Wattsburg. Our line was tremendous."

Whittelsey was one of several County players who caused a bit of a stir with their flowing hair. "They billed us as the first long-haired team to play in the Stadium," he said. "I played in a rock band and several other players like Jazenski and Jim Leopold had long hair. We kept our helmets on going down the steps to the field and some of the fans were throwing popcorn at us. But being the rebel I was, I kind of liked that."

Whittelsey would have liked to have had more of his Fort LeBoeuf teammates in the game. "We went undefeated but only had three guys on the team," he said. Jeff Oleson and Terry Dodd were the other LeBoeuf players selected. Being named to the Save-An-Eye was a special thrill. "The All-Star Game was a big deal," he said. "The crowds were huge (13,000 saw the 1970 game) and it's unfortunate that doesn't happen anymore. It's still pretty amazing the game has lasted for 75 years."

Cardboard Balloon didn't enjoy anywhere near that longevity. The rock band, including Gary Lindberg on bass, Jim Bonito on drums, Denny Taylor on guitar and Whittelsey handling keyboards, also formed LeBoeuf's starting backfield that season. Cardboard Balloon popped just one year after their senior season. "I didn't go to college because I thought I was going to be a rock and roll star," Whittelsey explained. "I was kind of skinny ... I played football at 165 pounds and wrestled at 145. I went to the University of South Dakota three years later, but they ran the veer and didn't throw the ball. I don't really know why they wanted me. I didn't like it and was only there one year."

Whittelsey has resided in Waterford ever since. He worked in Erie County Juvenile Probation for 28 years, retiring in 2012.

– Jim Camp

CITY SQUAD

1st Row — Frank Campbell, Paul Onorato, James Kozlowski, Rusty Tracy, Tony Verga, Gary Gasper, Ed Woodard, Don Evans.

2nd Row — Mike Nestor, Luther Gibbs, Edward Borgia, Fred Williams, Tom Locke, Tom Staszewski, Jim Gallesos, Nate Beard.

3rd Row — Bob Wright, John Matts, Bob Crawford, Randy Garrity, Bob Powell, Bob Spearman.

Coaches: Joe Kleiner, left; Don Zonno, right.

City

Max Alwens	Academy
Ken Brasington	Tech
Bob Casella	Strong Vincent
Mike Dropcho	Cathedral Prep
Tom Erdman	Cathedral Prep
Chuck Erickson	Strong Vincent
Ron Essigmann	East
Todd Froehlich	Cathedral Prep
William Gillespie	Academy
Odell Graves	East
Bob Hamilton	Academy
Tim Hughes	Cathedral Prep
Richard Kraus	Strong Vincent
Dave Lojewski	Tech
Rick Mangold	Cathedral Prep
Bill McManus	Academy
Paul Miller	East
Al Niemi	East
Mark Peters	Tech
Mike Pry	Tech
Kevin Rinn	Tech
Clint Roberts	Tech
Richard Rudenski	East
Tony Sansone	Strong Vincent
John Scypinski	Cathedral Prep
Cliff Smith	East
Gerry Steenberge	Cathedral Prep
Bob Stovall	Tech
Woody Thompson	East
David Vactor	East
Steve Wagner	Strong Vincent
Bob Williamson	Academy
John Zambroski	Cathedral Prep

Coaches: Bill Brabender of East, Jim Marnella of Tech

County

Glenn Anderson	Wattsburg
Mike Bartoszek	McDowell
Chuck Britton	McDowell
David Cline	Fort LeBoeuf
Dave Crowell	Corry
Jim Dohanic	Girard
John Downey	Corry
Ed Eller	Iroquois
Dan Harrison	General McLane
Bill Metzler	Girard
Walt Miller	Wattsburg
Steve Nolan	General McLane
Mike Palmer	McDowell
Joe Peagler	McDowell
John Randolph	Harbor Creek
Len Reuss	Iroquois
John Richardson	Fairview
Duffy Sample	Fairview
Mike Sequite	McDowell
Dennis Skelton	General McLane
Bob Songer	Northwestern
Richard Speicher	North East
Rodney Stage	North East
Scott Thomson	North East
Dan Tome	Girard
Ron Troyer	Fort LeBoeuf
Brent Willey	General McLane
Ted Willis	Girard
Bob Yamma	McDowell

Coaches: Jim McGowan of Fort LeBoeuf, Ron Jones of Fairview

COUNTY 20 - CITY 12

Mike Sequite of McDowell led the County to a comeback win. After trailing 12-6 at halftime, the County rallied before 13,000 fans. Sequite scored on a 4-yard run. Bob Stovall of Tech ran 14 yards for the game's first score. Ed Eller of Iroquois went 24 yards with a fumble recovery to tie the game.

Cliff Smith of East scored on a 34-yard interception return for the City late in the first half. Sequite then directed two second-half drives, which featured the running of Chuck Britton of McDowell and the pass catching of Jim Dohanic of Girard. Woody Thompson of East was in the City backfield. He later played for the University of Miami and the Atlanta Falcons of the NFL.

Clash In Annual Classic

... ~ will be the short, ~pected to be the starting halftime entertainment. Tick- better material for the game ~ack for Erie while ets are on sale at numerous and to accommodate the wish- ~ctor and Stovall outlets throughout the city and es of the coaches who said it ~field. also at the gate. was too much trouble breaking The Erie Lions Club s~on- up practice to take part in the

Raymond Carter says that he holds a distinction for the Save-An-Eye Game, even though he never played in the game. Carter spent the fall of 1970 playing for Wattsburg High, the forerunner of Seneca High. He was later selected to play in the 1971 game.

"I was the first black chosen to play for the County team, but I didn't play," Carter said. "I had enlisted and was the property of the United States Marine Corps and they didn't want damaged goods. Two days after the game I reported for duty."

Fred Butler – 1969
Raymond Carter – 1971

Actually, even if Carter had played in 1971 he would not have been the first black on a County team. Fred Butler of Iroquois holds that distinction. He played in the 1969 game won by the City, 14–0.

– Joe Mattis

Woody Thompson admits that his performance in the 1971 Save-An-Eye Game, won by his County team 20-12, was not his best performance on the gridiron. But he understood why and that was okay with him.

Thompson, who went on to be a productive fullback at the University of Miami and then with the Atlanta Falcons in the NFL, had played in the Big 33 Game in the summer of 1971. The Save-An-Eye Game came later in August. "I spent the summer in Miami and then went to Hershey for the Big 33 Game," Thompson recalled. "I had a big game and a lot of carries."

The coach for the City team was Bill Brabender, Thompson's coach at East. "He was very stern. He was a task master," Thompson said of Brabender. "He was also a tremendous motivator. He loved to win and he had players on the East team that loved to win." Brabender wanted to give every player an opportunity to show what he could do in the Save-An-Eye Game and he knew very well that Thompson had his showcase game earlier that summer. "He took that into account," said Thompson, a bruising runner. "I understood that and that was why I did not get many carries."

Woody Thompson – 1971

The 1971 game was not Thompson's initiation to the Save-An-Eye Game. He had viewed many of the previous games as a spectator.

"I began going to the games in grade school when we walked to the Stadium from (East) 3rd and Holland," he said. "I always wanted to play in the game. I looked forward to it."

Even though he played a small part in the game, one thing still stands out vividly in Thompson's memory. "We lost and I did not like that," he said. 'But my career was not complete until I played in the Save-An-Eye Game. And I did that. I'm proud to say I'm a member of the Save-An-Eye class of 1971."

– Joe Mattis

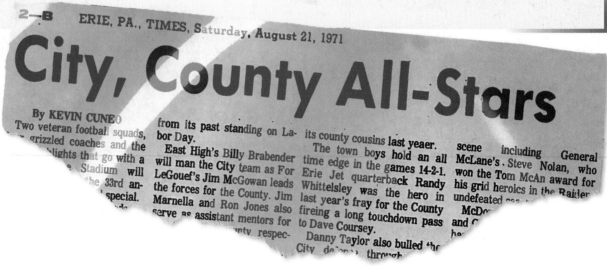

2—B   ERIE, PA., TIMES, Saturday, August 21, 1971

City, County All-Stars

By KEVIN CUNEO
Two veteran football squads, grizzled coaches and the lights that go with a Stadium will the 33rd an- special.

from its past standing on Labor Day.

East High's Billy Brabender will man the City team as For LeGouef's Jim McGowan leads the forces for the County. Jim Marnella and Ron Jones also serve as assistant mentors for nty respec-

its county cousins last yeaer.
The town boys hold an all time edge in the games 14-2-1. Erie Jet quarterback Randy Whittelsley was the hero in last year's fray for the County fireing a long touchdown pass to Dave Coursey.
Danny Taylor also bulled the City defense through

scene including General McLane's Steve Nolan, who won the Tom McAn award for his grid heroics in the Raider undefeated
McDo
and
h

Seven Area Players In Save An Eye Game

Seven area boys have been selected to play in the annual Erie Lions Club Save an Eye City-County All Star Football game.

Ted Willis, Jim Dohanic, Bill Metzler and Dan Tome from Union High; John Richardson and Duffy Sample from Fairview and Bob Songer from Northwestern will all play for the County All Stars.

The game traditionally has been played on Labor Day, but this year it has been advanced to Saturday, August 21, at 8:15 p.m. The Labor Day date made it impossible for some good players to participate because had already departed practice

extremely difficult for the coaches to conduct All Star practices and still devote sufficient time to their own teams.

Coaching the County All Stars this year will be Jim McGowan from Ft. LeBoeuf. Ron Jones from Fairview will be his assistant.

Advance tickets for this big attraction may be purchased at the Cosmopolite Herald and Hull's Cigar Store in Girard McCarty's in I... logel's IGA ...

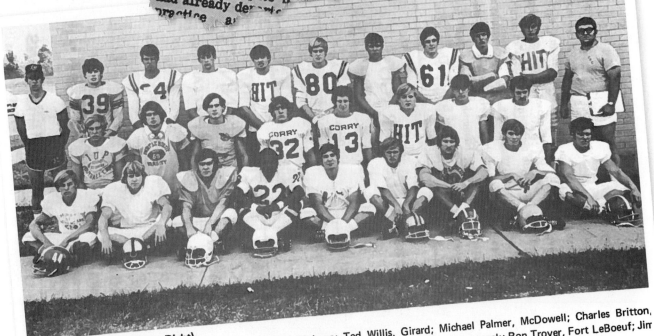

COUNTY SQUAD (Left to Right)

1st Row — Dan Harrison, General McLane; Ted Willis, Girard; Michael Palmer, McDowell; Charles Britton, McDowell; Michael Sequite, McDowell; John Randolph, Harborcreek; Ron Troyer, Fort LeBoeuf; Jim Dohanic, Girard; and Steve Nolan, General McLane.

2nd Row — Dennis Skelton, General McLane; David Cline, Fort LeBoeuf; Brent Willey, General McLane; Dave Crowell, Corry; John Downey, Corry; Joe Peagler, McDowell; Bill Metzler, Girard; Daniel Tome, Girard.

3rd Row — Jim McGowan, Coach; Ed Eller, Iroquois; Rodney Stage, North East; Jim May, Wattsburg; Walter Miller, Wattsburg; Scott Thomson, North East; Robert Songer, Northwestern; Richard Speicher, North East; Leonard Reuss, Iroquois; John Richardson, Fairview; Ron Jones, Coach.

66 My best memory of the game was that we won. Back then McDowell was considered a County school and I think that helped us out a little bit. My family was there watching me when I caught a pass.

Jim Dohanic – 1971

I played at Girard, but there was a pretty good camaraderie playing with the kids from other schools. I see Dennis Skelton from General McLane once in a while, and my buddy Ted Willis from Girard. He and I live just a couple of blocks from each other. After high school I went on to Kent State. I played one year there and I played with Jack Lambert (who was elected to the Pro Football Hall of Fame following an outstanding career with the Pittsburgh Steelers). 99

Willis, Dohanic Make Key Plays In City - County All Star Game

Although Ted Willis and Jim Dohanic did not get the opportunity to team up offensively, each came up with a key play in the County's 20-12 victory in the Lions Club Save-an-Eye All Star Game last Saturday night. Early in the second quarter, with the City holding a 6-0 lead, the Willis intercepted a City pass and returned it 23 yards to the City 19 setting up the County's first score.

Quarterback Mike Sequite from McDowell carried twice and scored on the second play to tie the game at 6 all. On the last play of the first half the City scored on an interception of an errant County pass

Neither team could mount a sustained offensive during the third period.

One of the most crucial plays in the game came midway through the final period when Dohanic beat his defender, hauled in a slightly underthrown pass from Sequite and moved the ball into City territory at the 27. That 37 yard play gave the County good field position that ultimately led to the winning score.

Bill Metzler and Dan Tome from Union High and John Richardson and Dufty Sample from ... also saw action in the

...lboy Gridders Honored

...hool foot-
...at last
...lub meet-
...ohn Pu-
...awards
...right
...neral]

McLane, his coach Bob Jamison; Mark Heinemann of Iroquois and his coach Ed Poly; Mike Bartoszek of McDowell and his coach Joe Moore; and Bob Smith of Prep and Rambler coaching aide Don Felix.

CITY SQUAD (Left to Right)

1st Row — Managers: Jim Gervase, Barry Kruise, Ken Kruise.

2nd Row — Mike Dropcho, Prep; Bill McManus, Academy; John Zambroski, Prep; Mark Peters, Tech; John Scypinski, Prep; Dave Lojewski, Tech; Bill Gillespie, Academy; Rich Mangold, Prep.

3rd Row — Paul Miller, East; Bob Cassella, Strong Vincent; Tom Erdman, Prep; Anthony Sansone, Strong Vincent; Al Niemi, Strong Vincent; Dave Vactor, East; Ron Essigman, East; Mike Pry, Tech.

4th Row — Max Alwens, Academy; Richard Kraus, Strong Vincent; Rick Rudenski, East; Chuck Ericson, Strong Vincent; Jerry Steenberge, Prep; Kevin Rinn, Tech; Robert Williamson, Academy.

5th Row — Bill Brabender, Coach; Bob Stoval, Tech; Cliff Smith, East; Woody Thompson, East; Odell Graves, East; Ken Brasington, Tech; Steve Wagner, Strong Vincent; Jim Marnella, Coach; Dave Kahl, Coach.

31st Annual Save An Eye All Star Football Game Sat., Aug. 21 - Talent Galore

Area football fans are reminded of the change of date for the Annual Lions Club "Save an Eye" City vs. County All Star game.

The game has traditionally been held on Labor Day but this year will be advanced to Saturday, August 21, 8:15 p.m., at Academy Stadium.

One of the most talented arrays of high school football stars ever to come out of the greater Erie area promises to make this gala 31st annual affair a football lover's dream.

The county team will be built around a strong nucleus of thirteen boys from three teams that lost only two ball games last year.

Union High, 8-1 last season, will be represented by last season's most valuable player, Dan Tome, plus the area's most prolific passing combination of quarterback Ted Willis and receivers Jim Behe of Fairview as his assistant.

Jones of Fairview as his assistant.

Bill Brabender of East High will direct the city's efforts with Jim Marnella of Tech as assistant.

This game has consistently drawn capacity crowds and the Lions Club sincerely hopes the change in date will not make this year an exception. Tickets are $1.50 at the gate and $1.25 in advance. Advance tickets in this area may be purchased at the Cosmopolite Herald office; and Hull's Cigar Store in Girard; and McCarty's in Lake City and Weisslogel's IGA in Fairview.

The Save an Eye program is the Lions Club of Erie's only program. Last year the club spent nearly $12,000 on eyeglasses for the needy. This year they have spent nearly $9,000 already. They help almost 1000 persons a year with the number

seeking help growing constantly. The fund also made a $2,000 grant in 1970 to the Erie Blind Center for the training of a mobility instructor who has already taught 20 Erie County blind persons to walk with white canes. The club bought large print books for the Erie Public Library for use by those with limited vision.

All this was made possible by the money raised by the 30-year old Save an Eye City - County All Star Football Game. The club spends just about every dollar it raises for eye care for the needy.

The Lions Club is hoping for another standing room only crowd.

If you want to see a bumper crop of athletes in a hard hitting football game -- don't miss this one. See the 21st Annual Save an Eye game at Academy Stadium, Saturday, August 21, at

Game 34 – August 19, 1972

City

Wayne Aldrich	Strong Vincent
David Bailey	Tech
Ed Beck	Cathedral Prep
John Bojarski	Cathedral Prep
David Brabender	Strong Vincent
David Britton	Strong Vincent
Marc Bush	Strong Vincent
Rick Byham	Strong Vincent
Merch Calabrese	Strong Vincent
Jim Caldwell	East
Gary Carson	Academy
Mike Coluzzi	Cathedral Prep
Gentle Cooley	Tech
Joshua Gilmore	East
Richard Haft	Tech
Don Herold	Strong Vincent
Jimmy Jones	Academy
Mike Mazanowski	East
Greg Oldach	Strong Vincent
Mike Panighetti	Tech
Gerald Rankin	Academy
Ed Rossman	Tech
Jeff Satyshur	East
Tim Schloss	Tech
Bill Scholz	Cathedral Prep
Ernie Scutella	Strong Vincent
Ron Steele	Strong Vincent
Tim Truitt	East
Alan Felix	Cathedral Prep
Don Wierbinski	Cathedral Prep
Nick Sambuchino	Tech
Bruce Dougherty	East
Bill Wisniewski	Tech
John Merski	Tech

Coaches: Glenn Barthelson of Strong Vincent, Jim McQuaide of McDowell

County

James Allen	North East
Gordon Bessetti	Wattsburg
Dave Ciacchini	McDowell
Ted Clark	McDowell
Al Cox	Girard
Charles Craft	Wattsburg
Mark Eller	Wattsburg
Tom Ferraro	Fairview
Mark Fitch	Iroquois
Mike Florek	General McLane
Jim Giacomelli	McDowell
Paul Goodwill	Corry
Jim Gratson	General McLane
Tim Haaf	Fort LeBoeuf
Robert Holiday	Northwestern
Robert Hopkins	Girard
Fred Hyde	Girard
Eric Johnson	Harbor Creek
Roger Jordan	Iroquois
Blaine Kibler	Girard
Dan Kosiorek	Wattsburg
Tom Lane	McDowell
Gary Lydic	Fort LeBoeuf
B.J. MacIntosh	Fort LeBoeuf
John Matcham	Iroquois
Dana Mays	Girard
Bruce Mick	Corry
Scott Millhouse	McDowell
Eric Newhall	General McLane
Dave Norton	Corry
Randy Nyberg	McDowell
Lloyd Prindle	Girard
Sam Tome	Girard
Bill Wagner	Northwestern
Jeff Yahn	McDowell

Coaches: Jim Sisson of Girard, Jon Christensen of Northwestern

COUNTY 14 - CITY 12

*S*cott Millhouse of McDowell passed to Blaine Kibler of Girard for two touchdowns. The tosses of 39 and 20 yards gave the County a 14-0 halftime edge before the City rallied with 10,000 fans watching. Millhouse hit 5 of 11 passing for 112 yards and rushed for 30 yards. Tom Ferraro of Fairview led the County ground game. Dave Ciacchini of McDowell had a punt return to set up the first touchdown. Millhouse then fired 39 yards to Kibler on the next play. The Millhouse-to-Kibler combo clicked again from 20 yards out with 4 seconds left in the half.

Ciacchini ran the pivotal 2-point conversion. Jeff Satyshur of East took over at quarterback for the City in the second half. Jimmy Jones of Academy, who had 85 yards on 19 rushes, had the first City touchdown on a 2-yard run. He later scored from 1 yard out, but the PAT was stopped short to preserve the win with 24 seconds left.

Dear Friend:

The Downtown Erie Lion's Club is devoted to providing eye care and promoting sight conservation. For more than 30 years, we have furnished eye examinations and glasses to all less-advantaged girls and boys in the City and throughout the County of Erie. This past year we helped more than 800 young people. In addition, we help to provide aid to the blind and those with vision handicaps.

As we serve, our service has become ever more depended upon and more costly. But, we're all in this together. By your attendance this evening, you make it possible that no girl or boy will go without needed eye care. This is our 32nd annual Save-An-Eye All-Star Football Game. The proceeds support our whole program. In a very real sense, you are helping to save the eyes of many girls and boys in our County-wide community.

We also acknowledge with sincere appreciation the contributions of all those who have donated their time and energy to make this game the success and spectacular it is: the All Stars and their coaches, the game officials, the police, the groundskeepers, the ambulance service, our halftime entertainers and the game committee, and those who support our efforts by purchasing the advance tickets and the ads in this program. Bless them all and each of you for being here this evening. Enjoy the game, with the knowledge that even if your team should lose, you are helping to make winners out of a lot of girls and boys. And come back next year.

Sincerely,

William Eckert

William Eckert, King Lion

City		County	
Steve Bohun	East	Dan Armbruster	Iroquois
Kim Carrara	Cathedral Prep	Barry Baker	Corry
Greg Cieslak	Cathedral Prep	Fred Baney	Fort LeBoeuf
David Cronin	Cathedral Prep	Hubert Brock	Iroquois
Don Detzel	Strong Vincent	Bob Bross	Harbor Creek
Joe Dipre	Cathedral Prep	John Buscemi	North East
Bill Drabina	Cathedral Prep	Dan Clapper	General McLane
Tom Dutkosky	Cathedral Prep	Tom Comstock	Iroquois
Jeff Ellis	Tech	Jim Corbett	McDowell
John Gannon	Strong Vincent	Rod Grettler	Girard
Rich Gavin	East	Greg Hampe	McDowell
John Hanhauser	Cathedral Prep	Ron Hanson	Iroquois
Bob Latimer	Academy	Doug Henry	Harbor Creek
Bill Maniece	East	Don Herbe	McDowell
Mark Miller	Tech	Dennis Kubiak	Corry
Mike Minton	Strong Vincent	Rick Kurt	Iroquois
Mark Newcamp	Tech	Mike Lane	McDowell
Joe Noonan	Tech	Steve Lane	McDowell
Mike Palkovic	Cathedral Prep	Felix Lucero	Fairview
Jim Palkovic	Cathedral Prep	Steve Merritt	Harbor Creek
Vernon Peterson	Cathedral Prep	Tom Morano	Harbor Creek
Greg Pochatko	Tech	Mike Nulph	Northwestern
Bob Rebar	Tech	Joe Pfeiffer	Wattsburg
Jeff Shaw	Tech	Perry Rodland	Harbor Creek
Mike Sherbin	Tech	Bill Ruhl	General McLane
Bruce Snyder	Tech	Sam Scott	Girard
Tibor Solymosi	Cathedral Prep	Tim Sherrange	McDowell
Mike Speros	East	Darrel Sisson	Girard
Bob Staab	Tech	Steve Spiegel	Iroquois
Joe Sullivan	East	Greg Spilko	Fort LeBoeuf
Jerry Tate	East	Fred Wilson	Fairview
Pat Wagner	Strong Vincent	Jim Zahner	North East
Tom Weber	Academy	Mark Zimmerman	Northwestern
Mark Zonno	Cathedral Prep		

Coaches: Bill Cutcher of Cathedral Prep, Joe Kleiner of Strong Vincent

Coaches: Tony Sanfilippo of Harbor Creek, Jim Concilla of North East

CITY 22 - COUNTY 6

*T*ibor Solymosi of Prep rushed for 151 yards on 21 carries and a touchdown for the City, with 12,000 in attendance. Joe Noonan of Tech hit on 5 of 9 passes for 88 yards and two touchdowns. The City put together three long drives for touchdowns. Solymosi had runs of 16, 13 and 23 yards in a 98-yard march. Noonan passed 16 yards to Solymosi for the touchdown. An 80-yard drive was ignited by Solymosi's 28-yard burst. Noonan connected with Dave Cronin of Prep for 26 yards before Joe Dipre of Prep scored from 1 yard out. Noonan passed to Jeff Ellis of Tech for the PAT. A 98-yard march featured a 27-yard run by Dipre and a 19-yarder by Bob Staab of Tech before Noonan hit Mark Zonno of Prep for a 22-yard touchdown. Richie Gavin of East ran for the 2-point conversion.

Sam Scott passed 57 yards to former Girard teammate Rod Grettler to set up the lone County touchdown. Joe Pfeiffer of Wattsburg scored from 6 yards out. Dipre had 61 yards on 10 carries while Rick Kurt of Iroquois ran for 25 yards on 10 attempts.

COUNTY SQUAD (Left to Right)

1st Row — Coach Concilla; Mike Nulph, Northwestern; Mark Zimmerman, Northwestern; Jim Corbett, McDowell; Greg Hampe, McDowell; Don Herbe, McDowell; Tim Sherrange, McDowell; Darrell Sisson, Girard; Felix Lucero, Fairview.

2nd Row — Coach Sanfilippo; Fred Baney, Ft. LeBoeuf; Greg Spilko, Ft. LeBoeuf; Dan Clapper, General McLane; Bill Ruhl, General McLane; Joe Pfeiffer, Wattsburg; Dennis Kubiak, Corry; Tom Morano, Harborcreek; Perry Rodland, Harborcreek.

3rd Row — Rick Kurt, Iroquois; Fred Wilson, Fairview; Dan Armbruster, Iroquois; Doug Henry, Harborcreek; Bob Bross, Harborcreek; Jim Zahner, North East; John Buscemi, North East.

4th Row — Jim Smith, Northwestern; Steve Merritt, Harborcreek; Rod Grettler, Girard; Sam Scott, Girard; Hubert Brock, Iroquois; Tom Comstock, Iroquois; Steve Spiegel, Iroquois; Ron Hanson, Iroquois.

Tibor Solymosi was at a crossroads approaching the Save-An-Eye Game of 1973. The Cathedral Prep running back had suffered a major ankle injury midway through his senior season, leaving a promising college football career in jeopardy. "I had a bad fracture and torn ligaments and limped through the remainder of the season," Solymosi remembered. "The injury caused all of the Division I schools to back off recruiting me. I was all set to go to Allegheny and play for coach Sam Timer, but the Save-An-Eye was going to be a determination of whether I could play college ball or not. "This was to be a big test . . . I guess I passed the test pretty well."

Those who watched him run that night would likely give him an A for his efforts. Solymosi hammered out 111 yards on 13 carries . . . in the first half. He saw limited action in the second half and finished with 151 yards on 21 attempts. "I was so sore after the first half I didn't finish the game," he said. "I had only been out of the cast for six weeks, but it was a great night for me. With it came the realization that I was going to be able to play in college."

Solymosi's efforts helped the City pound out a 22-6 win. It also provided him the chance to play one last time for Prep (and City) coach Bill Cutcher. "It was nice to play a final game for coach Cutcher," Solymosi said. "He really inspired me and made me believe in myself. He brought a touch of professionalism to high school coaching in Erie."

Tibor Solymosi – 1973

Now an Erie attorney, Solymosi had plenty of friends on both sides at the Save-An-Eye. "There were a lot of great players on those two teams that night," he said. "My teammates Joe Dipre, John Hanhauser and Kim Carrara played for the City. And I grew up with Rick Kurt from Iroquois." Only a family move prevented Kurt and Solymosi from teaming up in high school. "If we had not moved to the City, Ricky and I would have been in the same backfield at Iroquois," Solymosi said. "That would have been something." Kurt won the Thom McAn Award as Erie County's top player that year. Solymosi was also in the mix to win the honor, despite the ankle injury.

Solymosi has attended many of the Save-An-Eye Games since playing 40 years ago. "I make it a point to go each year," he said. One game he recalls in particular was in 2001. My son Mick (Fairview) played and it was kind of fun to watch him in the game," the senior Solymosi said. "It's really nice to see the tradition has been carried on by the Lions Club."

– Jim Camp

CITY SQUAD (Left to Right)

1st Row — Bob Rebar, Tech; Joe Sullivan, East; Don Detzel, Strong Vincent; Mark Zonno, Prep; Tibor Solymosi, Prep; David Cronin, Prep; Bob Latimer, Academy; and Jerry Tate, East.

2nd Row — Bob Staab, Tech; Mark Newcamp, Tech; Gary Cieslak, Prep; Tom Weber, Academy; Jeff Shaw, Tech; Mark Miller, Tech; Greg Pochatko, Tech; and John Hanhauser, Prep.

3rd Row — Coaches Kleiner and Cutcher; Mike Minton, Strong Vincent; Pat Wagner, Strong Vincent; John Gannon, Strong Vincent; Bill Drabina, Prep; Joe Noonan, Tech; Kim Carrara, Prep; Tom Dutkosky, Prep; Vernon Peterson, Prep; Bill Maniece, East; and Joe Dipre, Prep.

City

Craig Abbey	Academy
Alex Arrington	Academy
Lee Barthelmes	Academy
John Calabrese	Cathedral Prep
Mark Cicero	Cathedral Prep
Mark Cieslak	Cathedral Prep
Dave Cimino	Strong Vincent
Mel Darby	East
Jerry DiGello	Tech
Pat Driscoll	Academy
Mark Filipowski	Cathedral Prep
Bob Flak	East
Dan Fuhrman	Academy
Dana Gibbs	East
Dave Gunther	Tech
Mike Hale	Academy
Chuck Hintz	Strong Vincent
Mike Jensen	Tech
Pete Karuba	East
Joe Lomax	East
Tom Masi	Tech
Joe McAndrew	Tech
Pat McKenrick	Strong Vincent
Dan Pilewski	Cathedral Prep
Tony Pol	Cathedral Prep
George Quick	Cathedral Prep
Mark Rafalowski	Academy
Frank Rossman	Tech
Steve Scutella	Strong Vincent
Gene Seip	Tech
Eric Sonnenberg	Tech
Kelly Tompkins	Strong Vincent
Ron Weber	Tech

Coaches: Bill Brabender of East, Carney Metzgar of East

County

Don Adams	Northwestern
Brian Barham	Fort LeBoeuf
Scott Barth	Fairview
Harold Blount	General McLane
Gary Colvin	Harbor Creek
Larry Davies	General McLane
Dave Ellwood	Harbor Creek
Harry Evanoff	Iroquois
Bob Ferrando,	Fairview
Dave Fisher	McDowell
Andy Fritz	Iroquois
Phil Giewont	Wattsburg
Dan Jenks	Fort LeBoeuf
Dale Jennings	McDowell
Jim Johnson	Harbor Creek
Dave Kranking	Fort LeBoeuf
Bill Kruse	McDowell
Roy Laws	McDowell
Tom McShane	Iroquois
Bill Michael	Fairview
Tom Narus	McDowell
Paul Nicholson	Northwestern
Jim Nowakowski	Harbor Creek
Dan Petrush	Northwestern
Vance Richmond	Iroquois
Brad Shields	Fort LeBoeuf
Dan Stearns	Girard
Doug Stratton	North East
Gary Thompson	Wattsburg
Ron Walcheck	Northwestern
Rich Way	North East
Gregg Yeager	Fairview
Jeff Zuravleff	Iroquois

Coaches: Bob Jamison of General McLane, Jim Paul of McDowell

CITY 22 - COUNTY 8

$\mathcal{J}$erry DiGello of Tech ran for 130 yards on 15 carries and scored two touchdowns with 8,500 fans looking on. DiGello scored on runs of 4 and 6 yards. Eric Sonnenberg of Tech had a 2-yard touchdown run. Dana Gibbs of East, who rushed 21 times for 67 yards, kicked two extra points. Gibbs also passed to Pat McKendrick of Strong Vincent for a two-pointer. Mark Filipowski of Prep connected on 8 of 15 passes for 84 yards. McKendrick was his top receiver.

Harry Evanoff of Iroquois passed 13 yards to Bill Kruse of McDowell for the County touchdown. Evanoff also tossed to Kruse on the 2-point conversion play. Evanoff hit on five passes during the final County drive. The County also threatened at the end of the first half when Ron Walcheck of Northwestern hit three passes and ran 21 yards to the 2-yard line before being stopped as the half ended. Walcheck and Bob Ferrando of Fairview led the County offense.

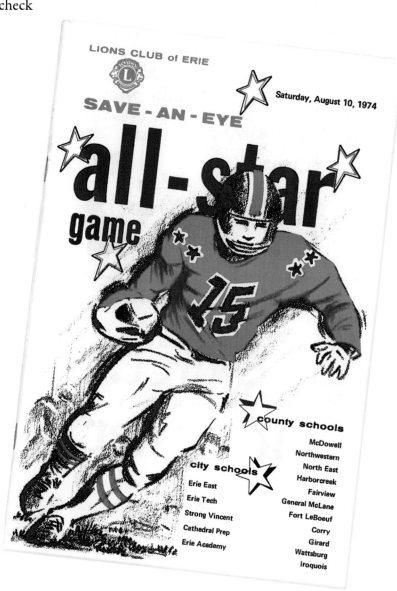

LIONS CLUB of ERIE

Saturday, August 10, 1974

SAVE - AN - EYE

all-star game

county schools

McDowell
Northwestern
North East
Harborcreek
Fairview
General McLane
Fort LeBoeuf
Corry
Girard
Wattsburg
Iroquois

city schools

Erie East
Erie Tech
Strong Vincent
Cathedral Prep
Erie Academy

66 I was a defensive halfback. I was scrawny — 5'6", 135 pounds. (East's Bill) Brabender was the coach. I didn't really know him. We had a good defense. I played most of the first half of the game, but Brabender said there would be no stars. Everyone would play half the game. Everyone would have fun.

Pretty much at the end of the game I wasn't playing. I was just standing there. There were about 3 minutes left in the game and we were on offense. Brabender turned around and said, 'Who hasn't been in for a while?' So I raised my hand. I wasn't going to college. I was a scrawny kid. It was the last time I was ever going to be in uniform.

Eric Sonnenberg – 1974

Brabender turned to me and said, 'Sonnenberg, go in for (Tom) Masi and run a 31 dive.' Tom Masi was Tech's fullback. He knew me and knew I wasn't on offense. As I'm running into the game I'm yelling, 'Masi, Masi.' So he runs out. I get into the huddle and like a big guy I said, '31 dive.' The quarterback kinda stood up and said, 'No way.' And so I said, '31 dive.'

It was on the 3-yard line and I walked in (for the touchdown). A 135-pound fullback scored. It was nice. (Brabender) let a guy who he really didn't know go in (for the touchdown). I think a lot of him for doing that.

The next day there was an article in the paper. Jack Polancy wrote that Tech defensive stalwart Eric Sonnenberg got his chance and made the most of it.

I look at my kids now and say, 'I was a fullback in the Save-An-Eye Game. 99

THE HALF TIME SHOW

THE STRONG VINCENT MARCHING BAND

The present organization was put in effect in September, 1972, and grew from fifty members to the present 160. Under the direction of Mr. James Crumbly, the band is noted for its swinging half-time shows. Modern rock music is its forté.

The organization consists of the instrumental section, twirlers, color guard, flags and fire batons.

Tonight the audience will observe every type of marching style from formal military to a fast bounce step based on the Pitt Marching Band. Also will be the songs Parade Rock and Beginnings, some colorful movement from the guard, a swinging dance by the twirlers fronted by the flags sophisticated routine and a truly daredevil display by the fire batons.

So, sit back and enjoy pre-game and half time with the swinging Strong Vincent Marching Band of 1974.

City

David Andrews	Academy
Jim Barabas	Cathedral Prep
Bob Bengel	Cathedral Prep
Rick Bengel	Cathedral Prep
James Bolden	Academy
Tim Cacchione	Academy
John Coleman	Academy
Anthony Dabrowski	Tech
Paul Deane	Strong Vincent
Bob Dixon	East
Mark Dylewski	Tech
David Feick	Tech
Tim Holland	Cathedral Prep
Jim Horton	Strong Vincent
Joe Jaruszewicz	Cathedral Prep
Doug Krugger	Tech
Bob Lee	Tech
Tom Lesniewski	Cathedral Prep
Russ Madonia	Cathedral Prep
Bob Miller	East
Prince Mobley	Academy
Tom Moske	Cathedral Prep
Archie Page	Academy
Mark Rebar	Tech
Shawn Roy	East
Ron Rugare	Academy
Gary Satyshur	East
John Sestak	East
Dan Sitter	Tech
Dan Truitt	East
Tim Tyzinski	Cathedral Prep
Jim Wolf	Academy

Coaches: Jon Christensen, Lee Larsen of Academy

County

Mike Burns	Iroquois
John Crotty	Iroquois
Jeff Daub	McDowell
Rock Deitsch	McDowell
Larry Fish	Fort LeBoeuf
Bill Giewont	General McLane
David Hanlon	Fort LeBoeuf
Jim Hedlund	Harbor Creek
Jeff Herman	Fort LeBoeuf
Kevin Horton	McDowell
Larry Loper	Fairview
Jerry Lorei	Seneca
Philip Lorenz	McDowell
Gus Maas	North East
Bob McGahen	Fort LeBoeuf
Harold Merritt	Northwestern
Matt Messmer	Kanty Prep
Joe Miller	Northwestern
Vern Mueller	Seneca
Mike Paris	McDowell
Ron Pushinsky	Fairview
Mike Randall	Iroquois
Galen Rogers	Seneca
Jeff Rosthauser	Seneca
Tom Rozantz	Fairview
Ray Smith	Iroquois
Joe Stahon	Iroquois
Wes Stull	Fort LeBoeuf
Tim Uglow	Harbor Creek
Jay Veith	Girard
Mike Weidler	Northwestern
Dan Wells	Seneca

Coaches: Jim McGowan of Fort LeBoeuf, John Gillette of Northwestern

CITY 16 - COUNTY 10

*R*uss Madonia of Prep rushed 22 times for 100 yards and the City squelched a County comeback. Madonia's production was aided by the blocking of Tim Holland of Prep. Dave Andrews of Academy had a 1-yard touchdown run. Tim Tyzinski of Prep ran 12 yards for a touchdown. Andrews threw to Rick Bengel of Prep for one conversion and Madonia ran for another.

Kevin Horton of McDowell kicked a 32-yard field goal for the County. Tom Rozantz, Fairview's All-County quarterback, led a second-half rally despite suffering from a knee injury. Rozantz hit former Fairview teammate Larry Loper with an 11-yard touchdown. Larry Fish of Fort LeBoeuf gained 20 yards rushing on the drive. Bob Bengel intercepted a Rozantz pass with 1:38 left to halt the final County drive. It was Bengel's second interception. Andrews hit 6 of 10 passing for 64 yards. Rozantz connected on 3 of 6 throws for 37 yards.

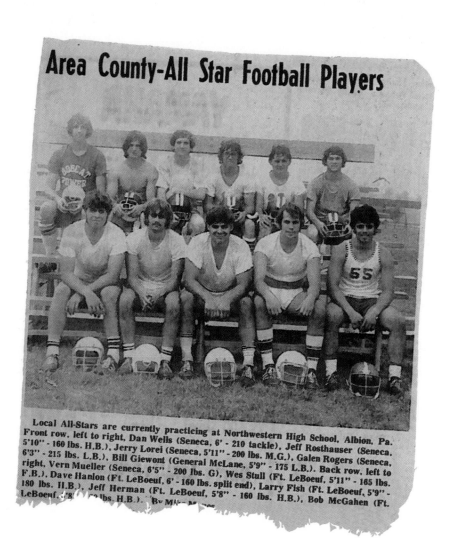

Area County-All Star Football Players

Local All-Stars are currently practicing at Northwestern High School, Albion, Pa. Front row, left to right, Dan Wells (Seneca, 6' - 210 tackle), Jeff Rosthauser (Seneca, 5'10" - 160 lbs. H.B.), Jerry Lorei (Seneca, 5'11" - 200 lbs. M.G.), Galen Rogers (Seneca, 6'3" - 215 lbs. L.B.), Bill Giewont (General McLane, 5'9" - 175 L.B.). Back row, left to right, Vern Mueller (Seneca, 6'5" - 200 lbs. F.B.), Dave Hanlon (Ft. LeBoeuf, 6' - 160 lbs. split end), Wes Stull (Ft. LeBoeuf, 5'11" - 165 lbs. F.B.), Jeff Herman (Ft. LeBoeuf, 5'8" - 160 lbs. H.B.), Larry Fish (Ft. LeBoeuf, 5'9" - 180 lbs. H.B.), Bob McGahen (Ft. LeBoeuf, 5'8" ... lbs. H.B.). By Mike Myers

> For Seneca, I played both ways (on offense and defense). In that game I played defensive end. Our coach was John Gillette. I believe at that time he was the coach at Northwestern. He was fantastic. He treated me extremely well. In fact, I think he singled me out and spent a lot of time with me. He made a big impression. I said, 'What a great guy he was.' After the game he came up and congratulated me even though we lost.

Vern Mueller – 1975

We lost and it was a bummer. We had an all-star basketball game and (the County) won. We had an all-star baseball game and (the County won). I guess two out of three ain't bad. And I played in all three games. I forgot about (Gillette). Apparently he switched schools (to General McLane). I was away on business in Brazil. I think it was 1998. CNN International News was on and I heard them say, 'Edinboro, Pennsylvania.' I had to wait for the next hour until they repeated it to find out what happened. It was shocking. It was terrible.

(On April 24, 1998, John Gillette was shot and killed by a 14-year-old student; another teacher and two students were wounded in a shooting at Nick's Place during an eighth grade party.)

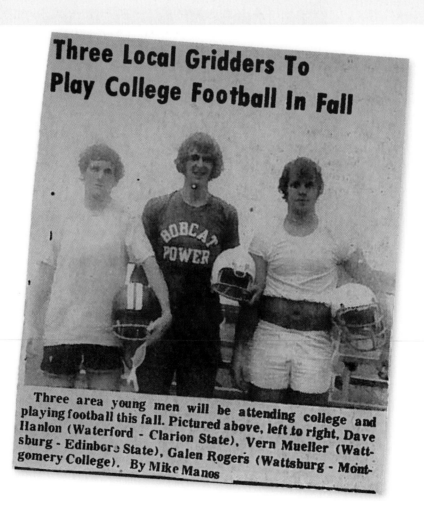

Three Local Gridders To Play College Football In Fall

Three area young men will be attending college and playing football this fall. Pictured above, left to right, Dave Hanlon (Waterford - Clarion State), Vern Mueller (Wattsburg - Edinboro State), Galen Rogers (Wattsburg - Montgomery College). By Mike Manos

66 They were throwing around names of who scored the first touchdown in the whole series. Somebody said, 'Clark Tysinski', and (long time game chairman) Tyco (Swick) said, 'Correct.' I was floored. I didn't know that.

(Tim's father, Clark Tysinski, changed the spelling of his last name to Tyzinski after World War II.)

I went home and said, 'Dad, did you score the first touchdown in the 1939 game?' He said, 'Yeh, I did.' I think he caught a touchdown pass or threw the touchdown pass, but he was part of the scoring combination. I had no idea until that time. He was very quiet about it and never brought things up. (Clark Tysinski threw a 21-yard touchdown pass to East teammate Jim Flanigan in the second quarter.)

Tim Tyzinski – 1975

About 15 or 20 years ago after Dad passed away, Mom was going through some things. She found a jersey and showed it to me. I said, 'That's really unique.' It was amazing going back over the articles that Mom had.

I played in 1975. My best memory was just the atmosphere. Coming up through the ranks, it was a big honor being selected to play. My concern was being able to play because of a college commitment. I played at Slippery Rock. It held more weight playing in the Save-An-Eye (Game) than it did going to the next level. That Save-An-Eye Game was the highlight of my career. 99

City

Steve Barney	Academy
Marty Beck	Cathedral Prep
Charles Blanks	Tech
Tony Bozich	Cathedral Prep
Jerry Carr	Tech
Mike Cuzzola	East
Rich Dandrea	Cathedral Prep
Mike DiBello	Cathedral Prep
Jeff Dolak	Tech
Mark Driscoll	Cathedral Prep
Ken Gustafson	Academy
John Hall	Cathedral Prep
Mickey Hintz	Strong Vincent
Jim Hogan	Tech
Dan Horn	Strong Vincent
Doug James	Tech
Don Kosobucki	Kanty Prep
Greg Loomis	Tech
Matt Malinowski	Kanty Prep
Randy Marzka	Academy
Pat Masterson	Cathedral Prep
Joe Monocello	Cathedral Prep
Vernon Payne	Strong Vincent
Doug Pierce	East
Alan Powell	Strong Vincent
Jay Ruggerio	Strong Vincent
Scott Steffey	Academy
Rich Vicary	Strong Vincent
Stan Walkiewicz	East
Dan Wenner	Strong Vincent
Don Wheeler	Strong Vincent
Mark Wilwohl	Cathedral Prep

Coaches: Glenn Barthelson of Strong Vincent, Gerry Drabina of Cathedral Prep

County

Ron Biletnikoff	Seneca
Larry Casciere	North East
Tom Cleary	Harbor Creek
Dan Diffenbacher	Seneca
Mark Elllis	Fort LeBoeuf
Stan Grandy	McDowell
Tim Hagmaier	Union City
Russ Halmi	McDowell
Jeff Hemler	Girard
Greg Hershelman	Northwestern
Brad Horky	McDowell
Tony Hughes	Fairview
Jim Kujan	Harbor Creek
Joe Kurung	Fairview
Pete Laboda	Iroquois
Matt Lascak	Northwestern
Ron McClelland	Harbor Creek
Chuck McConnell	Girard
Jamie Mead	Fairview
Mike Merritt	Harbor Creek
Ray Michael	Fairview
Jeff Miller	Seneca
Steve Mongera	Seneca
Phil Nagy	McDowell
Tom Peters	Fairview
Steve Potter	Fairview
MarkWroblewski	Seneca
Rich Smith	Northwestern
Brian Sprague	General McLane
Loel Tubbs	McDowell
Rick Wright	Seneca
Bill Wykoff	Harbor Creek

Coaches: Jack Bestwick of Fairview, Tony Ferrari of Fairview

CITY 13 - COUNTY 12

Steve Barney of Academy scored both City touchdowns and Jeff Dolak of Tech kicked a huge extra point as 9,000 watched. Barney tallied on runs of 16 and 17 yards. Ron Biletnikoff of Seneca had two touchdown catches. Dolak intercepted a pass on the opening County drive which led to the first City touchdown. Allan Powell of Strong Vincent gained 25 yards as the City moved 80 yards in the second quarter. Barney found Dolak for a key 19-yard gain, and Barney went the final 17 yards for the touchdown.

Tom Cleary of Harbor Creek recovered a fumble in the third quarter. Joe Kurung of Fairview passed 26 yards to Biletnikoff, then tossed 6 yards to Biletnikoff for the touchdown. The PAT pass fell incomplete. Kurung passed 27 yards to Brad Horky of McDowell on the other County march. Biletnikoff grabbed a 16-yarder for the touchdown. A pass for the extra point failed. Powell rushed 16 times for 96 yards. Doug James of Tech netted 44 yards on nine carries. Kurung hit 8 of 18 passing for 108 yards. Horky had two catches for 41 yards. Rich Smith of Northwestern rushed seven times for 31 yards.

Game 39 – August 13, 1977

City		County	
Mike Applebee	Tech	Keith Bille	Fairview
Don Applebee	Tech	Tim Boothby	Northwestern
Dean Barthelmes	Academy	Rod Brooks	Seneca
David Barthelmes	Academy	Doug Brumagin	Seneca
Oliver Bryant	East	Pat Comer	Iroquois
Clayton Carothers	Strong Vincent	Don Farver	Fairview
Ray Carr	Academy	Steve Ferrando	Fairview
Phil Chenard	Cathedral Prep	Rick Goleniewski	Fairview
Randell Coleman	Academy	Mark Green	McDowell
Ed Dalton	Strong Vincent	Joe Hampy	McDowell
Tom Dill	Cathedral Prep	Dave Herbe	McDowell
Marshall Dobbs	Cathedral Prep	Erik Johnson	Corry
Tim Dougan	Cathedral Prep	Nick Konzel	Harbor Creek
Mike Fox	Cathedral Prep	Tim Lascek	Northwestern
Bill Gazewski	Kanty Prep	Jack Lee	Fort LeBoeuf
Bob Gianelli	Tech	Ron Leuschen	McDowell
A.J. Grack	Tech	Tom Lindemuth	Fairview
Bob Hammer	Tech	Rick Maas	North East
David Hammons	Academy	Mike Nemeyer	Iroquois
Gene Karnes	East	Bill Ochalek	Northwestern
Scott Klimow	Academy	Richard Parks	Corry
Ed Lewicki	Tech	Jim Petrunger	General McLane
Kirk Loomis	Tech	Paul Randolph	Iroquois
Fran Mifsud	Cathedral Prep	Eric Ryan	General McLane
Mark Petruso	Academy	Kevin Sakuta	Girard
Mike Piotrowski	Cathedral Prep	Matt Seth	General McLane
Patsy Pontillo	Strong Vincent	Matt Shesman	General McLane
Richard Quadri	Cathedral Prep	Brian Stull	Fort LeBoeuf
Roger Ratcliff	Strong Vincent	Dennis Teed	Northwestern
Bob Scharrer	Tech	Mike Tome	Girard
Tom Smogorzewski	Cathedral Prep		
Pat Sorek	East		
John Toran	Academy		

Coaches: Jerry Mifsud of East,
Jim Marnella of Tech, Joe Bufalino of East

Coaches: Ed Poly of Iroquois,
Jim Tonks of Seneca

CITY 8 - COUNTY 8

*T*he game was played in a driving rainstorm, yet drew a crowd of 9,000. John Toran of Academy recovered a fumble to set up the City touchdown in the third quarter. Fran Mifsud of Prep carried six straight times on the drive, going the final 7 yards for the touchdown. Kirk Loomis of Tech ran for the 2-point conversion.

The County put together a 76-yard march, featuring the running of Keith Bille of Fairview, Mike Tome of Girard, Joe Hampy of McDowell and Ron Leuschen of McDowell. Hampy scored on a 1-yard plunge. Bille tacked on the 2-point conversion on a run for the 8-8 tie. Both teams threatened in the fourth quarter. Steve Ferrando of Fairview intercepted two passes to end City threats. Dave Barthelmes of Academy recovered a fumble to end a County march. Mifsud was the leading ball carrier with 123 yards on 24 attempts. Leuschen gained 69 yards on the ground. Tome had 11 carries for 63 yards and Bille ran 13 times for 38 yards.

"I played defensive tackle in the 1977 game. This was the last game played in the old brick Stadium with a cinder track around the field. After this game the Veterans Memorial Stadium was completely renovated. This was an intense game with many strong willed players. Ed Poly coached the County team who I played for and my high school was Fort LeBoeuf. Ed Poly was Iroquois' head coach. The game ended in an 8-8 tie.

During the game, two good size fights broke out. After the second one, the refs told our coaches if it happened again, they would call the game. That helped settle things down because both sides wanted to win. Late in the second half we had a severe thunderstorm with heavy rain. The stands emptied out and we kept playing. In 1977, high school football continued to play no matter what the weather was like.

Jack Lee – 1977

Ironically, when FLB played Iroquois the past season, FLB had a very good team and Iroquois struggled a bit. FLB had a poor game with many penalties. Somehow FLB managed to be winning 8-6 late in the game. With 9 seconds left to play, Pat Comer of Iroquois kicked a 37-yard field goal to beat us, 9-8. Pat played in our 1977 Save-An-Eye Game and had the same opportunity late in the game to kick a long game-winning field goal. The ball fell short of the goal post and the final score was 8-8. In Pat's defense, the ball was wet and heavy because of all the rain. It always haunted me because I wished his field goal would have fallen short against FLB and would have made it in the Save-An-Eye Game. **"**

Game 40 – August 12, 1978

City

Steve Allen	East
Al Barnett	East
Terry Carson	East
Jim Clark	Academy
Mark D'Amico	Cathedral Prep
John Dahlstrand	Strong Vincent
Gary Danowski	Strong Vincent
Andy Dawson	East
Earl Dawson	East
Mike Delahunty	Academy
Ron Delinski	Tech
Tony Donikowski	Tech
Mike Feldman	Cathedral Prep
Mike Finotti	Tech
Tony Finotti	Tech
Jeff Guild	Tech
Bob Kalivoda	Tech
Al Murawski	East
Mike Murzynski	Tech
Chris Nowak	Prep
Dave Noziglia	Strong Vincent
Ron Potocki	Cathedral Prep
Brian Roderick	Strong Vincent
Mark Saunders	Academy
Tim Sisinni	Cathedral Prep
Jim Tarkowski	Cathedral Prep
Jeff Thompson	Tech
Mike Tighe	Cathedral Prep

Coaches: Joe Bufalino of East,
Bruce Decker of Strong Vincent

County

Vic Antolik	Fairview
Jeff Blose	Harbor Creek
Mark Cadden	Iroquois
Randy Clark	Girard
Mike Cragg	Corry
Dan D'Amico	Seneca
Dan Dugan	Fairview
Chris Dunn	Girard
Tom Gage	Northwestern
Greg Ganzer	Harbor Creek
Scott Gehr	Northwestern
Kenny Gerzina	Corry
Brian Hackenberg	Harbor Creek
Wayne Helmbreck	General McLane
Barry Holes	Fort LeBoeuf
Chris Hornick	Corry
Rich Kennedy	Fairview
Scott MacKelvey	Fairview
Randy McDonald	Fairview
Tom McLaughlin	Fairview
Steve Miller	Union City
Pat Murphy	Girard
Pat Otteni	General McLane
Rich Passerotti	Harbor Creek
Nick Pelusi	General McLane
Phil Pieri	McDowell
Milt Preston	Girard
Jim Pruckner	McDowell
Mark Scarpino	Harbor Creek
Dave Seifert	Fort LeBoeuf
Mike Stanford	North East
Keith Swart	Corry
Gary Wilson	Girard

Coaches: Jim McGowan of Fort LeBoeuf,
John Gillette of Northwestern

CITY 27 - COUNTY 18

*T*his game was played at McDowell's Gus Anderson Field due to Veterans Stadium renovations. Attendance was 6,000. Andy Dawson of East scored twice and had 189 yards rushing on 18 carries. He had a 73-yard touchdown run and another gain of 57 yards.

Mike Delahunty of Academy threw a 78-yard touchdown pass to Mike Tighe of Prep. Delahunty also hit Chris Nowak of Prep for a 10-yard touchdown. Dawson had a 1-yard touchdown run. His 73-yard touchdown came with 49 seconds left. Dawson ran for one PAT and Ron Delinski of Strong Vincent had a conversion kick.

The County had two punt returns for touchdowns. Dave Seifert of Fort LeBoeuf had a 65-yard run back and Mike Cragg of Corry scored on a 56-yard return. The two also teamed for the third touchdown when Cragg passed 19 yards to Seifert. The Strong Vincent duo of John Dahlstrand and Ron Delinski was outstanding on defense for the City.

CITY STARS TOP COUNTY

BY JIM LeCORCHICK

Unheralded Andy Dawson of East High School sparked the City All-Stars to a 27-18 victory over the County All-Stars Saturday night in the annual Save-An-Eye game at McDowell's Gus Anderson Field.

A crowd of over 6,000 grid fans sat in perfect weather conditions as they were treated to one of the most exciting contests played in the history of the classic.

Dawson, who played mostly defense for the Warriors last season, came into his own — much to the dismay of the County team — as he carried the ball 18 times for 189 yards and two scores, including runs of 57 and 73 yards.

The final run breaking the back of a spirited County rally that had the crowd roaring to the end.

Dawson heroics were needed to offset the losers' dynamic duo of Fort LeBoeuf's Dave Seifert and Corry's Mike Cragg.

A strong City defense paced by Vincent's John Dahlstarnd and Ron Delinski kept the County attack pretty much in check, but the winners were unable to cope with the special teams of the County scored on one sustained march in the fourth period, but added two TD jaunts on punt returns — Seifet scampering 65 yards, Cragg returning for 56.

The County squad completely dominated the opening period as they ran off 18 plays to six for the City while threatening twice, but they were unable to put that elusive six points on the scoreboard.

The first time, the County had the ball fourth and inches on the City 19 but a very familar scene to Vincent's Metro champion fans was there to halt the attack.

Seifert tried the middle of the line but with no success as Dahlstrand and Delinski were there to stop him for no gain.

However, three plays later, the County was again knocking on the door as Girard's Mike Murphy recovered a City fumble to give his team the ball on the opponent's 28-yard-stripe.

The County moved for one first down; but the City defense — led by Delinski and Dahlstrand (of course) pushed the County back 30-yards as they forced a punt.

The City took over on their own 14 and moved to a first down behind three rushes by Dawson, but a holding penalty moved them back to first and 15 before they gained 10 of that back on a spurt up the middle by Dawson.

With a second and 15 facing his team, quarterback Mi[...]

Dawson set up his own run with a 57-yard scamper.

The County answered that score with its best drive of the night as they gave their faithful some hope with a 75-yard scoring drive that ended when halfback Cragg drilled a pass to Seifert that was good for 19-yards and the score. However, the County was unable to convert and still trailed 21-12 with more than nine-minutes of action left.

With the County defense up for the occasion, the City was forced to punt and Cragg took the ball in full stride and used blocks by Seifert and Rich Passerotti to race to paydirt from 56-yard out.

Again the County failed to convert as they trailed 21-18 with 6:13 left and the crowd now on its feet — to stay.

The City was unable to move the ball and the County took over with 4:49 on the clock and 45-yards separating them from a great comeback win, but the City was equal to the task and forced a punt.

Following one-first down, Dawson took the ball up the middle, broke two tackles — and the hearts of the County fans — as he outraced the County secondary to complete a 73-yard run and wrap up the scoring with 49 seconds left.

The extra point try was blocked, but it didn't matter as the City finally had a safe lead — 27-18.

GAME NOTES — Jim McGowan and John Gillette coached the County, Joe

Buffalino and Bruce Decker handling the City duties and both staffs did a great job. It was a treat for the fans as both teams came up with tremendous efforts...Only unfortunate incident came when a City player got a late hit in third period and full-scale scuffle broke out lasting about five minutes...Delahunty and Tighe were good combination as they took pressure off of Dawson...Cragg and Seifert were outstanding for County. Cragg set an Erie County League scoring record last season with 144 points, Seifert ended third with 78. Cragg will be concentrating on baseball in college...Official John Bradford worked his 38th all-star game...One bank of lights were down as McDowell officials were making repairs but it had no affect on play...City team was without two of its best backs as Narchie Coleman and Cliff Coleman (no relation) didn't play. Narchie was a no show and Cliff was unable to play because of college commitment.

County	0	6	12	—	18
City	8	14	7	6	—	27

CITY — Tighe 78-yard pass from Delahun (kick failed). CITY — Nowak 10-yard pass from Delahunty (Dawson run). COUNTY — Seifert 65-yard punt return (pass failed) CITY — Dawson one-yard plung (Delinski kick). COUNTY — Seifert 19-yard pass from Cragg (pass failed). COUNTY — Cragg 56-yard punt return (pass failed). CITY — Dawson 73-yard run (kick failed). ATT — 6,000.

City

John Barzano ....Strong Vincent
Mark Beskid.. East
Jamie Bulk............................Strong Vincent
Aaron Carson .... Academy
John Corkan ....Strong Vincent
Bill Dietz ....Cathedral Prep
Mike Easterling ....Strong Vincent
Pat Erdman .... Tech
Mark Fachetti .... East
Jay Grafius .... Tech
Lamar Hamilton .... East
Greg Hedrick.........................Strong Vincent
Pete Kaiser.. Tech
Tony Lee .... East
Mike Lesniewski ....Cathedral Prep
Kevin Litz .... Tech
Mike Magdalena ....McDowell
Tim Mahoney.....................Cathedral Prep
Mike May ....Cathedral Prep
Jerry McCormick.....................Kanty Prep
Doug Mercier ....McDowell
Gary Metzgar......................Cathedral Prep
Jeff Norris...............................McDowell
Gary Page .... Academy
Andy Penna..........................Cathedral Prep
John Popoff.. East
Greg Riley .... Tech
Dan Schloss...........................McDowell
Don Smith ....McDowell
Mike Smith .... Tech
Andrew Tate .... Academy
Don Weber........................... Academy
Tommy Woodard...................................... East
Jeffrey Young................................ Academy

Coaches: Joe Kleiner of Strong Vincent,
Tom Calabrese of Cathedral Prep,
Dave Kordich of Cathedral Prep

County

Joe Amann ....Iroquois
Tom Bojarski ....Harbor Creek
Wayne Boyd ....Harbor Creek
Jim Cardman ....Fairview
Dave Clabbatz ....Fort LeBoeuf
Brian Coon ....Girard
Doug Cottrell ....Seneca
Kevin Cudicio ....Harbor Creek
Steve Dronsfield..............General McLane
Mike Dylewski ....Fairview
Dan Eller ....Fort LeBoeuf
Steve Ellis ....Fairview
Rob Haley ....Iroquois
Ron Hamrick............................ Union City
Keith Harned...................General McLane
Chris Herman.......................Fort LeBoeuf
Ken Kirsch ....North East
Chris Kohler ....North East
Scott Lee.................................Fairview
Peter Logan ....Harbor Creek
John Maloney ....Corry
Randy McKinney..........................Fairview
Mike McLaughlin ....Fairview
Mark Northrup .... North East
Joe Pfadt ....Fort LeBoeuf
Dave Pratt ....Girard
Chip Rappe................................Fairview
Tony Rushin................................. Corry
Andy Shupala ....Fairview
Dave Uglow ....Harbor Creek
Steve Wall................................Harbor Creek
Clark Wren ....Fairview
Jim Yosten ....Seneca

Coaches: John Ballard, Dan Budziszewski,
Tom Blose, Paul Moneta, Tom Uglow of
Harbor Creek

CITY 14 - COUNTY 0

*B*oth City touchdowns came as the result of turnovers. Kevin Litz of Tech had a 41-yard interception return for a touchdown in the first quarter. Mike Easterling of Strong Vincent ran back a fumble recovery 55 yards for a touchdown in the third period. Tony Lee of East added the two-point conversion on a run.

The County drove to the City 9-yard line behind the running of Wayne Boyd of Harbor Creek and Steve Ellis of Fairview before John Corkan of Strong Vincent recovered a fumble. The County threatened again in the fourth quarter with a first down on the City 8-yard line. Defensive plays by Mike Smith of Tech, Mike May of Prep and Bill Dietz of Prep produced a fourth-and-11. Gary Metzgar of Prep then threw the quarterback for a loss to preserve the shutout.

Other City defensive stars included Tim Mahoney of Prep, Aaron Carson of Academy and Pat Erdman of Tech. Dave Uglow of Harbor Creek, Brian Coon of Girard and John Maloney of Corry excelled on defense for the County. Litz and Lee led the City rushing game. Boyd and Ellis were the top carriers for the County. This was the first year that McDowell players were on the City team.

DEDICATION

The Erie Lions Club, and the coaches, officials and players of the "1979 Save-An-Eye Game" are proud to honor the "Dean of the Officials," Mr. John A. Bradford. John has participated as our official or honorary official in all the 40 games since 1939. He is an honorary member since his retirement in 1971 of the Erie County Football Officials Association which is affiliated with the Pennsylvania Interscholastic Athletic Association.

John still bowls a respectable duck pin score, but was very active in all sports during the '40's, '50's, and '60's. While football is his first love, he blew the whistle, started or timed in the following: Swimming, Football, Basketball, Track, Soap-Box Derby, and Model Airplane competitions. He refereed amateur and professional boxing and wrestling, was active in Little League Baseball and Parochial Little Gridders. He says very humbly that the honor really belongs to his dear wife, Alice, who stayed home while he was blowing the whistle.

Eagles
M McDonald
Doobie Bros
Journey
Foreigner

"Aiden"
10 yrs old
5th gr.

6334 Dave & Colleen Reiser
6332 Patti Belfiglio
6330 Kathryn Burge
6329 Dave & Diane Blake
6326 Gayle Elmer
6324 "Ellie"

- Access to a
tower somewhere
in Erie

- "best place to
shoot video in
Erie Co."

- Dress like a
golfer & carry
a club to hike
through Golf Course

Open 7 days
7A
6:30 weekends
Until dark

GENIUS!

→ App to make
your phone ring
at a certain time
(or alarm set to
sound at certain time)

Tomorrow - Walk through G Course
?? to Grubb flea home (w/ club)

- Bear Run route

- Trout Run route

Chapter 6

*C*apped by the 50th anniversary game, the decade of the 1980s featured close battles as the City earned a 6-4 advantage. Jim Wade of Fort LeBoeuf powered the County to a win in 1989, accounting for 178 yards on pass receptions, two kickoff runbacks and a 66-yard touchdown punt return. The City won the first three games, including a 40-14 blowout in 1980. Tech grads Amos Tate and R.J. Costello led the way. Tate (81 yards rushing) scored on two runs and an 80-yard kickoff return. Costello ran for 82 yards and threw a touchdown pass. Greg Harayda of Academy fired two touchdown passes. Bill Nantes of Harbor Creek had a game record four interceptions.

The 1980s

Lee Barney of Academy and Lance Trott of Cathedral Prep scored in a 14-0 win in 1981. The City made it five straight the next year, scoring the final 18 points after trailing 10-0. The County took advantage of a fumble recovery in 1983, Pat Herr scored the lone touchdown. A passing attack featuring Matt McKinley of Fairview and Chris Blakeslee of North East spiced a 30-12 County romp in 1984.

Three field goals, including a 50-yarder by Charlie Baumann of Prep, boosted the City to a 16-13 edge in 1985. Greg Lewis of McDowell led the ground game. Chris Stablein of McDowell threw for two touchdowns and set up the other two scores in a 26-20 victory in 1986. The touchdown passes went to Mark Knight of Tech and B.J. Baumann of McDowell.

The passing skills of Eric Mikovch of Northwestern (148 yards, two scores) produced a 21-6 win in 1987. The City won in 1988 in a game called with 1:31 left due to a fight on the field. Jim Toohey of Prep passed to Brian Stablein of McDowell and Sam Carroll of Tech ran 3 yards for City scores in the 13-6 contest.

Game 42 – August 9, 1980

City

Nick Anderson	East
John Applebee	Tech
Henry Baskin	East
Lyle Bostick	McDowell
John Caporale	Cathedral Prep
R.J. Costello	Tech
Jeff Crockett	McDowell
John Engel	McDowell
Greg Giannelli	Tech
Greg Harayda	Academy
Pat Hart	East
Ron Haughsdahl	Strong Vincent
Melvin Hobson	Academy
Scott Martin	East
Pat McAndrew	Tech
Steve McGregor	McDowell
Chris Mrozowski	Tech
Don Palermo	Tech
Ray Paris	McDowell
George Perry	East
Paul Przepierski	Academy
Mike Redinger	McDowell
Jim Sampson	Academy
Bill Sandusky	Strong Vincent
Joe Serbati	Cathedral Prep
Doug Sesler	Academy
Pat Smrekar	Cathedral Prep
John Suminski	Cathedral Prep
Amos Tate	Tech
Gary Zamieroski	Cathedral Prep
Craig Ziegler	Tech

Coaches: Ron Costello of Tech,
Jim Marnella of Tech

County

Joe Amoroso	Corry
Doug Bailey	Corry
Kevin Baird	North East
Scott Beam	Girard
John Bergquist	Fairview
Jeff Biletnikoff	Seneca
Roger Boothby	Northwestern
Kevin Brooks	Seneca
Stuart Carr	Fort LeBoeuf
Mike Clark	Union City
Bert Cox	Girard
Mel Dinger	Girard
Gary Dougan	Harbor Creek
Tom Gido	Girard
Roger Harrington	Seneca
Harry Jones	Girard
Glenn Kirsch	North East
Scott Korb	Girard
Jim Leasure	Kanty Prep
Tom Marcinko	General McLane
Steve McEldowney	Corry
Bill Nantes	Harbor Creek
Rick Nash	North East
Quentin Nichols	Corry
Keith Osinski	Fairview
Kevin Palermo	Kanty Prep
Mark Paradise	Harbor Creek
Jeff Perino	North East
Chris Peterson	Fort LeBoeuf
Mike Sawtelle	Fairview
Steve Stahon	Iroquois
Tim Wilkins	Fairview
Dan Wingerter	Fairview

Coach: Arnold "Rip" Simmons of
North East

CITY 40 - COUNTY 14

*A*mos Tate of Tech scored three touchdowns as the City dominated. Bill Nantes of Harbor Creek set a Save-An-Eye record with four interceptions. Tate scored on a 20-yard run, 1-yard run and an 80-yard kickoff return. He finished with 81 yards rushing. R.J. Costello of Tech was another standout for the City, with his dad Ron doing the coaching. Costello had 82 yards rushing on seven runs. His 32-yard rollout set up Tate's second touchdown.

Costello passed 6 yards to Henry Baskin of East for another touchdown. Greg Harayda of Academy tossed a 40-yard touchdown pass to Paul Przepierski of Academy and capped the scoring with a 32-yard pitch to John Caporale of Prep. Ray Paris of McDowell caught a pair of 2-point conversion passes. Joe Amoroso of Corry scored the County touchdowns on runs of 1 and 5 yards. Tim Wilkins of Fairview kicked both extra points. Amoroso led the County with 92 yards on 20 carries. Harayda connected on 4 of 7 passes for 56 yards. Costello hit 3 of 6 for 54 yards. Rick Nash of North East had five receptions for 84 yards.

> **"** I believe we had the most players on the City squad from Tech that year. We took the Metro (League) championship. There were no state playoffs then.
>
> I was the left guard and I was on the kickoff team. On the opening kickoff of the game I tackled the receiver and he fumbled the ball. We got the ball on the 10-yard line. On the next play we scored a touchdown.

Chris Mrozowski – 1980

> R.J. Costello was the quarterback. It was supposed to be a pass play. I was supposed to pass protect for him, but there was only one defender in front of us. So I was waving R.J. to follow me.
>
> I ran into R.J.'s mother (Carol Costello) at the hall of fame last year. She told me she would never forget that play. **"**

Carol Costello hopes to attend the 75th Save-An-Eye Game. And why not? The Save-An-Eye has a special meaning for her. Carol's husband Ron, who died in 1996, was the quarterback for the City in the 1957 game, and was the City coach in 1969, 1980 and 1987. Her oldest son, R.J., was quarterback for the City in 1980 while playing for his father.

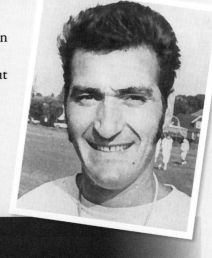

An interesting fact about the four games that included Ron or R.J. as a player or coach—the City won all of those games. But winning is not what Carol Costello remembers most about the tradition of the game. She has other memories.

"I don't even know the score when Ron played," she said on the phone while in Florida this spring. "But I know it was a big deal for him to play. He was very excited about it."

For the record, Ron was quarterback for the City and threw a touchdown pass in a 12-2 win.

Ron Costello – Coach 1980
Son, R.J. Costello – 1980

It was also a big deal when Ron coached in the gam... ...e as always happy to coach, because it was a volunteer thing for him. He enjoyed coaching the elite players, but that wasn't the biggest thing. It was the bonding he had with the players."

Carol Costello vividly remembers one play from the 1980 game in which the City trounced the County 40-14. R.J. rolled out and ran for 32 yards to the 1-yard line. The City scored on the next play.

"R.J.'s best friend was Chris Mrozowski, who was nicknamed Moose. When R.J. ran on that play, Moose was out in front of R.J. waving for R.J. to follow him. I think that picture was in the newspaper," Carol said. R.J. Costello and Mrozowski were best friends and teammates at Tech back then. They are still close. They get together when R.J. returns to Erie from his home in Florida, where he has lived for more than 25 years.

Another close friend of R.J. is Mike Sawtelle, who was on the County team in 1980. Sawtelle, a Fairview grad, was injured, but was on the County sideline when Costello made his long run. "Mike said he wanted to trip R.J. when he ran by, but he thought twice and realized it wasn't a good idea," Carol Costello said. "Mike and R.J. both went to West Virginia. After they graduated, they drove down to Florida and changed their clothes in the car to go to job interviews." They both landed jobs and even coached together for some time. R.J. is the godfather of Sawtelle's oldest son, Niko. "R.J. still talks about the game," Carol said. "He thinks the 40 points was the highest score for any team." It was for 25 years, until the City topped that in a 44-7 win in 2006.

Ron and Carol's other son, Craig, was selected to play in the 1983 game. But Craig, another Tech grad, went to West Virginia University and the coaching staff would not let him play in the Save-An-Eye Game. "It was something special for Ron when he coached R.J. in the 1980 game," Carol said. "Both of our boys had a wonderful opportunity to play for Ron at Tech. I wish my grandsons could have played for him, too."

– Joe Mattis

R.J. rambles

Erie Times-News

WEEKENDER
Sports & LEISURE

R.J Costello of Tech

City		
Phil Agnello	McDowell
Lee Barney	Academy
Rich Boesch	Cathedral Prep
Tim Church	Cathedral Prep
Mark Clark	Cathedral Prep
Terry Colvin	Cathedral Prep
Ted DeSanti	Academy
Mike Fuhrman	Academy
John Fulton	Cathedral Prep
Mark Gnacinski	Strong Vincent
Mike Hawley	McDowell
Ed Heidt	Cathedral Prep
Henry Howze	Academy
Jeff Johnson	East
V.J. Kaiser	Cathedral Prep
Rich Karsh	Academy
Tim Lakari	Strong Vincent
Keith Latzo	East
Mark Manna	Academy
Gilbert Marsh	East
Rich Michael	Tech
Bob Moss	Strong Vincent
Carl Nicholson	East
Bob Nies	Cathedral Prep
Bob Pivetta	McDowell
Lavonne Rowan	Academy
James Sherrod	Cathedral Prep
Rick Skonieczka	Academy
Mick Stepnoski	Tech
Jim Sturm	Cathedral Prep
Lance Trott	Cathedral Prep
Rob Wierbinski	Strong Vincent
David Zurn	Strong Vincent

Coaches: Dan DiTullio, Jim Piekanski
of Academy

County		
Mark Adams	Northwestern
John Baker	Girard
Mike Barberini	Harbor Creek
Dave Carner	Fairview
Rich Carniewski	Fort LeBoeuf
Dick Carver	Harbor Creek
Luke Dugan	Fairview
Tom Eck	Corry
Mike Emerson	North East
Nick Felice	Fort LeBoeuf
Gary Fish	Fort LeBoeuf
Scott Gilbert	General McLane
Chuck Gresh	Girard
Mike Jenkins	Fairview
Keith Kmecik	Girard
Mike Kuzilla	Harbor Creek
Ray Liebel	Fairview
Dave Lynch	Harbor Creek
Scott MacEwen	Girard
Sean Maloney	Corry
Tom May	Harbor Creek
Jeff McShane	Iroquois
Mark Miller	Corry
Keith Mitchell	Corry
Craig Newell	Fort LeBoeuf
Darryl Nirmaier	Union City
Dave Ramsdell	Seneca
Craig Sanders	Fort LeBoeuf
Dave Sawtelle	Harbor Creek
Mike Sornberger	Fairview
Ben Spitzer	Girard
Dave Urban	General McLane
Paul Zampino	Northwestern

Coaches: Joe Sanford, John Wilson
of Corry

CITY 14 - COUNTY 0

*T*he City scored early and late while keeping the County off the scoreboard. A 56-yard drive in the first period was spiced by a 13-yard pass from Keith Latzo of East to Rick Skonieczka of Academy. Latzo then threw 31 yards to Lee Barney of Academy for the touchdown. Barney ran the conversion for an 8-0 lead. The City engineered another drive late in the game, featuring a 17-yard pass from Mark Gnacinski of Strong Vincent to Skonieczka. Lance Trott of Prep ran the final 3 yards for the touchdown with 1:22 to play.

Bob Moss of Strong Vincent ended the biggest County threat with an interception on the 10-yard line. Ray Liebel of Fairview had two interceptions for the County. Another star for the City was Gilbert Marsh of East, who continually pinned the County deep with his punting. The game featured 13 players who had signed to play for coach Tony DeMeo at Mercyhurst College.

City All-Stars Stop County,

BY JIM LeCORCHICK

The City All-Stars, scoring touchdowns in the first and fourth quarters, stopped the County Stars 14-0 in the 42nd Annual Lions Club Save-An-Eye football game Saturday night at Erie Veterans Stadium.

A crowd of 5,500 sat in on a bruising defensive battle that saw the two defensive units of both teams repeatedly stymied by their opposition.

In the end, it was the larger City crew that held the edge. Though the County squad never gave up, they couldn't come up with the needed big-play against the talented City team.

For the game, the winners ended up with five first downs and 164 total yards -- 84 rushing and 80 passing. The County ended the evening with eight first downs and 140 yards on 103 rushing and 37 through the air. The County showed most of their offense in the opening half as they dominated most of the play.

However, it was the City that scored the only touchdown of the first half as they took the opening kick-off and moved 56 yards in five plays for the score. With former East star at quarterback, the City looked like a team that had been playing together for years as they marched smartly down the field for the score.

Latzo, who hit Academy's Rick Skonieczka for 13 yards during the drive, got the City on the scoreboard with 9:47 left in the opening period when he hit former Lion Lee Barney with a 35-yard scoring strike. Barney made a great catch -- over a County defender at the five-yard line -- and then took the ball the remainder of the way for six points. It was Barney again on the conversion as he took the ball on a flanker-around and circled the left side to give his team an 8-0 lead.

The County dominated the rest of the first quarter and the second ...za but the City defense contin... came up with the big play wh... appeared the County had enoug... mentum going to reach the end ...

Poor field condition and a sw... ing City defense kept the Coun...

BOB FELLER

Baseball Legend A Classic Entry

By FRANK DeSANTIS
Times-News Sports Editor

Former baseball great Joe Di-aggio, in his appearances here, ...ade a hit with the Greater Erie ...arity Golf Classic.

Now it's a former foe of ...aggio's, a star in his ow... ...ho will make a... ...urnament.

Bullet B... ...nd J...

He signed with the Tribe when he was just an Iowa farmboy of 16 and, like his lightning fastball, zoomed to stardom.

He beca...

City

John Baker	East
Jeff Barnes	McDowell
Scott Byerly	Academy
John Chiarelli	Strong Vincent
Scot Chiffon	Tech
Matt Chilcott	East
Bob Corritore	Cathedral Prep
Doug Dalton	Cathedral Prep
John Danilov	McDowell
Mark Deitsch	McDowell
Chris DeRose	Tech
David Gorring	Tech
Mike Graves	Academy
Mike Guerassimoff	East
Reggie Haugsdahl	Strong Vincent
Todd Hetrick	Strong Vincent
John Hummell	McDowell
Kevin Kreidinger	Tech
Doug Phillips	Strong Vincent
Frank Pizzo	Tech
Ronnie Porter	East
Doug Puckly	McDowell
Jim Reiser	Tech
Dan Rossman	Tech
Mike Salter	East
Brent Sesler	McDowell
Andrew Space	Strong Vincent
Doug Stewart	Academy
Terry Tighe	Cathedral Prep
Bob Uhlman	Cathedral Prep
Anthony Viglione	Cathedral Prep
John Vogel	Tech
Mark Williams	East

Coaches: Jack Costello of Strong Vincent, Phil Koval of East, Dave Zewe of Strong Vincent, Jeff Shaw of Tech

County

Richard Blosser	Harbor Creek
Stephen Brown	Fort LeBoeuf
Curt Cardman	Fairview
Doug Craker	Corry
Craig Feldman	Fairview
Richard Fox	General McLane
Scott Frisina	Corry
Darrell Hall	Corry
Tim Hanzelka	Girard
Dave Haupt	Harbor Creek
Russell Henry	Iroquois
Rich Jacobitz	Iroquois
Mark Jacobs	Fairview
Tim Johnson	Corry
Baron Joles	Union City
Shaun Kennedy	Fairview
Steve Korb	Girard
Roger Kravitz	Fairview
Mark Lane	Fairview
Joe Ledford	Union City
Mike Marcinko	General McLane
Jim Mershon	Girard
Scott Otteni	General McLane
David Rutledge	North East
Matt Sheridan	North East
Greg Sidun	Harbor Creek
Tim Skarupski	Fairview
Eric Swanson	Seneca
Rick Turiczek	North East
Bill Turner	Fairview
Eric Warner	Girard
Kent Whitaker	Fairview

Coaches: Arnold "Rip" Simmons, Jeff Perino, Carl Karsh of North East

CITY 18 - COUNTY 10

The City rallied from a 10-0 deficit to win. The County took the lead on an 8-yard touchdown run by Curt Cardman of Fairview. Kent Whitaker of Fairview kicked the extra point. Scott Otteni of General McLane recovered a fumble to ignite the drive, which was highlighted by a 17-yard Cardman pass to Rich Jacobitz of Iroquois. Cardman teamed up with Baron Joles of Union City for a 53-yard toss in the second quarter.

Doug Dalton of Prep made a saving tackle at the 11-yard line. The County settled for a 32-yard field goal by Whitaker for the 10-0 edge. John Chiarelli of Strong Vincent scored the first City touchdown in the third quarter on a 9-yard run after John Danilov of McDowell had recovered a fumble at the 12-yard line. Mark Deitsch of McDowell followed with a 55-yard touchdown run as the City moved in front. The last touchdown was scored on a 1-yard run by Chiarelli. The final City march featured a 16-yard run by Deitsch and a 20-yard pass from Matt Chilcott to former East teammate Mark Williams.

THE TIMES-LEADER
August 12th

County vs. City All Star Gridders To Clash In Save-An-Eye Classic Friday

By Mike Manos
Sports Editor

Erie, Pa. — Area football fans are once again eagerly awaiting this Friday's 44th Annual Erie Lions Club's Annual Save-An-Eye football classic, which will feature the top county and city senior gridders at Erie Veterans Stadium.

Last year, the City edged the County, 18-10 as the Slickers upped their lead in the series to a comfortable 22-6-2 margin.

The annual contest is staged for the benefit of the Erie Lions Club's SAVE-AN-EYE Fund, a most worthy cause and a great kick off for the upcoming 1983 area scholastic football season. Game time is set for 7:30 p.m.

Save-An-Eye Grid Officials Boast 86 Years Of All Star Experience

The officials for this Friday's 44th Annual Lions Club SAVE-AN-EYE All Star football game will again as in the past, be donating their services to the charity classic for gratis. This year's contest will be handled by eight of Erie County's finest, boasting a combined 86 years of SAVE-AN-EYE All Star game service.

Pictured above front row (l-r): Joe Sivak (1), Dave Wiley (2), Vinnie Marchant (24) and Fred Trott (13).

Back row (l-r): Dick McCrillis (1), John Edler (18), Huck Lininger (9) and Don Stoltz (19).

photo by Mike Manos

66 I was a defensive end and tight end. What was really neat about that game was I went to Prep and Prep-McDowell was the big rivalry. I played next to John Danilov, who happened to be a McDowell product. He had a temper that was worse than mine.

During the game he kept keying on the guy in front of him. They kept beating each other up. I was like, 'Don't worry about that guy. The guy with the ball is the prize.' He ended up listening to me and we both had good games. That was a memory I've always had. That was fun.

Tony Viglione – 1982

We were down at the half and we ended up squeaking up a win in the second half. With my immediate family, I took the kids to the game ever since they were young. It's been a family event every year for us. Last year was the first one I missed in years, and it was only because it was our 30th class reunion. I was getting updates at the reunion. I was celebrating my 30th reunion and my son (Luca) was celebrating his fifth. Both of my sons played in the game. Luca Viglione graduated in 2007, and V.J. Viglione graduated in 2010. **99**

★ CITY ALL-STARS ★

Erie Lion Tim Baird, City coach Jack Costello, County coach Rip Simmons and Erie Lion Mike Cottrell pose at a press conference for the 1982 game.

Viglione family ties with the Save-An-Eye go back three generations beginning with Chris Flipkowski Sr. 1947, Tony Viglione 1982, Nick Viglione 1989, and Tony's two sons, Luca Viglione 2007, and V.J. Viglione 2010. Going to the Save-An-Eye game is an annual event attended by the family.

City

Tyrone Battles......................Strong Vincent
Tim Beverage............................. Tech
Craig Bryant .... East
Mark Bujnoski.....................McDowell
Sam Campanella ....Strong Vincent
Tom Cermak.....................Cathedral Prep
Lavon Clark .... Tech
Ron Cleaver ....Cathedral Prep
Craig Costello .... Tech
Bobby Curry ....Strong Vincent
Tim Davis.........................McDowell
Doug DeHart ....McDowell
Jim Dilimone ....Cathedral Prep
Dana Dobbs.........................McDowell
Joe Dolak .... Tech
Lee Geiger ....Strong Vincent
Abdul Hakim............................. Academy
Robert Henderson.............................. East
Brian Horn .... Tech
Joe Kleiner.........................Cathedral Prep
Ray Kovalesky...........................McDowell
Chris Letkiewicz .... Tech
Ron Lomax .... East
Mike Mastrog ....McDowell
Mike Matos .... East
Matt McCormick ....Strong Vincent
Tony McCullum........................... Academy
Mike Monahan........................... Academy
Phil Ochalek.........................McDowell
Andre Overton............................. Academy
Anthony Pierce....................Strong Vincent
Tom Rupczewski.................................. Tech

Coaches: Jon Christensen of McDowell, Lee Larsen of McDowell, Joe Cuzzola of McDowell

County

Mike Agnello ....Girard
Ned Bailey.............................Corry
Richard Barber ....Fairview
Clare Blakeslee .... Union City
John Brandt ....Iroquois
Tim Campbell ....Fort LeBoeuf
Jeff Carpin ....Harbor Creek
Charles Cummings ....Fairview
Chris Ellis................................Fairview
Matt Ellis..................................North East
Dan Englert ....Fort LeBoeuf
Bryan Griswold ....Corry
Randy Gunther ....Fort LeBoeuf
Pat Herr ....Fort LeBoeuf
Jonathan Karsh..........................North East
Pat Kennedy.............................. Union City
Brian Laird .... Union City
Joe Lasky..........................General McLane
Lou Lazzera...............................North East
Mike Learn...........................Harbor Creek
Dennis McDonald ....Girard
Jim Muscarella ....North East
Frank Myers ....General McLane
Chip Nuzzo ....Corry
Mike Palmer...............................Fairview
Jerry Port ....Fort LeBoeuf
Scott Redinger...............................Fairview
Robert Reynolds ....Iroquois
Gary Smialek ....Girard
Gary Smith.................................Seneca
Roy Stanford..............................North East
Carl Wolfrom ....Fort LeBoeuf
Thomas Woods...............................Fairview

Coaches: Arnold "Rip" Simmons of North East, Carl Karsh, Jeff Perino, Tom Erdman, Ed Schneider

COUNTY 7 - CITY 0

*T*he only touchdown in this defensive battle came after the City was guilty of a bad snap on punt formation. The County recovered at the City 7-yard line. Pat Herr of Fort LeBoeuf took a handoff from Chip Nuzzo of Corry and went the distance on the next play. Jon Karsh of North East kicked the extra point. The lone score enabled the County to end an 11-year winless drought in the Save-An-Eye series. The County had the game's best drive in the second period, reaching the City 12-yard line behind Rich Barber of Fairview and Herr before the threat ended.

The City squelched scoring opportunities set up by interceptions by Brian Horn of Tech and Ron Lomax of East. Mark Bujnoski of McDowell and Andre Overton of Academy led the ground game for the City.

Erie Lion Carney Metzgar, City coach Jon Christensen, County coach Rip Simmons and Erie Lion Tim Baird discuss the upcoming 1983 game.

Pat Herr still marvels at the confidence of the County team entering the 1983 Save-An-Eye Game. The Fort LeBoeuf athlete remembered his team as brimming with optimism despite a long string of success by the City. The County had lost 10 of the 11 previous games, with only a tie in 1977 to mar the City's extended run. "Even though the City had won several Save-An-Eye games in a row, we sort of expected to win for whatever reason," Herr said. "We felt good about our chances entering the game and played like that."

Times were different in the early 1980s, Herr noted. "There was no social media back then, so we only knew these guys as competitors before the game. We only saw them when we had our helmets strapped on."

Despite the unfamiliarity with new teammates, the County meshed quickly. "We had two great weeks of practice and we really clicked as a group," Herr said. "I remain good friends with a lot of those guys to this day." The Bison running back suffered a setback in the days leading to the game. "I injured my Achilles tendon a couple days into practice for the game and was probably about 50 percent, but I was still able to play a lot," he recalled.

Pat Herr – 1983

Despite being slowed, County coach Rip Simmons of North East made good use of Herr in the game. "Coach Simmons kept giving me the ball," he recalled. The County took advantage of a turnover when a City punt attempt misfired. "After we recovered the fumble deep in their territory, coach called a play that I had run so many times during the season," Herr said.

The 7-yard burst resulted in the only touchdown in the 7-0 County win. About the touchdown run, Herr commented, "My former teammate, left guard Dan Englert, did what he usually did and blew his guy out. I tucked up inside him and was able to score." Herr took a handoff from Chip Nuzzo of Corry on the decisive play. Jon Karsh of North East kicked the PAT for the final 7-0 score. The LeBoeuf grad thought line play was pivotal in the County's win, saying, "Overall I thought our defensive and offensive lines controlled the game. They were solid."

For many Save-An-Eye players, the game was a final chance to perform with family and friends watching. "There were no playoffs at the time, so this game was a way to get a last shot at playing," Herr said. "It was just a lot of fun." Herr continued his football career and received his degree at Washington & Jefferson University. He now serves as Director of Community Shelter Services of Erie.

– Jim Camp

Do you remember the term, "Seeing eye dog?" Dogs with that label were once common as part of the halftime shows during Save-An-Eye Games.

One such dog was a beautiful German shepherd named Sasha, who belonged to Rich and Marianne Borkowski. Sasha and her pups were on display at halftime in 1983 at Veterans Stadium, 20 years after Rich, an all-city lineman at Tech, played for the winning City team in the Save-An-Eye Game.

In those days, there was a program for training dogs to help the blind. It was called the Erie County 4-H and Lions Leader Puppy Program. Even though many puppies entered the program, it was a special few who actually became leader dogs.

"Actually, Sasha was a brood bitch for leader dogs," said Marianne Borkowski. "She had a litter of 10 puppies, and two of them became leader dogs for the blind. They told us it was rare to have more than one (become a leader dog)."

Dogs on the Field

Actually, it was by fate that the Borkowski family became the owners of Sasha. It came about because of an item in the Erie newspaper placed by Proud Land Kennels. "There was an ad with a photo of Sasha that said, 'Sasha needs a home,' " Marianne Borkowski said. "Right then I knew it was the dog for us."

The Borkowski's son, Ricky, was on the field that night in 1983 with Sasha and her puppies. Ricky was not a football player, but he played soccer. Alex Davis, a Northwest Pennsylvania Collegiate Academy grad and all-state lineman for Strong Vincent, played in the rain-shortened 2010 City win. Marianne Borkowski had the pleasure of watching Davis, her grandson, in that game as she thought about how her husband Rich, who died in 2004, would have loved the game.

– Joe Mattis

ERIE COUNTY 4-H
AND
LIONS LEADER
PUPPY PROGRAM

Game 46 – August 10, 1984

City

Gordy Burns	East
Tim Carlin	McDowell
Paul Church	Cathedral Prep
Kevin Cooper	Academy
Terry Costello	Strong Vincent
Paul Cousins	McDowell
Denny Crotty	McDowell
Craig DeMarco	Cathedral Prep
Dave Dombkowski	Tech
Shannon Glover	Academy
Scott Gorring	Tech
Willie Heidelberg	Cathedral Prep
Al Hilling	McDowell
Tony Hollingsworth	East
Dick Jenkins	Strong Vincent
Dana Kubiak	Cathedral Prep
Don Michael	Tech
Gary Moore	Academy
Mark Olesky	McDowell
Tony Onorato	McDowell
Greg Page	Academy
Roosevelt Price	East
Marvin Ridgeway	Academy
Phil Sorensen	Cathedral Prep
Mike Stadtmiller	Cathedral Prep
Mark Strain	Tech
Steve Thomas	Tech
Doug Vroman	Tech
Jeff Wagner	Academy
Mike Wayne	Tech
Rob Young	Strong Vincent
Al Zenner	Cathedral Prep

Coach: Phil Koval of East

County

Greg Billings	Northwestern
Chris Blakeslee	North East
Dan Bokol	Iroquois
Charlie Buckshaw	Corry
Chris Concilla	North East
Norm Crenshaw	Harbor Creek
Jeff Cross	Fairview
Jim Dahlstrand	Girard
Dave Faulkenhagen	Harbor Creek
Dave Greene	Iroquois
Chet Kempinski	Fairview
Bill Klenz	North East
Brad Klomp	Harbor Creek
Kevin Lane	Fairview
Rob Laskey	General McLane
Tom Lathrop	Corry
Pat Levonduskie	Harbor Creek
Mike Magee	Union City
Denny Maguire	Harbor Creek
Bill Markle	Seneca
Matt McKinley	Fairview
Dave Michael	General McLane
Greg Mitchell	Harbor Creek
Keith Morris	Corry
Jack Pettis	Northwestern
Dave Polk	Fairview
John Shade	Northwestern
Ty Sornberger	Fairview
Jim Sykes	Fairview
Dana VanTassel	Girard
Bob Vaughan	General McLane
Roger Williams	Fort LeBoeuf
Eric Wingrove	Iroquois
Mark Woodrow	General McLane

Coaches: Tony Nunes of Girard,
Ray Pegg of Girard

COUNTY 30 - CITY 12

The County dominated with a strong passing game spotlighting quarterbacks Matt McKinley of Fairview and Chris Blakeslee of North East. The two combined to connect on 19 of 31 passes for 245 yards. Greg Mitchell of Harbor Creek had four catches for 84 yards and two touchdowns. Dan Bokol of Iroquois had seven receptions for 65 yards. Mitchell grabbed a 6-yard scoring toss from McKinley and a 41-yard touchdown throw from Blakeslee. Dave Michael of General McLane hauled in a 19-yard touchdown pass from McKinley. That score came on a fourth-and-6 play. John Shade of Northwestern posted the final touchdown on a 1-yard run with 2 seconds left in the game. Kevin Lane of Fairview kicked two conversions. Mitchell scored a 2-pointer on a run and Bokol grabbed a conversion pass.

Roosevelt Price of East and Scott Gorring of Tech had the City touchdowns. Price ran 2 yards for his score, which was set up when Greg Page of Academy hooked up with Gorring for a 59-yard completion. Gorring hauled in a 21-yard pass from Page for the other touchdown.

County seeks 2nd straight

By JIM SHAW
NEWS Sports Writer

The County goes looking for a second straight victory in the 46th annual Lions Club Save-An-Eye Football Classic Friday at Veterans Memorial Stadium.

A year ago the County capitalized on a City mistake to score the only touchdown it needed in posting a 7-0 victory. The win ended an 11-year drought for the suburbanites.

In the game the County recovered at the City seven-yard line and on the first play from scrimmage, Fort LeBoeuf's Pat Herr covered the distance for the only score of the game. The win was only the seventh in 32 games for the County.

In the 8 p.m. contest which pits the County and City senior All-Stars, Tony Nunes and Ray Pegg will call the shots for the County with Phil Koval handling the City reins. Nunes' and Pegg's assistants are Rich Radock, Ron Brunot and Paul Gilewicz. Koval is assisted by Jeff Shaw, Mike Alexa, John Popoff and Dale Lewis.

Nunes, formerly of Northwestern, expects to come out throwing against the City counterparts. "Our offense will be wide open," said Nunes. "The wider the better, because we have some fine athletes. We have a couple of great quarterbacks and scads of good receivers. This game is going to be one of the most exciting games ever — like Army-Navy. I think you're going to see the County and City play on even terms from here on out. The City domination is over."

Girard's Pegg, who will direct the defense, continued, "This game is eas[y] to prepare for defensively because these guys are so well-coached. We're restricted to a 52 defense and no blitzing, so all we can really do to confus[e] them is stunt the linemen and move the defensive backs around. We just h[ave] [o]ur guys to use good strategy and make sure they're in the [rig]ht [spots.]"

City		County	
Mike Allen	Tech	Jeff Booser	Seneca
Charlie Baumann	Cathedral Prep	David Brown	General McLane
Kevin Beard	Strong Vincent	Mike Bruno	General McLane
John Blanks	Strong Vincent	Brian Burns	Seneca
Robert Bobango	Cathedral Prep	Jeff Cass	Harbor Creek
Yod Bowers	Strong Vincent	Scott Cervik	Iroquois
Chris Brown	McDowell	Don Cox	Corry
Tony Campanella	Strong Vincent	Greg Deemer	Fort LeBoeuf
Craig Christensen	McDowell	David Ellsworth	North East
Erik Christensen	McDowell	Paul Foltz	Fort LeBoeuf
Bill Cook	Cathedral Prep	Matt Greer	Fairview
Robert Dombkowski	Tech	Pat Hart	Fairview
Don Gajewski	Cathedral Prep	Mike Harvey	Fort LeBoeuf
Joe Grippe	McDowell	Scott Hess	Fairview
Greg Lewis	McDowell	Jeff Holes	Fort LeBoeuf
Mike Lubak	East	Joseph Hosey	Northwestern
Marty Lynch	McDowell	David Hudson	Fairview
Jim Mitchel	East	Tim Jewell	Union City
Mike Nagy	East	Dan Lindquist	Corry
Bill Nemenz	Cathedral Prep	Kevin McEldowney	Corry
Ray Nicolia	Cathedral Prep	Jim Nelson	Iroquois
Tom Nunes	Cathedral Prep	Joe Newara	North East
Daryhl Page	Academy	Tom Nichols	Corry
Chris Pesch	McDowell	Bill Nirmaier	Union City
Eric Seggi	Academy	John Oldach	Harbor Creek
Mike Smith	Strong Vincent	Mike Pavolko	Northwestern
Tim Thomas	McDowell	Joe Rizzo	North East
David Torres	Academy	John Root	Fairview
Frank Vicary	Academy	John Saxon	Seneca
Dean Vomero	McDowell	Jim Schiefferle	Fairview
Matt Williams	McDowell	Rick States	Seneca
Pete Williams	McDowell	Mike Vogt	Fort LeBoeuf
		Douglas Wilbur	Fairview

Coaches: Pete Donatucci, Ed Dalton, Tim Cacchione of Strong Vincent

Coaches: Tony Nunes, Ray Pegg, Jack Pettis of Girard

CITY 16 - COUNTY 13

*C*harlie Baumann of Cathedral Prep was the star, kicking three field goals of 33, 50 and 43 yards. The 50-yarder is a Save-An-Eye record. Baumann later kicked for West Virginia. Greg Lewis of McDowell had 85 yards rushing on 14 carries. He also had two interceptions. Matt Williams of McDowell hit 6 of 11 passes for 104 yards. His twin brother Pete caught three balls for 95 yards. Joe Rizzo of North East got the County on the board with a 5-yard run. The drive was sparked by passes from Jeff Cass of Harbor Creek to Jim Nelson of Iroquois for 20 and 26 yards. The County took the lead when Cass tossed 13 yards to Greg Deemer of Fort LeBoeuf for a touchdown. David Ellsworth of North East kicked the point for a 13-9 score.

The last City drive was spiced by a 25-yard pass from Matt to Pete Williams and a 21-yard burst by Lewis. Matt Williams went the final 2 yards for the score. Baumann's kick gave the City a 16-13 lead. The final County threat ended when Bill Nemenz of Prep broke up a fourth down pass. Cass hit 7 of 16 passes for 129 yards and rushed six times for 61 yards. Deemer was the County's top rusher with 12 carries for 93 yards.

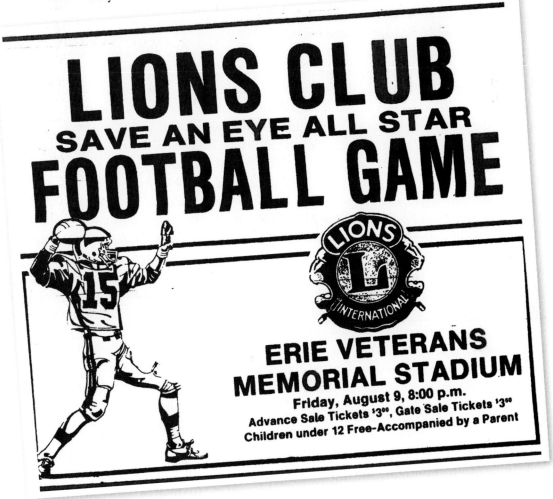

LIONS CLUB
SAVE AN EYE ALL STAR
FOOTBALL GAME

LIONS INTERNATIONAL

ERIE VETERANS
MEMORIAL STADIUM
Friday, August 9, 8:00 p.m.
Advance Sale Tickets $3⁰⁰, Gate Sale Tickets $3⁰⁰
Children under 12 Free-Accompanied by a Parent

Charlie Baumann didn't get many chances to kick field goals at Cathedral Prep. Coach Mina George was not a big proponent of field goals, despite having a quality kicker on the roster. "I only tried 12 field goals and made six kicking at Prep for three years," Baumann recalled. That all changed in the 1985 Save-An-Eye Game. Baumann attempted four field goals and connected on three that night, including a 50-yarder that still stands as a game record. His efforts helped the City post a 16-13 win. He also was true on kicks from 33 and 43 yards out. His only miss of the night came from 49 yards. That success provided a huge impetus for Baumann, already headed to West Virginia University on a full scholarship. "I used that game as a catalyst to go in and win the starting job at West Virginia as a true freshman," he recalled. "I was named the starter when I was still 17. I turned 18 on August 25 and a week later played my first college game."

Charlie Baumann – 1985

Charlie Baumann with the New England Patriots

Having a familiar holder in Cathedral Prep teammate Tom Nunes also aided Baumann in the Save-An-Eye. "It really helped me with Tom being there," he said. "That game meant a lot. I had some very good feedback." Playing in the Save-An-Eye was an experience Baumann had anticipated for years. "As a young boy you wonder if you're good enough to play in the game someday," he said. "It was really a neat experience, very competitive but at the same time fun and a loose atmosphere. It was an honor to play." The game also provided one last chance to kick in Erie. "This was your big sendoff to college," he said. "It was really a big deal to be selected for the game and you got to play in front of a huge crowd at the Stadium."

The future WVU kicker knew several of the players on both teams entering the game. "There were a lot of good players in that game," he said. "A good friend of mine, Billy Nemenz of Prep, broke up a pass to save the game for us." Nemenz picked off the throw to stop the County's final drive in the fourth quarter. "Running back Greg Lewis of McDowell had a really good game, along with Matt and Pete Williams of McDowell." Baumann "knew quite a few of the guys from youth football" entering the Save-An-Eye. "Jeff Cass was the County quarterback. I knew him all the way back to little gridders playing ball at Jefferson School. I played against other guys in that game going back to third grade."

Following his success in the Save-An-Eye Game and four solid years at West Virginia, Baumann made several stops on the professional level. He kicked for Miami and New England in the NFL, converting 20 field goals and 37 extra points. He also had stints with Buffalo, Minnesota, Pittsburgh and the New York Jets. He last kicked for two seasons (1996–97) for the Orlando Predators in the Arena League. Baumann also earned two masters' degrees and is now the Chief Financial Officer for U.S. Medical Group of Florida and the president and minority owner of the Brevard County Manatees, a minor league affiliate of the Milwaukee Brewers.

– Jim Camp

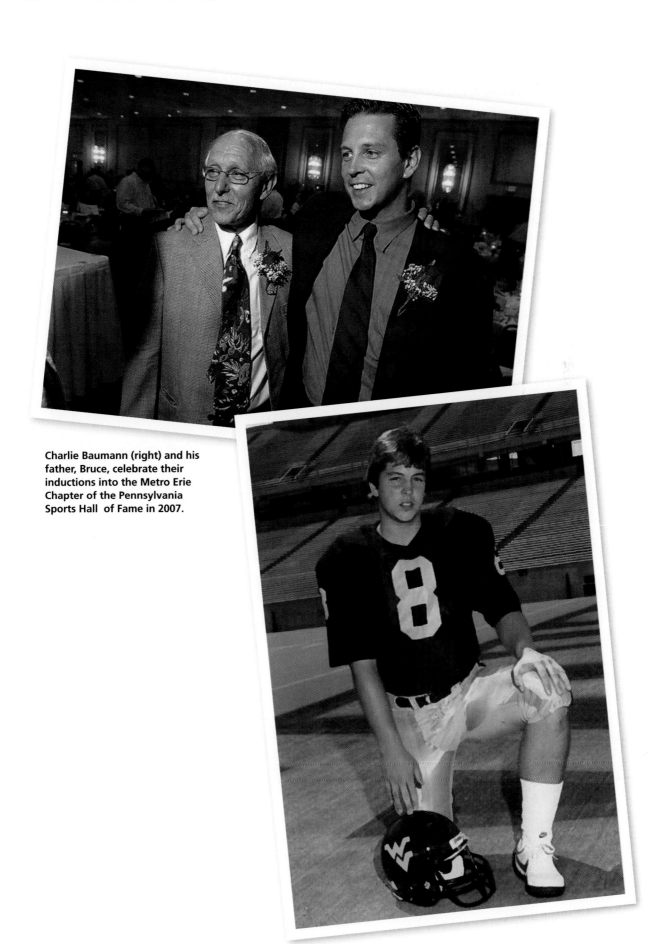

Charlie Baumann (right) and his father, Bruce, celebrate their inductions into the Metro Erie Chapter of the Pennsylvania Sports Hall of Fame in 2007.

Charlie Baumann as a West Virginia Mountaineer

City

Avis Anderson	Tech
B.J. Baumann	McDowell
Earnest Blakney	Academy
Mike Clark	Tech
Gary Coleman	Tech
Ed Cousins	McDowell
Todd DeBello	McDowell
Doug Dombkowski	Tech
Alan Frampton	East
Mike Franz	Academy
Mark Giza	McDowell
Mark Hubbart	East
Joe Iannello	Cathedral Prep
Bob Kaczenski	Cathedral Prep
Paul Kelvington	Cathedral Prep
Wade King	McDowell
Mark Knight	Tech
Jeff Kujawinski	Tech
Thomas Lynde	Academy
Dennis Misko	Cathedral Prep
Gary Myers	Academy
Mike Nedreski	East
Dave Ott	Cathedral Prep
Nate Overton	Tech
Jeff Porter	East
Larry Raimondi	Cathedral Prep
Ron Raimondi	Cathedral Prep
Brad Schnell	Strong Vincent
Chris Stablein	McDowell
Ben Stanback	East

Coaches: Mina George, Pat Czytuck, John Berchtold of Cathedral Prep

County

Mike Artise	North East
Lance Blakeslee	North East
Seth Bremmer	Fairview
Jamie Cipalla	Northwestern
Eric Conley	Iroquois
Scott Craig	Seneca
Sean Curry	Iroquois
Joe Dahlstrand	Girard
Joel Delavern	Girard
Michael Endean	Northwestern
Jon Fogel	Corry
Bob Frantz	General McLane
Glenn Hinkle	Fairview
Gary Kempinski	Fairview
J Knablein	Fort LeBoeuf
Ron McGahen	Fort LeBoeuf
Skip Metcalf	Fairview
Mike Miczo	Northwestern
Kevin Mihalik	Northwestern
Keith Mitchell	Harbor Creek
Jeff Morey	Seneca
Tadas Norvaisa	North East
Doug Pulling	Fairview
Brian Quirk	Corry
Aaron Reynolds	Union City
Brian Rizzo	North East
Bill Saborsky	Corry
Frank Semelko	North East
Scott Siergio	Harbor Creek
Kevin Soles	Iroquois
Les Utegg	Corry
Kary Valentine	Northwestern
Loren Wilshire	Corry

Coaches: Don Costa, Terry Bowersox, Don Adams, Blair Hrovat of Northwestern

CITY 26 - COUNTY 20

Chris Stablein of McDowell passed for 131 yards and two touchdowns . His passing also set up the other two City scores. Stablein's touchdown throws went for 37 yards to Mark Knight of Tech and 10 yards to B.J. Baumann of McDowell. Dave Ott of Prep had a 5-yard touchdown run and Larry Raimondi of Prep had a 1-yard touchdown run. Paul Kelvington of Prep kicked two extra points. Mike Miczo of Northwestern scored twice for the County on a 5-yard pass from Jon Fogel of Corry and a 1-yard run. Jamie Cipalla of Northwestern hauled in a 5-yard Fogle pass for a touchdown. Sean Curry of Iroquois had two conversion kicks.

Bob Kaczenski of Prep had three receptions for 67 yards. Knight had two catches for 43 yards. Ott led a balanced running game with seven carries for 33 yards . Baumann had 11 runs for 31 yards, Gary Myers of Academy 10 for 23 yards and Todd DeBello of McDowell four for 22 yards. Miczo ran 22 times for 105 yards. Fogel cashed on 5 of 10 passes for 71 yards and Brian Rizzo of North East hit 3 of 8 for 60 yards. Cipalla was the top receiver with three catches for 36 yards.

City, County clash in Save-An-Eye

BY JACK POLANCY
NEWS Sports Writer

The 1986 high school football season is just about at hand.

Kicking off the local campaign, as usual, is the Erie Lions Club Save-An-Eye All-Star Football Game.

The 48th annual affair gets itself played into the record books Friday night, kickoff at Erie Veterans Memorial Stadium set for 8 p...

The game f...

once aga...

seni...

ern High School to a share of the Erie County League crown — and the first-ever District 10 Division II playoff championship, will be heading the County coaching staff — assisted by Terry Bowersox, Don Adams and Blair Hrovat.

The County will featuring the passing of Corry's Jon Fogel and North East's Brian Rizzo nd the running of ...rthwestern and Seth

rials for 664 yards and four six-pointers last season.

Corry's Les Utegg, at 6-1 and 210, also hauled in 47 passes a year ago.

good for 805 yards and five touchdowns.

Jamie Cipall...
Northw...

★★ All-Star Rosters ★★

CITY ALL-STARS   Prep

10-Paul Kelvington — K
11-Gary Myers — TB
15-Gary Coleman — QB
15-Chris Stablein — QB
17-Earnest Blakney — DE
18-Mike Nedreski —
20-Nate Over...
21-Brad B...

<table>
<tr><td colspan="2">City</td></tr>
</table>

Curtis Barney	Academy
Randy Baughman	East
Kevin Carlin	McDowell
Dan Church	Cathedral Prep
Pat DelFreo	Cathedral Prep
Pat DiPaolo	Cathedral Prep
Dwight Esters	East
Rodney, Evans	Tech
Art Gamble	Academy
Herman Gamble	Tech
Mike Goodelle	McDowell
Mike Jenkins	Academy
Chris Johnson	East
Steve Lakari	Strong Vincent
Tim Malinowski	Strong Vincent
John Marzka	Academy
Steve Menosky	Academy
John Mundy	Cathedral Prep
Mike Nolan	Strong Vincent
Dave Onorato	McDowell
Pat Parra	Strong Vincent
Jeff Piaza	Tech
Mark Soboleski	McDowell
Steve Spearman	Academy
Steve Trejchel	Cathedral Prep
Tom Valerio	Academy
Darren Weber	McDowell
Aaron Young	McDowell

Coach: Ron Costello of Tech

County

Scott Barber	General McLane
Scott Bojarski	Harbor Creek
Rick Borgeson	Fairview
Terry Brown	General McLane
Chad Buell	Union City
Mike Burlingham	Harbor Creek
Ted Byham	Girard
Mike Carnahan	Fairview
Pete Cross	Fairview
Paul Ellis	Fort LeBoeuf
Paul Hartmann	Harbor Creek
Ron Hayes	Fort LeBoeuf
Terry Hayes	Corry
Ed Hess	Harbor Creek
Doug Kubiak	Fort LeBoeuf
Dennis Kukola	Seneca
Lou LaFuria	North East
Scott Lane	Fairview
Doug Leicht	Northwestern
Brian McGowan	Fort LeBoeuf
Scott Merritt	Northwestern
Eric Mikovch	Northwestern
Dean Platz	Fairview
Dan Renick	General McLane
Dave Schuster	Northwestern
Bill Schwab	Fort LeBoeuf
Jim Triana	North East
Scott Turner	Fairview
Mike Vaughan	General McLane
Dave Walker	Fairview
Pete Wegley	Iroquois
Vinny White	Fort LeBoeuf
Eric Willow	Fairview

Coach: Joe Shesman of Fort LeBoeuf

COUNTY 21 - CITY 6

$\mathcal{E}$ ric Mikovch of Northwestern threw for 148 yards and two touchdowns. Mikovch found his target on 8 of 14 throws. He connected with Doug Kubiak of Fort LeBoeuf for a 17-yard touchdown pass and fired 27 yards to Lou LaFuria of North East for another score. Terry Brown of General McLane contributed an 18-yard touchdown run. Scott Lane of Fairview had three conversion kicks. The only City touchdown came with 1:38 left and went to Herman Gamble of Tech on a 13-yard pass reception from Mark Soboleski of McDowell. That score was set by a fumble recovery by Dean Platz of Fairview. Kubiak had four catches for 74 yards and LaFuria had two grabs for 39 yards. Brown was the top County ground gainer with 14 runs for 60 yards. Ted Byham of Girard had three carries for 32 yards and Ed Hess of Harbor Creek had six for 30 yards.

Randy Baughman of East went 4 for 5 passing for 57 yards. Soboleski was 4-for-12 for 41 yards. Mike Jenkins of Academy had four receptions for 53 yards and Gamble had three catches for 22 yards. Mike Nolan of Strong Vincent had 10 runs for 61 yards.

Chapter 6 ‖ The 1980s   **153**

Game 50 – August 5, 1988

City

Mike Anderson	Tech
Bob Bland	East
Dennis Brady	Academy
Bob Buerger	Tech
Sean Carlson	Strong Vincent
Sam Carroll	Tech
Tim Cook	Academy
Sean Cooney	McDowell
Melvin Crosby	Academy
Mark Cunningham	McDowell
Andrew English	McDowell
Jim Fessler	Cathedral Prep
Darrell Gamble	Tech
Jeff Gibbons	Strong Vincent
Carl Goodwine	East
Pat Green	McDowell
Chris Grychowski	Cathedral Prep
Joe Hughes	Tech
Rob LaBar	McDowell
Tom Maciulewicz	McDowell
Jon Nolan	Tech
Pat Ott	Cathedral Prep
Jeff Pasinski	McDowell
Tony Quinn	Strong Vincent
Armand Rocco	Strong Vincent
Brian Rutkowski	Cathedral Prep
Garrett Skindell	Cathedral Prep
Brian Stablein	McDowell
Scott Stablein	McDowell
Michael Swift	McDowell
Tony Szabo	Tech
Jim Toohey	Cathedral Prep
Chris Wiesner	McDowell

Coach: Joe Sanford of McDowell

County

Scott Bacon	Union City
Todd Baker	Girard
Kelly Bender	Girard
Tim Burkett	General McLane
James Chimera	Harbor Creek
Jim Chorney	Fairview
Matt Cozad	North East
Eric Deemer	Fort LeBoeuf
Mark Dickson	General McLane
Peter Ferguson	Harbor Creek
Bill Flynn	Union City
Kyle Frank	General McLane
Mitch Fuhrer	Fort LeBoeuf
Mark Ginn	Corry
Steve Graeca	Corry
Kevin Kruszewski	Harbor Creek
Craig Kuhn	Fort LeBoeuf
Bill Long	Union City
David McDonald	General McLane
Bill O'Brien	Northwestern
Terry O'Connor	Harbor Creek
Sonny Paris	Iroquois
Gary Picheco	Northwestern
Scott Price	Northwestern
Ray Puzarowski	Harbor Creek
Todd Schneider	Seneca
Jeff Sorenson	Fort LeBoeuf
Scott Spaulding	Northwestern
John Steger	North East
Craig Vergotz	Fort LeBoeuf
Benjie Westfall	Northwestern
John Wolf	Seneca
Craig Zarzeczny	Harbor Creek

Coach: Jim Vogt of Iroquois

CITY 13 - COUNTY 6

*T*his game ended early when officials stopped play with 1:31 on the clock after a brawl broke out. Sean Cooney of McDowell had just intercepted a pass to end a final County drive before the skirmish erupted. The County took the early lead on a 42-yard run by John Wolf of Seneca. The City answered when Jim Toohey of Prep found Brian Stablein for a 24-yard touchdown pass. The kick by Bob Bland of East moved the City ahead 7-6. Sam Carroll of Tech added the other touchdown on a 3-yard run with 6 minutes to play. Darrell Gamble of Tech had 103 yards rushing on 18 carries. Pat Ott of Prep and Carroll both finished with 33 yards on the ground. Wolf had 10 runs for 80 yards. Toohey clicked on 2 of 5 passes for 34 yards. Stablein had both City receptions.

Jeff Sorenson of Fort LeBoeuf hit 4 of 13 passes for 54 yards and also caught a pass for 20 yards. Terry O'Connor of Harbor Creek had two catches for 37 yards. Chris Grychowski of Prep was outstanding at defensive end. He was credited with 15 tackles and four sacks. Cooney's interception and a fumble recovery by Craig Zarzeczny of Harbor Creek were the only turnovers. Stablein went on to play at Ohio State and in the NFL.

Slick City gets in its licks

By JIM CAMP
WEEKENDER Sports Editor

The 49th Save-An-Eye Game will long be remembered. Unfortunately, the contest won't be recalled for hard-hitting football, but for uncontrolled slugging that produced an early finish.

A bench-clearing fight, the last of several scuffles, forced officials to halt the game with 1:31 showing on the clock.

The City emerged with a 13-6 win before 7,000 fans at Veterans Memorial Stadium in the abbreviated tiff.

The County grabbed a 6-0 edge in the third quarter on John Wolf's 42-yard dash, the City answering later in the period on Jim Toohey's 24-yard toss to Brian Stablein. Bob Bland booted the PAT.

Sam Carroll's three-yard burst with six minutes left provided the final margin, the City now with a 26-9-2 edge under the current format.

Sean Cooney intercepted a County pass on the final play of the ... the brawl breaking o... turn down ...

point to avoid further problems.

Neither coach liked the way the game finished, but both ... pleased with their te... ance

City-County All-Stars renew rivalry

...e County All-Stars hope to contin-... luck against the City ... nual Save-An-Eye ...ght at

SAVE AN EYE GAME

Guards: McDowell's ... : McDow...

Crosby; McDowell's Mark Cunn...ham; Tech's Jon Nolan.

Centers: Tech's Bob ...ball mo...ian ...ning att...

"Jim ... able jo... playing ... And Ch... standing ... great tale...ness and i...

"This w... They're f... very proud...

Vogt rep... anything g...fense. The...tough to ta... Westfall ... quarter re... move some... Kruszewski...

"This was ... to work wit... to coach th...

The City ... cally as w... The winne... rushing and ...County net...

City quarterback Jim Toohey hands o...
...tkowski and Sean Carlson appl...

City

John Baumann......................Cathedral Prep
Jeff Buerger................................. Tech
Rob Carr..............................Cathedral Prep
Sonny Carson ....Strong Vincent
Dennis Clemente ....Strong Vincent
Randy Dovichow ....Cathedral Prep
Brett Erven.........................Cathedral Prep
Kyle Ferrick.......................Cathedral Prep
Mike Heberle ....Cathedral Prep
Daryl Herman .... Academy
Mike Higgins............................. Academy
Maurice House .... East
Albert Jones .... East
Eric Konieczny ....McDowell
Tim Kujawinski............................ Tech
Tom Laska..............................McDowell
Matt Leubin ....McDowell
Mark Odom .... Tech
Sean Perseo .... Tech
Jim Reddinger ....McDowell
Rich Riley............................Cathedral Prep
Derek Sanford ....McDowell
Aaron Satyshur........................McDowell
Tom Schelhammer...................McDowell
Tom Shade ....Cathedral Prep
George Silay................................. East
John Smith ....Cathedral Prep
Mike Szymanski .... East
Nick Viglione ....Cathedral Prep
Pat Vona.................................... Academy
John White ....Strong Vincent
Dan Wolf................................. Tech

County

Doug Baker ....Corry
Derek Brown ....General McLane
Mark Byham ....Girard
Pat Camp.......................Northwestern
Tom Cass.............................Iroquois
Joe Corbin...........................Fairview
T.J. Elliott ....Fairview
Mike Fitzgerald ....Harbor Creek
Jeff Fox ....Fairview
Mark Frushone ....Corry
Gary Gilbert ....General McLane
Rob Glus ....Northwestern
Chris Konieczny ....Fairview
Shawn Kuffer ....General McLane
Mike Kujan ....Harbor Creek
Kip Kuzmin ....Northwestern
Mike Lazzara ....North East
Joe Lichtinger ....Fort LeBoeuf
Paul Luke..........................North East
Jason MacQuarrie.................Harbor Creek
Mike Martin ....Fairview
Scott McClellan ....Corry
Neil Pickens ....Northwestern
Darrel Pound ....Seneca
Matt Schiefferle..............................Fairview
David Skelly ....Fairview
Doug Slater ....North East
Shawne Smith.......................... Union City
Tom Tracy ....Fort LeBoeuf
Jim Wade ....Fort LeBoeuf
Rob Weis ....Corry
Sean Wolfrom.....................Fort LeBoeuf
Ron Wygant.............................Girard

Coaches: Mina George, Pat Czytuck, Mike Alexa, Rick Grychowski of Cathedral Prep

Coaches: Don Costa, Eric Mikovch, Terry Bowersox, Pat Comer, Don Adams, Gary Picheco of Northwestern

COUNTY 20 - CITY 13

Jim Wade of Fort LeBoeuf was a star in the 50th anniversary game. He had four pass receptions for 42 yards, two kickoff returns for 70 yards and a punt return for a 66-yard touchdown. Jeff Fox of Fairview with a 1-yard run and Gary Gilbert of General McLane with a 4-yard run scored the other County touchdowns. Rob Glus of Northwestern kicked two extra points for the County.

Sonny Carson of Strong Vincent scored from 1 yard out and Aaron Satyshur of McDowell took a 22-yard pass from Mike Heberle for the City touchdowns. John Baumann of Prep kicked the extra point. Paul Luke of North East gained 106 yards on 21 carries for the winners. Heberle passed for 107 yards. Kip Kuzmin of Northwestern clicked on 6 of 12 passes for 63 yards. Carson had 39 yards rushing and 53 returning kicks. A City drive was stopped at the County 23-yard line as time expired.

City Coaches

(Left to right): Pat Czytuck (Assistant Coach - Cathedral Prep); Mina George (Head Coach - Cathedral Prep); Mike Alexa (Assistant Coach - Cathedral Prep); Rick Grychowski (Assistant Coach - Cathedral Prep); Mark Kresse (Trainer - Saint Vincent's Sports Medicine)

County Coaches

(Left to right): Coach Eric Mikovich (QB, OB); Head Coach Don Costa; Terry Bowersox (DB); Pat Comer (OL); Absent when picture was taken – Don Adams (DL); Gary Picheco (LB).

Chapter 7

The return of Brian Milne, a glittering performance by Aaron Slocum and a stadium shift due to artificial turf installation marked this decade. Milne's comeback helped draw a crowd of 11,000 in 1991. The powerful Fort LeBoeuf running back had missed his senior season due to Hodgkin's Disease. With a Penn State scholarship in hand, Milne piled up 164 yards on 30 carries. He scored all the County points on a pair of 1-yard rushes and a 2-point conversion. Milne's heroics, however, were not enough.

The 1990s

The City won 18-14 when former Tech teammates Randy Davis and A.J. Jimerson combined on a 35-yard halfback option pass with seconds remaining.

Slocum was outstanding in 1998. The McDowell grad played three positions, scored both City touchdowns on pass receptions, carried for 47 yards, completed a pass for 11 yards, caught three balls for 41 yards and returned a punt. He also was a defensive standout in a 17-6 win.

The 1995 and 1996 games were moved to General McLane during renovations at Veterans Stadium. The County won the first game when McLane products Luke Kuffer and Jaimen Gallo teamed for a late 45-yard touchdown pass. That spoiled a strong showing by Roosevelt Benjamin of Central, who tallied twice, one on an 86-yard run. The City rebounded with a 20-6 victory in 1996. Mike Miodus of Strong Vincent hit Tom Palmer of McDowell with a 97-yard touchdown pass.

The most lopsided game of the 1990s came when the City breezed 37-8 in 1992. The winners were sparked by 11 players from the Strong Vincent state championship team. Tim Malesiewski of North East ran for a 10-yard touchdown late in the game as the County won a defensive struggle 7-0 in 1993. Competition was tight during the decade, the City with a 6-4 overall edge in wins.

City	
Tony Akins	Tech
David Ashton	Strong Vincent
William Bailey	Strong Vincent
Randy Baumann	Cathedral Prep
John Burkell	Academy
Keith Burns	Cathedral Prep
Jim Ciecierski	East
Jason Cox	Strong Vincent
Chris Cyterski	Cathedral Prep
Phil Ferrare	Cathedral Prep
Mike Gashgarian	McDowell
Vincent Harvey	Strong Vincent
Brian Holland	Cathedral Prep
Jeff Holt	Strong Vincent
Chaun Johnson	East
Matt Koket	McDowell
Eric Kuhn	Strong Vincent
Bob Lee	Strong Vincent
Sean Madura	Tech
Joe Orlando	Strong Vincent
Shamus Petrucelli	Cathedral Prep
Bob Rehberg	McDowell
Sean Reichard	Tech
Matt Reiser	Academy
John Rumbaugh	McDowell
Jeff Scully	Academy
Pat Tighe	Cathedral Prep
V.J. Trapolsi	Cathedral Prep
DeMoyne White	Academy
Pat Williamson	Cathedral Prep
Tom Wolf	Tech

Coach: Dan DiTullio of Academy

County	
Rich Ardillo	Iroquois
Rick Ballard	General McLane
Tim Beal	Corry
David Case	General McLane
Bill Cole	Northwestern
Sean Conley	Iroquois
Steve DeMichele	Harbor Creek
Todd Dunda	Iroquois
Tim Eriksen	Fort LeBoeuf
Tom Ferguson	Corry
Chris Fuller	Northwestern
David Gianelli	Harbor Creek
Matt Gillette	Northwestern
John Hughes	Girard
Charles Hutchinson	Iroquois
Scott Kemling	Northwestern
Andrew Kerr	General McLane
John Langer	Fairview
John Mackanos	Girard
Don Mosher	Union City
Jason Myers	Fairview
Jamie Neuberger	General McLane
Gabe Oros	Fairview
Mike Rittenhouse	Corry
Eric Schrimper	Fort LeBoeuf
Jeff Sheldon	Iroquois
John Skalos	Seneca
Jon Swart	Corry
Chad Taylor	North East
Shawn Triana	Iroquois
Matt Walker	General McLane
Eric Watters	Girard
Pat Worley	Fort LeBoeuf

Coach: Ken Walker of General McLane

CITY 14 - COUNTY 3

*S*ean Madura of Tech and Pat Tighe of Prep led the City ground game. Madura gained 56 yards on 12 carries while Tighe ran for 34 yards on 11 attempts. Eric Kuhn of Strong Vincent directed the attack at quarterback, hitting 6 of 12 passes for 62 yards. William Bailey of Strong Vincent caught five passes for 46 yards. Madura scored on a 4-yard run. Chaun Johnson of East returned an interception 64 yards for the other score. Randy Baumann of Prep kicked both extra points.

John Mackanos of Girard kicked a 42-yard field goal for the only County points. John Skalos of Seneca gained 48 yards on 12 carries. Jeff Sheldon of Iroquois had 29 yards on five attempts. Matt Walker of General McLane hit on 6 of 29 passes for 57 yards. Andrew Kerr of McLane had three catches for 33 yards . Steve DeMichele of Harbor Creek, who recovered a fumble to set up the County field goal, had two receptions for 20 yards. The County was limited to nine first downs and never penetrated inside the City's 20-yard line.

> **❝** Rival, opponent, adversary, foe, even enemy...these are words that have often been used to describe the relationships between the football players at McDowell High School and Cathedral Prep. Honestly, I spent my four years playing football at McDowell despising the Prep players. After all, there is no bigger rivalry in the area.

Matt Koket – 1990

This all changed for me, however, when I was asked to play in the Save-An-Eye Game in the summer of 1990. First, I was thrilled with the honor of being viewed as an all-star and perhaps role model for younger players. And then it dawned on me . . . I will be placed on a team with players that I despised all year, and that I fought battles against in the trenches for the past four years. There was no way archrivals could get along, right? But somehow during the month of practices, not only did a team develop, so did friendships. I guess even enemies with a common cause can come together . . . and our cause was to beat the County! As a result we became friends.

One Prep player (Pat Tighe) in particular came to be a lasting friend of mine. That fall, I attended Syracuse University and he was headed off to Colgate University (about an hour away.) What followed was four years of car pools home, road trips, weekend parties and hanging out. All those good times we had during our college years still put a smile on my face today. When I think back, none of those special memories would have happened if not for the Save-An-Eye Game of 1990. I learned the true meaning of a team. So, with that, I want to thank the Save-An-Eye Game Committee not only for the experience of playing in the game but the opportunity to spawn new and lasting friendships. **❞**

Game 53 – August 2, 1991

City

Tory Benning......................Strong Vincent
Dan Danowski ....Cathedral Prep
Randy Davis.. Tech
Bryan Delio................................. Academy
Steve DeLuca.....................Strong Vincent
Robert DiGello .... Tech
Glenn Duck .... Tech
Ric Giles .... East
David Grack.......................Strong Vincent
Matt Grisik ....McDowell
Chris Harris ....McDowell
Andrew Hilling...................Cathedral Prep
Mike Jack .... East
Dietrich Jells .... Tech
Richard Jenkins .... East
A.J. Jimerson .... Tech
Terry Johnson .... Tech
Chris Kozlowski....................McDowell
Randy Kulesza....................Cathedral Prep
Joe Laska.................................McDowell
Steve Lunger ....McDowell
Chris Merski ....Cathedral Prep
David Peterson ....McDowell
Matt Pollock ....Strong Vincent
Jim Romanski ....Cathedral Prep
Josh Schneidmiller..............Cathedral Prep
Chris Schroyer............................. Academy
Dave Seyboldt ....Cathedral Prep
Matt Tressler.....................Strong Vincent
John White .... East
Corey Zieziula....................Cathedral Prep

Coaches: Paul Petrianni, Ray Pegg, Tom Torok, Tony Nunes, Ron Pontoriero of Tech

County

Mark Amenta ....Girard
Jason Anderson ....Fairview
C.J. Barbaro ....General McLane
Kevin Bayer.................................Fairview
Don Bernatowicz.................Harbor Creek
Chris Bonanti.............................Fairview
Al Chorney ....Fairview
Brandon Crotty..............................Corry
Chris Curtis ....Harbor Creek
Paul Ebert.............................Fort LeBoeuf
Jeff Englert ....Fort LeBoeuf
Steve Eriksen ....Fort LeBoeuf
Shaun Fawcett ....Northwestern
Art Greishaw ....Fort LeBoeuf
Jay Johnson....................General McLane
Tom Kranz ....Fairview
Chad Kuffer ....General McLane
T.J. Malesiewski.........................North East
Mike Mariani....................General McLane
Jim McAndrew................General McLane
Glenn McCall..........................North East
Keith McCracken .... Union City
Brian Milne...........................Fort LeBoeuf
Chris Oswalt............................Iroquois
Sean Siggins ....Harbor Creek
Dan Smith......................General McLane
Chris Snyder ....Seneca
Glenn Surrena.........................Fort LeBoeuf
Craig Villa ....General McLane
Darby Walsh ....Corry
Jamie Ward....................................Girard
Bill Wolfe ....Fort LeBoeuf
Dennis York ....Harbor Creek

Coaches: Joe Shesman, Bob Sensor, Jeff Nichols, Ed Orris, Bill Naughton, Steve Nishnick, Lou Benko of Fort LeBoeuf

CITY 18 - COUNTY 14

The City won in dramatic fashion, scoring on a 35-yard tailback option pass from Randy Davis to former Tech teammate A.J. Jimerson with 38 seconds left. Davis took a pitch from quarterback Josh Schneidmiller of Prep, then connected with Jimerson. Ric Giles of East scored on a 62-yard run on the first play from scrimmage. The game marked the return of Brian Milne to the field. He had missed his senior season due to Hodgkin's Disease.

The Fort LeBoeuf star carried 30 times for 164 yards and scored both County touchdowns on 1-yard plunges. He also ran for a 2-point conversion. Andy Hilling of Prep scored on a 2-yard run. Schneidmiller hit 10 of 15 passing for 127 yards and Davis connected on 5 of 8 throws for 74 yards. Chris Snyder of Seneca had six rushes for 57 yards and Al Chorney of Fairview had 10 runs for 48 yards. A crowd of 11,000, the largest since the renovation of Veterans Memorial Stadium, was on hand.

City All-Stars

County All-Stars

The Save-An-Eye Game has meant many things to many players, but probably not as much to anyone as Brian Milne.

To set the background to Milne's appearance in the 1991 game, we have to go back to when he was a junior at Fort LeBoeuf. He had an outstanding season as the featured running back for the Bisons. Actually, outstanding probably is an understatement.

Brian Milne – 1991

Here are Milne's numbers for that 1989 season: 2,419 rushing yards, 6.9 yards per carry, 31 touchdowns, 190 points. Twice he ran for more than 300 yards in a game. He racked up 312 yards and six touchdowns against General McLane, and he posted 301 yards with four touchdowns against Seneca.

Milne was receiving scholarship offers from virtually every major college in the country. He was a hot commodity as a future football player, and he was a PIAA champion in the discus during the track and field season.

Then came the news that changed everything. Milne was diagnosed with Hodgkin's disease. "It was stage 3B," Milne recalled of the diagnosis of his cancer. "They said I had a 60 percent chance to live." Milne was down but certainly not out. Chemotherapy sapped him of his strength, but he vowed to come back, not only to football but to throwing the discus again. While he was hospitalized, his college future was decided. "Many of the schools that offered me scholarships dropped off because I was sick," Milne said. "I think the schools didn't know how to handle it. But (Penn State) coach (Joe) Paterno stepped up. He called me in the hospital and told me that I had a full scholarship, even if I never played football at Penn State."

Milne missed his senior football season in 1990. When the spring of 1991 rolled around, Milne was a dominant athlete in track and field. In the PIAA championship, he threw the discus 206 feet, 3 inches to set a Class AA record. But football was still on his mind. He was determined to get ready for the Save-An-Eye Game which was scheduled for August 2. "I remember starting to run to get my wind back," Milne said. Brought up on a farm, he ran along the country roads. "I would sprint as far and as fast as I could until I lost my breath. Then I would do it again. I wanted to be ready. It was important to represent (Fort LeBoeuf) coach (Joe) Shesman and Fort LeBoeuf."

He represented them well. Although the City won 18-14 with a touchdown in the last minute, Milne was outstanding. Playing in his first football game in more than one and one-half years, he ran for 160 yards and scored all of the County's 14 points. In an emotional interview with Mike Gallagher of WJET-TV after the game, Milne said that he was back. "It was all the emotions that we have locked up, but when you get in certain situations you let it out," he said of that interview. "It was sincere. It was a love of football and running the ball."

The Save-An-Eye Game was a stepping stone for Milne. He went on to play on the 1993 Penn State team that won the Citrus Bowl, the 1994 team that won the Rose Bowl (when the Nittany Lions were undefeated and ranked No. 2 in the country), and the 1995 team that won the Hall of Fame Bowl.

Milne wore uniform No. 22 at Penn State, the same number that Brian Piccolo wore during his career at Maryland. That is not the only similarity between Milne and Piccolo, who died of cancer while a member of the Chicago Bears and is immortalized in the movie, "Brian's Song." "My mother saw the movie (Brian's Song) when she was pregnant with me and she named me after Brian Piccolo," Milne said.

Drafted by the Baltimore Colts in 1996, Milne played five seasons in the NFL for the Cincinnati Bengals, Seattle Seahawks and the New Orleans Saints.

During a telephone interview from his home in Cincinnati, Milne said, "The Save-An-Eye Game was an incredible, incredible thing. It was the first step to coming back. It was huge, and it was an honor."

– Joe Mattis

County's Milne finds room to roam

Brian Milne eludes tackler Randy Simitoski and heads downfield during third quarter of Friday's Save-An-Eye Game at the Stadium. Milne's County teammates C.J. Barbaro (42) and Chris Bonanti (14) follow the play. City scored last TD for 18-14 win before 11,000 fans.

Weekender photo / Ken Ziegler

City

Barry Akins	Tech
Charles Altman	Strong Vincent
Greg Baney	Strong Vincent
Craig Bennetti	Strong Vincent
Scott Bolheimer	McDowell
Paul Carr	East
Duane Conner	Academy
Jamaal Crawford	Strong Vincent
Dan Davis	Tech
Rick DiBacco	Cathedral Prep
Mike DiFilippo	McDowell
Mark Fetzner	Cathedral Prep
David Grandinetti	East
David Guilianelli	Academy
Charles Hanmore	Strong Vincent
Bill Lyons	Academy
Malik Martin	Strong Vincent
Brian O'Hara	Strong Vincent
Dan Olson	Strong Vincent
Quentin Orlando	Strong Vincent
Brian Palotas	Cathedral Prep
Ranfis Perez	Cathedral Prep
Garrick Perkins	Cathedral Prep
Jerry Roberts	Tech
Terry Roberts	Tech
Tony Robie	Strong Vincent
Tim Romanski	Strong Vincent
Paul Schaaf	Cathedral Prep
Craig Shupenko	Cathedral Prep
Jim Sitter	Cathedral Prep
Maolo Stewart	Tech
John Teel	Academy
Scott White	Academy
Craig Woodard	Mercyhurst Prep

Coach: Joe Bufalino of Strong Vincent

County

Chris Anthony	Union City
Jason Beckwith	Corry
Dave Brady	Iroquois
Chris Breese	Northwestern
Brian Brozell	Girard
Ben Corbin	Fairview
Eric Dudenhoeffer	Seneca
Darren Eller	Seneca
Robert Englert	Harbor Creek
Mike Gerlach	Harbor Creek
Mike Goard	Iroquois
Dana Harrington	Corry
Jay Herberg	Corry
Rob Heubel	Fairview
Aaron Hoover	Seneca
Matt Laniewicz	Iroquois
David Leri	Harbor Creek
Dave Mayer	General McLane
Eric McCray	Corry
Rick Miles	North East
Nick Mitchell	Corry
Scott Moneta	Harbor Creek
Bob Murray	Fairview
Greg Nelson	Fort LeBoeuf
Tim Newara	Iroquois
Mike O'Connor	Harbor Creek
Mark Patmore	Harbor Creek
Jay Sarvis	Harbor Creek
Sean Sherman	Northwestern
Eric Sittinger	Iroquois
Troy Stenger	Iroquois
Chad Vogt	Harbor Creek
Ted Wisniewski	Fort LeBoeuf

Coach: Dan Budziszewski of Harbor Creek

CITY 37 - COUNTY 8

*S*trong Vincent coach Joe Bufalino had 11 players from his state championship team. Three Vincent backs had big nights. Tim Romanski carried seven times for 96 yards, Tony Robie had 13 attempts for 56 yards and Quentin Orlando had 13 carries for 54 yards. Robie scored from a yard out, Orlando had a 5-yard touchdown run and Romanski capped the scoring with a 52-yard touchdown. Craig Woodard became the first Mercyhurst Prep player to perform in the Save-An-Eye Game. He had a 54-yard touchdown run. Bill Lyons of Academy accounted for the other touchdown on a 7-yard run. David Guilianelli of Academy kicked four extra points and a 33-yard field goal. Chad Vogt of Harbor Creek scored the only County touchdown on a 5-yard keeper. Vogt had a superb showing in a losing cause. He hit 10 of 28 passes for 139 yards, rushed six times for 15 yards, caught a pass for 6 yards and had a 33.7 yard punting average. The crowd was 8,500.

Top: City Team, Bottom: County Team

Football, and the Save-An-Eye Game in particular, runs strong in the Vogt family. Jim played for the County for coaches Joe Moore and Bill Vorsheck in the near-miraculous 1967 game where the County demolished their rival City players 25-0. He's hard pressed to decide the best part of the experience, being coached by Moore and Vorsheck, the decisive victory or being able to play on the same team with his cousin and friend, Gene Vogt.

Jim Vogt – 1967
Son, Chad Vogt – 1992
Son, Casey Vogt – 1995

Jim Vogt

Jim went on to coach the game as head coach in 1988, assistant coach in 1992 under Dan Budziszewski, assistant coach in 1998 under Phil Glass, and as defensive coach in 2010 under Coach Gerry Drozdowski.

There's no doubt that the best part of coaching in 1992 was the fact that Jim's son, Chad, was a member of the County roster. His son, Casey, played in 1995. Casey went on to become a coach like his father, heading up the team at Mercer University in Macon, Georgia.

The Save-An-Eye is not just about good memories for Jim and his family though. On game day in 2002, Jim's son, Chad, fell off a ladder while working and died of his injuries. Jim recalls learning that the crowd became completely silent for a moment to pay their respects to this fallen player who was later buried in his Save-An-Eye jersey. He says it did not surprise him that players and fans alike would take this moment to mourn the loss of a Save-An-Eye player for the game is one of respect as well as rivalry.

Chad Vogt

– Linda Hackshaw

Joe Bufalino has a long history with the Save-An-Eye Game.

It began in 1966 when, as a Cathedral Prep grad, Bufalino ran for 50 yards for the City team that beat the County 12-7. He also coached the City team several times. Bufalino remembers the 1992 game vividly. His Strong Vincent team had won the PIAA Class AAA championship the previous fall while relying heavily on their precise execution of the Wing-T offense. Eleven seniors from that team were selected to compete for the City. When practice began, there was one problem. The Wing-T, which Bufalino wanted his team to run, can be a complicated offense. Only the Vincent players were fully schooled in running it. According to Bufalino, that problem disappeared quickly.

"All of our kids became coaches," Bufalino said. "They coached the other kids to run the Wing-T." That turned out to be good strategy as the City rolled past the County 37-8 with Vincent grads Tim Romanski, Tony Robie and Quentin Orlando combining for 206 rushing yards.

Bufalino also remembers the great job the defense did in holding the County, led by Harbor Creek quarterback Chad Vogt, to just one touchdown. "The kids from Tech were really outstanding, especially in the secondary," Bufalino said.

Joe Bufalino – Coach 1992

Bufalino remembers one other thing that happened before the 1992 game was played. "We only had room for 33 kids on the team," he said. "When we selected the players, the 34th was one of the Roberts twins." Bufalino was referring to Jerry and Terry Roberts, twins from Tech. "The one who wasn't selected came to practice every day," Bufalino said. "When (the people from) the Lions Club found out, they added him to the roster." The brothers were both part of the Tech contingent that stood out on defense.

So which one of the Roberts twins—Jerry or Terry—was selected and which one was added to the team? "I really don't know," Bufalino said.

– Joe Mattis

Game 55 – August 6, 1993

City

Dustin Berarducci	Central
John Berarducci	Strong Vincent
Michael Burke	East
Chris Conrad	Central
Jason Crilley	Cathedral Prep
Corey Delio	Central
Tony DiNicola	Cathedral Prep
Cory Gehrlein	McDowell
John Gore	East
Spike Hanlin	Strong Vincent
Mike Hopkins	McDowell
Harry Izbicki	Cathedral Prep
Shawn Kendrick	Cathedral Prep
Jason Kleps	Strong Vincent
Mike Liebel	Cathedral Prep
Eric Lindsey	Central
Mark Miller	McDowell
Demon Moffett	East
Jamie Peterson	McDowell
Jamie Potosnak	Strong Vincent
Bryan Robie	Cathedral Prep
Jerry Schwenk	McDowell
Chris Serafini	Cathedral Prep
Chris Slawson	McDowell
Tony Tate	Mercyhurst Prep
Randy Terizzi	Cathedral Prep
Sheldon Thomas	Cathedral Prep
Dan Turley	Cathedral Prep
Steve Ulrich	Strong Vincent
Chris Valimont	Mercyhurst Prep
Jerry Varich	McDowell
Matt Wells	Cathedral Prep
Josh Wright	Strong Vincent

Coach: Ron Rudler of McDowell

County

Jason Barnett	Union City
Dan Bell	Fort LeBoeuf
Steve Coughlin	Seneca
Andy Crozier	Iroquois
Adam D'Ambrosio	Fairview
Sean Day	Iroquois
Jason Delp	Harbor Creek
Todd Eaglen	Harbor Creek
Greg Featsent	Fairview
Tim Gage	Northwestern
Mike Garner	Iroquois
Phil Glass	Iroquois
Dale Gregory	Fairview
Preston Griffith	Corry
James Hagle	Iroquois
Joseph Hassak	General McLane
Dan Heitzenrater	Fairview
Jamie Howard	Northwestern
David Kranz	Fairview
Ron Leeds	Fairview
Tim Malesiewski	North East
Mike Manning	Harbor Creek
Augie Mennen	Corry
Lee Owens	Fairview
Aaron Phanco	North East
Nick Price	Iroquois
Jody Rindfuss	Fort LeBoeuf
Scott Schnars	Iroquois
Craig Stocker	Girard
Jody Sutton	Harbor Creek
Doug Tracy	Fort LeBoeuf
Joe Weber	Harbor Creek
Greg Wilson	Corry
Pete Wisniewski	Northwestern

Coach: Jack Bestwick of Fairview

COUNTY 7 - CITY 0

$\mathcal{T}$im Malesiewski of North East had a 10-yard touchdown run with less than 3 minutes left for the game's only score. The run capped a 73-yard drive. The key play in the march was a 40-yard pass from Ron Leeds to former Fairview teammate Dale Gregory. Nick Price of Iroquois added the conversion. Malesiewski was the game's leading ball carrier with 10 attempts for 51 yards. Leeds connected on 8 of 13 passes for 79 yards. Gregory caught four passes for 50 yards and Pete Wisniewski of Northwestern caught three for 19 yards. Harry Izbicki of Cathedral Prep hit 12 of 22 passes for 95 yards. Chris Conrad of Central caught six passes for 70 yards. Sheldon Thomas of Prep was the City's leading ball carrier with 33 yards on 11 rushes and Mark Miller of McDowell had seven carries for 20 yards. This defensive battle marked the final appearance on the sidelines for retiring Fairview coach Jack Bestwick.

Here's the City squad for tonight's Save-An-Eye Game: first row, left to right, Eric Lindsey, Dustin Berarducci, Jamie Potosnak, Chris Serafini, Jerry Varich, Cory Gehrlein; second row, Harry Izbicki, John Gore, Jamie Peterson, Chris Slawson, Mark Miller, Tony Tate; third row, Corey Delio, Matt Wells, Steve Ulrich, Mike Burke, Dan Turley, Chris Vallimont, Mike Hopkins; fourth row, Josh Wright, Randy Terrizzi, Jason Kleps, Jerry Schwenk, Jason Crilley, Tony DiNicola, Shawn Kendrick, Mike Liebel.

City

Chris Bielak	Central
Mike Bowers	McDowell
Terry Capitol	Central
Harry Carpenter	Mercyhurst Prep
James Carr	East
Kareem Carson	Strong Vincent
Vince Clark	Central
Cliff Crosby	East
John Hare	Central
Eric Hicks	Mercyhurst Prep
Scott Johnson	McDowell
Curtis Jones	Mercyhurst Prep
Eric Kempisty	Central
Andy Kish	McDowell
Kevin Klemm	Central
Gregg Kuzma	Cathedral Prep
Joe Muldrew	Central
Brian Ostrum	Mercyhurst Prep
Mike Palmer	McDowell
Ron Pilarski	Cathedral Prep
Ryan Rezzelle	McDowell
Ray Salmon	McDowell
Greg Sivik	Central
Russ Smith	Mercyhurst Prep
Randy Tecza	Cathedral Prep
Richard Thornton	East
Mo Troop	Central
Craig Wilfong	East
Jason Williams	Central

County

Brian Andrychowski	Iroquois
Jacob Andrzejczak	General McLane
Greg Baney	Fort LeBoeuf
Ryan Beason	Harbor Creek
Howard Bolte	Northwestern
Ken Brown	Northwestern
Andy Bufalino	General McLane
Greg Burek	Union City
Sean Byars	Northwestern
Joe Cerce	Corry
Micah Chernicky	General McLane
Brad Costolo	Harbor Creek
William Davis	North East
Joel Dinger	Fort LeBoeuf
Scott Engle	Corry
Adam Fiscus	General McLane
D.J. Hough	Northwestern
Chip Johnson	General McLane
Chris King	Harbor Creek
Brian Komisarski	Seneca
Jason Locke	North East
Mike MacDonald	North East
Jason Patterson	Corry
Bill Quay	Northwestern
Anthony Sanfilippo	Harbor Creek
Brett Sproveri	Corry
Dennis Stauffer	Harbor Creek
Mike Stetson	North East
Jeffrey Strait	Northwestern
Jeremy Swartzfager	Fairview
Bill Szympruch	Girard
Steve Taylor	Corry
Bryan Turnbull	Fort LeBoeuf

Coaches: Tim Holland, Joe Tarasovitch, Ken Brasington, Bob Hoffman, Joe Kleiner, Steve Galich, Brian Holland, Gary Hess of Central

Coaches: John Wilson, Dan Clark, Bill Ross of Corry, Ed Margie of Union City

CITY 21 - COUNTY 0

*T*he City used a big play offense, with 15 plays gaining 10 yards or more. Mo Troop of Central hit on 7 of 9 passes for 120 yards, including a 27-yard touchdown pitch to Mike Palmer of McDowell. Cliff Crosby of East scored on a spectacular 17-yard run, aided by a crushing block by Kevin Klemm of Central. Eric Kempisty of Central kicked the PAT. Andy Kish of McDowell went 2 yards for the final City touchdown. The 87-yard drive came after Klemm recovered a County fumble. The march featured runs of 15 and 14 yards by Crosby. Brian Ostrum of Mercyhurst Prep passed to Kareem Carson of Strong Vincent for the two-point conversion. Curtis Jones of Mercyhurst had 72 yards on 15 carries and Crosby finished with 63 yards on seven trips. D.J. Hough of Northwestern led the County with 55 yards on 11 carries and two receptions for 12 yards. Strait had 48 yards on five carries. Brett Sproveri of Corry returned three kicks for 101 yards. The win went to Tim Holland, who had recently retired as Central's coach. The game featured Crosby and Eric Hicks of Mercyhurst Prep, who would both later play in the NFL after collegiate careers at Maryland.

The Mercyhurst Prep players pose with their Laker coaches (From left to right): Harry Carpenter, Eric Hicks (Kansas City Chiefs), Coach Terry Costello, Coach Ron Costello, Curtis Jones, Brian Ostrum, and Russ Smith

Chris King has been involved with the Save-An-Eye Game for quite some time. He is currently the president of the Erie Lions Club that annually sponsors the game. He is also the Director of Vision Services of the Sight Center of Northwest Pa., the organization that works hand in hand with the Lions Club to provide services to those who are visually impaired.

King's association dates back to 1994, the year he graduated from Harbor Creek High School. That was the year that he played in the Save-An-Eye Game.

Chris King – 1994

"One of the things that I remember is something that the Lions Club did not think of," King said. "That was the travel." John Wilson of Corry was the County coach in 1994 and King and his Harbor Creek teammates – Dennis Stauffer, Brad Costolo, Ryan Beason and Anthony Sanfilippo – would car pool to the practices at Corry. "I can't imagine what it was like for the players from schools like Girard and Northwestern when they had to go to practice," King said.

King also remembers the player introductions. Or, make that the large glasses that the players ran through (they still do to this day) when their names were called over the public address system. "I didn't want to be the one to trip on them," he said. "I hopped over them."

King was a defensive end for the County, which lost to the City 21-0. He had to line up against two huge City linemen, Mercyhurst Prep's Eric Hicks (a future NFL player) and McDowell's Ryan Rezelle. King was not a match for them size-wise. Instead, he used quickness and movement. After one play, Hicks pulled King aside. "What's with all this juking?" King said that Hicks asked him. So King replied, "If I was 6'5" and 260 pounds, I wouldn't need to do that."

King, who went on to play at Thiel College, enjoyed the moment. "It was actually the most fun I had in a football game, either in high school or college. I spent more time talking to opposing players, but it was in a good way. We weren't trying to get on each other."

One play sticks out in King's mind to this day. The City snapped the ball and "it was like the Red Sea parted," King said. "I had a clear path to (quarterback) Mo Troop. I hit him as hard as I could. He was hurt, but still played in the game. As I turned around, I realized I gave myself a whiplash." Later in the game, King went head-to-head with Kevin Klemm, a teammate of Troop's at Central. "Klemm reminded me of how bad my neck was bothering me," King said.

King's feelings about the Save-An-Eye Game have not diminished over the years. "I love it as an event," he said. "It was one of the highest accomplishments in my career. I'm more than happy to be associated with it today."

– Joe Mattis

Save-An-Eye Game reaches 55

K...

Metro, ECL players meet tonight in annual Save-An-Eye Game

By JIM CAMP
Of the Erie Daily Times

The local football season gets its usual kickoff Friday night when the 55th Save-An-Eye Game unfolds at Veterans Memorial Stadium.

The annual matchup of the outstanding seniors from the Metro and Erie County League teams begins at

know they're a talented team, especially the Central group that went so far with Coach Holland last fall. We're very aware of their ability and the size up front. They have big people and are very quick. We're going to try to use ball control and force them into some mistakes. We'll put a lot of pressure on our defensive ends and hope our people can stop ...m up front."

...e game is a farewell of sorts for ....h retired from the .... as Central

The annual matchup of the outstanding seniors from the Metro and ECL teams begins at 8 p.m.

ready at end are Steve Taylor (Cor-ry) and D.J. Hough (Northwestern).

Bryan Turnbull (Fort LeBoeuf) and Jason Locke (North East) open at linebackers. Others availa... Wilson ...cL...e).

(Central) and Wilfong sharing t... there. Tecza is the strong sa... backed by Palmer, with Ost... Bowers and Crosby a reliable st... safety trio.

Gates at the Stadium are s... open at 7 p.m. Tickets are pri... $4 apiece, with children under ... companied by a parent adm... free.

ALL-STAR...

City

Chris Bailey	Central
Roosevelt Benjamin	Central
Joe Bires	Strong Vincent
Richard Blatt	Strong Vincent
Duvall Braxton	McDowell
Charles Carson	Central
Josh Chiocco	McDowell
Jamall Cooper-Stewart	Central
Bill Ehegartner	McDowell
Ray Ferritto	East
Maurice Goodwine	East
Melvin Grady	East
Dan Greulich	Cathedral Prep
Mario Hall	East
Bernie Hessley	Cathedral Prep
Derrick Huff	East
Jody Irwin	Cathedral Prep
Justin Izbicki	Cathedral Prep
Sean Kaday	McDowell
Misael Kercado	East
Sean Kostef	Cathedral Prep
Craig Kulesza	Cathedral Prep
Tom Laird	Cathedral Prep
David Massing	Strong Vincent
Mike McIntire	Strong Vincent
Kenny Mitchell	East
Tyler Phenneger	Cathedral Prep
Matt Pierce	McDowell
Dan Rzepecki	Cathedral Prep
Bashan Stewart	Central
Lou Strelecki	McDowell
Tim Stumpf	McDowell
Donnie Tatum	Strong Vincent
Brian Ulrich	Strong Vincent

Coaches: John Dahlstrand, Bob Kwiatkowski, Phil Koval, Joe Dahlstrand, George Ogeka, Bill Shotta, Doug Bubna of East

County

Dan Baney	Fort LeBoeuf
Joe Benden	North East
Jared Bigelow	Harbor Creek
Travis Black	Girard
Dennis Carver	Harbor Creek
Mike Ferritto	Iroquois
Jaimen Gallo	General McLane
Benji Gaston	Fort LeBoeuf
Chad Jantzi	Corry
Ray Kavelish	General McLane
Larry Kerr	General McLane
Keith Knauff	Union City
Jack Kuchcinski	North East
Luke Kuffer	General McLane
Jeremy Lear	Northwestern
Shawn LoDovico	Corry
Dan Long	Northwestern
Dan Lovett	Girard
Scott Malesiewski	North East
Anthony Marino	Northwestern
Brad Mitchell	Corry
Brent Neal	Fort LeBoeuf
Mike Polakowski	General McLane
Fred Price	Fairview
Gary Scutella	Seneca
Chris Smith	General McLane
Jason Sokol	Harbor Creek
Dan Stablein	Fort LeBoeuf
J.C. Strait	Northwestern
Jaime Tecza	General McLane
Matt Triana	North East
Casey Vogt	Harbor Creek
Cliff Wynkoop	Seneca

Coaches: John Ballard, John Beaumont, Keith Reynolds, Regan Tanner, Steven Wall, Mike MacDonald of North East

COUNTY 15 - CITY 12

Due to renovations at Veterans Stadium, this game was played at General McLane. It marked the first time the game was held at an Erie County League location. The contest spotlighted a pair of McLane players. Luke Kuffer threw a 45-yard touchdown pass to Jaimen Gallo late in the fourth quarter to decide the outcome. Scott Malesiewski of North East fired 10 yards to Brad Mitchell of Corry for the other County touchdown. Jason Sokol of Harbor Creek kicked one PAT and Kuffer scored the other on a two-pointer on a keeper. Roosevelt Benjamin of Central scored both City touchdowns on runs of 4 and 86 yards. Benjamin gained 109 yards on eight carries despite sitting out the second half with a shoulder injury.

2-B   ERIE, PA., MORNING NEWS, Friday, August 4, 1995

City All-Stars

The City team for tonight's Save-An-Eye Game: first row, left to right, Brian Ulrich, Lou Strelecki, Sean Kaday, Craig Kulesza, Dan Greulich, Sean Kostef, Duvall Braxton, Rich Blatt, Tim Stumpf; second row, Ray Ferritto, Roosevelt Benjamin, Jamaal Cooper, Mario Hall, Donnie Tatum, Maurice Goodwine, Melvin Grady, Chris Bailey, Dan Rzepecki, David Massing, Tom Laird; third row, Matt Pierce, Mike McIntire, Joe Bires, Kenny Mitchell, Misael Kercado, Bill Ehegartner, Josh Chiocco, Justin Izbicki, Bernie Hessley, Jody Irwin, Chuck Carson.

All-Star contest tonight at McLane

Continued from Page 1-B

up.

Dahlstrand will open with Justin Izbicki (Prep) at quarterback. Kenny Mitchell (East) will also see time. Matt Pierce (McDowell) operates at fullback. Chuck Carson (Central) and Donnie Tatum (Strong Vincent) get the nod at running backs, with Bernie Hessley (Prep) and Roosevelt Benjamin (Central) also ready.

Tom Laird (Prep) gets the call at split end while Tim Stumpf (McDowell) and Mike McIntire (Vincent) will alternate at tight end.

Along the front, Duvall Braxton (McDowell) and Dan Greulich (Prep) are the tackles, Chris Bailey (Central) and Joe Bires (Vincent) the guards, Sean Kostef (Prep) at center. Brian Ulrich (Vincent) will see time at both center and guard while Rich Blatt (Vincent) is ready for duty at tackle.

Ballard has worked with three complete backfield units in practices. Luke Kuffer (McLane) is likely to open at quarterback, with J.C. Strait (Northwestern) and Scott Malesiewski (North East) slated to get equal time.

County tailbacks include Shawn Lodovico (Corry), Jeremy Lear (Northwestern) and Fred Price (Fairview). Sharing fullback chores are Dan Stablein (Fort LeBoeuf), Larry Kerr (McLane) and Dennis Carver (Harbor Creek).

A host of receivers are ready for the ECL crew. Flankers include Benji Gaston (Fort LeBoeuf), Matt Triana (North East), Jaimen Gallo (McLane), Gary Scutella (Seneca) and Brent Neal (LeBoeuf). The split end corps boasts Anthony Marino (Northwestern), Jared Bigelow (Harbor Creek) and Dan Lovett (Girard). Four tight ends are available: Mike Polakowski (McLane), Brad Mitchell (Corry), Mike Ferritto (Iroquois) and Travis Black (Girard).

The subbing will continue along the front. Ticketed for action at tackle are Ray Kavelish (McLane), Dan Baney (LeBoeuf), Cliff Wynkoop (Seneca), Jack Kuchcinski (North East) and Keith Knauff (Union City). Guards are Chad Jantzi (Corry), Casey Vogt (Harbor Creek), Chris Smith (McLane) and Dan Long (Northwestern). Splitting time at center will be Jaime Tecza (McLane) and Joe Benden (North

East).

That County offensive unit will square off with the City defense, anchored by Jody Irwin (Prep) at nose-guard. The tackles are Melvin Grady (East), Craig Kulesza (Prep) and Sean Kaday (McDowell). Ray Ferritto (East), Jamaal Stewart (Central) and Bill Ehegartner (McDowell) will work at defensive ends.

Dahlstrand is pleased with his linebacking crew of Mario Hall (East), Lou Strelecki (McDowell), McIntire and Dan Rzepecki (Prep). The cornerbacks are Maurice Goodwine (East) and Josh Chiocco (McDowell). Mitchell and Misael Kercado (East) are the City safeties. Reserve secondary help comes from Tyler Phenneger (Prep) and Derick Huff (East).

The County defense includes Knauff, Benden and Smith sharing time on the nose, with Wynkoop, Kavelish, Kuchcinski and Long at tackles, Polakowski, Kuffer, Ferritto, Carver and Mitchell the defensive ends.

The linebacking unit includes Vogt, Jantzi, Black, Price and Tecza. In the secondary, Gallo, Gaston, Scutella, Malesiewski and Lovett are the corners, Lear, Strait, Triana, Kerr, Neal, Marino and Lodovico the safeties.

Jason Sokol (Harbor Creek) will handle the kicking chores, Malesiewski and Kuffer both capable punters. Lodovico and Lear will be back for both punt and kickoff runbacks.

Tatum will punt for the City, with David Massing (Vincent) the place-kicker. Benjamin will bring back punts and join Kercaco on kickoff returns.

Forecasting the game, Dahlstrand said, "Both of our quarterbacks can run and that's a nice dimension. And we're definitely not lacking in speed. The County has some quality people and we're expecting a mixture of run and pass from them."

Ballard commented, "We'll try to take advantage of our abilities and look to see what the players can do best. The City has big linemen and good running backs and we figure they'll try to run the ball."

A large crowd is anticipated for the contest, fans reminded to secure seats (and spots on the McLane grassy areas) early.

County All-Stars

The County squad for Friday's Save-An-Eye Game: first row, left to right, Travis Black, Gary Scutella, Shawn Lodovico, Brad Mitchell, Chad Jantzi, Luke Kuffer, J.C. Strait, Fred Price, Dan Stablein; second row, Jaime Tecza, Keith Knauff, Joe Benden, Jeremy Lear, Anthony Marino, Jaimen Gallo, Mike Ferritto, Dan Lovett, Scott Malesiewski, Benji Gaston; third row, Cliff Wynkoop, Larry Kerr, Mike Polakowski, Dan Long, Chris Smith, Matt Triana, Dan Baney, Ray Kavelish; fourth row, Casey Vogt, Dennis Carver, Jason Sokol, Jared Bigelow, Jack Kuchcinski.

City

Keith Balko	McDowell
Chuck Bizzarro	McDowell
Stephen Bryan	Strong Vincent
Rich Clark	East
Eugene Crosby	Cathedral Prep
Ramone Ellis	Cathedral Prep
Eric Faulkner	McDowell
Matt Frano	McDowell
Steve Franz	Central
Owen George	Cathedral Prep
Tony Grack	Strong Vincent
Quincy Jones	Strong Vincent
Jamie Kaiser	Mercyhurst Prep
Ramown Kinnard	Central
Jason Larson	Cathedral Prep
Justin Lustig	Cathedral Prep
Joe Magorien	McDowell
Mike Miodus	Strong Vincent
Dwight Morgan	East
Greg Morgan	Mercyhurst Prep
Brian Myers	Mercyhurst Prep
Ken Nickson	Central
Brad Orlando	McDowell
Tom Palmer	McDowell
Rausaan Powell	Cathedral Prep
Ed Serafini	Cathedral Prep
Andrew Tamilin	Strong Vincent
Pat Testrake	Strong Vincent
Ato Troop	Central
Harry Watkins	East
Eric Wilkosz	Cathedral Prep

Coaches: Mina George, Mike Leibel, Kyle Ferrick, Tony Jenco, Jeff Joint of Cathedral Prep

County

Ryan Andrews	Iroquois
John Angerer	Harbor Creek
Jerry Baker	Corry
Mike Ball	Fort LeBoeuf
Joe Bish	Northwestern
John Feketi	Seneca
Doug Friedman	Fort LeBoeuf
Justin Gallo	General McLane
Brent Goodenow	Fort LeBoeuf
Marty Gray	North East
Rob Haibach	Fort LeBoeuf
Dennis Hinkler	Fort LeBoeuf
Aaron Holmes	Fairview
Jeremiah Hovis	Northwestern
Tom Kaliszewski	Iroquois
Chris Karsznia	Harbor Creek
Jamie Keeney	General McLane
Justin King	Fairview
Scott Lafuria	North East
Frank Longo	Iroquois
Joe Lukac	Corry
Chad Maleski	Union City
Shane McChesney	Corry
Mark McManus	Fairview
Brad Mongera	Fort LeBoeuf
Brian Polk	Girard
Keith Rocca	General McLane
Jared Rosendahl	Fairview
Mike Smyklo	Iroquois
Jeff Spires	General McLane
Shawn Thompson	Seneca
Mike Williams	Fairview
Buddy Williamson	General McLane

Coaches: Craig MacKelvey, Dale Lewis, Rick Graziani, Gerry Drabina, Tom Laska, Orr Weislogel, Jeremy Friel, John Hardy of Fairview

CITY 20 - COUNTY 6

*A*rtificial turf problems at Veterans Stadium forced the switch to General McLane for the second straight year. The longest play in Save-An-Eye history helped the City win. Mike Miodus of Strong Vincent connected with Tom Palmer of McDowell for a 97-yard scoring pass. The play came after a County drive was stopped at the 1-yard line. Owen George threw 34 yards to former Prep teammate Ramone Ellis and Ato Troop of Central ran 7 yards for the other City scores. Miodus hit 5 of 7 passes for 185 yards. Palmer had all five receptions. Aaron Holmes of Fairview kicked two field goals for the only County points. Brad Orlando of McDowell stopped another County threat with an interception at the 4-yard line.

Football returns as GM hosts 57th Save-An-Eye

By JIM CAMP
Of the *Erie Daily Times*

Football and the Save-An-Eye Game make returns this evening.

The fall sport gets its customary early start when the 57th version of the All-Star attraction goes back to General McLane for the second straight time.

Kickoff for the annual extravaganza is listed for 8 o'clock.

Artificial turf woes at Veterans Memorial Stadium for the second successive year forced the switch to Linden Field, where the County rallied for a 15-12 win in 1995.

That was just the 12th win for the ECL crew against 30 City victories and two ties under the current format. The game is the oldest of its type in the country.

The Erie Lions Club sponsors the popular event, which provides eye care for needy children throughout Erie County. The Lions have raised over a half-million dollars through the game, and every cent goes to the charity.

A unique aspect of this year's renewal involves the opposing coaches, Mina George and Craig Mackelvey. Both have changed positions. George resigned after a long run at Cathedral Prep and later took the job at Girard. Mackelvey left as the head man at Fairview and is now a member of Ron Rudler's McDowell staff.

Both coaches predict a fun game ... with plenty of passing, ... wholesale substi- ... both offen...

City All-Stars

No.—Player	School	Ht.	Wt.	Pos.
10 — TOM PALMER	McDowell	5-10	170	CB
12 — MIKE MIODUS	Vincent	6-0	185	QB
14 — OWEN GEORGE	Prep	6-2	170	QB
16 — ERIC WILKOSZ	Prep	5-8	150	K
18 — ERIC FAULKNER	McDowell	6-3	215	DE
20 — STEVE FRANZ	Central	5-10	160	CB
21 — RAMONE ELLIS	Prep	5-9	165	CB
22 — BRAD ORLANDO	McDowell	6-0	218	RB
23 — THEO HAMMOND	Vincent	5-9	190	RB
24 — RAMOWN KINNARD	Central	5-8	200	CB
25 — DWIGHT MORGAN	McDowell	5-10	175	FB
26 — CHUCK BIZZARRO	Central	5-8	140	DB
28 — ATO TROOP	East	5-9	190	RB
30 — RICH CLARK	M'hurst	6-1	200	S
32 — BRIAN MYERS	Prep	5-8	205	FB
34 — JASON LARSON	Prep	6-0	215	NG
36 — ED SERAFINI	Central	5-11	165	LB
41 — ERIC DEFELICE	Vincent	5-8	195	K
43 — ANDREW TAMILIN	McDowell	5-8	215	LB
48 — JOE MAGORIEN	Vincent	6-0	190	FB
51 — CHRIS STAROCCI	M'hurst	6-5	280	OG
52 — JAMIE KAISER	Vincent	5-9	200	OG
53 — TONY GRACK	Prep	6-1	275	DT
68 — EUGENE CROSBY	M'hurst	5-11	230	OG
70 — GREG MORGAN	Vincent	6-2	250	DT
73 — PAT TESTRAKE	McDowell	6-1	280	DT
75 — KEITH BALKO	East	5-10	265	OT
76 — HARRY WATKINS	Central	6-4	300	OT
78 — KEN NICKSON	Vincent	6-2	200	DE
86 — STEPHAN BRYAN	Vincent	6-2	190	TE
89 — QUINCY JONES				

County All-Stars

No.—Player	School	Ht.	Wt.	Pos.
10 — RYAN ANDREWS	Iroquois	6-2	210	LB
12 — AARON HOLMES	Fairview	6-0	175	K
16 — JOE SMYKLO	Iroquois	6-0	175	QB
20 — JUSTIN GALLO	McLane	5-8	180	RB
21 — BRAD MONGERA	LeBoeuf	5-9	185	FB
22 — JOE LUKAC	Corry	5-11	170	DB
23 — SHANE MCCHESNEY	Corry	5-7	160	LB
24 — TOM KALISZEWSKI	Iroquois	5-10	165	DB
25 — BRIAN POLK	Girard	5-9	165	DB
30 — CHAD MALESKI	Un.City	6-0	190	TB
32 — DENNIS HINKLER	LeBoeuf	5-11	205	DE
34 — SHAWN THOMPSON	Seneca	5-9	180	TB
36 — JOHN FEKETI	Seneca	5-10	175	K
40 — JOE BISH	N'western	5-8	200	LB
42 — MIKE BALL	LeBoeuf	6-2	170	WR
44 — JEFF SPIRES	McLane	5-10	200	RB
50 — BRENT GOODENOW	LeBoeuf	5-11	180	C
51 — BUDDY WILLIAMSON	McLane	5-7	210	G
52 — FRANK LONGO	Iroquois	5-7	155	DL
53 — ROB HAIBACH	LeBoeuf	5-11	180	DT
60 — MARK MCMANUS	Fairview	6-2	210	C
62 — JAMIE KEENEY	McLane	6-0	215	T
68 — CHRIS KARSZNIA	H'Creek	5-11	218	G
71 — MARTY GRAY	N.East	6-3	220	T
75 — JERRY BAKER	Corry	6-2	240	T
76 — JOHN ANGERER	H'Creek	6-5	300	T
77 — MIKE WILLIAMS	Fairview	6-2	282	TE
80 — JEREMIAH HOVIS	N'western	6-2	170	WR
82 — KEITH ROCCA	McLane	5-8	160	DE
83 — DOUG FRIEDMAN	LeBoeuf	6-1	190	QB
84 — SCOTT LAFURIA	N.East	6-0	155	DE
90 — JUSTIN KING	Fairview	6-3	200	TE
99 — JARED ROSENDAHL	Fairview	6-5	215	

...uria available to share ...chores. Mackelvey ...unior backs. ... Hovis, Jared Rosendahl, Doug Friedman at tight end. ...front. ...outfit has ...

Greg Mor... Pat Testra... son, Euge... and ends... Faulkner, ... Morgan.

The back... Magorien, ... lin, Chris ... Chuck Bizz... Hammond, ... Ellis, stron... nard and ... Owen Geo... Miodus.

Switchin... Metro pass... George giv... QB. The fu... ers, Magor... mond, Dwi... are flanke... at tailbacks... split ends... Franz, Eric ... Clark and ti... ner, Jones a...

The fron... Frano, gua... Morgan, B... Testrake, ... Watkins.

That offer... a County I... Karsznia, ... tackles Ba... Hinkler, W... King, Keer... Friedman.

The back... liamson, ... Mongera, M... ney and Spi...

City

Rasheed Allen	Central
Reynaldo Batista	McDowell
Jeff Brzezinski	Cathedral Prep
Brian Caldwell	McDowell
Shawn Carlson	Strong Vincent
Randy Carson	Central
Matt Catalino	McDowell
Matt DiRaimo	Cathedral Prep
Jason Elwell	McDowell
Keith Featsent	Cathedral Prep
Stephen Greulich	Strong Vincent
Doug Grieshaber	East
Mitch Groszkiewicz	Cathedral Prep
Chuck Heid	Mercyhurst Prep
Aaron Hertel	Cathedral Prep
Eric Hinkler	Cathedral Prep
John Howard	East
Chris Loomis	Cathedral Prep
Eric Lynde	Central
Steve Musone	Central
Jeff Ohrn	McDowell
Geoff Radziszewski	Central
Steve Scheloske	Strong Vincent
Gary Stanbro	Strong Vincent
Jeff Van Volkenburg	Cathedral Prep
Tanner Youkers	Strong Vincent
Andrew Young	Central
Nick Zappia	Strong Vincent
Michael Zona	Cathedral Prep

Coaches: Jeff Nichols, Brad Darrow, Mike Parmenter, Doug Schreiber, Dave Reichard of Mercyhurst Prep

County

Jared Alexander	Northwestern
Bill Baker	Girard
Malcolm Beall	Fairview
Ryan Bogert	Corry
Tim Case	Harbor Creek
Loren Chase	Corry
Mike Chase	Northwestern
Greg Dore	General McLane
Mike Downey	Corry
Mark Dubrosky	Corry
Phil Dunlap	General McLane
Erik Glus	Northwestern
Kurt Haibach	Fort LeBoeuf
Dana Keeler	Corry
Geoffrey Kelly	Fort LeBoeuf
Chris Luker	Northwestern
Dave Merritt	Northwestern
Kyle Millet	Iroquois
Todd Minor	General McLane
Doug Mitchell	Corry
Shawn Mitchell	Corry
Sam Newara	Iroquois
Brandon Nishnick	Fort LeBoeuf
Carl Patterson	General McLane
Ryan Randolph	Harbor Creek
Nick Sargent	Fort LeBoeuf
Cale Schultz	North East
Eric Sharie	Seneca
Mike Stablein	Fort LeBoeuf
Jeff West	Northwestern
Corey Williams	Union City
Dave Wojtecki	Union City
Errick Woodard	Fort LeBoeuf

Coaches: John Wilson, Joe Lukac, Bill Ross, Mike Anthony, Mike Daniels, Marty Rimpa of Corry

COUNTY 17 - CITY 7

$\mathscr{E}$rrick Woodard of Fort LeBoeuf scored both County touchdowns. Woodard took an 11-yard pass from Erik Glus of Northwestern for one touchdown and also ran 2 yards for a score. Woodard carried 11 times for 71 yards. Mike Stablein of Fort LeBoeuf kicked a 30-yard field goal and two extra points. The City earned its only touchdown on a 4-yard run by Randy Carson of Central. Keith Featsent of Prep kicked the PAT. Doug Mitchell of Corry was a defensive standout with 11 tackles and two sacks. Glus hit 4 of 9 passes for 65 yards. Carson rushed 19 times for 76 yards for the City. Jeff Brzezinski of Cathedral Prep was the leader of the City defense. This marked the first game on the new artificial turf at Veterans Memorial Stadium.

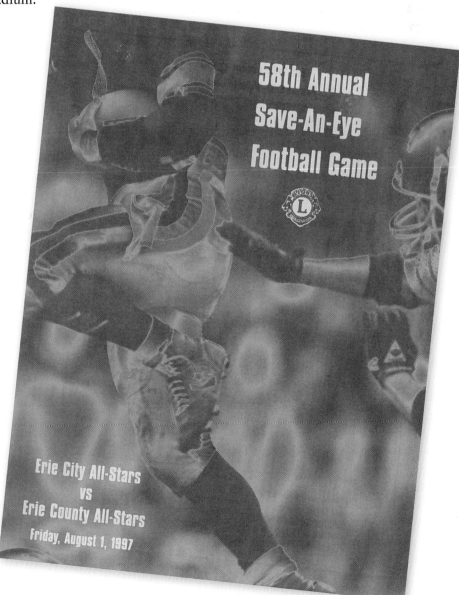

58th Annual Save-An-Eye Football Game

Erie City All-Stars
vs
Erie County All-Stars
Friday, August 1, 1997

City

Bill Adams	Strong Vincent
Mike Allgeier	Mercyhurst Prep
Mike Bennett	Central
Tony Bowers	Cathedral Prep
Travis Bricker	McDowell
Kevin Brzezinski	Cathedral Prep
Jeff Brzostowski	Central
Ryan Cappelletty	McDowell
Joey Ciminella	McDowell
Todd Dipre	Cathedral Prep
Mike Driehorst	Mercyhurst Prep
Chris Dudley	Cathedral Prep
Greg Dufala	Cathedral Prep
Ryan Erven	McDowell
Eric Farrell	Central
Kevin Gorman	Strong Vincent
Rob Grygier	McDowell
James Hartken	McDowell
Geoff Heyl	McDowell
Corey Kinnard	Central
Ed Kowalski	Cathedral Prep
Marc Limano	Cathedral Prep
Zac Martin	McDowell
Nick Mehall	McDowell
Brent Meyer	McDowell
Fine Nai	McDowell
Ryan Nietupski	Cathedral Prep
Ryan Paszkowski	Mercyhurst Prep
Tim Prior	Central
Gary Reed	East
Scott Reichard	Mercyhurst Prep
George Siegel	McDowell
Aaron Slocum	McDowell
Greg Tarbell	McDowell
Jerry Troop	Central
Craig Wilczynski	Cathedral Prep

Coaches: Ron Rudler, Mike Burke, Craig MacKelvey, Paul Yoculan, Tim Cacchione, Mark Soboleski of McDowell

County

Aaron Anderson	Seneca
Jason Brown	Northwestern
Dave Buzard	Northwestern
Nick Cadie	Northwestern
Chett Fisher	Northwestern
Brad Freeman	Fairview
Jason Fuhrer	Fort LeBoeuf
Aaron Jelley	North East
Jeremy Keith	Northwestern
James Kerns	Union City
Joel Knight	Fort LeBoeuf
David Lanagan	Iroquois
Eric McCommons	Northwestern
Mike McGuigan	North East
Mike McKinney	Union City
Josh Miller	Fort LeBoeuf
Nick Miller	North East
Jason Norton	Northwestern
Adam Orsefskie	Iroquois
Jim Presley	General McLane
Nate Rizzo	North East
Kevin Sabol	Northwestern
T.J. Schaffner	Fairview
Mike Schroeder	North East
Jeffrey Smith	Fort LeBoeuf
Andy Stritzinger	Harbor Creek
Brian Swift	Northwestern
Dan Waisley	General McLane
Dave Wethli	Fort LeBoeuf
Jeremy Young	Harbor Creek

Coaches: Dave Merritt, Rob Glus, Tom Gage, Jim Brown, Eric Mikovch, Tony Kitchen, Dennis Teed, Harold Merritt of Northwestern

CITY 17 - COUNTY 6

Aaron Slocum of McDowell had a huge night while playing quarterback, wide receiver and defensive back in the 60th annual game. He scored both City touchdowns on pass receptions of 28 and 16 yards from Jerry Troop of Central. Slocum had nine carries for 47 yards, hit 1 of 2 passes for 11 yards, and had three receptions for 41 yards and one punt return for 11 yards. The versatile Slocum also made three solo tackles and broke up two passes. Joey Ciminella of McDowell was the top rusher with 13 carries for 79 yards. Ryan Nietupski of Prep had two catches for 20 yards and netted 70 yards on kick returns. Jason Brown of Northwestern accounted for the County touchdown on a 32-yard run.

60th anniversary Save-An-Eye Game tonight at Stadium

By JIM CAMP
Staff writer

The Save-An-Eye Game is about numbers, and not just those on the Veterans Stadium scoreboard.

Tonight's contest is the 60th in the series sponsored by the Erie Lions Club, with over 3,500 athletes competing since its inception. More importantly, over 17,000 Erie County children have received the equivalent of more than $3,000,000 worth of eye care from game proceeds.

One number that has changed this year is the starting time. Kickoff will be at 7:30 p.m., Stadium gates opening at 6:15.

The 60th anniversary game will have a distinctive Albion flavor. Head coaches Ron Rudler and Dave Merritt were teammates and both later coached at Northwestern High School.

And this year's game is being dedicated to the memory of John Gillette, who played and coached at both Northwestern and in the Save-An-Eye. Gillette, who participated in the All-Star classic in 1967 and coached in 1975-78, will be honored during pre-game ceremonies.

McDowell boss Rudler and Merritt, who resigned at Northwestern after last season, were pleased with workouts and looking forward to tonight's battle.

"We practiced hard," Rudler said. "But these guys responded and things have fallen into place. It's been a pleasure to coach this group. They've gotten along quite well. They're all used to being first-... ...to set

their egos aside and just play."

Merritt noted, "It's nice to work with people you don't have to teach every little thing to. You tell them once and they know what they're doing. It's been a good experience."

Both coaches are well aware the City has an advantage in both numbers and size entering the game.

"They probably have the edge in agility while we're bigger," Rudler said. "But Dave will have his guys well prepared and he has a lot of his Northwestern kids that will help them."

"We're not big, but we're very competitive," Merritt remarked. "The City is just huge up front and with their big linemen they might try to power it. But they can also pass, so we don't know what to expect. Our players want to play a good game and represent the County well."

Merritt will alternate a pair of quarterbacks, with Jason Norton of Northwestern and Mike Schroder of North East both available. Jason Brown of Northwestern will likely open at fullback, backed by Joel Knight of Fort LeBoeuf and James Kerns of Union City.

Nick Miller of North East and T.J. Schaffner of Fairview will start at wingbacks, with Kevin Sabol of Northwestern, Aaron Anderson of Seneca and Brian Swift of Northwestern also ready. The County has four split ends, Eric McCommons of Northwestern, Mike McGuigan of North East, Dave Lanagan of Iroquois and Jim Presley of General McLane all capable receivers.

See SAVE-AN-EYE, Page 4C

City	
Nevin Baker	McDowell
Joe Boyer	Cathedral Prep
Brian Bubna	East
Mike Caldwell	McDowell
Josh Carrick	McDowell
Rory Carroll	Cathedral Prep
Jason Cassano	East
Matt Dubowski	Mercyhurst Prep
Jason Gabbard	Mercyhurst Prep
Peter Gervase	Cathedral Prep
Bryan Gore	East
Dave Jones	Mercyhurst Prep
Alan Kelley	Central
Rick Kraus	McDowell
James Kuhn	McDowell
Fred Munch	McDowell
Steve Noonan	Cathedral Prep
Maurice Page	Strong Vincent
Kyle Presogna	Cathedral Prep
Ravaire Prince	Central
Cory Rush	Mercyhurst Prep
Jason Russell	McDowell
Craig Sauers	Central
Matt Snippert	Central
Donnie Staaf	Mercyhurst Prep
Chris Testrake	Strong Vincent
Matt Testrake	Strong Vincent

County	
Matt Angerer	Harbor Creek
Aaron Briggs	Fort LeBoeuf
Lincoln Bufalino	General McLane
Daryl Burek	Union City
Nate Burnett	Harbor Creek
Josh Clark	Harbor Creek
Mike Cooklis	North East
Clark Ellsworth	North East
Scott Flick	Iroquois
Gregg Gebhardt	General McLane
Tom Kirdahy	General McLane
Jim Kuhl	Seneca
Geoff Lewis	Fairview
Dan Madden	Northwestern
Marty Mariani	General McLane
Matt McMaster	General McLane
James Miller	Fort LeBoeuf
Josh Miller	Girard
Tom Newara	Iroquois
Mark Nipper	Fairview
Brian Peters	Iroquois
Matt Puskar	Seneca
Andy Resinger	Harbor Creek
Nick Schneider	Harbor Creek
Joel Schreiber	Seneca
Chad Sheehan	Iroquois
Chad Smith	Girard
Chris Smith	Fort LeBoeuf
Mike Steigerwald	Fort LeBoeuf
Brian Tech	Seneca
Jeremy Thompson	Northwestern
Nick Weston	Seneca
Jeremiah Winnie	Fairview

Coaches: Bob Kwiatkowski, Maurice "Mo" Troop, Rich Boesch, Tom Slomski, Bill Schroth, Dale Lewis, Mark Knight, Doug Bubna, George Ogeka of East

Coaches: Joe Shesman, Walley Mahle, Carm Bonito, Bill Naughton, Sean Wolfrom, Rich Goodenow, Bob Sensor, Ed Orris, Marty Rimpa, Lou Benko, Steve Nishnick of Fort LeBoeuf

COUNTY 23 - CITY 9

*C*oach Joe Shesman of Fort LeBoeuf switched from his usual running game as the County racked up 201 yards passing. Chris Smith of LeBoeuf connected on 7 of 9 passes for 163 yards and two touchdowns. Josh Clark of Harbor Creek had touchdown receptions of 89 and 34 yards. Jeremy Thompson of Northwestern hit 3 of 4 passing for 38 yards and connected with Matt Puskar of Seneca for a 25-yard touchdown. Maurice Page of Strong Vincent scored on a 1-yard run and Peter Gervase of Prep kicked a 24-yard field goal for the City's points. Lincoln Bufalino of General McLane was the top County rusher with 41 yards on 16 carries. Bryan Gore of East led the City runners with 60 yards on 15 carries. Page added 52 yards on 12 carries. The City completed 2 of 11 passes for 6 yards.

Save-An-Eye game sees fans into season

... season officially kicks off ... the 61 ... ual Save-An-...
...es open at 6:15.

■ The 61st annual Save-An-Eye Game between City and County All-Star teams starts tonight at 7:30 at Veterans Stadium. Gates open at 6:15.

...ning game.

pleased with the play of his team in practi...
"We've had some pretty spirited ...tices," he reported. "The kids have ...ing a great effort."

For Shesman, there was ... taking players from 10 ... molding them into ... ...aid ... "Adi...

Save-An-Eye football game always sight to behold

PLAYERS in the first Save-An-Eye Game were outfitted in leather helmets and high-top black cleats. Those durable athletes of 1939 had no face masks, no multi-colored shoes, no sophisticated padding. Equipment, like the sport itself, has evolved steadily over the past six decades. So, better-protected players will produce the popping sounds of plastic-on-plastic Friday when the 61st charity game unfolds at Veterans Stadium.

While appearances change, much about the second-oldest game of its kind in the country remains intact. The crowd likely will be second to none this season. And it's still City vs. County with last year's seniors doing battle.

Needy children from throughout the county will receive free eye services thanks to the game. The Erie Lions Club has used proceeds to aid 17,000 kids with over $3,000,000 worth of eye care since it all started.

The Save-An-Eye has distinct memories for thousands who h... watched, played or coac...

Jim Camp

annual attraction. We've seen our share of games through the years and fondly recall certain moments.

AARON SLOCUM of McDowell last August concocted perhaps the most impressive individual performance in the game's history. Playing three positions, he was spectacular as the City earned a 17-...ed both tou...

and 16-yard passes from Central's Jerry Troop. Slocum carried nine times for 47 yards, caught three balls for 41, completed one pass for 11 and returned a punt for 11 yards Defensively, he had three tackles and two broken-up passes to cap his busy evening. Slocum played last year at Edinboro, earning a starting job at defensive back before a mid-season injury sidelined him. He was transferred to Geneva and intends to play there, we're told.

MIKE MIODUS of Strong Vincent and Tom Palmer of McDowell teamed for a record 97-yard touchdown pass and run in 1996 when the City prevailed 20-6. That game and the '95 contest were played at General McLane due to Stadium renovation. The County won 15-12 four years ago when Luke Kuffer hit Jaimen Gallo with a 45-yard touchdown strike late in the fourth quarter. Both were McLane grads.

BRIAN MILNE'S return to football was spoiled when the City won 18-14 in 1991. A throng of 11,000 saw ...is toss a 35-yard tailback...

mate A.J Jimerson for the deciding score with 38 seconds left. Milne, who missed his senior year at Fort LeBoeuf because of Hodgkin's Disease, carried 30 times for 164 yards and both County scores.

JIM WADE of LeBoeuf proved his versatility as the County earned a 20-13 victory in 1989. He caught four passes for 42 yards, returned two kickoffs for 70 and brought back a punt for 66. Paul Luke of North East rushed for 106 yards.

CHARLIE BAUMANN of Prep kicked field goals of 33, 50 and 43 yards in the City's 16-13 win in 1985. Dan Bokol of Iroquois caught seven passes for 65 yards, and Greg Mitchell of Harbor Creek added four more receptions for 84 as the County romped 30-12 in '84.

FRAN MIFSUD of Prep, playing for brother and City coach Jerry Mifsud, ran for 123 yards in a driving rainstorm in the 8-8 tie in 1977. Russ Madonia of Prep picked up 100 yards on the ground in the City's 16-10 win in 1975 when Kevin Horton of McDow...all kicked the City's first ... of 32...

TIBOR SOLYMOSI of Prep rushed for 151 yards as the City won 22-6 in 1973. Tony Major of Iroquois piled up 200 yards receiving in the County's 25-0 win in 1967 before 16,000 fans, the largest crowd since '47.

DAVE WENRICK of Prep quarterbacked the City to a 21-0 win in 1965 as 14,000 watched. The year before, Mina George of East hit Prep's Pat Lupo with a 7-yard TD pass with one second left to produce a 6-6 tie.

These are but a few of the thousands of athletes who have played in the 60 Save-An-Eye games. They all undoubtedly carry memories of the experience.

One tradition that changed a couple years ago is worth mentioning. This year, the County will be the home team. That means fans of the ECL team will sit on the West side of Veterans Stadium while City supporters occupy the East seats.

Regardless where they sit, those attending will get a first taste of football for this year. And, like previous games, this one should provide ...ments to savor.

Chapter 8

*T*he first decade of the new millennium for the Save-An-Eye Game featured record-shattering individual and team performances. Highlighting these 10 games were the sensational Jovon Johnson of Mercyhurst Prep and the 2006 City team. Johnson rolled up an incredible 344 yards to pace a 26-17 win in 2002. The future Iowa star accounted for 109 yards on two kickoff returns, 107 yards on two pass receptions, 86 yards on a punt return, 31 yards on a pass interception and 11 yards on two rushing tries. Johnson erupted on the game's first play, going 80 yards for a touchdown after taking a halfback pass from Ryan Sherwood-Ericsson of McDowell. Johnson scored later on the 86-yard punt return.

The 2000s

The 2006 City squad pounded out a 44-7 decision, setting game records for points scored and margin of victory. Javon Rowan of Cathedral Prep ignited a second-half blitz with a 92-yard kickoff return. He also intercepted three passes. Gary Williams of Strong Vincent bolted 92 yards after an interception and Daniel Graham of East scored twice in the lopsided win. Strong defense helped the City prevail in 2000 and 2001. The County claimed a 28-3 win in 2003, with three scoring plays of at least 50 yards.

Chris Hoderny of McDowell threw for 233 yards and three scores in a 35-28 shootout in 2004. The passing combination of Rob Mattis of McDowell to Andre Henderson of Strong Vincent led a win in 2005. The City win streak reached four thanks to a defense that allowed just seven first downs in 2007.

The County got back on top when Tyler Sargent of Fairview rushed for 225 yards and three scores in 2008. Corey Ratliff of East hit Brandon Marlow of Strong Vincent with a 59-yard touchdown pass in the closing seconds to decide a tense 21-17 contest in 2009.

City

Player	School
Mike Baker	McDowell
Jeff Bomba	Cathedral Prep
Garrison Brown	Central
Eric Carlson	Cathedral Prep
David Dickerson	East
Jason Dolak	Cathedral Prep
Kevin Farr	Strong Vincent
Brandon Green	McDowell
Randy Hawkins	Central
Pat Hoderny	McDowell
Mike Jones	Central
Mike Krahe	Cathedral Prep
Scott Kucinski	Cathedral Prep
Greg Kujawa	Cathedral Prep
Mark Laska	McDowell
Chris Lilley	East
Chad Lino	Cathedral Prep
Jake Lynch	Cathedral Prep
Garrett Mays	Cathedral Prep
Joe McFadden	Mercyhurst Prep
Tom Morgan	Cathedral Prep
Steve Murosky	McDowell
Mike Murzynski	McDowell
Eric Neavins	Central
Matt Palermo	McDowell
Don Potts	East
Owen Rhodes	Central
Jonathan Sitter	Cathedral Prep
Dante Spain	Central
Mike Stanbro	Strong Vincent
Ishmael Trainor	Mercyhurst Prep

Coaches: Tom Cacchione, Scott White, Dan Olson, Matt Morgan, Brian Moles, Jeff Gibbons, Jeff Dahlstrand, Armand Rocco of Strong Vincent

County

Player	School
Daniel Arkwright	Northwestern
Greg Baker	Girard
Dave Banta	General McLane
Trevor Cawley	North East
Chad Eades	North East
Josh Fiske	Fort LeBoeuf
Dave Frank	Iroquois
Greg Giannelli	Harbor Creek
Matt Glass	Iroquois
Robert Hammer	Fort LeBoeuf
Matt Hopkins	General McLane
Eric Hubler	Iroquois
Steve Jackson	Fort LeBoeuf
Adam Johnson	Iroquois
Joe Julian	Northwestern
John Laboski	Harbor Creek
Jason Lantzy	Fort LeBoeuf
Kevin Loftus	Iroquois
Kevin Lyons	Seneca
Jack McIntire	Fort LeBoeuf
Matt McKinney	Union City
Dave McQuiston	Harbor Creek
Ryan Miller	Corry
Mike Nelson	Northwestern
Kris Oros	Fairview
Justin Platz	Girard
Matt Riccomini	General McLane
Terry Smith	Girard
Mike Soltis	Northwestern
Dusty Soudan	Girard
Tim Stafford	General McLane
Jake Tobolewski	Girard
Jim Vaughn	Iroquois

Coaches: Phil Glass, Jim Vogt, Matt Shesman, Jerry Drozdowski, John Falk, Bernie Fitch, Pete Szoszorek of Iroquois

CITY 14 - COUNTY 7

A solid City defense limited the County to 63 yards of total offense. The County had quality runners in Josh Fiske of Fort LeBoeuf, Justin Platz and Greg Baker of Girard, but was held to 18 yards on 19 carries. Garrison Brown of Central scored the deciding touchdown on a 60-yard punt return. The other City touchdown came on an 11-yard pass from Eric Carlson of Prep to Kevin Farr of Strong Vincent. Farr had four catches for 30 yards. Jason Dolak of Prep kicked two extra points. Matt Riccomini of General McLane had a 2-yard run for the only County touchdown. Mike Soltis of Northwestern added the conversion kick. Pat Hoderny of McDowell passed for 139 yards on just five completions.

County sets sights on 2nd straight win

City to rely on pair of strong-armed QBs in Save-An-Eye game

When the City All-Stars opened practice for tonight's 62nd annual Save-An-Eye All-Star Football Game in the second week of July, Strong Vincent coach Tom Cacchione told his players to forget about their past skirmishes with each other and try and focus on being a team.

"I told them to be best friends for a month," he said. "I don't care what they do after that. They've taken the game very seriously. We've been blowing our whistles real quick in practice to keep the kids from lumping on each other."

The annual charity game that kicks off the local high-school football season gets underway tonight at 7:30 at Veterans Stadium. The City holds a 32-14-2 advantage in the series, but the County won last year's contest, 23-9.

Save-An-Eye
■ City vs. County
■ Today, 7:30 p.m.
■ Veterans Stadium

Veteran Iroquois head coach Phil Glass will guide the County.

Cacchione has been working out his team for the past three weeks, and he expects a competitive contest.

"I think our strong point is at quarterback with Eric Carlson and Pat Hoderny," Cacchione said. "Our speed is good and size-wise, we match up well."

The City will run a Wing-T offense, but its most potent weapon, Cathedral Prep's Demond Sanders, will not play. Sanders played in the Big 33 All-Star Game two weeks ago and is preparing to report to the University of Iowa for preseason practice.

Hoderny, who is headed to the University of Pittsburgh, has been named the starting quarterback. He will be joined in the backfield by McDowell's Mike Murzynski and East's David Dickerson at halfback, and Cathedral Prep's Chad Lino at fullback.

Up front, the City will start Prep's Greg Ku-

jawa at center, Prep's Jeff Bomba and Jon Sitter at guard, and Central's Eric Neavins and Prep's Scott Kucinski at the tackle. Central's Mike Jones is the starting tight end, with Prep's Garrett Mays opening at split end.

"I expect we'll be able to run the ball," Cacchione said. "The real pleasure has been working with the two quarterbacks – Hoderny and Carlson. It's been very easy to teach this offense to both of them. Both have done a great job."

The City's defensive starters include East's Chris Lilley at nose guard, Sitter and Neavins at tackle, and Prep's Mike Krahe and McDowell's Mike Baker at the end.

■ Please turn to COUNTY / 6C

During his long career coaching baseball, football and volleyball at Iroquois, Phil Glass had the opportunity to coach all-star teams in several sports. Among those was the 2000 Save-An-Eye Game with his son, Matt, as the County quarterback. "I coached the (City-County) baseball game, but the Save-An-Eye Game was much more competitive," Phil Glass said. "Matt told me that it was the hardest hitting game of his career." Part of the reason for that was the quality of players.

Phil Glass – 2000

The City team featured 11 members from Cathedral Prep, a team that lost in the PIAA Quad-A championship game the previous fall. Two County players – Bobby Hammer of Fort LeBoeuf and Dave McQuiston of Harbor Creek— played for the Erie Explosion of the Continental Indoor Football League.

The quality of the players made for some tough decisions for Glass. "We had a special group of kids. The talent was unbelievable. You tried to be fair to all the kids and get them a chance to play," he said. "We still wanted to win, so that was a big challenge to the coaches." Even with all the talent on both teams, it was a low-scoring game with the City prevailing 14-7. "I remember that the defenses were outstanding," Glass said. "Neither team could move the ball. The special teams had to be huge." It turned out to be a special team touchdown, a 60-yard punt return by Garrison Brown of Central, that decided the game.

Another quandary for Glass was installing an offense that players from 11 different schools could learn in a limited number of practices. Glass' Iroquois teams could choose from more than 200 plays. "It was hard to put in an offense. We cut (the Iroquois offense) down to about 10 plays," Glass explained.

The 2000 game was special for Glass because he was able to coach his youngest son in Matt's final appearance on the gridiron. "That was very, very special," said Phil Glass.

In 1993 another of Glass' sons, also named Phil, played in the game won by the City 7-0. "That was a little different because I was a fan at that game and not a coach," said Big Phil as the elder Glass was called. "Actually, Phil had an easier time than Matt did playing for his father. He was a defensive end and tight end. Matt was at a high profile position and always in the limelight."

Glass has a story to show the difference between being a coach and a player. The year was 1991 and Eisenhower and Iroquois were battling in the District 10 Class A championship game. In overtime, the Knights faced a fourth and goal on the 1-yard line. A touchdown would win the game for Eisenhower. But the Braves stopped the play and won 13-10 in the second overtime.

"We were almost home when coach (Sam) Talarico told me it was my son Phil that made the key tackle to keep the Knights out of the end zone," Phil Glass said. "Any parent or fan would have known, but I was so involved in the game that I didn't know who made the tackle."

One thing about the 1993 game that Glass remembers is a play late in the game. Scott Schnars, the Iroquois quarterback, went out of bounds on the City sideline. "He didn't reappear right away," Glass said. "There were a little extra curricular activities going on before Scott got back onto the field." That was the competitive nature of the Save-An-Eye games.

– Joe Mattis

WCTL's award-winning sportscasters David Harms (far left), Ron Raymond (center) and Adam Q. Frase (right) call the action from their vantage point in the press box at Veterans Stadium. Recognizing the importance of the game both as a fundraiser to assist those needing help with eye care in the community and as a final opportunity for many of the area's student athletes to showcase their talents on the football field, WCTL is honored to have been pre-promoting and providing live play-by-play coverage of the annual contest since 2000. The radio station covers the action live in the local area at 106.3 FM and 105.9 FM and streams the game for interested parties around the world at wctl.org.

City

Steve Barron	McDowell
Ed Brown	Cathedral Prep
Dan Bukowski	Mercyhurst Prep
Jarrod Carr	Central
Mike Cody	Central
Tim Dance	Cathedral Prep
Jason Easter	Cathedral Prep
Jay Ernst	Strong Vincent
Joe Evans	East
Eric Field	Cathedral Prep
Justin Grzegorzewski	Cathedral Prep
Nathan Hain	Strong Vincent
Mike Hromyak	Cathedral Prep
Alan Kantorowski	Strong Vincent
Kevin Klino	East
Chris Kuhn	McDowell
Josh Lustig	Cathedral Prep
Ryan Miller	McDowell
Rob Munch	McDowell
Mike Musone	Central
Kyle Orth	McDowell
Jesse Owens	Central
Mike Panighetti	McDowell
Matt Parsons	Cathedral Prep
Derek Rudler	McDowell
Joe Slomski	East
Jason Terry	Strong Vincent
Mark Vommaro	Mercyhurst Prep
Eric Weber	McDowell
Brad Wernicki	Cathedral Prep
Dale Williams	Cathedral Prep
Dwaon Woodard	Central
Chris Woodard	Strong Vincent

Coaches: Mike Mischler, Pat Czytuck, Rick Grychowski, Chris Grychowski, John Moore, Mark Knight, Ryan Abbott, Jim Skindell, John M. Csir, Dave McDonald of Cathedral Prep

County

Pat Aretz	General McLane
Adam Beck	General McLane
Jason Beer	Fort LeBoeuf
Aaron Bluey	Fairview
Zach Boswell	General McLane
Clay Brocious	Girard
Doug Carson	Girard
Dan Cypher	Harbor Creek
Josh Dinger	Northwestern
Zach Fuhrer	Fort LeBoeuf
Craig Gourley	Harbor Creek
Andy Griffith	General McLane
Dan Harris	Fort LeBoeuf
Mike Jaruszewicz	Fairview
Bill Jasper	Girard
Nick Krasa	Corry
Corey Lear	Northwestern
Josh Maher	Girard
Mike Mangel	Union City
Rob McGahen	Harbor Creek
Zach Meeder	Fairview
Andy Mullen	North East
Robert Mulligan	Fort LeBoeuf
Adam Podufal	Girard
Mike Roach	Girard
Luke Rohler	Girard
Joe Scott	Fort LeBoeuf
Dan Shields	Fort LeBoeuf
Mick Solymosi	Fairview
Mike Sowers	Girard
Dave Sundberg	Fairview

Coaches: Mina George, D.J. Vendetti, Bob Vasik, Jamie Cipalla, Mike Liebel, Jim Senyo, Dan Senyo, Ed Heidt, Jeff Joint of Girard

CITY 17 - COUNTY 6

The speed of the City and the mistakes of the County were deciding factors in this game. The County had turnover problems, losing five fumbles and a pass interception. Tim Dance of Prep, despite nursing a bruised shin, had 10 carries for 74 yards. Both City touchdowns were on passes, a 50-yarder from Joe Slomski of East to Joe Evans of East and an 8-yarder from Mike Panighetti of McDowell to Josh Lustig of Prep. Kyle Orth of McDowell kicked a 42-yard field goal and two extra points. Dan Shields of Fort LeBoeuf scored the County touchdown on a 10-yard run. Corey Lear of Northwestern led the County ground game with 11 carries for 48 yards.

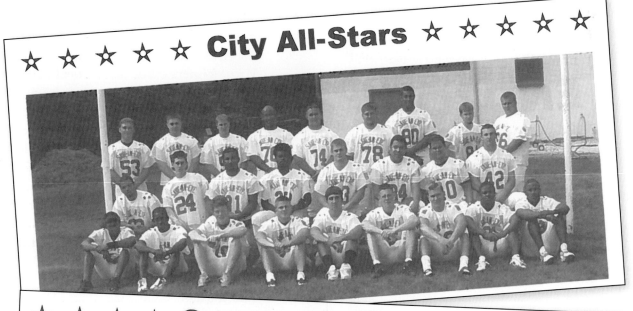

★ ★ ★ ★ ☆ **City All-Stars** ★ ★ ★ ★ ★

★ ★ ★ ☆ **County All-Stars** ★ ★ ★ ★ ★

City

Todd Aldrich	McDowell
Mike Bean	McDowell
Eric Cruz	East
Nathan Evers	McDowell
Mike Fisher	McDowell
Jesse Francis	Central
Ryan Gaines	Strong Vincent
Justin Gannoe	Mercyhurst Prep
Nick Gordon	East
Joe Grack	McDowell
Mark Harrington	Cathedral Prep
Dijon Jefferson	Central
Shane Johnson	Strong Vincent
Jovon Johnson	Mercyhurst Prep
Antonio Jones	Central
Daryl Joyce	East
Nick Lubahn	McDowell
Phil Lupo	Cathedral Prep
Gary Magorien	McDowell
Matt Magyar	Cathedral Prep
Arsenio McAdory	East
Dan Milhisler	Cathedral Prep
Gene Natale	Cathedral Prep
Derick Page	Central
Matthew Parker	McDowell
Robert Robison	Strong Vincent
Dywon Rowan	Mercyhurst Prep
Ryan Sherwood-Ericsson	McDowell
Jason Sibley	Mercyhurst Prep
Ebbo Skadhague	Cathedral Prep
Goral Soldo	Central
Steve Thomas	Central
Ashley Watts	Strong Vincent
Andy Willis	Mercyhurst Prep
Peter Wishnok	McDowell

Coaches: Pat DiPaolo, Roosevelt Benjamin, Andre Bridgett, Jerry Carr, Doug England, Chris Gaub, Tom Laird, Ken Nickson of Central

County

Scott Brumagin	Seneca
Jason Danowski	Harbor Creek
Paul Duran	Fort LeBoeuf
Jacob Fiske	Fort LeBoeuf
Jim Folmar	North East
Brent Freeburg	Fort LeBoeuf
Jeff Goodwill	Corry
Jay Grochulski	Iroquois
Tony Hammer	Fort LeBoeuf
Dave Jazenski	Iroquois
Chris Kelly	North East
Rob Klus	Union City
Dan Kubiak	General McLane
Ben Kuchta	North East
Andy Kuzma	Corry
Shawn Leehan	Northwestern
Matt Maisner	Fort LeBoeuf
Pat Murzynski	Iroquois
Ed Pfeiffer	Seneca
Joe Piazza	Seneca
Kevin Porath	General McLane
Seth Randall	North East
Greg Renker	Harbor Creek
Larry Skeel	Northwestern
Brad Skelton	Fort LeBoeuf
Greg Smialek	Girard
Josh Vogel	Harbor Creek
Dave Vrenna	Iroquois
Tate Warren	Seneca
Eric Weidler	Girard
Matt Widdowson	Harbor Creek
Joe Yuhas	Girard

Coaches: Randy Gunther, Dana Anderson, Dave Buzard, Terry Dawley, Darren Galkowski, Rob Grygier, Bill Hoffman, J Knablein, Dave Murosky, Eric Sharie, Jim Sheldon, Paul Yoculan of Seneca

CITY 26 - COUNTY 17

*J*ovon Johnson of Mercyhurst Prep put on one of the finest individual performances in game history. The future Iowa defensive back piled up 344 total yards, with 109 yards on two kickoff returns, 107 yards on two pass receptions, 86 yards on a punt return, 31 yards on a pass interception and 11 yards on two rushing attempts. Johnson set the tone on the game's first play when he took a halfback pass from Ryan Sherwood-Ericsson of McDowell and went 80 yards for a touchdown. Johnson also scored on the 86-yard punt return. Dywon Rowan of Mercyhurst Prep ran 7 yards and Sherwood-Ericsson plunged 1 yard for the other City scores. Josh Vogel of Harbor Creek had a 31-yard touchdown run and Dave Jazenski of Iroquois returned a fumble 31 yards for a touchdown for the County. Matt Widdowson of Harbor Creek kicked a 41-yard field goal.

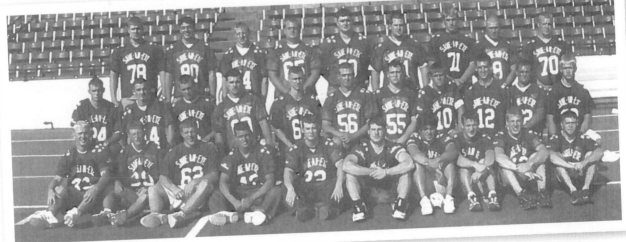

Top: City Team, Bottom: County Team

When the City team scored on the first play from scrimmage in the 2002 Save-An-Eye Game, it was a surprise to most of the fans in the stands. Well, almost everyone. One spectator who was not caught off-guard was longtime Erie detective and District Judge Dom DiPaolo. Actually, he expected it.

"The City team was practicing at Central that summer because my son, Pat, was coaching the team," DiPaolo said. "He would stop over every day after practice. The week of the game he told me, 'Wait 'til you see what we open with. We'll catch them sleeping.'"

Pat DiPaolo – Coach 2002

On the play after the opening kickoff, McDowell halfback Ryan Sherwood-Ericsson took a handoff and ran to his right before stopping and lofting a pass to Jovon Johnson who completed the 80-yard pass play for a touchdown. "We were so excited about the play," said Cathedral Prep's Dan Milhisler, who played middle linebacker in the City's 26-17 win in front of 7,500 fans at Veterans Stadium. "We knew that they would be looking at Ryan because he was such a threat and that Jovon would be open. That opening play lit a fire under us."

Pat DiPaolo, who has a serious health problem with Lyme Disease, is unable to talk about the play today. But immediately after the game, nothing else was on his mind. Here is how he related it in the Erie Times-News. "A couple of weeks ago I was sitting there thinking that if we put Ryan and Dywon (Rowan) in the backfield and we run student body right, they would all come flying up because they want to smack somebody," DiPaolo said.

Following the offensive flow, County players smacked someone all right, but none of them was even close to Johnson after he caught the pass and sped down the sideline.

Johnson, who went on to play defensive back for the University of Iowa, the Pittsburgh Steelers and for several teams in the Canadian Football League, had an outstanding performance that will be difficult to duplicate. "Pat never coached against Johnson because Central did not play Mercyhurst," Dom DiPaolo said. "But after one (Save-An-Eye) practice, he said, 'Jovon is the real deal.'"

After graduating from Cathedral Prep in 1987, Pat DiPaolo was selected to play for the City as a placekicker. A pulled hamstring just days before the game put him on the sideline, but DiPaolo made sure his City team made a quick statement in the game when he returned to coach 15 years later.

– Joe Mattis

Certificate of Appreciation
awarded to
Fred Ferraro

for Outstanding Athletic Ability
and for his contribution to the
promotion of athletics
in the City and County of Erie, Penna.

and as an expression of thanks
for his participation in the 1943

LIONS CLUB ANNUAL "SAVE AN EYE"
ALL STAR
EAST-WEST FOOTBALL GAME

Sponsored for the Conservation of Eyesight
in our Community

_____
PRESIDENT

_____
SECRETARY

Ferraro's experience in the 1943 Save-An-Eye Game was important
to him–so important that he stayed connected to it and went on to
become the Lions Club President in 2002

City

Donnye Aiken	Central
William Bell	Strong Vincent
Brian Bell	Strong Vincent
Brian Bixby	Cathedral Prep
Zack Brandt	Mercyhurst Prep
Don Brown	Cathedral Prep
Mike Cacchione	McDowell
Kyle Caldwell	McDowell
Justin Carr	Central
Tom Danias	East
David Edwards	Cathedral Prep
Greg Flick	McDowell
Joe Gabbard	McDowell
James Grygier	McDowell
David Hauser	Cathedral Prep
John Hersch	Cathedral Prep
Sean Hoffman	McDowell
Willie Jordan	Strong Vincent
Brett Krizanik	McDowell
Ryan Marovich	McDowell
Travis Matson	Mercyhurst Prep
Brian McCullough	Strong Vincent
Willie Murel	Central
Eric Newlin	McDowell
Dave Pernice	McDowell
Matthew Rapp	McDowell
Jermaine Selby	Strong Vincent
Justin Senita	Cathedral Prep
Jason Senita	Cathedral Prep
Kory Smith	Cathedral Prep
Kyle Snoke	Cathedral Prep
Donnell Tangle	Central
Tom Wallace	Central
Jovan Williams	Strong Vincent

Coaches: Jon Cacchione, Bob Hoffman, Joe Bufalino, Mike Bowers, Mark Soboleski, Jeff Brzezinski, Chris Caldwell, Pat Mifsud, Brad Orlando, Dave Grack, Mark Chludzinski of McDowell

County

Shawn Adams	Union City
Ben Behringer	Girard
D.J. Bross	Seneca
Billy Brown	Northwestern
Casey Cleveland	Girard
Joel Czurnecki	Harbor Creek
Jason Dersch	Northwestern
Shane Donnelly	General McLane
Pat Duda	Harbor Creek
Adam English	Northwestern
Ben Fenell	Northwestern
Jared Flowers	Harbor Creek
Paul Garofalo	General McLane
Justin Herring	Girard
Joe Kowle	North East
Patrick Kurtz	Fort LeBoeuf
Jonathan Kutterna	North East
Ryan Learn	Harbor Creek
Jeremy Lightner	Fairview
Paul Nies	Seneca
Dan Palmer	Northwestern
Mike Pruveadenti	General McLane
Jarad Roach	General McLane
Nick Roseberry	General McLane
Seth Rotko	Northwestern
Bob Sargent	Northwestern
Zack Schafer	Northwestern
Matt Seth	General McLane
Kyle Smith	Harbor Creek
Lucas Vance	Corry
Bill Warner	Northwestern

Coaches: Jim Wells, Luke Graham, Scott Jenco, Rob Lange, Don Chludzinski, D.K. McDonald of General McLane

COUNTY 28 - CITY 3

Big plays paved the way for the County. Shawn Adams of Union City returned a fumble recovery 75 yards for a score. Two other touchdowns came on long passes, a 62-yarder from Matt Seth of General McLane to Ryan Learn of Harbor Creek and a 50-yarder from Ben Fenell to former Northwestern teammate Dan Palmer. Fenell also ran for a 1-yard touchdown. Kyle Snoke of Cathedral Prep kicked a 33-yard field goal for the City's only points. Fenell completed 7 of 12 passes for 96 yards. Seth led the County with 61 yards on seven carries and caught four passes for 36 yards. The County owned a 324-160 edge in total yards. Jeremy Lightner of Fairview had two interceptions for the County and Pat Duda had 13 tackles.

65th Annual Save An Eye Football Game

August 1, 2003
Erie Veterans Memorial Stadium

Presented by
HAMOT
SPORTS MEDICINE

Recalled by Ben Fenell's mother, Janine Fenell

"" In 1955, Tony Nunes earned the All-City quarterback position and capped his high school career with a brilliant performance in the Lions Club Save-An-Eye All-Star football game. Tony went on to play and coach football until 2003 when he retired.

Tony Nunes

Tony Nunes – 1955
Ben Fenell – 2003

Ben Fenell

In 2002, Ben Fenell, Tony's cousin, earned the All-County quarterback position as well as All-County punter. The County beat the city big that year. Ben has also gone on to coach area football working with Rob Glus at Conneaut Valley and now with Coach Leonard Ford at East.

Both men were true team players and their love of football runs deep. ""

★ City All-Stars ★

TOP ROW: Dave Pernice; Ryan Marovich; Kyle Caldwell; Kory Smith; Justin Senita; David Hauser; David Edwards; Willie Jordan; Jason Senita; Brian Bixby; Sean Hoffman.
MIDDLE ROW: Matthew Rapp; Justin Carr; Brian McCullough; Gregory Flick; Michael Cacchione; Jovan Williams; Brian Bell; Don Brown; Kyle Snoke; John Hersch; Zack Brandt; Willie Murel; Thomas Wallace.
BOTTOM ROW: William Bell; Jermaine Selby; Donnye Aiken; Brett Krizanik; James Grygier; Thomas Danias, Jr.; Eric Newlin; Travis Matson; Joe Gabbard.
ABSENT: Donnell Tangle

County All-Stars

TOP ROW: Shawn Adams; Ben Behringer; Bill Warner; Benjamin Fennell; D. J. Bross; Jason Dersch; Nick Roseberry; Justin Herring.
MIDDLE ROW: Patrick Kurtz; Casey Cleveland; Lucas Vance; Adam English; Mike Pruveadenti; Jarad Roach; Pat Duda; Seth Rotko.
BOTTOM ROW: Jared Flowers; Bob Sargent; Zack Schafer; Ryan Learn; Paul Nies; Matt Seth; Paul Garofalo; Shane Donnelly.
ABSENT: Dan Palmer; Billy Brown; Jeremy Lightner; Joe Kowle; Joel Czurnecki; Jonathan Kutterna; Kyle Smith.

Mike Baniszewski .... Mercyhurst Prep
J.B. Britton .... McDowell
Tyrone Buckner .... Cathedral Prep
Tommy Clanton .... Central
Deonte Colley .... Central
Eric Costello .... Central
Nick Curry .... McDowell
Anthony Dabrowski .... Cathedral Prep
Ryan Drabina .... Cathedral Prep
Jeff Ernst .... Strong Vincent
Mike Freeman .... Cathedral Prep
Kyle Frost .... East
Mike Golson .... East
Roland Haines .... East
Chris Hoderny .... McDowell
Marquelle Knight .... Cathedral Prep
Desuan Lindsey .... Cathedral Prep
Josh Mezzacapo .... Cathedral Prep
Hardin Moss .... East
David Nesselhauf .... Cathedral Prep
Paul Petruso .... McDowell
Mike Pistone .... McDowell
Jonathan Quinn .... East
Matt Raun .... Cathedral Prep
Mike Savelli .... Cathedral Prep
Bryan Sechrist .... Cathedral Prep
Vince Senita .... McDowell
Matt Shields .... East
Brian Shreve .... McDowell
Dan Sockett .... McDowell
Tim Taylor .... Cathedral Prep
Scott Wilcox .... East
Peter Yeaney .... Cathedral Prep

Coaches: Jeff Dahlstrand, Tiger LaVerde, Tom Lenox, Gary Hess, Kevin Horton, Joe Dahlstrand, Steve Boucher of East

John Basco .... Girard
Matt Beidler .... Fort LeBoeuf
Brent Boyd .... Seneca
Tim Campbell .... Fort LeBoeuf
Russell Chase .... Girard
Mike Coletta .... North East
Ken Cox .... Iroquois
Andy Duran .... Fort LeBoeuf
Mike Dworakowski .... Girard
Tim Finegan .... General McLane
Denny Gray .... North East
Chris Grettler .... Girard
Matt Griffith .... General McLane
Brett Hall .... Northwestern
Matt Hedlund .... Harbor Creek
Jared Johnson .... Fort LeBoeuf
Joe Koech .... Girard
Cory Lamison .... Fort LeBoeuf
Matt McShane .... Iroquois
Matt Nelson .... Girard
Doug Osborn .... Fort LeBoeuf
Steve Puskar .... Seneca
Jason Sadowski .... Union City
Dan Sheridan .... Harbor Creek
Ryan Stephenson .... Fairview
Rickie Thompson .... North East
Mike Tripp .... Girard
Kevin Walker .... General McLane
Chris Wheeler .... General McLane

Coaches: Joe Tarasovitch, John Campbell, Tom Shade, Jim Schoonover, Tim Holland, Jason Beer, Chris Hudnol, Bob Hoffman, Bob Hammer of Fort LeBoeuf

CITY 35 - COUNTY 28

$\mathcal{C}$hris Hoderny of McDowell completed 7 of 10 passes for 233 yards and three touchdowns. Hoderny hit Bryan Sechrist of Cathedral Prep for scoring passes of 45 and 58 yards and threw 86 yards to Tyrone Buckner of Prep on a screen pass for another touchdown. Sechrist caught three passes for 123 yards. Tommy Clanton of Central and Vince Senita of McDowell scored on short runs for the City. Fort LeBoeuf quarterback Cory Lamison threw for 136 yards, including a touchdown pass to Doug Osborn of Fort LeBoeuf. Rickie Thompson of North East scored on runs of 1 and 5 yards and Mike Tripp of Girard ran 1 yard for County scores. The game ended when Kevin Walker of General McLane returned an intercepted pass 57 yards before being stopped. The City was forced to pass in the closing seconds to meet the minimum requirement under Save-An-Eye rules.

Passing drama

Tyrone Buckner of Cathedral Prep, left, runs for a few of his 90 yards for the City team as the County's Kevin Walker of General McLane pursues during the Save-An-Eye Game Friday at Veterans Stadium.

GREG WOHLFORD/Erie Times-News

Facing quota, City nearly throws away Save-An-Eye Game

By JOE MATTIS
joe.mattis@timesnews.com

The City was leading by a touchdown and had the ball with seconds remaining in the Erie Lions Save-An-Eye G... Friday at V...

turf after returning the ball 57 yards could the City breathe easy with a 35-28 victory.

"I knew I had the pick," Walk-...

"It really doesn't get any better than this," winning coach Jeff Dahlstrand said. "These people got their money's worth."

Each team showed their offensive power in the high-scoring game

and Prep's Peter Yeaney kicked five extra points.

Fort LeBoeuf qua... Cory Lamison ... yards ...

A pair of Mikes—Freeman and Savelli—began playing football together as fifth-graders for the St. Andrew Spartans in 1996. Their coach, for only one season before he went on to East High, was Jeff Dahlstrand.

Fast forward to 2004. Both Freeman, a wide receiver, and Savelli, a defensive back, had concluded their high school playing days at Cathedral Prep. But both had one more game. They would be teammates for the City team in the Save-An-Eye game coached by . . . Jeff Dahlstrand. "I was so happy they were selected to play in the game," Dahlstrand said. "They were both great kids, and they were both good football players."

Dahlstrand was aware of something else that Freeman and Savelli had in common. They each had a parent die while they were in high school—Freeman's mother Janice and Savelli's father Mario.

Jeff Dahlstrand – Coach 2004

When Dahlstrand gave his pre-game talk to this team, he remembered something he told all the players. "I made mention that we had guys that lost family members," Dahlstrand said. "I didn't say their names, but we dedicated the game to them. The other kids responded. You could see it in their eyes."

The City beat the County 35-28 in that game. The rules almost allowed the County to score a touchdown and possibly tie the game on the last play. General McLane's Kevin Walker picked off a City pass and returned in 57 yards before being tackled. "The rules say we have to throw 15 passes," said Dahlstrand as he leafed through the instructions he was given by members of the Erie Lions Club that summer. "We had to pass (on the last play) because of the rules."

McDowell's Chris Hoderny was the City's starting quarterback, even though Dahlstrand said Hoderny wasn't the Trojan starter as a senior. "I knew he could fit into our offense," Dahlstrand said of Hoderny. "He was tall, poised, and had a nice touch. And he had a great game that helped him go to Gannon." Hoderny was outstanding, throwing for 233 yards and three touchdowns, two of them to Prep's Bryan Sechrist. But the pass play that Dahlstrand remembers the most was an 86-yard screen pass from Hodeny to Prep speedster Tyrone Buckner. "That screen play was our ace in the hole," Dahlstrand said. "I got that play from Tiger Laverde, who had coached at Franklin."

Freeman's mother had died of cancer so in 2008 he initiated the Courage Cup for the regular season game between Cathedral Prep and McDowell. A portion of each ticket sold was earmarked for cancer research in the Erie Area. That game was renamed the Cureage Cup the following year and continues to be played annually.

– Joe Mattis

Lions ⓛ Club

66th Annual Save An Eye
All Star Football Game
To Benefit Eye Care for Needy Children

City All Stars

County All Stars

Erie Veterans Memorial Stadium
Friday August 6, 2004

Presented by **HAMOT SPORTS MEDICINE** **Hamot**

City

Emanuel Beason	Strong Vincent
Tony Bozich	Cathedral Prep
Demetric Braxton	McDowell
James Carson	Cathedral Prep
Joe Chevalier	Mercyhurst Prep
DeShawn Crosby	Strong Vincent
Pat Evans	Cathedral Prep
Christian Fleming	Strong Vincent
Bryan Gaines	Strong Vincent
Markus Graham	Cathedral Prep
Vince Graham	Strong Vincent
Duane Hemphill	Strong Vincent
Andre Henderson	Strong Vincent
Mario Henry	Strong Vincent
Matt Hintz	Cathedral Prep
Todd Kinnear	Mercyhurst Prep
Matt Kozer	McDowell
Adam Krizanik	McDowell
Jay Marquis	McDowell
Rob Mattis	McDowell
Rashad McAdory	East
T.J. McGraw	McDowell
Brandon McLaurin	Strong Vincent
Jesse Meade	McDowell
Sean Nutter	Cathedral Prep
Ronald Palmer	Central
Andy Parshall	McDowell
Derek Selby	Strong Vincent
Lonnie Spearman	Strong Vincent
Craig VanTassel	Strong Vincent
Dupre Wallace	Central
Joe Welton	Central
Jayson White	McDowell

Coach: Tom Cacchione, Jeff Gibbens, Scott White, Lonnie Wright, Chris Starocci, Dan Olsen, Tony Hollingsworth, Tracy Lindsey, John Ferrare, Chris Spooner, Keven Boxer of Strong Vincent

County

Jamie Agresti	General McLane
Mike Artise	North East
Chad Baccus	Fairview
Brandon Baker	Fort LeBoeuf
Jason Beebe	Seneca
Jordan Belosh	General McLane
Josh Best	North East
Mark Brooks	Harbor Creek
Jake Comer	Harbor Creek
Mitch Dabrowski	Iroquois
John DiMattio	Girard
Jim Gdanetz	General McLane
Dan Howell	Iroquois
Andrew Kimmy	North East
Zach Kuchta	North East
Chad Lander	North East
Craig Lawrence	Fairview
Dave Murzynski	Harbor Creek
Mike Proctor	Fort LeBoeuf
Nick Schafer	Northwestern
Mark Schinke	Girard
Ryan Schulz	Fort LeBoeuf
Jerahmy Smith	Iroquois
Branden Stearns	General McLane
Phil Stuczynski	Girard
Andy Swift	General McLane
Kevin Tolon	Harbor Creek
Tom Voelker	Iroquois
Andy Walczyk	Fort LeBoeuf
Josh Warren	Harbor Creek
Mike Williams	North East
Kiel Wolf	Corry
Kyle Wunz	Northwestern

Coach: Matt Shesman, Joe Shesman, Rich Goodenow, Walley Mahle, Bob Sensor, Ed Orris, Shawn Humes, Paul Pennington of North East

CITY 24 - COUNTY 12

$\mathcal{A}$ndre Henderson of Strong Vincent caught six passes for 169 yards including a 41-yard touchdown pitch from Rob Mattis of McDowell. Mattis completed 6 of 11 passes for 126 yards. Mattis and Jayson White of McDowell each scored on 1-yard runs for the City. The Mattis score was set up by a 39-yard interception return by T.J. McGraw of McDowell. Pat Evans of Cathedral Prep kicked three extra points and a 39-yard field goal for the winners. The field goal was set up when Christian Fleming blocked a punt and former Strong Vincent teammate Emanuel Beason recovered at the County 21-yard line. Chad Baccus of Fairview scored both County touchdowns on runs of 4 and 2 yards.

City wraps up County

Henderson helps put game out of reach early

By JOE MATTIS
joe.mattis@timesnews.com

Andre Henderson waited a month to get the opportunity to play on offense.
After playing only on defense in the PSFCA All-Star Game in Altoona in June, Henderson showed the crowd of 6,500 fans at Veterans Stadium what he could do as a wide receiver Friday.

City..............24
County 12

■ **Key stat:** City led 24-0 at halftime.

➤ **Inside:** Summary, 4D

The Strong Vincent grad caught six passes for 169 yards and one touchdown to lead the City to a 24-12 win in the 67th Erie Lions Club Save-An-Eye Football Game.
"I've been ready," said Henderson, a first-team selection on the Pennsylvania Football News All-State team as a defensive back. "I waited to get my hand back on the ball. They gave me a couple of passes and I made the plays."
One of Henderson's catches was on a 41-yard pass from McDowell's Rob Mattis that gave the City a 21-0 lead in the second quarter.

➤ Please see EYE, 4D

GAME BREAKER

Andre Henderson
City
■ **Position:** wide receiver
■ **Ht:** 6-1 ■ **Wt:** 180

Receptions...................6
Yards 169
TDs 1

JIMMIE PRESLEY/Erie Times-News

County All-Stars running back Zach Kuchta, right, gets tackled by City All-Star DeShawn Crosby as Markus Graham, left, moves in on the play during the 67th Erie Lions Club Save-An-Eye Football Game at Veterans Stadium on Friday. Kuchta led the County with nine carries for 45 yards.

City

Andrew Adamus	Cathedral Prep
Jake Agresti	Mercyhurst Prep
Rob Barger	Mercyhurst Prep
Hank Bink	Mercyhurst Prep
John Csir	Cathedral Prep
Antonio Foster	Central
Jordan Fracassi	Central
Anthony Fuhrman	Strong Vincent
Adlen Gilmore	East
Justin Gomes	McDowell
Daniel Graham	East
Mike Gray	East
Aaron Grill	Mercyhurst Prep
Tony Haefner	East
Matthew Hawryliw	Mercyhurst Prep
Frank Hazlett	Cathedral Prep
Tony Henderson	Central
Jake Jurkiewicz	Strong Vincent
John Koester	McDowell
Eric Komar	Mercyhurst Prep
Kyle Latzo	Cathedral Prep
Daniel LeFaiver	Mercyhurst Prep
Matthew Lewis	Strong Vincent
Travis Litz	Central
Terrance McLaren	Mercyhurst Prep
Brett Niemeic	Cathedral Prep
Brian Ras	McDowell
Javon Rowan	Cathedral Prep
William Thames	East
Anthony Weaver	McDowell
Jonathan Wentz	Cathedral Prep
Gary Williams	Strong Vincent

Coaches: Matt Morgan, Dan DiTullio, Drew Botelho, Joe Chevalier, Mike Baniszewski, Ryan Abbott, Rich Krafty, Nate Hain of Mercyhurst Prep

County

Tyler Amy	Corry
Dan Barringer	Iroquois
Steve Barringer	Iroquois
Stephen Blose	Harbor Creek
Aaron Brown	Girard
Nicholas Carson	Corry
Tom Dodd	Union City
Jeremy Dornhoefer	Iroquois
Jimmy Douglas	Northwestern
Jeff Erdman	General McLane
Adam Farrell	Fort LeBoeuf
Shawn Giewont	Seneca
Dan Goodman	Seneca
Michael Hedlund	Harbor Creek
Andy Herget	Iroquois
Derrick Johnson	Girard
Greg Lane	Fairview
William McCray	Corry
Todd Morse	Northwestern
Jarryd Pearson	Iroquois
Ty Perry	Fairview
Matt Pfadt	Harbor Creek
Erik Pollard	Fairview
Alex Retcofsky	Fairview
Matt Scheuer	Girard
Austin Schroder	North East
Kevin Stephenson	Fairview
Brendan Taylor	Girard
Adam VanHooser	Iroquois
Joshua Voelker	Harbor Creek
Greg Waples	Fairview
Steven Woods	General McLane
Jonathan Wroblewski	Seneca

Coaches: Dan Budziszewski, John Ballard, Tom Blose, Marty Dale, Chris Carpin, Mark Brooks, Tom Erdman of Harbor Creek

CITY 44 - COUNTY 7

The City ran wild in the first game played on the new Veterans Stadium artificial turf. The 44 points and the 37-point difference were both Save-An-Eye records. The City scored 34 unanswered points in the second half. A 92-yard kickoff return by Javon Rowan of Cathedral Prep to open the second half ignited the romp. Rowan also intercepted three passes. Daniel Graham of East scored two touchdowns on runs of 60 and 4 yards. John Csir of Prep ran 1 yard, Jon Wentz of Prep ran 8 yards and Gary Williams of Strong Vincent went 92 yards with an interception return for other City touchdowns. Justin Gomes of McDowell kicked a 29-yard field goal and five extra points. The County's only score came on a 22-yard pass from Dan Barringer of Iroquois to Shawn Giewont of Seneca. Stephen Blose of Harbor Creek kicked the PAT. Anthony Weaver of McDowell rushed 13 times for 103 yards.

68TH ANNUAL SAVE-AN-EYE GAME

JANET B. CAMPBELL/Erie Times-News

City running back I. Daniel Graham outruns the County's Jonathan Wroblewski on the way to scoring the first touchdown of the Save-An-Eye Game on Friday. Graham scored twice in the game.

City stampede

CITY   Rowan, Graham lead City to rout nty team

Game 69 – July 27, 2007

City

Craig Baniszewski	Mercyhurst Prep
Jordan Bukowski	McDowell
Chris Buzas	Cathedral Prep
Jovan Crosby	East
Tony D'Albora	Central
Garrick Drabina	Cathedral Prep
Brandon Dunn	Central
Neal Eicher	Mercyhurst Prep
Eric Fenton	McDowell
Matt Fome	McDowell
Donte Harden	Strong Vincent
Markel Hubbart	East
Ashton Jones	Strong Vincent
Jared Kaufmann	Cathedral Prep
Sam Kinnear	Mercyhurst Prep
Marcus Kouczynski	McDowell
Andy Kunic	Mercyhurst Prep
Lamont McWilliams	Strong Vincent
Dan Muldowney	McDowell
Jayson Nickson	Mercyhurst Prep
Mike Noble	Strong Vincent
Chad Noce	McDowell
Buddy O'Leary	Mercyhurst Prep
David Orlando	Cathedral Prep
Dave Roach	Cathedral Prep
Todd Russell	Central
Abe Satterfield	Cathedral Prep
Jon Sayles	Central
Kyle Sliker	McDowell
David Tate	Strong Vincent
Brent Thompson	Cathedral Prep
Luca Viglione	Cathedral Prep
Durfey Wells Jr.	Strong Vincent

Coaches: Mark Soboleski, Ron Rudler, Todd Strasenburgh, Craig Villa, Gary Magorian, Kim Parker of McDowell

County

Anthony Azevedo	Iroquois
Kyle Beebe	Seneca
Mike Bell	Iroquois
Greg Bush	North East
Brad Callan	General McLane
Craig Catalfu	Corry
Shane Cyphert	Seneca
Jeremy Ditzler	Iroquois
Brandan Eck	Corry
Paul Flick	Corry
Corey Frantz	Iroquois
Kyle Gates	Corry
Mike Gdanetz	Seneca
Jesse Heubel	Seneca
Tori Holes	Fort LeBoeuf
Cameron Johnson	Northwestern
Kyle Koeth	Girard
John Mangol	Union City
Jim Mathers	North East
Jack McCann	Fairview
Matt Michael	Fairview
Robert Moore	Northwestern
Kelly Ponsoll	General McLane
J.R. Porter	North East
Jake Randolph	Iroquois
Joe Rizzo	North East
Josh Schneider	Harbor Creek
Dan Skelton	General McLane
Travis Trojan	Harbor Creek
Frank Vicary	North East
Mike Wright	Girard

Coaches: Jamie Cipalla, D.J. Hough, Tim Neal of Northwestern

CITY 34 - COUNTY 7

A solid defense paved the way to the City's fourth straight win and a 39-15-2 lead in the series. The County managed only seven first downs and 142 yards of offense. Durfey Wells of Strong Vincent and Brent Thompson of Cathedral Prep were defensive standouts. Wells had three sacks while chasing County quarterbacks the entire game. Thompson had two interceptions, returning one for a touchdown. He also recovered a fumble to set up another touchdown. Lamont McWilliams of Strong Vincent raced 54 yards for a touchdown on the second play from scrimmage. Thompson's fumble recovery on the County 9-yard line set up a 1-yard plunge by Donte Harden of Strong Vincent. Thompson then picked off a pass and went 52 yards for another City score. Brandon Dunn of Central grabbed a 16-yard touchdown pass from Dave Roach of Prep and Craig Baniszewski of Mercyhurst Prep tossed 2 yards to Abe Satterfield of Prep for the other City touchdowns. Jared Kaufmann of Prep kicked two extra points and Harden ran for a 2-point conversion. The only County score came on a 1-yard plunge by Frank Vicary of North East. The touchdown was set up by a fumble recovery by Dan Skelton of General McLane. Jeremy Ditzler of Iroquois kicked the County PAT.

Save an Eye City football player and Cathedral Prep graduate Abe Satterfield prepares for practice at Gus Anderson Field recently. Satterfield said he plans to enjoy his last venture on a high school football field and hopes his team wins the 69th annual game Friday.

JANET B. CAMPBELL/Erie Times-News

Looking forward to a ...
Fun finish

Versatile Satterfield hopes focused, enjoyable practices pay off for City

...ATTIS
...mesnews.com

they are always joking around and keeping us loose."

"Those two are the leaders of the band, and I mean that in a good way," City coach ...boleski said of the two Strong Vin-... "They don't let ...

...Frida... ...th

READY FOR SOME FOOTF...
■ **What:** 69th Save An E...
Football Game
■ **When:** Frid...
■ **W...**

66 I played linebacker, long snapper and left guard. I remember more from the practices than I do from the game. Everyone that you are playing with was your rival for four years of high school. Practices were pretty intense trying to get along with some of the guys you hated seeing line up across from you the last four years. Sometimes there was a little bad blood and you tried to get that out to move on and be teammates in the game.

Luca Viglione – 2007

We got to know everyone and became friends instead of enemies. 99

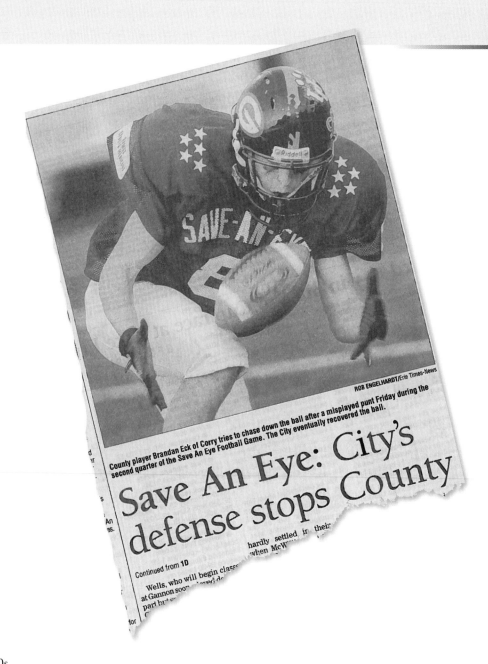

ROB ENGELHARDT/Erie Times-News

County player Brandan Eck of Corry tries to chase down the ball after a misplayed punt Friday during the second quarter of the Save An Eye Football Game. The City eventually recovered the ball.

Save An Eye: City's defense stops County

Continued from 1D

Wells, who will begin class at Gannon soon...
part b...

hardly settled in their when McW...

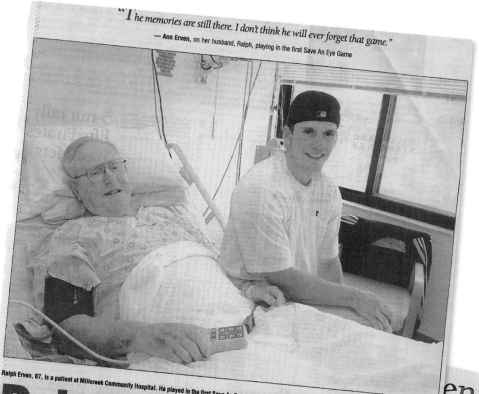

"The memories are still there. I don't think he will ever forget that game."

— **Ann Erven**, on her husband, Ralph, playing in the first Save An Eye Game

Ralph Erven, 87, is a patient at Millcreek Community Hospital. He played in the first Save An Eye Game in 1939. His grandson, Corey Frantz, will play in today's game.

JACK HANRAHAN/Erie Times-News

Relative excitement

Ralph Erven played in the first Save An Eye Game in 1939. Today, he hopes to leave the hospital and watch his grandson play in the game.

By JOE MATTIS

second-half touchdown in the West's

Erven expected to be back at Veterans Stadium tonight, when the City plays the County in the 69th charity game.

Erven had a special reason to do so. His grandson, Corey Frantz of Iroquois, will play for the City as they meet the City's

Ervens ha he will play in the game. He 19 great. has practiced at quarterback, running back, wide receiver, free safety and strong safety. Because of that, he has earned a new nickname.

"(General McLane's) Kelley Ponsoll called me 'Utility,' and that's my nickname now," Frantz said.

Frantz, who also wrestled and played baseball for the Braves, has learned some more things about his grandfather's playing days.

"They called him 'Bull' because he played on the defensive line," Frantz said. "I guess he was an animal."

Erven said he weighed 180 pounds when he played at Fairview, big for a lineman in those days. He said that every player saw action in the first half of the Save An Eye Game, and then the coaches selected those who performed the best to play in the second half.

Now that he knows of his grandfather's exploits in that game nearly 70 years ago, Frantz has a special rea play well.

"That do

If Erven cannot attend the game, Frantz and se nty teammat Ce. b and do about my s not sure what posi-

Former Iroquois player Corey Frantz, left, will play in the Erie Lions Club Save An Eye All-Star Football Game tonight, nearly 70 years after his grandfather, Ralph Erven, played in the first game.

JANET B. CAMPBELL/Erie Times-News

said. "The greatest thing would be if I could block a punt late in the game, and then be on up on him by ru for a

bragging rig love that

City

Nick Arrigo	Mercyhurst Prep
Brendan Barber	Cathedral Prep
Nate Beaman	McDowell
Mike Blount	Cathedral Prep
Jeremy Burroughs	McDowell
Melquwan Carson	East
James Cowles	Mercyhurst Prep
Billy D'Andrea	Mercyhurst Prep
Jason Dorich	Mercyhurst Prep
Nick Galich	McDowell
Rob Guriel	McDowell
Calyn Hamilton	Strong Vincent
Nick Harpster	McDowell
Dave Herbe	McDowell
Joe Jelinek	Mercyhurst Prep
Mike Keller	Strong Vincent
Bryant Kimball	McDowell
Marquis Knight	Strong Vincent
Alex Macrino	Mercyhurst Prep
Mike Mathis	East
Tajh Pacley	East
Mike Parsons	Cathedral Prep
Josh Prischak	Cathedral Prep
Kyle Protho	Central Tech
Joe Rumberger	Cathedral Prep
Tywan Salter	Strong Vincent
Akeem Satterfield	Cathedral Prep
Albert Scott Jones	East
Branden Seyler	Cathedral Prep
Andy Shaffer	McDowell
Dajour Stewart	East
Maleek Toran	Central Tech
Dan Vasil	McDowell
Robert Ward	McDowell
Jesse Wattle	Strong Vincent

Coaches: Maurice "Mo" Troop, Ed Williams, Tywonn Taylor, Kevin Klemm, Michael Cutter, Ron Hayes, Andre Bridgett, Eric Neavins of East

County

Jordan Babcock	Fairview
Adam Benko	Fort LeBoeuf
Troy Budziszewski	North East
Ken Burnett	Harbor Creek
Tom Cermak	Seneca
Dave Cimino	Girard
Eric Divell	Harbor Creek
Aaron Gluvna	Corry
Shane Goodwin	Fairview
Seth Grolemund	Harbor Creek
Justin Haney	Fairview
Kyle Johnson	Harbor Creek
Bryan Kirsch	North East
E.J. Kruse	Fairview
Jake Lightner	Fairview
Tim McAndrew	Harbor Creek
Josh McAnulty	Harbor Creek
Shawn McFadden	General McLane
Pat Michael	Fairview
Marcus Paradise	Northwestern
Casey Patton	Fairview
Mike Podskalny	Harbor Creek
Jeff Pollard	Fairview
Tyler Sargent	Fairview
Ryan Sheridan	Harbor Creek
Jordan Shields	Union City
Ryan Skelton	General McLane
Jim Stalford	Seneca
Matt Sundberg	Fairview
Phil Thomas	Iroquois
Shawn Walker	General McLane
Andy Wallen	Iroquois
Rich Widdowson	Seneca
Josh Williams	Fort LeBoeuf

Coaches: Jerry Lightner, Malcolm Beall, Jim Brinling, Dave Hudson, Jeff Nichols, Aaron Bluey, Mike Parmeter of Fairview

COUNTY 29 - CITY 8

$\mathcal{T}$yler Sargent of Fairview helped the County end a four-year City victory string. Sargent rushed 26 times for 225 yards and three touchdowns. He scored on runs of 2, 56 and 1 yards. The County defense also played a pivotal role in the victory. The City did not pick up a first down in the first half and ended with only 146 total yards for the game. With Sargent the big weapon, the County gained 263 yards on the ground and 354 yards overall. After Troy Budziszewski of North East kicked a 25-yard field goal in the first quarter, Sargent scored on a 2-yard run in the second period. Budziszewski's PAT produced a 10-0 halftime difference. Sargent broke free for a 56-yard touchdown romp in the third quarter.

The City ended its scoreless drought when Dave Herbe hit former McDowell teammate Robert Ward for a 27-yard touchdown pass. Herbe tossed to Tywan Salter of Strong Vincent for the 2-point conversion.

Jim Stalford of Seneca passed 3 yards to Justin Haney of Fairview for a County touchdown in the fourth quarter. Sargent completed the scoring with a 1-yard plunge. Haney caught four passes for 21 yards. Marquis Knight of Strong Vincent led the City ground game with 10 carries for 46 yards.

SAVE AN EYE GAME | COUNTY 29, CITY 8

UNSTOPPABLE

Sargent's rushing, County's defense prove too much for City to handle

By JOHN DUDLEY
john.dudley@timesnews.com

After three weeks of ramming fruitlessly against the County's tough defense, Tyler Sargent finally found some room to run on Friday night.

Sargent, a former Fairview star bound for New Hampshire as a defensive back, rushed for 225 yards and three touchdowns to help the County snap a four-year losing streak against the City 29-8 before a crowd of 5,800 in the Save An Eye game at Veterans Stadium.

In one of the dominant performances in the game's 70-year history, Sargent carried 26 times and

gcerie

First online:
Reported Friday
at 10:39 p.m.
On GoErie.com

Jackson King had a promising future in football. He became a starter for coach Randy Gunther as a sophomore at Seneca in 2005.

But all that changed on May 9, 2006 when King was involved in a horrific auto accident on his way to school. In that accident, he suffered a serious brain injury. He remains homebound to this day.

King would have been a senior in 2008, and he probably would have been selected to play in the Save-An-Eye Game along with Seneca teammates Tom Cermak, Jim Stalford and Rich Widdowson. Someone came up with the idea of having King as an honorary captain of the County team, and the notion was presented to game chairman, Tyco Swick. Swick had no problem with it, but he said it first had to be approved by County coach Jerry Lightner. That became just a formality when, after being presented with the proposition, Lightner immediately agreed.

Jackson King – 2008

Just prior to the game, King's father, Jack, took Jackson onto the field in his wheelchair to join the County captains for the coin toss. In a surprise move before the official tossed the coin, he presented King with a football that was autographed by all of the referees. "He should have been out there," said Widdowson about King, his best friend in school. "It was a good thing they did. It was the right thing."

King (front) with Seneca teammates Jim Stalford (left), Rich Widdowson (center) and Tom Cermak

Widdowson's father, also Rich, played for the County team that lost to the City 26-0 in 1968. The two Widdowsons would go to Save-An-Eye games together and the younger Widdowson wanted to some day play in the game. "I always dreamed about it," he said. "I used to talk to Jackson about it."

The County beat the City in the 2008 game 29-8. Stalford threw a touchdown pass in the fourth quarter. "We were kind of the underdog," said Widdowson, who now lives and works in Pittsburgh. "It was a combination of hard work and determination. We had our eyes set on the goal of winning. We went out there and did it." Widdowson gave a lot of credit for the win to the County coaching staff, headed by Coach Lightner and assisted by his Fairview staff. "We were all really competitive," Widdowson said. "To get us all together was great.

The coaches were a huge part of that." Widdowson recalls King's sophomore season when they both played for Coach Gunther. "Jackson was a huge part of our team," Widdowson said. "We expected to have a great senior season. If Jackson was there, he would have been very helpful. He had a lot of heart." Widdowson also remembers some other things about King. "He always pumped me up," Widdowson said. "He was driven. He was inspiring. He was a true leader."

After the Save-An-Eye Game, when King had his photo taken with his three former Seneca classmates and teammates, he still had that football sitting on his lap. It remains in his bedroom at home today.

– Joe Mattis

TONIGHT: 70th annual Save An Eye all-star football game

FILE PHOTO ROB ENGELHARDT/Erie Times-News

General McLane's Shawn Walker, right, and other County players run through drills in preparation for tonight's game.

OPENING KICK

Back injury keeps County's Divell on sideline; City aims for 5th straight win in annual game

By JOE MATTIS
joe.mattis@timesnews.com

After the fine football season Harbor Creek's Eric Divell had in the fall, he fully expected to be selected to play in today's Save An Eye football game.

What he did not expect was to be watching the game from the sideline.

Divell was winner of the Chad Vogt Award as the Region 5 player of the year after earning first-team honors at running back, kicker and punter. When he suffered two fractures in a vertebra, he had to end his high school baseball season after nine games.

"... is wearing a back ...

baseball season. I had been working hard all winter on strength and endurance."

Divell does not know exactly when the injury occurred. He started noticing it when he began pitching in March. He said it could ha happened during a s ulty soccer game such as wc ca

City

Christian Andrews	Cathedral Prep
Ray Blanks II	Cathedral Prep
Darrell Brooks	Strong Vincent
Robert Carson	Mercyhurst Prep
Tim Corder	Cathedral Prep
Joshua Edwards	Strong Vincent
Jason Faipler	Cathedral Prep
Jerrod Gibbs	East
Brad Gore	McDowell
Erick Green	Cathedral Prep
Marshall Huntsman	Mercyhurst Prep
Robert Joyce	Strong Vincent
Jordan Koper	McDowell
Dylan Lane	McDowell
Antre Lindsey	Strong Vincent
Christian Magee	Central Tech
Bob Mahoney	Cathedral Prep
Donny Mallin	Cathedral Prep
Brandon Marlow	Strong Vincent
Chawn McCowien	Mercyhurst Prep
Kaylon Mims	Central Tech
Qiydaar Muhammed	East
Corey Ratliff	East
Tim Shaloiko	Mercyhurst Prep
Austin Smith	Cathedral Prep
Zack Stano	McDowell
Demetris Stevenson	Central Tech
David Stromenger	McDowell
Tyler Wingrove	McDowell

Coaches: Jason Beer, Joe Tarasovitch, Jim Schoonover, Jeff Gibbens, Steve Musone, Bob Hammer, William Muriel, Thomas Muriel of Central Tech

County

Eric Albrecht	Union City
Curtis Bailey	North East
Michael Brandt	General McLane
Thomas Brooks	Harbor Creek
Michael Brown	Corry
Aaron Carney	Corry
Jeff Carniewski	North East
Ryan Coleman	Union City
Tyler Dawson	Union City
Patrick Dunn	Girard
Colin Feeney	Fort LeBoeuf
Brian Foley	Iroquois
Jon Gredler	Harbor Creek
Nick Grow	North East
Jeff Harvey	Iroquois
Joseph Hewel	Seneca
Blake Hockett	Fort LeBoeuf
Todd Jackson	Union City
Adam Krahe	Iroquois
Brooks Linkoski	Fairview
Tyler Lutton	Corry
Kyle Maio	Northwestern
Kyle Majewski	General McLane
Neil McCord	North East
Joe McIntire	Fort LeBoeuf
Jordan Mosher	Corry
Glenn Murphy	North East
Kellen O'Neill	General McLane
Kyle Peirson	Northwestern
Zach Poulson	Iroquois
Donald Sanfilippo	North East
Garrett Sheely	General McLane
Garrett Stolz	Fairview

Coaches: Homer DeLattre, Brian Patten, Bill Ross, Mark Chludzinski, Travis Carey, Jeff Goodwill, Adam Walstrom, Josh Kerns, Ed McMahan of Corry

CITY 21 - COUNTY 17

A 59-yard touchdown pass with 58 seconds remaining vaulted the City to a thrilling 21-17 win. Corey Ratliff of East hit Brandon Marlow of Strong Vincent with the decisive toss. The City got its final chance when Robert Joyce of Strong Vincent intercepted a pass at the City 26 with 1:44 remaining. Ratliff began the closing drive by finding Robert Carson of Mercyhurst Prep for a 15-yard completion. After an incompletion, he connected with Marlow on the County 15. The 240-pound tight end shook off a tackle and powered into the end zone. The touchdown catch was the second of the night for Marlow, who hauled in a 20-yarder from Ratliff in the second quarter. Ratliff fired 39 yards to Joyce for the City's opening score. Ray Blanks of Cathedral Prep kicked all three extra points. The County tied the game at 7-7 on a 1-yard run by Eric Albrecht of Union City. The score was set up by a 42-yard pass from Kellin O'Neill of General McLane to Fairview's Brooks Linkoski. Colin Feeney of Fort LeBoeuf's recovery set the stage for Adam Krahe of Iroquois to kick a 24-yard field goal, leaving a 14-10 City lead at the half. Curtis Bailey of North East fired 6 yards to Northwestern's Kyle Maio early in the fourth quarter to lift the County in front 17-14. Garrett Stolz of Fairview kicked both extra points. Ratliff hit on 6 of 13 passes for 166 yards. Marlow caught three for 100 yards. Brooks rushed 14 times for 60 yards.

71ST ANNUAL SAVE-AN-EYE GAME | TODAY, 7 P.M. | VETERANS STADIUM

In 2008, it was County 29-8. This year, just ...

FORGET ABOUT IT

City promises different game this time around

By TOM REISENWEBER
tom.reisenweber@timesnews.com

Strong Vincent graduate Robert Joyce didn't attend last year's Save-An-Eye game.

The wide receiver/linebacker was attending college camps and going through the recruiting process before his senior season.

► Save-An-Eye Game rosters, 3C
► Past games, 3C

So Joyce wasn't there, and he doesn't care about the result of the game.

"It doesn't matter what happened last year," Joyce said. "We are ready to play. Who knows, maybe the 2009 City team would smash last year's City team."

While Joyce might not know about the County's 29-8 rout of the City, most of this year's players and coaches are aware and out for revenge.

"They (County) did put a whoopin' on us last year, but I wasn't on that team," Vincent graduate Josh Edwards said. "This is our year and we are looking to get the title back to the City. A big thing for us is our unity, man. I'm going to be honest: We have a lot of people out here doing their thing, but as brothers."

► Please see GAME, 3C

City coach Jason Beer of Central Tech gives instructions to Brandon Marlow of Strong Vincent, left, during practice for the Save-An-Eye game.

ROB ENGELHARDT/Erie Times-News

goerie | CAN'T GET TO THE GAME? THE LIVE BLOG IS BACK. VISIT GOERIE.COM/BLOGS/VARSITY FOR REPORTS.

Chapter 9

The City earned three straight wins in the games leading up to the 75th Game. The most decisive victory came in 2011 and featured a stingy defense that limited the County to only 26 yards rushing. The County also was strong defensively, not allowing an offensive touchdown while losing 16-6. All the scoring for the winners came on special teams play, including three field goals. Noah Ackerman of Cathedral Prep connected from 29 and 34 yards in the second quarter. Ryan Mong of McDowell booted a 35 yard field goal with just under two minutes to play to complete the scoring.

2010 to 2013

The only touchdown for the City came on a 51-yard punt return by Jermaine Thornton of East midway through the fourth quarter. The County grabbed a 6-3 lead as Ryan Myers of Union City threw a 45-yard touchdown pass to Josh Niswonger of General McLane.

The 2010 Save-An-Eye came to a sudden stop when Lions officials were forced to end the action due to lightning and driving rain. Despite the tight 20-14 final score, the City claimed a wide 215-52 edge in total yards. Shyquawn Pullium of Cathedral Prep produced the winning touchdown on a 13-yard run. Pullium earlier hit his cousin Courtney Harden-Pullium of Strong Vincent for a 14-yard touchdown pass. Brandon Akins-Jones of Vincent scored the other City touchdown on a 15-yard dash. Both County touchdowns came on fumble recoveries by General McLane grads Kevin Kulka and Kyle Ponsoll.

The entertaining 2012 game was finally decided in overtime when Denzel Jones of Strong Vincent scored on a two-point conversion. Jones was driven out of bounds, but stretched the ball over the goal for the 21-20 win. He also threw a 43-yard touchdown pass to Kimani Smith of Prep. The overtime decision gave the City its 43rd win under the current format against 16 losses and two ties.

City

Brandon Akins-Jones	Strong Vincent
Gary Brown Jr.	McDowell
Trevor Colvin	Mercyhurst Prep
Tony Cordovano	Mercyhurst Prep
Michael Cruz	Mercyhurst Prep
Alex Davis	Strong Vincent
Dusty Galich	McDowell
Kasey Gallagher	McDowell
John Gianoni Jr.	Cathedral Prep
Zach Greenawalt	McDowell
Alondre Hamilton	East
Phil Hampy	Cathedral Prep
Courtney Harden-Pullium	Strong Vincent
Scott Harris	McDowell
Sean Herron	Strong Vincent
Damian Jefferson	East
Jacob Johnson	Central Tech
Rob Kaiser	Mercyhurst Prep
Greg Koester	McDowell
William Lubahn	Cathedral Prep
Jonathan Pohl	McDowell
Shyquawn Pullium	Cathedral Prep
Markese Pullium	Strong Vincent
Thomas Robishaw	Cathedral Prep
Davon Stovall	Central Tech
ReSean Thrower	Cathedral Prep
V.J. Viglione	Cathedral Prep
Emmanuel Wells	Strong Vincent
Logan Woznicki	Mercyhurst Prep
DeJon Young	McDowell

Coaches: Mike Mischler, Jim Skindell, Matt Melle, Brad Orlando, Ryan Drabina, Aaron Slocum, Pat Czytuck, Jeff Bomba, John P. Csir, Stephen Hiegel of Cathedral Prep

County

Jimmy Bailey	North East
Ryan Bunce	North East
Joe Bundy	Harbor Creek
Jared Burger	Union City
Jordan Drohn	Seneca
Andrew Enterline	Fort LeBoeuf
Scottie Frisina	Corry
Tim Gilson	Fairview
Zac Henry	North East
Robbie Hollis	Union City
Blaine Iskula	Northwestern
Peter Jackson	Fairview
Matthew Kowle	Fort LeBoeuf
Kevin Kulka	General McLane
T.J. Lawrence	Fairview
Nick Lombardo	General McLane
Craig Marti	Corry
Nicholas Maskrey	Northwestern
Corey McWilliams	Fort LeBoeuf
Brandon Miller	Corry
Ryan Murphy	Seneca
Louis Neff	North East
Patrick Papale	North East
Kyle Ponsoll	General McLane
Joshua Rzepecki	Harbor Creek
Bill Sobucki	Girard
B.J. States	Iroquois
Jake Szoszorek	Iroquois
Jesse Vazquez	Union City
Braidy Westfall	Corry
Joshua Williams	Girard
Josh Young	Northwestern

Coaches: Gerry Drozdowski, Jim Vogt, Mike Whitney, Jeff McShane, Mark Srnka, Pete Szoszorek, Roman Boykin, Pat Callahan of Iroquois

CITY 20 - COUNTY 14

The weatherman ended the 72nd renewal of the City-County Game early after the City controlled things in the first half. Game officials made the decision to halt the game following a 37-minute delay due to lightning and pouring rain. Before conditions brought the contest to a halt, the City had rolled up a 215-52 advantage in total yardage. The City took the lead when Brandon Akins-Jones of Strong Vincent went 15 yards for a touchdown in the first quarter. Another touchdown came in the second period when Courtney Harden-Pullium of Vincent caught a 14-yard pass from his cousin Shyquawn Pullium of Cathedral Prep. V.J. Viglione of Prep kicked both extra points.

The County tied the score on a pair of fumble returns for touchdowns by General McLane grads. Kevin Kulka went 36 yards and Kyle Ponsoll grabbed a bad pitch and dashed 31 yards for a score. Zac Henry of North East added the two conversion kicks. Shyquawn Pullium bolted 13 yards with 1:28 to play in the half for the go-ahead touchdown. The weather worsened at that point and caused Erie Lions Club officials to eventually call a stop to the game during the halftime intermission.

The City dominated the statistics in the shortened game, running 52 plays to just 16 for the County and owning a 17:42-6:16 edge in time of possession. Shyquawn Pullium hit on 5 of 7 passes for 101 yards and ran for 57 yards on 12 tries. Akins-Jones had 33 yards on nine carries. Scottie Frisina of Corry hit 5 of 9 passing for 36 yards for the County.

SAVE-AN-EYE GAME

Area football fans can get one more look at Cathedral Prep's Shyquawn Pullium before he begins his career at Penn State.

After back-to-back 2,000-yard passing seasons, Corry's Scottie Frisina will cap his high school career in the Save-An-Eye game.

Final showcase
& top quarterbacks
ll-star game

GREG WOHLFORD/Erie Times-New

Stephen Hiegel, 23, is the water boy for the Cathedral Prep football team, although he is blind and suffers from epilepsy, cerebral palsy and diabetes. Coach Mike Mischler, right, met Hiegel when he coached at Iroquois High School and invited Hiegel to come to Prep with him. Hiegel was working at the Prep Events Center in Erie on Saturday. Hiegel also will be the water boy for the City team at the Save-An-Eye Game on Friday.

City

Noah Ackerman ....Cathedral Prep
Jeremy Baronner.........................McDowell
Aaron Bell ....Strong Vincent
Andrew Bennett........................McDowell
Jacob Breakstone........................McDowell
DeAndre Connor ....Mercyhurst Prep
Tyler Covato ....McDowell
Brandon Czerwinski ....Mercyhurst Prep
John Dahlstrand.........................McDowell
Krishawn Day .... East
Jake Geanous ....Cathedral Prep
Jared Gillespie..........................McDowell
Peter Hamilton................................ East
Manuel Holmes.....................Central Tech
Aaron Horton ....Mercyhurst Prep
Markel Keys ....Cathedral Prep
Colin Kimball ....McDowell
Chris Kurzik ....Mercyhurst Prep
Jorge Luiggi............................Central Tech
Joshua Marques ....Strong Vincent
Zach Mayr ....McDowell
Ryan Mong..................................McDowell
Zach Murzynski ....Mercyhurst Prep
Martin Oduho ....McDowell
Zach Palmer.....................Mercyhurst Prep
Tyler Pullium...................Mercyhurst Prep
Mario Sanders.....................Cathedral Prep
Eddie Theiss ....Cathedral Prep
Jermaine Thornton .... East
Tony Twillie.......................Strong Vincent
Mike Weissinger.........................McDowell
Dearis Williams ....Cathedral Prep

Coaches: Mark Soboleski, Joe Magorien,
Steve Musone, Chris Spooner,
Chris Caldwell, Joe Wanson,
Brad Whitman, Todd Strasenburgh,
Kim Parker, Andre Bridgett of McDowell

County

Cody Bootes ....Harbor Creek
Travis Bryant.....................General McLane
Alan Buckel......................General McLane
Nate Carr................................Fort LeBoeuf
Spencer Cornelius.......................North East
Hunter Erdman...............................Girard
Josh Gdanetz ....Fairview
Alec Gluvna .... Corry
Jake Green ....Fort LeBoeuf
Luke Hetrick.............................. Union City
Josh Klenz ....North East
Zach Lucas ....General McLane
Justin Miller ....Corry
Alex Mobilia ....North East
Jacob Muye.................................Seneca
Ryan Myers .... Union City
Josh Niswonger ....General McLane
Cory Owens..................................Corry
Casey Pace ....Fort LeBoeuf
Josh Paradise ....Northwestern
Greg Reinke .... Union City
David Robinson ....North East
Austin Schied ....North East
Derek Schultz ....General McLane
Timothy Schwenk ....Harbor Creek
Kyle Shinn.........................General McLane
Joe Sobucki ....Girard
Anthony Stuart ....Girard
Steven Turner ....Fairview
John Vogel......................................Girard
Adam Zimmerman ....Corry

Coaches: Jim Funk, Pat Erdman,
Mike Zona, Tracy Dinger, Bill McNally,
Ron Platz, Jason Johnson of Girard

CITY 16 - COUNTY 6

A staunch City defense limited the County to 26 rushing yards and made key plays down the stretch in the 73rd City-County Game. The County defense was also solid, keeping the City offense off the board. All 16 points for the winners came on special teams. Noah Ackerman of Cathedral Prep kicked field goals of 29 and 34 yards in the second quarter. After Ackerman's first kick, the County went ahead when Ryan Myers of Union City connected with Josh Niswonger of General McLane for a 45-yard touchdown pass. The extra point was blocked. The score remained tied until six minutes remained in the fourth quarter when Jermaine Thornton of East fielded a punt at the City 49, raced down the left sidelines and then cut right to complete the 51-yard touchdown romp. Ackerman's point-after conversion boosted the lead to 13-6. The County had two more chances to score. The first ended when Chris Kurzik of Mercyhurst Prep intercepted a pass on a tipped ball. Kurzik raced 50 yards before Casey Pace of Fort LeBoeuf ran him down and punched the ball loose. Spencer Cornelius of North East secured the fumble recovery. The County's following second chance drive ended on a turnover on downs. Ryan Mong of McDowell sealed the win with a 35-yard field goal with 1:55 left. Colin Kimball of McDowell rushed 20 times for 72 yards and hit on 2 of 5 passes for 57 yards. Jeremy Baronner of McDowell had 31 yards on the ground. Cody Bootes of Harbor Creek passed for 110 yards and Joe Sobucki of Girard had four catches for 74 yards. Niswonger and Anthony Stuart of Girard each had three receptions.

SAVE-AN-EYE GAME

Kyle Shinn, bottom, of General McLane, tackles the City's John Dahlstrand, of McDowell, during the first quarter of the 73rd annual Save-An-Eye Game on Friday at —dium. The City won 16-6.

JANET B. CAMPBELL/Erie Times-News

This is a true story. Only the names have been changed for confidentiality purposes.

On September 22, 2011, Catherine Valerio, President of the Erie Lions Club, was contacted by Dr. X, an ophthalmologist from Pittsburgh who specializes in corneal and external eye diseases. The call regarded Steve, an 8-year-old boy living in Northwest Pennsylvania. He suffered from an extremely rare genetic condition, ligneous conjunctivitis, caused by a hereditary deficiency of plasminogen in the blood, resulting in aggressive tumors emanating from the upper eye lid. The tumors covered over half of his right eye, blocking the pupil, so light could not enter to produce vision. If not treated quickly, the vision in that eye would be permanently lost, since the visual cortex in the brain was not receiving sufficient stimulation to develop vision.

The complicating problem was that simply surgically removing the tumors activated the body's normal healing mechanism, and without plasminogen the tumors regrew with a vengeance.

Steve's Story – 2011

Dr. X did diligent research and discovered strong anecdotal evidence that plasminogen was being used in Europe to treat this condition with positive results. Although the use of plasminogen was approved for human use in Europe, it was not yet approved in the United States for human use.

Through a colleague, who also had a child with the condition, Dr. X learned that another doctor had received FDA approval to use plasminogen on a baby with the eyelid tumors, and the tumors did not regrow.

Based on that information, Dr. X sought approval from the Food and Drug Administration (FDA) to use the drug for Steve. At that point Steve could only see shadows, so time was critical or the vision loss would be permanent. Because plasminogen had been used successfully and because Steve's condition had deteriorated so drastically, the FDA gave immediate approval to use plasminogen, usually only meant for laboratory use, on this one child.

Little did Dr. X know that obtaining the drug was going to be a taxing ordeal despite quick FDA approval. Since the plasminogen was not FDA approved for the general public, but for this one child only, the cost would not be covered by any state or private insurance. Based on the dosages used in the previous surgeries, Dr. X estimated that a minimum of $5,000 worth of plasminogen would be needed for the surgery. After months of unsuccessful pleas for donated plasminogen from the various drug manufacturers, Dr. X finally turned to the Erie Lions Club for assistance in funding to personally purchase the plasminogen.

The Erie Lions immediately pledged $1,000 to the Eye Surgery Trust Fund of Lions District 14F to purchase the drug; the Trust Fund matched the $1,000 donation with an additional $2,000 grant; other Lions Clubs in the District pledged the remaining amount, and the surgery was performed.

It has been about a year since the surgery, and there has been no recurrence of tumors with the application of plasminogen eye drops daily. Because this is pioneering surgery in this country it is not known how long Steve will receive the drops, but we are pleased to report that, because of the success of the surgery, the drug company has donated more plasminogen to maintain the therapy.

Even though Steve's successful surgery is over, his story is not. It will be repeated for future Steves who suffer from this genetic disorder. Hopefully the struggles Dr. X experienced will enable other children with this rare disorder to be treated much earlier in their lives, resulting in even more successful development and maintenance of their vision.

The successful outcome of this "experimental" treatment was possible only because of the Erie Lions Club Save-An-Eye Fund that is supported primarily through the Save-An-Eye All-Star Football Game. It is the combined efforts of the players, coaches, referees, fans, and patrons that make the game successful.

The Save-An-Eye Game is a sports classic that stands on its own merits; but it is also a venerated charity with an impeccable history of service to the vision needs of children and low income adults in Erie County.

– Tyco Swick

JACQUELINE CONNOR/Erie Times-News

Fort LeBoeuf football players Jake Green, 18, Casey Pace, 18, and Nate Carr, 18, will take the field for today's Save-An-Eye game thinking about B.J. Arrowsmith, who was injured in a July 11 car accident along Old State Road that killed two others.

Dudley: LeBoeuf stars will play with injured teammate in mind

City

Josh Agresti	Mercyhurst Prep
Michael Amendola Jr.	Cathedral Prep
Zach Baker	McDowell
Jeff Biggie	Central Tech
Christopher Bleggi	Cathedral Prep
Dwayne Canady	Mercyhurst Prep
Luke DeHart	McDowell
Darrin Donikowski	Mercyhurst Prep
Anthony Ernst	Cathedral Prep
Nicholas Fenton	McDowell
Levonte Ford	East
Mason Giacomelli	McDowell
Khlique Harris	McDowell
Demarcus House	East
Robert Jones Jr.	Strong Vincent
Denzel Jones	Strong Vincent
Paul Kemper	McDowell
Anthony Lecce	McDowell
D.J. Mahoney	Mercyhurst Prep
James Malone	Cathedral Prep
Nathan McLaurin	Cathedral Prep
Josh Meade	McDowell
Paul Moyak	Cathedral Prep
Mike Neavins Jr.	Strong Vincent
Joe Oduho	Cathedral Prep
Blake Quirk	Strong Vincent
Anthony Raucci	McDowell
Noel Ruiz	Central Tech
Kimani Smith	Cathedral Prep
Ben Tarcson	Mercyhurst Prep
Tywonn Taylor	East
Michael Weber	Mercyhurst Prep
P.J. Wycech	Mercyhurst Prep

Coach: Matt Morgan, Scott Gorring, John Graeb, James Cowles, Rich Krafty, Zack Palmer, Jake Szoszorek, Pete Szoszorek, Nate Hein, Drew Barelho, Jayson Nickson of Mercyhurst Prep

County

Matt Astorino	General McLane
Cody Bailey	Corry
Cory Bailey	North East
Justin Bengel	Union City
Tyler Bretz	Harbor Creek
Parrish Brown	Iroquois
Drew Browning	General McLane
John Cragg	Corry
John Drozdowski	Iroquois
Mickey Ferrare	Fairview
Joey Gierlak	General McLane
Andrew Hajec	Corry
Tyler Johnson	North East
Hunter Jones	Girard
Max Knight	North East
Chad Kulka	General McLane
Dustin Lee Sweet	North East
Brady Lynn	North East
Stephen Maskrey	Northwestern
Matt Mongera	Seneca
Aaron Morley	Northwestern
Lucas Morton	Harbor Creek
Brandon Phillips	Harbor Creek
Josh Ponsoll	General McLane
Jeremy Powers	Fort LeBoeuf
Mitchell Schauble	Harbor Creek
Eddie Sheldon	North East
Ethan Strobel	General McLane
Brian Suminski	General McLane
Alex Svetz	North East
Parris Warner	Harbor Creek
Michael Wydro	North East

Coach: Jim Wells, Luke Graham, Bill Frick, Brad Wheeler, Elliot LaPlaca, Bobbie Stauffer, Dan Skelton, Scott Balheimer of General McLane

CITY 21 - COUNTY 20

*I*t went down to the final play in overtime in the 74th City-County Game before Denzel Jones propelled the City to its fourth straight win. The entertaining contest was decided when Strong Vincent product Jones stretched the ball over the goal line on a two-point conversion. Jones scrambled left on the play and was knocked out of bounds, but not before reaching the ball past the line. More than 6,000 fans watched at Veterans Memorial Stadium. Neither team could score the final six minutes of the fourth quarter after Andy Hajec of Corry converted a 28-yard field goal to produce a 13-13 tie. Hajec earlier booted a 40-yard field goal.

Max Knight of North East got the County on the board first with a 21-yard touchdown run in the opening quarter. Hajec's PAT kick and his 40-yard field goal boosted the County lead to 10-0. Jones connected with Kimani Smith of Cathedral Prep for a 43-yard touchdown pass in the second. The PAT pass attempt failed. The City charged ahead in the third period when Dwayne Canady snagged a 5-yard touchdown pass from former Mercyhurst Prep teammate P.J. Wycech. Zach Baker of McDowell boosted the lead to 13-10 with the placement kick. Hajec's field goal was the only scoring in the fourth quarter, bringing about overtime.

The County clawed ahead when Alex Svetz of North East plunged 1 yard on fourth down for the touchdown. Hajec gave the County a 20-13 lead with the conversion. Noel Ruiz of Central Tech carried three straight times for the City, capped by a 4-yard touchdown run. Then the dramatic 2-point conversion by Jones decided things. Luke DeHart of McDowell led the City rushers with 58 yards on nine carries. The North East trio of Tyler Johnson (50 yards), Svetz (31) and Knight (24) paced the County ground game. Smith had three catches for 81 yards for the City, and Jones hit all

SATURDAY
July 28, 2012

Matt Martin
managing editor/sports
870-1704
matt.martin@timesnews.com

GoErie.com
Blogs, photos, scores

Erie Times-News
Sports

BACK ON TRACK
SeaWolves end eight-game losing streak, beat Flying Squirrels at Uht Park. 2C

SECTION
C

City upends County in OT

Jones' 2-point conversion on final play seals victory in Save An Eye Game

The City's Kimani Smith, of Cathedral Prep, celebrates after the City beat the County 21-20 in the 74th annual Save An Eye All-Star Game against the County at Veterans Stadium Friday. The City's Denzel Jones, of Strong Vincent, scored on a two-point conversion to win the game on the final play. View more photos from the game at GoErie.com/photos.

JANET B. KUMMERER/Eri

By TOM REISENWEBER
tom.reisenweber@timesnews.com

Strong Vincent graduate Denzel Jones was one of the most electrifying football players in Erie throughout his career with one

74TH ANNUAL SAVE AN EYE GAME

City 21
County 20

➤ Summary, 2C
➤ 5C

Squirrels (54-53) 7-6 in 15 innings.

conversion in overtime and give the City a thrilling 21-20 win over the County in the 74th annual Save An Eye All-Star Game Friday in front of more than 6,000 fans at Veterans Stadium.

"We had .... Brown (124) and Romero (123)

out in a quarterback sweep, faked a throw and I got in. We had a nice halftime speech from coach and got our heads on straight in the second half to get the win."

Corry's Andy Hajec tied the game at 13-13 with 6 minutes, 8 seconds left by drilling a 28-yard field goal. He hit a 40-yarder in the first quarter and executed three onside kicks that the County recovered in the first 12 minutes. Neither team could get much offense over the final 6:08 to ...... before he departed after the sixth.

send the game to overtime. The biggest play of the fourth quarter might have been Kimani Smith's interception with 1:04 left inside the City 20.

"I was so nervous because the ball seemed like it was in the air for years," said Smith, a Cathedral Prep graduate who will play outside linebacker for Robert Morris this fall. "I think I was still looking in the air when it hit my hands, and luckily I hung on."

➤ Please see SAVE AN EYE, 2C

Read the Extra Innings blog at GoErie.com/blogs/extrainnings.

Save An Eye: County wins in overtime

Continued from 1C

Smith's interception was part of a resurgent defensive effort by the City after halftime.

Alex Svetz carried the ball nine times for 31 yards, but his final carry in overtime put the County ahead 20-13. After working their way to the 1-yard line, the County went for it on fourth down and Svetz barely crossed the goal line.

The City had an easier time during its turn in overtime. Central Tech's Noel Ruiz ran the ball three times to bowl into the end zone and cut the lead to 20-19.

City coach Matt Morgan called a timeout to make the biggest decision of the game.

"We had some problems with special teams obviously and we wondered if we should even hang our hat on this game coming down to a special teams play," Morgan said. "The kids came off and said that we had to go for it. We had two options. Either stick with Ruiz on the iso up the middle or go with Denzel. He made an athletic play and got in the end zone."

Jones completed 3-of-3 for 44 yards, including a 43-yard touchdown pass to Smith. McDowell's Luke DeHart led the City with 58 yards on nine carries.

North East's trio of Tyler Johnson (50 yards), Svetz (31) and Max Knight (24) paced the County. Knight scored on a 21-yard .... in the first quarter.

The City's Denzel Jones, right, of Strong Vincent, is tackled by the County's Alex Svetz, of North East, during the Save An Eye Game at Veterans Stadium Friday night. The City won 21-20 in overtime when Jones ran in for a two-point conversion.

JANET B. KUMMERER/Erie Times-News

The County seemed to be in control in the first half with its triple-option offense. They were running the clock down and limited the City to only three first-half possessions.

The City rallied in the third

quarter as Mercyhurst Prep duo P.J. Wycech and Dwayne Canady hooked up for a 5-yard touchdown to give the City a 13-10 lead.

"We didn't really make any adjustments on defense because

of the Save An Eye rules," Morgan said. "Luke DeHart and Levonte Ford did a great job on stopping the run along with our defensive ends. The triple-option offense is tough to stop and even if you are physically better, it is an equalizer."

TOM REISENWEBER can be reached at 870-1707 or by e-mail. Follow him on Twitter at twitter.com/ETNreisenweber. Read the Varsity blog at GoErie.com/blogs/Varsity and post comments.

SAVE AN EYE GAME

City 21, County 20

	COUNTY	CITY
First Downs	14	10
Rushes-yards	44-203	29-113
Comp.-Att.-Int.	4-11-1	8-9-0
Passing yards	25	94
Total yards	228	207
Penalties-yards	1-6	6-44
Fumbles-lost	3-1	4-2

County	10	0	3	7	—	20	
City	0	6	7	0	7	—	21

First Quarter
CO — Max Knight 21 run (Andrew Hajec kick)
CO — Hajec 46 field goal

Second Quarter
CI — Kimani Smith 43 pass from Denzel Jones (James Malone pass failed)

Third Quarter
CI — Dwayne Canady 5 pass from P.J. Wycech (Zach Baker kick)

Fourth Quarter
CO — Hajec 28 field goal

Overtime
CO — Alex Svetz 1 run (Hajec kick)
CI — Noel Ruiz 4 run (Jones rush)

Rushing
CO: Tyler Johnson 5-50, Josh Ponscoll 9-40, Svetz 9-31, Knight 5-24, Cory Bailey 5-20, Ponsah Brown 4-20, Brian Sumirati 3-9; Harrison Jones 1-6, Matt Astorino 9-3.
CI: DeHart 9-58, Canady 5-21, Matt Astorino 9-3, Ruiz 4-7, Oduho 3-3, Wychech 1-2, Lecce 1-1.

Passing
CO: Poncoll 3-7-0-26, Bailey 1-3-1-(-1), Knight 0-1-0-0.
CI: Lecce 2-3-0-7, Jones 3-3-0-44, Wychech 3-3-0-43.

Receiving
CO: Knight 1-22, Johnson 1-2, Astorino 1-(-1).
CI: Smith 3-61, Canady 3-11, McLaurin 2-2.

'Hurst grads get one last game together

By DAN KUBACKI
daniel.kubacki@timesnews.com

It's time for one last hurrah.

Seven Mercyhurst Prep players will take the field together in Laker helmets for the final time when they play for the City team Friday night in the 74th annual Erie Lions Club Save An Eye all-star football game.

All seven had a role in leading the Lakers to a 31-4 record since 2009, one of the top marks in District 10.

"We're going to miss them a great deal," Mercyhurst Prep and City coach Matt Morgan said. "They've had four tremendous years. They're going to be missed, but they've

MORE INFORMATION

74th annual Save An Eye all-star football game
■When: Friday, 7 p.m.
■Where: Veterans Stadium
➤ City roster, 3C

definitely left a good legacy for kids coming up."

Running back Dwayne Canady, receiver Ben Tarcson, lineman Mike Weber and cornerback D.J. Mahoney each was named first-team all-region in 2011. Weber, a Hiram recruit, was an all-state and all-district pick as well.

Tight end Josh Agresti and

defensive end Darrin Donikowski made second-team all-region.

"It's almost kind of bittersweet to be playing with these guys one last time," said Tarcson, an Allegheny College recruit, "because I know most of them are going to college and playing ball, and I'll maybe see these guys again but probably not.

"They're my good friends; it's pretty much family between us," Mahoney said.

But the Save An Eye game is also an opportunity to play with some of the best football players Erie had to offer in 2011.

➤ Please see SAVE AN EYE, 3C

Mercyhurst Prep graduates, standing from left, Dwayne Canady, D.J. Mahoney and Ben Tarcson, and, seated from left, Darrin Donikowski, P.J. Wycech, Mike Weber and Josh Agresti, were instrumental in turning around the Lakers' football program. View more images from practice at GoErie.com/photos.

CHRISTOPHER MILLETTE/Erie Times-News

COMING UP: Chart your weekend fishing outing with the weekly FishOn! regional report. Friday

230   Chapter 9 ‖ 2010 to 2013

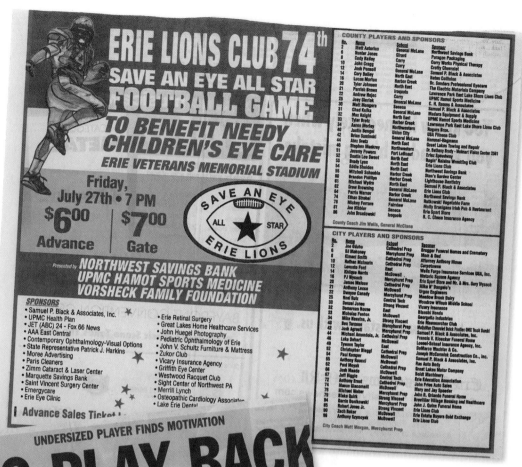

ERIE LIONS CLUB 74th SAVE AN EYE ALL STAR FOOTBALL GAME

TO BENEFIT NEEDY CHILDREN'S EYE CARE

ERIE VETERANS MEMORIAL STADIUM

Friday, July 27th • 7 PM

$6.00 Advance | $7.00 Gate

SAVE AN EYE ALL STAR ERIE LIONS

Presented by
NORTHWEST SAVINGS BANK
UPMC HAMOT SPORTS MEDICINE
VORSHECK FAMILY FOUNDATION

SPONSORS
• Samuel P. Black & Associates, Inc.
• UPMC Health Plan
• JET (ABC) 24 - Fox 66 News
• AAA East Central
• Contemporary Ophthalmology-Visual Options
• State Representative Patrick J. Harkins
• Moree Advertising
• Paris Cleaners
• Zimm Cataract & Laser Center
• Marquette Savings Bank
• Saint Vincent Surgery Center
• Emergycare
• Erie Eye Clinic
• Erie Retinal Surgery
• Great Lakes Home Healthcare Services
• John Huegel Photography
• Pediatric Ophthalmology of Erie
• John V. Schultz Furniture & Mattress
• Zukor Club
• Vicary Insurance Agency
• Griffith Eye Center
• Westwood Racquet Club
• Sight Center of Northwest PA
• Merrill Lynch
• Osteopathic Cardiology Associates
• Lake Erie Dental

Advance Sales Tickets

UNDERSIZED PLAYER FINDS MOTIVATION

BIG-PLAY BACK

County All-Star uses heart, to excel on field

COMING UP
74th annual Erie Lions Club
Save An Eye All-Star Football Game
Friday, 7 p.m., at Veterans Stadium
■ Get live updates from Friday's game on the Varsity blog.
Visit GoErie.com/blogs/Varsity

By DAN KUBACKI
daniel.kubacki@timesnews.com

By all means, call Hunter undersized for a football play
Then buckle up.
"I find it motivating bec always been told I'm too sma that I'll never be a premier b able to run between the tack Jones, 18, a Girard graduate. me work harder and show pe and weight don't mat ter. It's about heart and the will to play."
The 5-foot 5-inch, 147-pound running back scored 12 touch downs and ran for nearly 1,000 yards in his senior season at Girard Jones will get one last moment in the high school football spotlight as a member of the County squad in the 74th annual Erie Lions C An Eye All-Star Game Friday ans Stadium.
"It's a chance to play with the I've played against for years," J "I'm going to try to help County we haven't had one in a while,
It's exceptional outside sp Jones brings to bear, a skill th and General McLane coach Ji firmly aware of.
Wells' game plan against 2011 included shutting down the Lancers 48-7 victory. Jones aged 62 yards on 20 carries and touchdown run in the fourth q avert a shutout.
"He, among others (on the team), does have speed," Wells has the ability to play the edge.

ANDY COLWELL

Running back Hunter Jones, of Girard, runs a play during County team practice at General McLane fo Jones, who will play at Allegheny College, had a successful high school career despite being 5'
View photos from a recent County practice at GoErie.com/photos.

City Coach: Joe Bufalino   **County Coach:** Jack Bestwick

Chapter 10

Officials at any sport love to hear someone say, "I was at the game, but I never noticed you." Not being noticed on the field for a football official is a great compliment. It means that the officials called a great game with nothing out of the ordinary to call attention to their decisions.

The same is true for those who work at the Save-An-Eye Games. The officials play an integral part of the annual charity game, and they usually do it in anonymity.

On July 26, 2013, when the 75th Save-An-Eye Game is played, seven officials will make up the crew. That's a far cry from the early days of the game when as few as three officials worked on a game.

The Referees

In the beginning, the same crew would officiate game after game after game. That is how some of the officials were able to work so many Save-An-Eye Games. John Bradford has the record of number of games worked, 42 consecutive, from the first game in 1939 to 1980.

No one today can approach Bradford's longevity feat because of a change in the way officials are selected. In the past several years, five-man crews (which are used during the high school season) are rotated with two more officials added to make seven for the game.

There are only eight officials who have worked on the field for at least 20 years. They include Bradford, Don Stolz (38), Hank Galla (29), Bob DeMarco (28), John Edler (26), Vinnie Marchant (25), Frank Ropelewski (25) and Joe LeCorchick (24).

If you attend a Save-An-Eye Game in the future, it's okay to notice the officials. Actually, you should notice them but only for the good job they do in helping make the Save-An-Eye Game the wonderful charity event that it is.

Rick Johannesmeyer is a big high school football fan. He is also a high school referee. "I took my kids to games when they were smaller," he said. "Probably the most memorable was going to three of Cathedral Prep's state championship games."

He also makes it a point to go to the Save-An-Eye games, either as a spectator, a referee or a helper on the sideline.

Rick Johannesmeyer

Johannesmeyer was part of the crews that worked the 2005 and 2008 games. On other occasions he has helped Greg Deemer of the Lions Club make sure the coaches follow the special rules that are in effect for the game. One of those rules makes it mandatory that each team throw at least 15 passes in the game. "The rule is there so that a wide receiver can be a part of the offense," he said. "It also makes it more fun for players and fans."

Johannesmeyer remembers the help he received from fellow referees when he began officiating in 2001. Elmer Petrucelli, Bob DeMarco and Don Stolz were the veterans that Johannesmeyer worked with that year. "It was great traveling with them," Johannesmeyer said. "Not only did I learn a lot from them, but they told some great stories."

The atmosphere of the Save-An-Eye games is something that Johannesmeyer loves. It beats any other high school game that he has watched. "It's a nice friendly atmosphere, especially with the banquet and recognition," he said. "The kids get to play on a big stage at the Stadium. For most of them, it is their last moment of glory. I'm thrilled that I have been able to be a part of it."

With the Save-An-Eye Game reaching 75 years of continuity, Johannesmeyer hopes it never ends. "They should keep the game going," he said. "It's a great thing for the community"

– Joe Mattis

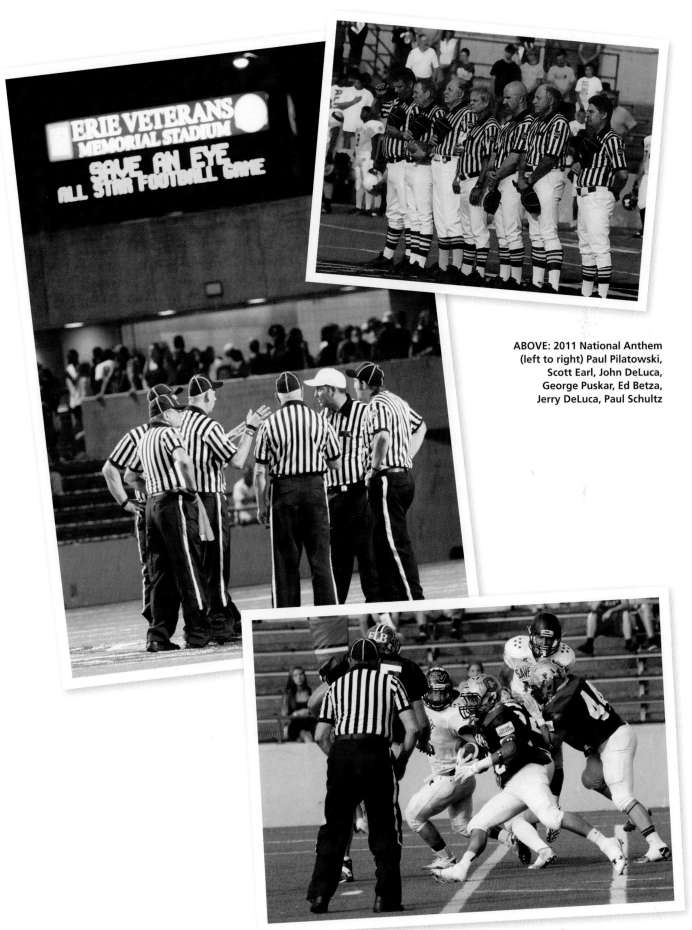

ABOVE: 2011 National Anthem (left to right) Paul Pilatowski, Scott Earl, John DeLuca, George Puskar, Ed Betza, Jerry DeLuca, Paul Schultz

Long time high school football and 38-year Save-An-Eye Game referee Don Stolz recently sat down in his dining room to talk about his experiences in the game and how he started as a football referee. Don began his adventure in his striped shirt in 1951 after coming out of college having played eight straight years of football in high school and Grove City College. He realized his love was still with the game when John Bradford asked him to consider learning to be a referee. Don and a fairly large group of others went through a six-week training program and passed a test to gain certification to handle the refereeing position.

When he started, there were just two striped shirts handling each game. Don says, "In those days, it was just plunge into the line and hope you and the cloud of dust could gain some yards." But after a few years, they added another man to help as plays became more complicated and fancy. But as Don says, "Then some smart coach must have been watching a few college games and decided they could pass too. This changed the game, and now referees on the wings had to be in the best of shape to keep up with the high school kids. At the time, that happened to be me because I was the youngest official on the field." Don said that when this became the norm, another referee was needed and began to be assigned to each game.

Don Stolz

When asked what were some of the best memories he had of the 1965 through 2001 and 2003 games he worked, he laughed and said we could be here for days. The biggest factor that he thought was important and very meaningful involved the long-term friendships that evolved between the players, coaches and referees. I mentioned to him that as we were putting this book together, we also experienced the special camaraderie that was generated by the Save-An-Eye Game participants.

When asked if there were any games or players that stuck in his mind after all his years of involvement, he quickly began talking about his second Save-An-Eye Game in 1966. This was the game in which Mike McCoy of Cathedral Prep, and a future Notre Dame and NFL star played. Of course, all the pre-game hype centered on McCoy, but Don says, "A little guy, only two-thirds the size of McCoy by the name of Gerry Mikovich from Girard, made Mike see what a starry night it was by putting him flat on his back most of the game. This little guy was fast and smart and played his heart out."

Another game he remembered was from a different perspective. Don was in the stands as a spectator. He still tries to make most of the games. This game was in 2002, two years after Don's injury. This was the game where Jovon Johnson of Mercyhurst Prep put on a real show for the crowd. Don said that, "He was like an eel, no one could hold onto him. They would have him stopped and all of a sudden he was free for another 15 yards." Don said he enjoyed that evening.

In the 1999 game, Don must have decided to leave the game with a bang. Don was on the sideline when a defensive back diving for the ball to stop a pass missed, and hit Don's leg just below the knee. When the dust cleared, Don's leg was straight, however his foot and ankle were at a 90 degree angle from the leg, and as one coach put it, "When I saw it, I nearly passed out." It was a long recovery for Don; however, the next year he was on the field again enjoying his love, "Refereeing the Save-An-Eye Game."

– Gene Ware

Referees posed for a referee chapter photo in this undated photo. Most of them officiated in at least one Save-An-Eye Game. The group includes in front (left to right): Lou Nardo, Chubbles DiFazio, Naz Servidio and John Bradford. In back: Bernard "Babe" Harkins, Joe Sivak Tom Fuhrman, Hank Galla, unidentified, Huck Lininger, Howard Kelly, George Kosterman, Frank Ropelewski, Nord Cofini and John Grassberger.

Appendices

Game	Date	Score	Attendance	Series
Game 1	December 2, 1939	West 18, East 6	NA	West 1-0
Game 2	December 6, 1940	East 12, West 7	NA	Tied 1-1
Game 3	November 27, 1941	West 14, East 0	NA	West 2-1
Game 4	November 26, 1942	West 13, East 0	NA	West 3-1
Game 5	November 27, 1943	East 25, West 0	NA	West 3-2
Game 6	November 24, 1944	East 13, West 6	NA	Tied 3-3
Game 7	November 23, 1945	West 11, East 0	NA	West 4-3
Game 8	November 23, 1946	East 6, West 0	NA	Tied 4-4
Game 9	November 21, 1947	West 21, East 7	14,000	West 5-4
Game 10	November 26, 1948	East 13, West 0	9,000	Tied 5-5
Game 11	November 24, 1949	East 20, West 6	NA	East 6-5
Game 12	December 2, 1950	West 19, East 0	5,000	Tied 6-6
Game 13	November 16, 1951	West 25, East 0	NA	West 7-6 *
Game 14	September 1, 1952	City 19, County 6	NA	City 1-0
Game 15	September 7, 1953	City 12, County 6	NA	City 2-0
Game 16	September 6, 1954	City 14, County 0	NA	City 3-0
Game 17	September 5, 1955	City 19, County 13	13,000	City 4-0
Game 18	September 3, 1956	City 33, County 12	14,000	City 5-0
Game 19	September 2, 1957	City 12, County 2	12,000	City 6-0
Game 20	September 1, 1958	City 13, County 6	12,000	City 7-0
Game 21	September 7, 1959	County 19, City 12	13,500	City 7-1
Game 22	September 5, 1960	City 13, County 6	NA	City 8-1
Game 23	September 4, 1961	County 14, City 0	11,000	City 8-2
Game 24	September 3, 1962	City 31, County 6	12,000	City 9-2
Game 25	September 2, 1963	City 18, County 0	12,000	City 10-2
Game 26	September 7, 1964	City 6, County 6 (tie)	NA	City 10-2-1
Game 27	September 6, 1965	City 21, County 0	14,000	City 11-2-1
Game 28	September 5, 1966	City 12, County 7	12,000	City 12-2-1
Game 29	September 4, 1967	County 25, City 0	16,000	City 12-3-1
Game 30	September 2, 1968	City 26, County 0	13,000	City 13-3-1
Game 31	September 1, 1969	City 12, County 0	15,000	City 14-3-1
Game 32	September 7, 1970	County 14, City 0	13,000	City 14-4-1
Game 33	August 21, 1971	County 20, City 12	13,000	City 14-5-1
Game 34	August 19, 1972	County 14, City 12	10,000	City 14-6-1
Game 35	August 11, 1973	City 22, County 6	12,000	City 15-6-1
Game 36	August 10, 1974	City 22, County 8	8,500	City 16-6-1
Game 37	August 9, 1975	City 16, County 10	NA	City 17-6-1
Game 38	August 14, 1976	City 13, County 12	9,000	City 18-6-1
Game 39	August 13, 1977	City 8, County 8 (tie)	9,000	City 18-6-2
Game 40	August 12, 1978	City 27, County 18	6,000	City 19-6-2 **

Save-An-Eye Game Results

Game	Date	Score	Attendance	Series
Game 41	August 11, 1979	City 14, County 0	NA	City 20-6-2
Game 42	August 9, 1980	City 40, County 14	NA	City 21-6-2
Game 43	August 8, 1981	City 14, County 0	NA	City 22-6-2
Game 44	August 14, 1982	City 18, County 10	NA	City 23-6-2
Game 45	August 12, 1983	County 7, City 0	NA	City 23-7-2
Game 46	August 10, 1984	County 30, City 12	NA	City 23-8-2
Game 47	August 9, 1985	City 16, County 13	NA	City 24-8-2
Game 48	August 8, 1986	City 26, County 20	NA	City 25-8-2
Game 49	August 7, 1987	County 21, City 6	NA	City 25-9-2
Game 50	August 5, 1988	City 13, County 6	NA	City 26-9-2
Game 51	August 4, 1989	County 20, City 13	NA	City 26-10-2
Game 52	August 3, 1990	City 14, County 3	NA	City 27-10-2
Game 53	August 2, 1991	City 18, County 14	11,000	City 28-10-2
Game 54	August 7, 1992	City 37, County 8	8,500	City 29-10-2
Game 55	August 6, 1993	County 7, City 0	NA	City 29-11-2
Game 56	August 5, 1994	City 21, County 0	NA	City 30-11-2
Game 57	August 4, 1995	County 15, City 12	NA	City 30-12-2 ***
Game 58	August 2, 1996	City 20, County 6	NA	City 31-12-2 ***
Game 59	August 1, 1997	County 17, City 7	NA	City 31-13-2
Game 60	August 7, 1998	City 17, County 6	NA	City 32-13-2
Game 61	August 6, 1999	County 23, City 9	NA	City 32-14-2
Game 62	August 4, 2000	City 14, County 7	NA	City 33-14-2
Game 63	August 3, 2001	City 17, County 6	NA	City 34-14-2
Game 64	August 2, 2002	City 26, County 17	NA	City 35-14-2
Game 65	August 1, 2003	County 28, City 3	NA	City 35-15-2
Game 66	August 6, 2004	City 35, County 28	NA	City 36-15-2
Game 67	July 29, 2005	City 24, County 12	6,500	City 37-15-2
Game 68	July 28, 2006	City 44, County 7	6,531	City 38-15-2
Game 69	July 27, 2007	City 34, County 7	7,000	City 39-15-2
Game 70	July 25, 2008	County 29, City 8	5,800	City 39-16-2
Game 71	July 24, 2009	City 21, County 17	6,500	City 40-16-2
Game 72	July 23, 2010	City 20, County 14	NA	City 41-16-2
Game 73	July 29, 2011	City 16, County 6	5,500	City 42-16-2
Game 74	July 27, 2012	City 21, County 20	6,000	City 43-16-2
Game 75	July 23, 2013			

* Last game played under East vs. West format
** Game played at McDowell's Gus Anderson Field
*** Game played at General McLane's Linden Field

A

Jack Aaronson, Wesleyville (1965, County)
Joe Abal, Tech (1967, County)
Craig Abbey, Academy (1974, City)
Richard Abbey, Conneautville (1947, West)
Henry Abbott, Waterford (1950, East)
Ed Abramoski, East (1950, East)
Noah Ackerman, Cathedral Prep (2011, City)
Bill Adams, Strong Vincent (1998, City)
Don Adams, Northwestern (1974, County)
Mark Adams, Northwestern (1981, County)
Sandy Adams, North East (1943, East)
Shawn Adams, Union City (2003, County)
Tom Adams, Strong Vincent (1966, City)
Andrew Adamus, Cathedral Prep (2006, City)
Red Adelhart, Millcreek (1953, County)
Mike Agnello, Girard (1983, County)
Phil Agnello, McDowell (1981, City)
Jake Agresti, Mercyhurst Prep (2006, City)
Jamie Agresti, General McLane (2005, County)
Josh Agresti, Mercyhurst Prep (2012, City)
Donnye Aiken, Central (2003, City)
Warren Aikens, Harbor Creek (1943, East)
James Akin, North East (1944, East)
Barry Akins, Tech (1992, City)
Tony Akins, Tech (1990, City)
Brandon Akins-Jones, Strong Vincent (2010, City)
John Alacce, East (1961, City)
Ralph Albert, Waterford (1944, East)
Eric Albrecht, Union City (2009, County)
Stan Albro, Kanty Prep (1950, West)
Dick Alcorn, Edinboro (1953, County)
William Alcorn, Waterford (1947, East)
Todd Aldrich, McDowell (2002, City)
Wayne Aldrich, Strong Vincent (1972, City)
Don Aleksiewicz, East (1969, City)
Bob Alex, Cathedral Prep (1964, City)
Pete Alex, Tech (1954, City)
Jared Alexander, Northwestern (1997, County)
Ray Alexander, Union City (1939, East)
Nick Alfieri, Harbor Creek (1959, County)
Chuck Allen, Academy (1961, City)
Craig Allen, Tech (1965, City)
James Allen, North East (1972, County)
Mike Allen, Tech (1985, City)
Rasheed Allen, Central (1997, City)
Steve Allen, East (1978, City)
Tom Allen, Harbor Creek (1956, County)
Joe Allesie, Wesleyville (1960, County)
Mike Allgeier, Mercyhurst Prep (1998, City)
Jerry Allison, Union City (1963, County)
Phil Almendinger, Millcreek (1956, County)
Bob Alo, Tech (1954, City)
Fred Alois, Tech (1939, East)

Charles Altman, Strong Vincent (1992, City)
Sam Alward, Strong Vincent (1948, West)
Max Alwens, Academy (1971, City)
Joe Amann, Iroquois (1979, County)
Michael Amendola Jr., Cathedral Prep (2012, City)
Art Amendola, East (1943, East)
Larry Amenta, St. Gregory (1960, County)
Mark Amenta, Girard (1991, County)
Bob Amon, Fort LeBoeuf (1965, County)
Joe Amoroso, Corry (1980, County)
Tyler Amy, Corry (2006, County)
Aaron Anderson, Seneca (1998, County)
Art Anderson, Lawrence Park (1947, East)
Art Anderson, Tech (1945, West)
Avis Anderson, Tech (1986, City)
Carl Anderson, Strong Vincent (1967, County)
Charles Anderson, North East (1943, East)
Earl Anderson, McDowell (1969, County)
Glenn Anderson, Wattsburg (1971, County)
Gus Anderson, Strong Vincent (1951, West; 1952, City)
Jack Anderson, Lawrence Park (1944, East)
Jason Anderson, Fairview (1991, County)
Jim Anderson, Cathedral Prep (1967, County)
John Anderson, Strong Vincent (1969, City)
John Anderson, Girard (1967, County)
Mike Anderson, Tech (1988, City)
Nick Anderson, East (1980, City)
Richard Anderson, Tech (1955, City)
Swede Anderson, Wesleyville (1941, East)
Christian Andrews, Cathedral Prep (2009, City)
David Andrews, Academy (1975, City)
Rich Andrews, Strong Vincent (1965, City)
Ron Andrews, Fairview (1965, County)
Roy Andrews, Academy (1950, East)
Ryan Andrews, Iroquois (1996, County)
Brian Andrychowski, Iroquois (1994, County)
Jacob Andrzejczak, General McLane (1994, County)
Bill Angelotti, Millcreek (1953, County)
Frank Angelotti, Strong Vincent (1950, West)
John Angerer, Harbor Creek (1996, County)
Matt Angerer, Harbor Creek (1999, County)
Arron Ankeny, General McLane (1969, County)
Frank Antalek, Cathedral Prep (1961, City)
Ken Antalek, Iroquois (1970, County)
Chris Anthony, Union City (1992, County)
Frank Anthony, Cathedral Prep (1949, West)
Joe Anthony, Academy (1964, City)
Tony Anthony, Cathedral Prep (1953, City)
Vic Antolik, Fairview (1978, County)
Don Applebee, Tech (1977, City)
John Applebee, Tech (1980, City)
Mike Applebee, Tech (1977, City)
Rich Ardillo, Iroquois (1990, County)
Pat Aretz, General McLane (2001, County)
Art Arkelian Strong, Vincent (1944, West)

John Arkelian, Strong Vincent (1946, West)
Daniel Arkwright, Northwestern (2000, County)
Dan Armbruster, Iroquois (1973, County)
Bob Arndt, Academy (1947, East)
Dana Arneman, Millcreek (1947, West)
Nick Arrigo, Mercyhurst Prep (2008, City)
Alex Arrington, Academy (1974, City)
Ed Arrington, East (1962, City)
Rich Arrington, East (1961, City)
Harold Arrowsmith, Strong Vincent (1960, City)
Mike Artise, North East (2005, County)
Mike Artise, North East (1986, County)
David Ashton, Strong Vincent (1990, City)
Matt Astorino, General McLane (2012, County)
Pat Atkins, Strong Vincent (1966, City)
Charles Augustine, Cathedral Prep (1955, City)
John Austin, Edinboro (1957, County)
Anthony Azevedo, Iroquois (2007, County)

Jordan Babcock, Fairview (2008, County)
Chad Baccus, Fairview (2005, County)
Paul Bacik, Fairview (1952, County)
Scott Bacon, Union City (1988, County)
Ray Baer, Academy (1943, East)
Stan Baginski, East (1959, City)
Tom Baginski, East (1961, City)
Dean Bagnoni, Tech (1969, City)
Bob Bailey, Corry (1959, County)
Chris Bailey, Central (1995, City)
Cody Bailey, Corry (2012, County)
Cory Bailey, North East (2012, County)
Curtis Bailey, North East (2009, County)
David Bailey, Tech (1972, City)
Doug Bailey, Corry (1980, County)
Jimmy Bailey, North East (2010, County)
Ned Bailey, Corry (1983, County)
Walter Bailey, Lawrence Park (1940, West)
William Bailey, Strong Vincent (1990, City)
Kevin Baird, North East (1980, County)
Alan Baker, Wattsburg (1949, East)
Art Baker, Academy (1957, City)
Barry Baker, Corry (1973, County
Bill Baker, Girard (1997, County)
Brandon Baker, Fort LeBoeuf (2005, County)
Dave Baker, Academy (1968, City)
Doug Baker, Corry (1989, County)
Greg Baker, Girard (2000, County)
Jerry Baker, Corry (1996, County)
John Baker, East (1982, City)
John Baker, Girard (1981, County)
Junior Baker, Cambridge Springs (1948, West)
Mike Baker, McDowell (2000, City)
Nevin Baker, McDowell (1999, City)
Robert Baker, Cambridge Springs (1949, West)

Todd Baker, Girard (1988, County)
Zach Baker, McDowell (2012, City)
Walter Baldauf, Fairview (1958, County)
Keith Balko, McDowell (1996, City)
Mike Ball, Fort LeBoeuf (1996, County)
Rick Ballard, General McLane (1990, County)
Henry Baltine, Tech (1951, East; 1952, City)
Eugene Bambauer, Strong Vincent (1942, West)
Dan Baney, Fort LeBoeuf (1995, County)
Fred Baney, Fort LeBoeuf (1973, County)
Greg Baney, Fort LeBoeuf (1994, County)
Greg Baney, Strong Vincent (1992, City)
Craig Baniszewski, Mercyhurst Prep (2007, City)
Dick Baniszewski, Cathedral Prep (1958, City)
Mike Baniszewski, Mercyhurst Prep (2004, City)
Dave Banta, General McLane (2000, County)
Jim Barabas, Cathedral Prep (1975, City)
Frank Baranowski, East (1943, East)
Tony Baranowski, Tech (1953, City)
C.J. Barbaro, General McLane (1991, County)
Brendan Barber, Cathedral Prep (2008, City)
Richard Barber, Fairview (1983, County)
Richard Barber, Tech (1949, East)
Scott Barber, General McLane (1987, County)
Mike Barberini, Harbor Creek (1981, County)
Bob Barclay, Strong Vincent (1939, West)
Ray Barczak, Tech (1947, West)
Rob Barger, Mercyhurst Prep (2006, City)
Richard Bargielski, Tech (1948, East)
Brian Barham, Fort LeBoeuf (1974, County)
Doug Barnes, Union City (1954, County)
Jeff Barnes, McDowell (1982, City)
Al Barnett, East (1978, City)
Bob Barnett, East (1964, City)
Jason Barnett, Union City (1993, County)
Curtis Barney Academy (1987, City)
Bob Barney, Academy (1967, County)
Don Barney, Academy (1948, East)
Lee Barney, Academy (1981, City)
Steve Barney, Academy (1976, City)
Paul Barone, Wesleyville (1943, East)
Jeremy Baronner, McDowell (2011, City)
Dan Barringer, Iroquois (2006, County)
Steve Barringer, Iroquois (2006, County)
Steve Barron, McDowell (2001, City)
Andy Bartfai, Albion (1950, West)
Scott Barth, Fairview (1974, County)
David Barthelmes, Academy (1977, City)
Dean Barthelmes, Academy (1977, City)
Lee Barthelmes, Academy (1974, City)
Mike Bartoszek, McDowell (1971, County)
John Barzano, Strong Vincent (1979, City)
John Basco, Girard (2004, County)
Henry Baskin, East (1980, City)
Jerry Baskin, Fairview (1940, East)

Seymour Baskin, Fairview (1942, West)
Reynaldo Batista, McDowell (1997, City)
Ike Battles, East (1962, City)
Tyrone Battles, Strong Vincent (1983, City)
Randy Baughman, East (1987, City)
B.J. Baumann, McDowell (1986, City)
Charlie Baumann, Cathedral Prep (1985, City)
John Baumann, Cathedral Prep (1989, City)
Randy Baumann, Cathedral Prep (1990, City)
Don Baumgardner, McDowell (1961, County)
Kevin Bayer, Fairview (1991, County)
Larry Bayle, McDowell (1969, County)
Tim Beal, Corry (1990, County)
Malcolm Beall, Fairview (1997, County)
Scott Beam, Girard (1980, County)
Nate Beaman, McDowell (2008, City)
Mike Bean, McDowell (2002, City)
Kevin Beard, Strong Vincent (1985, City)
Larry Beard, Harbor Creek (1959, County)
Nate Beard, East (1970, City)
Emanuel Beason, Strong Vincent (2005, City)
Ryan Beason, Harbor Creek (1994, County)
Bill Beatman, Academy (1940, East)
Ken Beatty, Girard (1939, West)
Jim Bebko, Tech (1966, City)
Bill Bechdel, Iroquois (1970, County)
Pete Bechtos, East (1945, East)
Adam Beck, General McLane (2001, County)
Ed Beck, Cathedral Prep (1972, City)
Marty Beck, Cathedral Prep (1976, City)
Jason Beckwith, Corry (1992, County)
Ed Bednarowicz, Tech (1955, City)
Jason Beebe, Seneca (2005, County)
Kyle Beebe, Seneca (2007, County)
Norm Beemis, North East (1958, County)
Jason Beer, Fort LeBoeuf (2001, County)
Fred Behnken, North East (1945, East)
Ben Behringer, Girard (2003, County)
Matt Beidler, Fort LeBoeuf (2004, County)
Leo Beill, East (1946, East)
Aaron Bell, Strong Vincent (2011, City)
Brian Bell, Strong Vincent (2003, City)
Dan Bell, Fort LeBoeuf (1993, County)
Frank Bell, Academy (1939, West)
Mike Bell, Iroquois (2007, County)
William Bell, Strong Vincent (2003, City)
Jordan Belosh, General McLane (2005, County)
Chuck Bemmus, Academy (1950, East)
Henry Benczkowski, Academy (1939, West)
Carl Benden, North East (1957, County)
Joe Benden, North East (1995, County)
Kelly Bender, Girard (1988, County)
Robert Bender, East (1946, East)
Charles Bendig, Harbor Creek (1939, East)
Don Bendig, Lawrence Park (1951, East; 1952, County)

Bob Bengel, Cathedral Prep (1975, City)
Justin Bengel, Union City (2012, County)
Rick Bengel, Cathedral Prep (1975, City)
Roosevelt Benjamin, Central (1995, City)
Adam Benko, Fort LeBoeuf (2008, County)
Andrew Bennett, McDowell (2011, City)
Fred Bennett, Union City (1959, County)
Mike Bennett, Central (1998, City)
Craig Bennetti, Strong Vincent (1992, City)
Tory Benning, Strong Vincent (1991, City)
Allan Benson, Strong Vincent (1945, West)
John Benson, Wesleyville (1942, East)
Steve Benson, Cathedral Prep (1964, City)
Arnold Bentley, Albion (1947, West)
Richard Benz, Academy (1959, City)
Carmen Berarducci, Tech (1969, City)
Dustin Berarducci, Central (1993, City)
Joe Berarducci, Strong Vincent (1958, City)
John Berarducci, Strong Vincent (1993, City)
Larry Berdis, Tech (1951, East)
John Bergquist, Fairview (1980, County)
Roy Bernardini, Tech (1942, East)
Don Bernatowicz, Harbor Creek (1991, County)
Ed Bernik, Tech (1940, West)
Dave Bertges, Wattsburg (1968, County)
Don Bertram, Cambridge Springs (1951, West; 1952, County)
Mark Beskid, East (1979, City)
Gary Besonson, Union City (1958, County)
Gordon Bessetti, Wattsburg (1972, County)
Josh Best, North East (2005, County)
Dan Betcher, Cathedral Prep (1967, County)
Donald Betts, Corry (1944, East)
Tim Beveridge, Tech (1983, City)
Don Bevilacqua, Strong Vincent (1942, West)
Carmen Bianco, Strong Vincent (1950, West)
Dom Bianco, Strong Vincent (1953, City)
Tom Bidwell, Union City (1965, County)
Tom Biel, Strong Vincent (1960, City)
Chris Bielak, Central (1994, City)
Ed Bielak, Tech (1964, City)
Ed Bielec, East (1947, East)
Robert Bierig, Strong Vincent (1949, West)
Jared Bigelow, Harbor Creek (1995, County)
Jeff Biggie, Central Tech (2012, City)
Jeff Biletnikoff, Seneca (1980, County)
Ron Biletnikoff, Seneca (1976, County)
Ron Biletnikoff, Academy (1954, City)
Sam Biletnikoff, Strong Vincent (1965, City)
Keith Bille, Fairview (1977, County)
Greg Billings, Northwestern (1984, County)
Hank Bink, Mercyhurst Prep (2006, City)
Joe Bires, Strong Vincent (1995, City)
Dick Bischoff, Millcreek (1954, County)
Joe Bish, Northwestern (1996, County)
Brian Bixby, Cathedral Prep (2003, City)

Save-An-Eye Game Players

Chuck Bizzarro, McDowell (1996, City)
Frank Bizzarro, Academy (1961, City)
Duane Black, McDowell (1959, County)
Travis Black, Girard (1995, County)
David Blackman, Cathedral Prep (1949, West)
Steve Blackman, McDowell (1969, County)
Dave Blake, Academy (1956, City)
Lowell Blake, Academy (1942, West)
Chris Blakeslee, North East (1984, County)
Clare Blakeslee, Union City (1983, County)
Jeff Blakeslee, North East (1968, County)
Lance Blakeslee, North East (1986, County)
Earnest Blakney, Academy (1986, City)
Grove Blanchard, Academy (1959, City)
Bob Bland, East (1988, City)
Ray Blanks II, Cathedral Prep (2009, City)
Charles Blanks, Tech (1976, City)
John Blanks, Strong Vincent (1985, City)
Richard Blatt ,Strong Vincent (1995, City)
Christopher Bleggi, Cathedral Prep (2012, City)
Greg Blinn, East (1965, City)
Bud Bloom, Wesleyville (1940, West)
Stephen Blose, Harbor Creek (2006, County)
Jeff Blose, Harbor Creek (1978, County)
Richard Blosser, Harbor Creek (1982, County)
Harold Blount, General McLane (1974, County)
Mike Blount, Cathedral Prep (2008, City)
Erwin Bloxdorf, Academy (1955, City)
Aaron Bluey, Fairview (2001, County)
Cleve Blunt, Lawrence Park (1965, County)
Dave Bobango, East (1965, City)
John Bobango, East (1958, City)
Robert Bobango, Cathedral Prep (1985, City)
Dave Bock, Lawrence Park (1942, East)
Rich Boesch, Cathedral Prep (1981, City)
Ryan Bogert, Corry (1997, County)
Steve Bohun, East (1973, City)
John Bojarski, Cathedral Prep (1972, City)
Scott Bojarski, Harbor Creek (1987, County)
Tom Bojarski, Harbor Creek (1979, County)
Dan Bokol, Iroquois (1984, County)
James Bolden, Academy (1975, City)
Scott Bolheimer, McDowell (1992, City)
Howard Bolte, Northwestern (1994, County)
Jeff Bomba, Cathedral Prep (2000, City)
Chris Bonanti, Fairview (1991, County)
Charles Bondurant, North East (1969, County)
Fred Bongiorno, Strong Vincent (1955, City)
Carm Bonito, Wesleyville (1940, West)
Joe Bonito, Wesleyville (1950, East)
Tony Bonito, Wesleyville (1943, East)
Bill Bonnett, Girard (1965, County)
Dick Bonniger, Iroquois (1966, County)
Sid Booker, East (1968, City)
Jeff Booser, Seneca (1985, County)

Cody Bootes, Harbor Creek (2011, County)
Roger Boothby, Northwestern (1980, County)
Tim Boothby, Northwestern (1977, County)
Rick Borgeson, Fairview (1987, County)
Ed Borgia, Prep (1970, City)
Otto Borgia, Cathedral Prep (1968, City)
Julius "Whitey" Borkowski, Academy (1948, East)
Rich Borkowski, Tech (1963, City)
Quinton Boroi, Harbor Creek (1964, County)
Lyle Bostick, McDowell (1980, City)
Zach Boswell, General McLane (2001, County)
Mike Bowers, McDowell (1994, City)
Tony Bowers, Cathedral Prep (1998, City)
Yod Bowers, Strong Vincent (1985, City)
Brent Boyd, Seneca (2004, County)
Wayne Boyd, Harbor Creek (1979, County)
Joe Boyer, Cathedral Prep (1999, City)
Bruce Boyle, Harbor Creek (1954, County)
Dennis Boyuzick, General McLane (1964, County)
Tony Bozich, Cathedral Prep (2005, City)
Tony Bozich, Cathedral Prep (1976, City)
Bill Brabender, Strong Vincent (1944, West)
Bob Brabender, Strong Vincent (1969, City)
David Brabender, Strong Vincent (1972, City)
Dave Brady, Iroquois (1992, County)
Dennis Brady, Academy (1988, City)
Fran Brady, Tech (1956, City)
Pat Brady, Tech (1966, City)
Phil Brady, Harbor Creek (1968, County)
Roger Brady, Wesleyville (1953, County)
Dave Brandell, Fairview (1964, County)
Don Brandon, Fairview (1955, County)
John Brandt, Iroquois (1983, County)
Michael Brandt, General McLane (2009, County)
Zack Brandt, Mercyhurst Prep (2003, City)
Dennis Brandyberry, Girard (1965, County)
Chuck Brasington, East (1946, East)
Ken Brasington, Tech (1971, City)
Demetric Braxton, McDowell (2005, City)
Duvall Braxton, McDowell (1995, City)
Jacob Breakstone, McDowell (2011, City)
George Brece, Albion (1941, West)
Ron Brecious, McDowell (1955, County)
Chris Breese, Northwestern (1992, County)
Robert Brei, Tech (1962, City)
Seth Bremmer, Fairview (1986, County)
Bob Bretz, Harbor Creek (1946, East)
Carl Bretz, Harbor Creek (1953, County)
Richard Bretz, Harbor Creek (1944, East)
Steve Bretz, Harbor Creek (1958, County)
Tyler Bretz, Harbor Creek (2012, County)
Charles Brewton, Tech (1965, City)
Wilbur Brezee, Lawrence Park (1946, East)
Pete Bricker, Millcreek (1940, East)
Travis Bricker, McDowell (1998, City)

Aaron Briggs, Fort LeBoeuf (1999, County)
Harley Briggs, North East (1942, East)
Joe Brink, Cambridge Springs (1950, West)
Chuck Britton, McDowell (1971, County)
David Britton, Strong Vincent (1972, City)
J.B. Britton, McDowell (2004, City)
Clay Brocious, Girard (2001, County)
Hubert Brock, Iroquois (1973, County)
Dave Brockelbank, Wesleyville (1941, East)
Bob Brockmyer, Strong Vincent (1969, City)
Darrell Brooks, Strong Vincent (2009, City)
Kevin Brooks, Seneca (1980, County)
Mark Brooks, Harbor Creek (2005, County)
Rod Brooks, Seneca (1977, County)
Thomas Brooks, Harbor Creek (2009, County)
Bob Bross, Harbor Creek (1973, County)
D.J. Bross, Seneca (2003, County)
Bob Brown ,Strong Vincent (1968, City)
Gary Brown Jr., McDowell (2010, City)
Aaron Brown, Girard (2006, County)
Billy Brown, Northwestern (2003, County)
Bob Brown, Cambridge Springs (1953, County)
Chris Brown, McDowell (1985, City)
David Brown, General McLane (1985, County)
Derek Brown, General McLane (1989, County)
Don Brown, Cathedral Prep (2003, City)
Ed Brown, Cathedral Prep (2001, City)
Elvin Brown, Cambridge Springs (1957, County)
Eugene Brown, Academy (1943, East)
Garrison Brown, Central (2000, City)
Gilbert Brown, Millcreek (1948, West)
Jason Brown, Northwestern (1998, County)
Ken Brown, Northwestern (1994, County)
Michael Brown, Corry (2009, County)
Parrish Brown, Iroquois (2012, County)
Stephen Brown, Fort LeBoeuf (1982, County)
Terry Brown, General McLane (1987, County)
Drew Browning, General McLane (2012, County)
Brian Brozell, Girard (1992, County)
Doug Brumagin, Seneca (1977, County)
Scott Brumagin, Seneca (2002, County)
Marc Brunner, Wesleyville (1953, County)
Mike Bruno, General McLane (1985, County)
John Bryan, Albion (1949, West)
Stephen Bryan, Strong Vincent (1996, City)
Craig Bryant, East (1983, City)
Oliver Bryant, East (1977, City)
Travis Bryant, General McLane (2011, County)
Al Bryon, Wesleyville (1964, County)
Jeff Brzezinski, Cathedral Prep (1997, City)
Kevin Brzezinski, Cathedral Prep (1998, City)
Jeff Brzostowski, Central (1998, City)
Brian Bubna, East (1999, City)
Jay Buchanan, Strong Vincent (1962, City)
Eric Bucheit, McDowell (1970, County)

Thomas Buck, Strong Vincent (1949, West)
Alan Buckel, General McLane (2011, County)
Jim Bucklin, Wattsburg (1962, County)
Tyrone Buckner, Cathedral Prep (2004, City)
Charlie Buckshaw, Corry (1984, County)
Troy Budziszewski, North East (2008, County)
Ben Budzowski, Edinboro (1953, County)
Chad Buell, Union City (1987, County)
Bob Buerger, Tech (1988, City)
Chuck Buerger, East (1960, City)
Jeff Buerger, Tech (1989, City)
Andy Bufalino, General McLane (1994, County)
Joe Bufalino, Cathedral Prep (1966, City)
Lincoln Bufalino, General McLane (1999, County)
John Buffington, North East (1954, County)
Bill Bujnoski, Cathedral Prep (1955, City)
Mark Bujnoski, McDowell (1983, City)
Tim Bujnowski, East (1956, City)
Dan Bukowski, Mercyhurst Prep (2001, City)
Jordan Bukowski, McDowell (2007, City)
Jamie Bulko, Strong Vincent (1979, City)
Dick Bullock, Cambridge Springs (1945, East)
Ryan Bunce, North East (2010, County)
Joe Bundy, Harbor Creek (2010, County)
Doug Burch, North East (1962, County)
Vance Burdick, Waterford (1950, East)
Daryl Burek, Union City (1999, County)
Greg Burek, Union City (1994, County)
Don Burger, Academy (1954, City)
Jared Burger, Union City (2010, County)
Terry Burgess, Academy (1945, East)
Tony Burgett, Edinboro (1958, County)
Robert Burick, Lawrence Park (1957, County)
Michael Burke, East (1993, City)
John Burkell, Academy (1990, City)
Paul Burkell, McDowell (1967, County)
Jim Burkett, Corry (1955, County)
John Burkett, Corry (1955, County)
Tim Burkett, General McLane (1988, County)
Mike Burlingham, Harbor Creek (1987, County)
Buff Burnett, Albion (1941, West)
Ken Burnett, Harbor Creek (2008, County)
Nate Burnett, Harbor Creek (1999, County)
Brian Burns, Seneca (1985, County)
Gordy Burns, East (1984, City)
Herb Burns, Union City (1946, East)
Keith Burns, Cathedral Prep (1990, City)
Mike Burns, Iroquois (1975, County)
Jeremy Burroughs, McDowell (2008, City)
Jim Burrows, Tech (1964, City)
Robin Burrows, Lawrence Park (1959, County)
Marlow Burt, Strong Vincent (1953, City)
Homer Bury, Wesleyville (1942, East)
John Buscemi, North East (1973, County)
Don Buseck, Fairview (1944, West)

Greg Bush, North East (2007, County)
Marc Bush, Strong Vincent (1972, City)
Dan Butler, East (1964, City)
Fred Butler, Iroquois (1969, County)
Joe Buto, Academy (1945, East)
Dave Buzard, Northwestern (1998, County)
Chris Buzas, Cathedral Prep (2007, City)
Bob Buzzanco, Strong Vincent (1968, City)
Bob Buzzard, Academy (1950, East)
Sean Byars, Northwestern (1994, County)
Scott Byerly, Academy (1982, City)
Mark Byham, Girard (1989, County)
Rick Byham, Strong Vincent (1972, City)
Ted Byham, Girard (1987, County)
William Byham, Girard (1949, West)

Lee Cabeloff, East (1951, East; 1952, City)
Mike Cacchione, McDowell (2003, City)
Tim Cacchione, Academy (1975, City)
Mark Cadden, Iroquois (1978, County)
Nick Cadie, Northwestern (1998, County)
John Cadwallader, Union City (1943, East)
Tom Cahill, Strong Vincent (1956, City)
John Calabrese, Cathedral Prep (1974, City)
Merch Calabrese, Strong Vincent (1972, City)
Brian Caldwell, McDowell (1997, City)
Jim Caldwell, East (1972, City)
Jim Caldwell, East (1966, City)
Kyle Caldwell, McDowell (2003, City)
Mike Caldwell, McDowell (1999, City)
Brad Callan, General McLane (2007, County)
Pat Camp, Northwestern (1989, County)
Sam Campanella, Strong Vincent (1983, City)
Tony Campanella, Strong Vincent (1985, City)
Bill Campbell, Strong Vincent (1963, City)
Frank Campbell, Strong Vincent (1970, City)
Harry Campbell, Tech (1951, East; 1952, City)
Jack Campbell, Strong Vincent (1947, West)
Larry Campbell, Academy (1965, City)
Lynn Campbell, General McLane (1966, County)
Tim Campbell, Fort LeBoeuf (2004, County)
Tim Campbell, Fort LeBoeuf (1983, County)
Dwayne Canady, Mercyhurst Prep (2012, City)
Nick Cancilla, Iroquois (1969, County)
Joe Canella, North East (1941, East)
Terry Capitol, Central (1994, City)
John Caporale, Cathedral Prep (1980, City)
Ryan Cappelletty, McDowell (1998, City)
Curt Cardman, Fairview (1982, County)
Jim Cardman, Fairview (1979, County)
William Carey, Cathedral Prep (1957, City)
Kevin Carlin, McDowell (1987, City)
Tim Carlin, McDowell (1984, City)
Brian Carlson, Strong Vincent (1962, City)

Dick Carlson, Tech (1946, West)
Eric Carlson, Cathedral Prep (2000, City)
Sean Carlson, Strong Vincent (1988, City)
Shawn Carlson, Strong Vincent (1997, City)
Mike Carnahan, Fairview (1987, County)
Dave Carner, Fairview (1981, County)
Aaron Carney, Corry (2009, County)
Jeff Carniewski , North East (2009, County)
Rich Carniewski, Fort LeBoeuf (1981, County)
Clayton Carothers, Strong Vincent (1977, City)
Harry Carpenter, Mercyhurst Prep (1994, City)
Tom Carpenter, East (1962, City)
Jeff Carpin, Harbor Creek (1983, County)
Ed Carr, East (1967, County)
Herb Carr, Millcreek (1957, County)
James Carr, East (1994, City)
Jarrod Carr, Central (2001, City)
Jerry Carr, Tech (1976, City)
Justin Carr, Central (2003, City)
Nate Carr, Fort LeBoeuf (2011, County)
Paul Carr, East (1992, City)
Ray Carr, Academy (1977, City)
Rob Carr, Cathedral Prep (1989, City)
Stuart Carr, Fort LeBoeuf (1980, County)
Kim Carrara, Cathedral Prep (1973, City)
Josh Carrick, McDowell (1999, City)
Robert Carrick, East (1947, East)
Alan Carroll, Fort LeBoeuf (1969, County)
Rory Carroll, Cathedral Prep (1999, City)
Sam Carroll, Tech (1988, City)
Aaron Carson, Academy (1979, City)
Charles Carson, Central (1995, City)
Doug Carson, Girard (2001, County)
Gary Carson, Academy (1972, City)
James Carson, Cathedral Prep (2005, City)
Kareem Carson, Strong Vincent (1994, City)
Melquwan Carson, East (2008, City)
Nicholas Carson, Corry (2006, County)
Randy Carson, Central (1997, City)
Robert Carson, Mercyhurst Prep (2009, City)
Sonny Carson, Strong Vincent (1989, City)
Terry Carson, East (1978, City)
Bud Carter, General McLane (1962, County)
Dave Carter, Academy (1958, City)
Jim Carter, General McLane (1960, County)
Dennis Carver, Harbor Creek (1995, County)
Dick Carver, Harbor Creek (1981, County)
Bill Caryl, Academy (1951, East; 1952, City)
Larry Casciere, North East (1976, County)
David Case, General McLane (1990, County)
Tim Case, Harbor Creek (1997, County)
Bob Casella, Strong Vincent (1971, City)
Jim Cash, Fairview (1969, County)
Jeff Cass, Harbor Creek (1985, County)
Jerry Cass, Harbor Creek (1963, County)

Save-An-Eye Game Players

Tom Cass, Iroquois (1989, County)
Jason Cassano, East (1999, City)
Craig Catalfu, Corry (2007, County)
Matt Catalino McDowell (1997, City)
Bill Cauley, General McLane (1963, County)
Trevor Cawley, North East (2000, County)
Bob Cenfetelli, Tech (1957, City)
Joe Cerami, Strong Vincent (1944, West)
Joe Cerce, Corry (1994, County)
James Cermak, Academy (1962, City)
Tom Cermak, Seneca (2008, County)
Tom Cermak, Cathedral Prep (1983, City)
Scott Cervik, Iroquois (1985, County)
Ernie Chandler, Northwestern (1970, County)
Floyd Chandler, McDowell (1960, County)
Dan Chase, Fairview (1964, County)
Loren Chase, Corry (1997, County)
Mike Chase, Northwestern (1997, County)
Russell Chase, Girard (2004, County)
Phil Chenard, Cathedral Prep (1977, City)
Micah Chernicky, General McLane (1994, County)
Joe Chevalier, Mercyhurst Prep (2005, City)
John Chiarelli, Strong Vincent (1982, City)
Scot Chiffon, Tech (1982, City)
Matt Chilcott, East (1982, City)
Art Chimenti, Tech (1939, East)
Ron Chimenti, Cathedral Prep (1962, City)
Frank Chimera, North East (1941, East)
James Chimera, Harbor Creek (1988, County)
Josh Chiocco, McDowell (1995, City)
Bill Chircuzzio, Corry (1950, East)
Don Chludzinski, Tech (1956, City)
Steve Chludzinski, Tech (1968, City)
Al Chorney, Fairview (1991, County)
Jim Chorney, Fairview (1988, County)
Michael Chriest, St. Gregory (1962, County)
Bob Christensen, Strong Vincent (1939, West)
Chip Christensen, Academy (1968, City)
Craig Christensen, McDowell (1985, City)
Erik Christensen, McDowell (1985, City)
Chet Chrzanowski, Cathedral Prep (1961, City)
John Chrzanowski, East (1965, City)
Martin Chulick, Girard (1946, West)
Dan Church, Cathedral Prep (1987, City)
Paul Church, Cathedral Prep (1984, City)
Tim Church, Cathedral Prep (1981, City)
Dave Ciacchini, McDowell (1972, County)
Sam Cianflocco, Strong Vincent (1948, West)
Mark Cicero, Cathedral Prep (1974, City)
Jim Ciecierski, East (1990, City)
Greg Cieslak, Cathedral Prep (1973, City)
Mark Cieslak, Cathedral Prep (1974, City)
Joey Ciminella, McDowell (1998, City)
Dave Cimino, Girard (2008, County)
Dave Cimino, Strong Vincent (1974, City)

Hubert Cioccio, East (1960, City)
Jamie Cipalla, Northwestern (1986, County)
Dave Clabbatz, Fort LeBoeuf (1979, County)
Tommy Clanton, Central (2004, City)
Byron Clapper, McKean (1941, West)
Dan Clapper, General McLane (1973, County)
Dick Clark, Strong Vincent (1953, City)
Ed Clark, Union City (1940, West)
Jim Clark, Academy (1978, City)
Josh Clark, Harbor Creek (1999, County)
Lavon Clark, Tech (1983, City)
Mark Clark, Cathedral Prep (1981, City)
Mike Clark, Tech (1986, City)
Mike Clark, Union City (1980, County)
Randy Clark, Girard (1978, County)
Rich Clark, East (1996, City)
Sherman Clark, Harbor Creek (1955, County)
Ted Clark, McDowell (1972, County)
Vince Clark, Central (1994, City)
Tom Cleary, Harbor Creek (1976, County)
Ron Cleaver, Cathedral Prep (1983, City)
Alex Clemente, Strong Vincent (1950, West)
Dennis Clemente, Strong Vincent (1989, City)
Casey Cleveland, Girard (2003, County)
David Cline, Fort LeBoeuf (1971, County)
Roy Cline, East (1943, East)
Augie Cocarelli, Tech (1950, East)
Mike Cody, Central (2001, City)
John Coffey, Strong Vincent (1966, City)
Bill Cole, Northwestern (1990, County)
Gary Coleman, Tech (1986, City)
John Coleman, Academy (1975, City)
Randell Coleman, Academy (1977, City)
Ryan Coleman, Union City (2009, County)
Mike Coletta, North East (2004, County)
Deonte Colley, Central (2004, City)
Bill Collins, Wesleyville (1950, East)
Mike Coluzzi, Cathedral Prep (1972, City)
Chuck Colvin, Cathedral Prep (1945, West)
Gary Colvin, Harbor Creek (1974, County)
Terry Colvin, Cathedral Prep (1981, City)
Trevor Colvin, Mercyhurst Prep (2010, City)
Jake Comer, Harbor Creek (2005, County)
Pat Comer, Iroquois (1977, County)
Tom Comstock, Iroquois (1973, County)
Craig Conboy, Strong Vincent (1960, City)
Chris Concilla, North East (1984, County)
Jim Concilla, North East (1955, County)
Joe Concilla, North East (1949, East)
Joe Concilla, North East (1946, East)
Bob Conley, Lawrence Park (1950, East)
Eric Conley, Iroquois (1986, County)
John Conley, Conneautville (1950, West)
Sean Conley, Iroquois (1990, County)
Walter Conn, Strong Vincent (1940, East)

Shad Connelly, Strong Vincent (1963, City)
Duane Conner, Academy (1992, City)
Andy Connor, Millcreek (1958, County)
DeAndre Connor, Mercyhurst Prep (2011, City)
Bill Connors, Albion (1942, West)
Dick Connors, Academy (1959, City)
Rich Conover, McDowell (1963, County)
Chris Conrad, Central (1993, City)
Bill Cook, Cathedral Prep (1985, City)
Bill Cook, Strong Vincent (1960, City)
Tim Cook, Academy (1988, City)
Mike Cooklis, North East (1999, County)
Gentle Cooley, Tech (1972, City)
Brian Coon, Girard (1979, County)
Chris Cooney, Cathedral Prep (1959, City)
Sean Cooney, McDowell (1988, City)
Kevin Cooper, Academy (1984, City)
Melvin Cooper, East (1965, City)
Jamall Cooper-Stewart, Central (1995, City)
Sam Copeland, East (1963, City)
Tom Corapi, Cathedral Prep (1955, City)
Dan Corbett, Corry (1969, County)
Jim Corbett, McDowell (1973, County)
Ben Corbin, Fairview (1992, County)
Joe Corbin, Fairview (1989, County)
Tim Corder, Cathedral Prep (2009, City)
Tony Cordovano, Mercyhurst Prep (2010, City)
John Corkan, Strong Vincent (1979, City)
John Corklin, Cambridge Springs (1954, County)
Spencer Cornelius, North East (2011, County)
Bob Corritore, Cathedral Prep (1982, City)
Craig Costello, Tech (1983, City)
Eric Costello, Central (2004, City)
R.J. Costello, Tech (1980, City)
Ron Costello, Cathedral Prep (1957, City)
Terry Costello, Strong Vincent (1984, City)
Brad Costolo, Harbor Creek (1994, County)
Doug Cottrell, Seneca (1979, County)
Steve Coughlin, Seneca (1993, County)
Dick Coursey, McDowell (1970, County)
James Coursey, Millcreek (1939, West)
Ed Cousins, McDowell (1986, City)
Paul Cousins, McDowell (1984, City)
Tyler Covato, McDowell (2011, City)
James Cowles, Mercyhurst Prep (2008, City)
Al Cox, Girard (1972, County)
Bert Cox, Girard (1980, County)
Don Cox, Corry (1985, County)
Jason Cox, Strong Vincent (1990, City)
Ken Cox, Iroquois (2004, County)
Travis Cox, Union City (1939, East)
Bill Coyne, East (1941, East)
James Coyne, Academy (1943, East)
Matt Cozad, North East (1988, County)
Charles Craft, Wattsburg (1972, County)

John Cragg, Corry (2012, County)
Mike Cragg, Corry (1978, County)
Bob Craig, Tech (1953, City)
Scott Craig, Seneca (1986, County)
Doug Craker, Corry (1982, County)
Don Crannell, Iroquois (1967, County)
Bob Crawford, Tech (1970, City)
David Crawford, Academy (1941, West)
Glen Crawford, Harbor Creek (1942, East)
Jamaal Crawford, Strong Vincent (1992, City)
Clarence Cray, Tech (1940, West)
Norm Crenshaw, Harbor Creek (1984, County)
Jason Crilley, Cathedral Prep (1993, City)
Jeff Crockett, McDowell (1980, City)
David Cronin, Cathedral Prep (1973, City)
Cliff Crosby, East (1994, City)
DeShawn Crosby, Strong Vincent (2005, City)
Eugene Crosby, Cathedral Prep (1996, City)
Jovan Crosby, East (2007, City)
Melvin Crosby, Academy (1988, City)
Jeff Cross, Fairview (1984, County)
Jim Cross, Millcreek (1953, County)
Norb Cross, Waterford (1957, County)
Pete Cross, Fairview (1987, County)
Richard Cross, McDowell (1955, County)
Paul Crossman, Girard (1944, West)
Bill Crotty, East (1940, West)
Brandon Crotty, Corry (1991, County)
Dave Crotty, Lawrence Park (1961, County)
Denny Crotty, McDowell (1984, City)
John Crotty, Iroquois (1975, County)
Dave Crowell, Corry (1971, County)
Russ Crowner, East (1964, City)
Andy Crozier, Iroquois (1993, County)
Eric Cruz, East (2002, City)
Michael Cruz, Mercyhurst Prep (2010, City)
John Csir, Cathedral Prep (2006, City)
Bob Cubbison, Academy (1951, East)
Kevin Cudicio, Harbor Creek (1979, County)
Jack Cugnin, Academy (1941, West)
Bob Culbertson, Corry (1964, County)
Charles Cummings, Fairview (1983, County)
Chris Ellis, Fairview (1983, County)
Mark Cunningham, McDowell (1988, City)
Bobby Curry, Strong Vincent (1983, City)
Dennis Curry, Fairview (1962, County)
Nick Curry, McDowell (2004, City)
Sean Curry, Iroquois (1986, County)
Chris Curtis, Harbor Creek (1991, County)
John Cutter, Tech (1963, City)
Joe Cuzzola, Cathedral Prep (1954, City)
Mike Cuzzola, East (1976, City)
Dan Cypher, Harbor Creek (2001, County)
Shane Cyphert, Seneca (2007, County)
Chris Cyterski, Cathedral Prep (1990, City)

Len Cyterski, Cathedral Prep (1950, West)
Brandon Czerwinski, Mercyhurst Prep (2011, City)
Joel Czurnecki, Harbor Creek (2003, County)

Tony D'Albora, Central (2007, City)
Adam D'Ambrosio, Fairview (1993, County)
Dan D'Amico, Seneca (1978, County)
Mark D'Amico, Cathedral Prep (1978, City)
Billy D'Andrea, Mercyhurst Prep (2008, City)
Jim D'Andrea, Strong Vincent (1960, City)
Anthony Dabrowski, Cathedral Prep (2004, City)
Anthony Dabrowski, Tech (1975, City)
Mitch Dabrowski, Iroquois (2005, County)
Don Daggett, Girard (1942, West)
Dave Dahlkemper, Cathedral Prep (1951, West)
Jerry Dahlkemper, Cathedral Prep (1963, City)
Jim Dahlstrand, Girard (1984, County)
Joe Dahlstrand, Girard (1986, County)
John Dahlstrand, McDowell (2011, City)
John Dahlstrand, Strong Vincent (1978, City)
Jim Dale, Fairview (1962, County)
Ed Dalglish, Lawrence Park (1953, County)
Doug Dalton, Cathedral Prep (1982, City)
Ed Dalton, Strong Vincent (1977, City)
Jack Dalton, Cathedral Prep (1949, West)
Gary Damico, Academy (1959, City)
Tom Damico, East (1952, City)
Tim Dance, Cathedral Prep (2001, City)
Rich Dandrea, Cathedral Prep (1976, City)
Tom Danias, East (2003, City)
Jim Daniels, Fort LeBoeuf (1969, County)
John Daniels, East (1954, City)
John Danilov, McDowell (1982, City)
Dan Danowski, Cathedral Prep (1991, City)
Gary Danowski, Strong Vincent (1978, City)
Jason Danowski, Harbor Creek (2002, County)
John Danowski, Academy (1948, East)
Terry Darada, Fort LeBoeuf (1962, County)
Mel Darby, East (1974, City)
Jeff Daub, McDowell (1975, County)
Bernard Daugherty, Tech (1942, East)
Bob Davenport, Conneaut Valley (1951, West; 1952, County)
Bob Davern, Girard (1942, West)
Larry Davies, General McLane (1974, County)
Alex Davis, Strong Vincent (2010, City)
Dan Davis, Tech (1992, City)
Dewey Davis, Millcreek (1945, West)
Ed Davis, Cathedral Prep (1957, City)
Howard Davis, Union City (1945, East)
John Davis, East (1940, West)
Paul Davis, Millcreek (1951, West; 1952, County)
Randy Davis, Tech (1991, City)
Ron Davis, Cambridge Springs (1959, County)

Tim Davis, McDowell (1983, City)
William Davis, North East (1994, County)
Andy Dawson, East (1978, City)
Earl Dawson, East (1978, City)
Tom Dawson, General McLane (1965, County)
Tyler Dawson, Union City (2009, County)
Krishawn Day, East (2011, City)
Sean Day, Iroquois (1993, County)
Walter Dean, Tech (1943, West)
Paul Deane, Strong Vincent (1975, City)
Todd DeBello, McDowell (1986, City)
Jack Debold, Millcreek (1953, County)
Bruce Decker, Academy (1960, City)
Bill DeDionisio, Harbor Creek (1963, County)
Dick Deeds, Cathedral Prep (1950, West)
Eric Deemer, Fort LeBoeuf (1988, County)
Greg Deemer, Fort LeBoeuf (1985, County)
Doug DeHart, McDowell (1983, City)
Luke DeHart, McDowell (2012, City)
Mark Deitsch, McDowell (1982, City)
Rock Deitsch, McDowell (1975, County)
Mike Delahunty, Academy (1978, City)
Jack Delavern, Millcreek (1956, County)
Joel Delavern, Girard (1986, County)
Fred Delfino, Academy (1961, City)
Pat DelFreo, Cathedral Prep (1987, City)
Jerry Delinski, East (1942, East)
Ron Delinski, Tech (1978, City)
Bryan Delio, Academy (1991, City)
Corey Delio, Central (1993, City)
John DeLiva, Strong Vincent (1942, West)
Don Delo, East (1958, City)
Jason Delp, Harbor Creek (1993, County)
Ed DeLuca, East (1955, City)
Steve DeLuca, Strong Vincent (1991, City)
Craig DeMarco, Cathedral Prep (1984, City)
Steve DeMichele, Harbor Creek (1990, County)
Bill Demyanovich, East (1948, East)
Paul Demyanovich, East (1954, City)
Chuck Dengel, Iroquois (1967, County)
Paul DeRaimo, Tech (1956, City)
Chris DeRose, Tech (1982, City)
Jason Dersch, Northwestern (2003, County)
Joe DeSanti, Tech (1959, City)
Ted DeSanti, Academy (1981, City)
Dan Desser, Cathedral Prep (1955, City)
Don Detisch, Academy (1959, City)
Bob Detzel, East (1944, East)
Don Detzel, Strong Vincent (1973, City)
Jim Detzel, North East (1968, County)
Rick DiBacco, Cathedral Prep (1992, City)
Mike DiBello, Cathedral Prep (1976, City)
Larry Dibler, Academy (1961, City)
David Dickerson, East (2000, City)
Rich Dickey, Strong Vincent (1954, City)

Mark Dickson, General McLane (1988, County)
Bill Dietz, Cathedral Prep (1979, City)
Bill Difenbach, Cathedral Prep (1961, City)
Dan Diffenbacher, Seneca (1976, County)
James Diffenbacher, Wesleyville (1949, East)
Mike DiFilippo, McDowell (1992, City)
Jerry DiGello, Tech (1974, City)
Robert DiGello, Tech (1991, City)
Dick Dilimone, Tech (1960, City)
Jim Dilimone, Cathedral Prep (1983, City)
Dick Dill, Cathedral Prep (1955, City)
Tom Dill, Cathedral Prep (1977, City)
John DiMattio, Girard (2005, County)
Bill Dimon, Northwestern (1970, County)
Joel Dinger, Fort LeBoeuf (1994, County)
Josh Dinger, Northwestern (2001, County)
Mel Dinger, Girard (1980, County)
John Dingfelder, McDowell (1959, County)
Ed DiNicola, Tech (1954, City)
Peter DiNicola, Harbor Creek (1949, East)
Phil DiNicola, Strong Vincent (1954, City)
Tony DiNicola, Cathedral Prep (1993, City)
Pat DiPaolo, Cathedral Prep (1987, City)
Tony DiPaolo, East (1951, East)
Lou DiPlacido, Cathedral Prep (1963, City)
Joe Dipre, Cathedral Prep (1973, City)
Todd Dipre, Cathedral Prep (1998, City)
Matt DiRaimo, Cathedral Prep (1997, City)
Art DiRienzo, Millcreek (1956, County)
Bob Dishinger, Tech (1942, East)
John Dittrich, Cathedral Prep (1953, City)
Richard DiTullio, Strong Vincent (1939, West)
Jeremy Ditzler, Iroquois (2007, County)
Eric Divell, Harbor Creek (2008, County)
Bob Dixon, East (1975, City)
Dana Dobbs, McDowell (1983, City)
Marshall Dobbs, Cathedral Prep (1977, City)
Terry Dodd, Fort LeBoeuf (1970, County)
Tom Dodd, Union City (2006, County)
William Dodge, East (1955, City)
Jim Dohanic, Girard (1971, County)
Jason Dolak, Cathedral Prep (2000, City)
Jeff Dolak, Tech (1976, City)
Joe Dolak, Tech (1983, City)
Bill Dolinsky, Cambridge Springs (1945, East)
Dave Dombkowski, Tech (1984, City)
Doug Dombkowski, Tech (1986, City)
Robert Dombkowski, Tech (1985, City)
Ray Dombrowski, Tech (1944, West)
George Donachy, Cambridge Springs (1953, County)
John Donahic, Girard (1945, West)
Sam Donato, Strong Vincent (1943, West)
Jerry Donatucci, Cathedral Prep (1950, West)
Pete Donatucci, Cathedral Prep (1956, City)
Jack Donihi, Academy (1944, East)

Darrin Donikowski, Mercyhurst Prep (2012, City)
Richard Donikowski, Tech (1957, City)
Tony Donikowski, Tech (1978, City)
Shane Donnelly, General McLane (2003, County)
Richard Doolittle, Strong Vincent (1957, City)
Greg Dore, General McLane (1997, County)
Jason Dorich, Mercyhurst Prep (2008, City)
Jeremy Dornhoefer, Iroquois (2006, County)
Ronald Doucette, Edinboro (1944, West)
Gary Dougan, Harbor Creek (1980, County)
Tim Dougan, Cathedral Prep (1977, City)
Tom Dougan, Harbor Creek (1967, County)
John Dougherty, East (1941, East)
Jimmy Douglas, Northwestern (2006, County)
Randy Dovichow, Cathedral Prep (1989, City)
Harold Dowler, Edinboro (1943, West)
John Downey, Corry (1971, County)
Mike Downey, Corry (1997, County)
Rich Doyle, Strong Vincent (1954, City)
Tom Doyle, St. Gregory (1964, County)
Bill Drabina, Cathedral Prep (1973, City)
Garrick Drabina, Cathedral Prep (2007, City)
Ryan Drabina, Cathedral Prep (2004, City)
Mike Driehorst, Mercyhurst Prep (1998, City)
Mark Driscoll, Cathedral Prep (1976, City)
Pat Driscoll, Academy (1974, City)
Jordan Drohn, Seneca (2010, County)
Steve Dronsfield, General McLane (1979, County)
Mike Dropcho, Cathedral Prep (1971, City)
John Drozdowski, Iroquois (2012, County)
Matt Dubowski, Mercyhurst Prep (1999, City)
Mike Dubowski, Tech (1969, City)
Mark Dubrosky, Corry (1997, County)
Glenn Duck, Tech (1991, City)
Pat Duda, Harbor Creek (2003, County)
Tom Dudenhoefer, Cathedral Prep (1951, West)
Eric Dudenhoeffer, Seneca (1992, County)
Chris Dudley, Cathedral Prep (1998, City)
Greg Dufala, Cathedral Prep (1998, City)
Dan Dugan, Fairview (1978, County)
Luke Dugan, Fairview (1981, County)
Jim Dunda, Northwestern (1967, County)
Todd Dunda, Iroquois (1990, County)
Dick Dundon, Edinboro (1951, West)
Phil Dunlap, General McLane (1997, County)
Brandon Dunn, Central (2007, City)
Chris Dunn, Girard (1978, County)
Ernest Dunn, Academy (1955, City)
Patrick Dunn, Girard (2009, County)
Andy Duran, Fort LeBoeuf (2004, County)
Paul Duran, Fort LeBoeuf (2002, County)
Gary Duris, Northwestern (1969, County)
Tom Dutkosky, Cathedral Prep (1973, City)
Mike Dworakowski, Girard (2004, County)
Mark Dylewski, Tech (1975, City)

Mike Dylewski, Fairview (1979, County)

Chad Eades, North East (2000, County)
Doug Eades, Harbor Creek (1947, East)
Dick Eaglen, Harbor Creek (1951, East)
Todd Eaglen, Harbor Creek (1993, County)
Dick East, Fairview (1942, West)
Jason Easter, Cathedral Prep (2001, City)
Mike Easterling, Strong Vincent (1979, City)
Clyde Eaton, Fairview (1955, County)
Ken Eaton, Fairview (1956, County)
Tom Eaton, North East (1968, County)
Bill Eberlein, Cathedral Prep (1958, City)
Paul Ebert, Fort LeBoeuf (1991, County)
Robert Ebisch, East (1939, East)
Brandan Eck, Corry (2007, County)
Tom Eck, Corry (1981, County)
Everett Eddy, East (1966, City)
Dennis Edmonds, Academy (1964, City)
David Edwards, Cathedral Prep (2003, City)
Don Edwards, Wesleyville (1946, East)
Joshua Edwards, Strong Vincent (2009, City)
Bill Ehegartner, McDowell (1995, City)
Neal Eicher, Mercyhurst Prep (2007, City)
Whitey Eiser, Harbor Creek (1962, County)
Len Ekimoff, Tech (1945, West)
Ted Elchynski, Corry (1954, County)
Dan Eller, Fort LeBoeuf (1979, County)
Darren Eller, Seneca (1992, County)
Ed Eller, Iroquois (1971, County)
Mark Eller, Wattsburg (1972, County)
John Elliott, Strong Vincent (1969, City)
T.J. Elliott, Fairview (1989, County)
Jeff Ellis, Tech (1973, City)
Mark Ellis, Fort LeBoeuf (1976, County)
Matt Ellis, North East (1983, County)
Paul Ellis, Fort LeBoeuf (1987, County)
Ramone Ellis, Cathedral Prep (1996, City)
Steve Ellis, Fairview (1979, County)
Clark Ellsworth, North East (1999, County)
David Ellsworth, North East (1985, County)
Bob Ellwood, Harbor Creek (1967, County)
Dave Ellwood, Harbor Creek (1974, County)
Doug Elwell, McDowell (1960, County)
Jason Elwell, McDowell (1997, City)
Moe Elwell, McDowell (1967, County)
Felix Emeideo, Tech (1957, City)
Mike Emerson, North East (1981, County)
Joe Emington, Lawrence Park (1939, East)
John Emington, Lawrence Park (1939, East)
Michael Endean, Northwestern (1986, County)
Bill Engel, McDowell (1969, County)
Frank Engel, Academy (1949, East)

John Engel, McDowell (1980, City)
Scott Engle, Corry (1994, County)
Dan Englert, Fort LeBoeuf (1983, County)
Jeff Englert, Fort LeBoeuf (1991, County)
Robert Englert, Harbor Creek (1992, County)
Adam English, Northwestern (2003, County)
Andrew English, McDowell (1988, City)
Andrew Enterline, Fort LeBoeuf (2010, County)
Jack Erb, Cathedral Prep (1940, East)
Hunter Erdman, Girard (2011, County)
Jeff Erdman, General McLane (2006, County)
Pat Erdman, Tech (1979, City)
Tom Erdman, Cathedral Prep (1971, City)
Bill Erickson, McDowell (1967, County)
Chuck Erickson, Strong Vincent (1971, City)
Orvid Erickson, Wesleyville (1940, West)
Steve Eriksen, Fort LeBoeuf (1991, County)
Tim Eriksen, Fort LeBoeuf (1990, County)
Dick Ernfeldt, Fairview (1943, West)
Anthony Ernst, Cathedral Prep (2012, City)
Jay Ernst, Strong Vincent (2001, City)
Jeff Ernst, Strong Vincent (2004, City)
Brett Erven, Cathedral Prep (1989, City)
Ralph Erven, Fairview (1939, West)
Ryan Erven, McDowell (1998, City)
Bernie Erwin, Wesleyville (1962, County)
Bill Essigmann, East (1969, City)
Ron Essigmann, East (1971, City)
Dwight Esters, East (1987, City)
Ross Etter, East (1949, East)
Chuck Evanoff, Academy (1960, City)
Harry Evanoff, Iroquois (1974, County)
Mike Evanoff, McKean (1940, East)
Ron Evanoff, Academy (1960, City)
Don Evans, East (1970, City)
Joe Evans, East (2001, City)
Pat Evans, Cathedral Prep (2005, City)
Rodney Evans, Tech (1987, City)
Nathan Evers, McDowell (2002, City)

Bill Fabian, Strong Vincent (1941, West)
Don Fabian, Strong Vincent (1942, West)
Mark Fachetti, East (1979, City)
Jason Faipler, Cathedral Prep (2009, City)
Donald Faller, Harbor Creek (1944, East)
Kevin Farr, Strong Vincent (2000, City)
Adam Farrell, Fort LeBoeuf (2006, County)
Duane Farrell, Union City (1959, County)
Eric Farrell, Central (1998, City)
Richard Farren, Wesleyville (1948, East)
Don Farver, Fairview (1977, County)
Dave Faulkenhagen, Harbor Creek (1984, County)
Chuck Faulkner, McDowell (1962, County)
Eric Faulkner, McDowell (1996, City)

Gary Faulkner, Girard (1970, County)
Ken Faulkner, McDowell (1962, County)
Shaun Fawcett, Northwestern (1991, County)
Greg Featsent, Fairview (1993, County)
Keith Featsent, Cathedral Prep (1997, City)
Bob Federoff, East (1956, City)
Colin Feeney, Fort LeBoeuf (2009, County)
Carl Feick, East (1953, City)
David Feick, Tech (1975, City)
Dick Feidler, Millcreek (1958, County)
Tait Feisler, McDowell (1970, County)
John Feketi, Seneca (1996, County)
Craig Feldman, Fairview (1982, County)
Mike Feldman, Cathedral Prep (1978, City)
Nick Felice, Fort LeBoeuf (1981, County)
Rusty Felix, Cathedral Prep (1969, City)
Ben Fenell, Northwestern (2003, County)
Eric Fenton, McDowell (2007, City)
Larry Fenton, North East (1966, County)
Nicholas Fenton, McDowell (2012, City)
Peter Ferguson, Harbor Creek (1988, County)
Tom Ferguson, Corry (1990, County)
Bob Ferrando, Fairview (1974, County)
Steve Ferrando, Fairview (1977, County)
Mickey Ferrare, Fairview (2012, County)
Mike Ferrare, Strong Vincent (1969, City)
Phil Ferrare, Cathedral Prep (1990, City)
Fred Ferraro, Harbor Creek (1943, East)
Tom Ferraro, Fairview (1972, County)
Kyle Ferrick, Cathedral Prep (1989, City)
Mike Ferritto, Iroquois (1995, County)
Ray Ferritto, East (1995, City)
Don Fessler, Cathedral Prep (1948, West)
George Fessler, Cathedral Prep (1956, City)
Jim Fessler, Cathedral Prep (1988, City)
Dave Fetzner, Tech (1968, City)
Leonard Fetzner, Tech (1939, East)
Mark Fetzner, Cathedral Prep (1992, City)
Rich Fetzner, Cathedral Prep (1968, City)
Harold Fiddler, Millcreek (1954, County)
Eric Field, Cathedral Prep (2001, City)
Rich Figaski, Cathedral Prep (1970, City)
Chris Filipowski, Cathedral Prep (1947, West)
Mark Filipowski, Cathedral Prep (1974, City)
Tim Finegan, General McLane (2004, County)
Ernest Finke, Harbor Creek (1939, East)
Joe Finney, Edinboro (1941, West)
Pat Finnucan, Conneaut Valley (1962, County)
Mike Finotti, Tech (1978, City)
Tony Finotti, Tech (1978, City)
Pete Fischer, Academy (1943, East)
Adam Fiscus, General McLane (1994, County)
Dennis Fiscus, North East (1960, County)
Gary Fish, Fort LeBoeuf (1981, County)
Larry Fish, Fort LeBoeuf (1975, County)

Chett Fisher, Northwestern (1998, County)
Dave Fisher, McDowell (1974, County)
Mike Fisher, McDowell (2002, City)
Jacob Fiske, Fort LeBoeuf (2002, County)
Josh Fiske, Fort LeBoeuf (2000, County)
Mark Fitch, Iroquois (1972, County)
Larry Fitzgerald, Wesleyville (1964, County)
Mike Fitzgerald, Harbor Creek (1989, County)
Robert Fitzgerald, Union City (1943, East)
Bob Flak, East (1974, City)
Jim Flanigan, East (1939, East)
John Flanigan, Cathedral Prep (1942, West)
Christian Fleming, Strong Vincent (2005, City)
Chuck Fleming, Corry (1954, County)
Greg Flick, McDowell (2003, City)
Jack Flick, Cambridge Springs (1947, East)
Paul Flick, Corry (2007, County)
Scott Flick, Iroquois (1999, County)
Mike Florek, General McLane (1972, County)
Jared Flowers, Harbor Creek (2003, County)
Stan Flowers, Tech (1940, West)
Bill Flynn, Union City (1988, County)
Gale Fobes, Albion (1941, West)
Jon Fogel, Corry (1986, County)
Robert Fogle, Strong Vincent (1948, West)
Brian Foley, Iroquois (2009, County)
Jim Folmar, North East (2002, County)
Paul Foltz, Fort LeBoeuf (1985, County)
Matt Fome, McDowell (2007, City)
George Foor, East (1954, City)
Bob Ford, Strong Vincent (1953, City)
Levonte Ford, East (2012, City)
Bob Formaini, Cathedral Prep (1939, West)
Harry Fornalczyk, Academy (1942, West)
Antonio Foster, Central (2006, City)
Dick Foster, Corry (1945, East)
Bob Fox, McDowell (1966, County)
Jeff Fox, Fairview (1989, County)
Mike Fox, Cathedral Prep (1977, City)
Richard Fox, General McLane (1982, County)
Robert Fox, Fairview (1949, West)
Al Fracassi, Academy (1945, East)
Joe Fracassi, Academy (1949, East)
Jordan Fracassi, Central (2006, City)
Larry Frame, Academy (1958, City)
Alan Frampton, East (1986, City)
Jesse Francis, Central (2002, City)
Dave Frank, Iroquois (2000, County)
Kyle Frank, General McLane (1988, County)
Matt Frano, McDowell (1996, City)
Bob Frantz, General McLane (1986, County)
Corey Frantz, Iroquois (2007, County)
Joe Franz, Academy (1953, City)
Mike Franz, Academy (1986, City)
Steve Franz, Central (1996, City)

Tom Franzkowski, Academy (1941, West)
Russ Fratto, Millcreek (1940, East)
Tom Freebourn, Strong Vincent (1956, City)
Brent Freeburg, Fort LeBoeuf (2002, County)
Bill Freeman, Academy (1947, East)
Brad Freeman, Fairview (1998, County)
Chuck Freeman, Millcreek (1952, County)
Jim Freeman, Cathedral Prep (1958, City)
Mike Freeman, Cathedral Prep (2004, City)
Tom Freeman, Tech (1949, East)
Connie French, Corry (1957, County)
Neil French, Lawrence Park (1940, West)
Jack Frey, Girard (1954, County)
Lawrence Frey, Girard (1948, West)
Harry Fried, Strong Vincent (1967, County)
Doug Friedman, Fort LeBoeuf (1996, County)
Jim Fries, Cathedral Prep (1965, City)
John Fries, Cathedral Prep (1956, City)
Scott Frisina, Corry (1982, County)
Scottie Frisina, Corry (2010, County)
Frank Frith, Wesleyville (1951, East)
Ron Fritts, Tech (1967, County)
Andy Fritz, Iroquois (1974, County)
Todd Froehlich, Cathedral Prep (1971, City)
Kyle Frost, East (2004, City)
Mark Frushone, Corry (1989, County)
Jason Fuhrer, Fort LeBoeuf (1998, County)
John Fuhrer, Fort LeBoeuf (1968, County)
Mitch Fuhrer, Fort LeBoeuf (1988, County)
Ron Fuhrer, Fort LeBoeuf (1964, County)
Zach Fuhrer, Fort LeBoeuf (2001, County)
Anthony Fuhrman, Strong Vincent (2006, City)
Bob Fuhrman, Strong Vincent (1942, West)
Dan Fuhrman, Academy (1974, City)
Mike Fuhrman, Academy (1981, City)
Chris Fuller, Northwestern (1990, County)
Gerry Fuller, General McLane (1960, County)
John Fuller, Conneautville (1949, West)
Rich Fuller, Edinboro (1954, County)
Vic Fuller, Edinboro (1939, West)
John Fulton, Cathedral Prep (1981, City)

Jason Gabbard, Mercyhurst Prep (1999, City)
Joe Gabbard, McDowell (2003, City)
Bill Gaber, Fort LeBoeuf (1961, County)
Gary Gaber, Academy (1966, City)
John Gage, Albion (1955, County)
Tim Gage, Northwestern (1993, County)
Tom Gage, Northwestern (1978, County)
Bryan Gaines, Strong Vincent (2005, City)
Ryan Gaines, Strong Vincent (2002, City)
Don Gajewski, Cathedral Prep (1985, City)
Dusty Galich, McDowell (2010, City)

Nick Galich, McDowell (2008, City)
Kasey Gallagher, McDowell (2010, City)
Jim Gallegos, East (1970, City)
Jaimen Gallo, General McLane (1995, County)
Justin Gallo, General McLane (1996, County)
Art Gamble, Academy (1987, City)
Art Gamble, Tech (1966, City)
Darrell Gamble, Tech (1988, City)
Herman Gamble, Tech (1987, City)
Justin Gannoe, Mercyhurst Prep (2002, City)
John Gannon, Strong Vincent (1973, City)
Greg Ganzer, Harbor Creek (1978, County)
Gary Garn, Wesleyville (1958, County)
Gene Garn, Wesleyville (1949, East)
Kay Garn, Wesleyville (1955, County)
Mike Garner, Iroquois (1993, County)
Edward Garnow, North East (1947, East)
Paul Garofalo, General McLane (2003, County)
Randy Garrity, Strong Vincent (1970, City)
Fred Gartner, North East (1940, West)
Chester Gasconi, North East (1939, East)
Mike Gashgarian, McDowell (1990, City)
Gary Gasper, Strong Vincent (1970, City)
Benji Gaston, Fort LeBoeuf (1995, County)
Kyle Gates, Corry (2007, County)
Ron Gates, Corry (1954, County)
Rich Gavin, East (1973, City)
Bill Gay, Harbor Creek (1951, East)
Bob Gay, Millcreek (1940, East)
Bill Gazewski, Kanty Prep (1977, City)
Jim Gdanetz, General McLane (2005, County)
Josh Gdanetz, Fairview (2011, County)
Mike Gdanetz, Seneca (2007, County)
Jake Geanous, Cathedral Prep (2011, City)
Gregg Gebhardt, General McLane (1999, County)
Scott Gehr, Northwestern (1978, County)
Cory Gehrlein, McDowell (1993, City)
Don Gehrlein, Cathedral Prep (1964, City)
George Geiger, Cathedral Prep (1948, West)
Lee Geiger, Strong Vincent (1983, City)
Jeff Gemler, Girard (1976, County)
Tony Genis, Academy (1967, County)
Jack Gentile, Fort LeBoeuf (1966, County)
Donald George, East (1944, East)
Mike George, Fairview (1962, County)
Mina George, East (1964, City)
Owen George, Cathedral Prep (1996, City)
Tom George, Fairview (1967, County)
Don Geraci, North East (1942, East)
Bob Gerbracht, Strong Vincent (1965, City)
Mike Gerlach, Harbor Creek (1992, County)
Peter Gervase, Cathedral Prep (1999, City)
Kenny Gerzina, Corry (1978, County)
Jim Getsinger, Conneautville (1957, County)
Bill Getz, Fairview (1941, West)

Jim Giacomelli, McDowell (1972, County)

Mason Giacomelli, McDowell (2012, City)

Ron Giacomelli, Tech (1953, City)

Bob Gianelli, Tech (1977, City)

David Gianelli, Harbor Creek (1990, County)

Greg Giannelli, Harbor Creek (2000, County)

Greg Giannelli, Tech (1980, City)

John Gianoni Jr., Cathedral Prep (2010, City)

Jeff Gibbons, Strong Vincent (1988, City)

Tommy Gibbons, Academy (1950, East)

Dana Gibbs, East (1974, City)

Jerrod Gibbs, East (2009, City)

Luther Gibbs, Tech (1970, City)

Robert Gibbs, North East (1949, East)

George Gido, Girard (1956, County)

Joe Gido, Girard (1952, County)

Tom Gido, Girard (1980, County)

Joey Gierlak, General McLane (2012, County)

Bill Giewont, General McLane (1975, County)

Larry Giewont, Wattsburg (1968, County)

Phil Giewont, Wattsburg (1974, County)

Shawn Giewont, Seneca (2006, County)

Ed Giglio, Tech (1963, City)

Vince Gigleimo, East (1940, West)

Gary Gilbert, General McLane (1989, County)

Scott Gilbert, General McLane (1981, County)

Ric Giles, East (1991, City)

Tom Gill Lawrence, Park (1943, East)

Jared Gillespie, McDowell (2011, City)

William Gillespie, Academy (1971, City)

John Gillette, Northwestern (1967, County)

Matt Gillette, Northwestern (1990, County)

Adlen Gilmore, East (2006, City)

Joshua Gilmore, East (1972, City)

Tim Gilson, Fairview (2010, County)

Mark Ginn, Corry (1988, County)

Mark Giza, McDowell (1986, City)

Gus Gladd, Albion (1942, West)

Bob Glasgow, Lawrence Park (1959, County)

Matt Glass, Iroquois (2000, County)

Phil Glass, Iroquois (1993, County)

Bill Glecos, Academy (1966, City)

Bob Glecos, Academy (1967, County)

Shannon Glover, Academy (1984, City)

Erik Glus, Northwestern (1997, County)

Rob Glus, Northwestern (1989, County)

Aaron Gluvna, Corry (2008, County)

Alec Gluvna, Corry (2011, County)

Mark Gnacinski, Strong Vincent (1981, City)

Bud Gnadge, Cambridge Springs (1949, West)

Mike Goard, Iroquois (1992, County)

Howard Godfrey, Millcreek (1943, West)

Bruce Goetz, Girard (1955, County)

Leo Goetz, Fairview (1943, West)

Rick Goleniewski, Fairview (1977, County)

Mike Golson, East (2004, City)

Justin Gomes, McDowell (2006, City)

Mike Goodelle, McDowell (1987, City)

Brent Goodenow, Fort LeBoeuf (1996, County)

John Goodill, Cathedral Prep (1939, West)

Dan Goodman, Seneca (2006, County)

Jim Goodman, Lawrence Park (1956, County)

Ed Goodrich, Strong Vincent (1962, City)

Bob Goodwill, Cathedral Prep (1963, City)

Ervin Goodwill, Corry (1951, East)

Jeff Goodwill, Corry (2002, County)

Paul Goodwill, Corry (1972, County)

Shane Goodwin, Fairview (2008, County)

William Goodwin, Girard (1949, West)

Carl Goodwine, East (1988, City)

Maurice Goodwine, East (1995, City)

Nick Gordon, East (2002, City)

Brad Gore, McDowell (2009, City)

Bryan Gore, East (1999, City)

John Gore, East (1993, City)

Kevin Gorman, Strong Vincent (1998, City)

John Gorney, Cathedral Prep (1956, City)

Ron Gorney, Cathedral Prep (1962, City)

David Gorring, Tech (1982, City)

Scott Gorring, Tech (1984, City)

Adam Gorski, Cathedral Prep (1946, West)

John Gorski, Tech (1950, East)

Bob Gossman, Girard (1943, West)

Craig Gourley, Harbor Creek (2001, County)

Don Gourley, Lawrence Park (1954, County)

John Grabowski, North East (1940, West)

A.J. Grack, Tech (1977, City)

David Grack, Strong Vincent (1991, City)

Joe Grack, McDowell (2002, City)

Tony Grack, Strong Vincent (1996, City)

Melvin Grady, East (1995, City)

Steve Graeca, Corry (1988, County)

Jay Grafius, Tech (1979, City)

Daniel Graham, East (2006, City)

James Graham, Academy (1955, City)

Markus Graham, Cathedral Prep (2005, City)

Paul Graham, Albion (1939, West)

Vern Graham, Fort LeBoeuf (1956, County)

Vince Graham, Strong Vincent (2005, City)

David Grandinetti, East (1992, City)

Stan Grandy, McDowell (1976, County)

Gene Graney, Academy (1952, City)

Bill Grant, Cathedral Prep (1941, West)

Jim Gratson, General McLane (1972, County)

Mike Graves, Academy (1982, City)

Odell Graves, East (1971, City)

Denny Gray, North East (2004, County)

Marty Gray, North East (1996, County)

Mike Gray, East (2006, City)

Charles Grebielski, Academy (1959, City)

Jon Gredler, Harbor Creek (2009, County)
Brandon Green, McDowell (2000, City)
Erick Green, Cathedral Prep (2009, City)
Jake Green, Fort LeBoeuf (2011, County)
Jim Green, Strong Vincent (1950, West)
Mark Green, McDowell (1977, County)
Pat Green, McDowell (1988, City)
Zach Greenawalt, McDowell (2010, City)
Dave Greene, Iroquois (1984, County)
Ben Greer, Albion (1958, County)
Matt Greer, Fairview (1985, County)
Dale Gregory, Fairview (1993, County)
Mike Gregory, Academy (1956, City)
Jim Greider, Iroquois (1966, County)
Art Greishaw, Fort LeBoeuf (1991, County)
Chuck Gresh, Girard (1981, County)
Chris Grettler, Girard (2004, County)
Rod Grettler, Girard (1973, County)
Dan Greulich, Cathedral Prep (1995, City)
Stephen Greulich, Strong Vincent (1997, City)
Dan Grey, Fort LeBoeuf (1963, County)
Dick Grieb, Lawrence Park (1946, East)
Doug Grieshaber, East (1997, City)
Jack Grieshober, Strong Vincent (1943, West)
Andy Griffith, General McLane (2001, County)
Karl Griffith, Union City (1953, County)
Matt Griffith, General McLane (2004, County)
Preston Griffith, Corry (1993, County)
Aaron Grill, Mercyhurst Prep (2006, City)
Joe Grippe, McDowell (1985, City)
Matt Grisik, McDowell (1991, City)
Bryan Griswold, Corry (1983, County)
Jay Grochulski, Iroquois (2002, County)
Ed Grode, Academy (1965, City)
Seth Grolemund, Harbor Creek (2008, County)
Barry Grossman, Strong Vincent (1964, City)
Mitch Groszkiewicz, Cathedral Prep (1997, City)
Nick Grow, North East (2009, County)
Merrill Grubbs, Fairview (1943, West)
Wilbur Grubbs, Fairview (1946, West)
Jim Grumblatt, Fort LeBoeuf (1961, County)
Chris Grychowski, Cathedral Prep (1988, City)
James Grygier, McDowell (2003, City)
Rob Grygier, McDowell (1998, City)
Justin Grzegorzewski, Cathedral Prep (2001, City)
Mike Guerassimoff, East (1982, City)
Don Guerrin, Cathedral Prep (1949, West)
Jeff Guild, Tech (1978, City)
Al Guilianelli, Strong Vincent (1950, West)
David Guilianelli, Academy (1992, City)
Bob Gumbert, Edinboro (1956, County)
Al Gunner, Academy (1953, City)
Don Gunter, Cathedral Prep (1967, County)
Dave Gunther, Tech (1974, City)
Randy Gunther, Fort LeBoeuf (1983, County)

Rob Guriel, McDowell (2008, City)
Charles Gurtson, Corry (1947, East)
Richard Gurtson, Corry (1947, East)
John Gustafson, Fairview (1961, County)
Ken Gustafson, Academy (1976, City)

Tim Haaf, Fort LeBoeuf (1972, County)
Bob Habel, Fairview (1953, County)
Bill Habersack, Cathedral Prep (1959, City)
Bert Hackenberg, Harbor Creek (1957, County)
Brian Hackenberg, Harbor Creek (1978, County)
Jerry Hadley, McDowell (1963, County)
Tony Haefner, East (2006, City)
Phil Haendler, Academy (1941, West)
Richard Haft, Tech (1972, City)
George Hagle, Cathedral Prep (1945, West)
James Hagle, Iroquois (1993, County)
Tim Hagmaier, Union City (1976, County)
Chuck Hagmann, Academy (1944, East)
Ron Hahn, Strong Vincent (1956, City)
Frank Haibach, Fort LeBoeuf (1962, County)
Kurt Haibach, Fort LeBoeuf (1997, County)
Rob Haibach, Fort LeBoeuf (1996, County)
Nathan Hain, Strong Vincent (2001, City)
Roland Haines, East (2004, City)
Charles Haise, Strong Vincent (1949, West)
Andrew Hajec, Corry (2012, County)
Mike Hakel, Tech (1961, City)
Abdul Hakim, Academy (1983, City)
Mike Hale, Academy (1974, City)
Dan Haley, Cathedral Prep (1965, City)
Rob Haley, Iroquois (1979, County)
Brett Hall, Northwestern (2004, County)
Culver Hall, Tech (1947, West)
Darrell Hall, Corry (1982, County)
John Hall, Cathedral Prep (1976, City)
Mario Hall, East (1995, City)
Charles Haller, Cathedral Prep (1949, West)
Russ Halmi, McDowell (1976, County)
Jim Hamike, Fairview (1962, County)
Alondre Hamilton, East (2010, City)
Bob Hamilton, Academy (1971, City)
Calyn Hamilton, Strong Vincent (2008, City)
Lamar Hamilton, East (1979, City)
Peter Hamilton, East (2011, City)
Bob Hammer, Tech (1977, City)
Ed Hammer, Academy (1969, City)
Robert Hammer, Fort LeBoeuf (2000, County)
Tony Hammer, Fort LeBoeuf (2002, County)
Jesse Hammerman, East (1941, East)
Jack Hammond, Academy (1946, East)
David Hammons, Academy (1977, City)
Greg Hampe, McDowell (1973, County)
Joe Hampy, McDowell (1977, County)

Phil Hampy, Cathedral Prep (2010, City)
Ron Hamrick, Union City (1979, County)
Justin Haney, Fairview (2008, County)
John Hanhauser, Cathedral Prep (1973, City)
Andy Hanisek, Girard (1968, County)
Jack Hanley, Union City (1947, East)
Larry Hanlin, Union City (1940, West)
Rex Hanlin, Union City (1967, County)
Spike Hanlin, Strong Vincent (1993, City)
David Hanlon, Fort LeBoeuf (1975, County)
Charles Hanmore, Strong Vincent (1992, City)
Mike Hanna, Corry (1963, County)
Art Hannah, Lawrence Park (1941, East)
Tom Hansen, Cathedral Prep (1970, City)
Ron Hanson, Iroquois (1973, County)
Tim Hanzelka, Girard (1982, County)
Harry Harabedian, Cathedral Prep (1946, West)
Frank Haraczy, Cathedral Prep (1955, City)
Claude Haraway, Tech (1963, City)
Greg Harayda, Academy (1980, City)
Harry Harbaugh, Girard (1958, County)
Donte Harden, Strong Vincent (2007, City)
Courtney Harden-Pullium, Strong Vincent (2010, City)
Grant Hare, Union City (1941, East)
John Hare, Central (1994, City)
John Harkins, Academy (1969, City)
Keith Harned, General McLane (1979, County)
Nick Harpster, McDowell (2008, City)
Dana Harrington, Corry (1992, County)
Don Harrington, East (1945, East)
Judd Harrington, Albion (1945, West)
Mark Harrington, Cathedral Prep (2002, City)
Roger Harrington, Seneca (1980, County)
Bud Harris, Union City (1951, East)
Chris Harris, McDowell (1991, City)
Dan Harris, Fort LeBoeuf (2001, County)
Khlique Harris, McDowell (2012, City)
Randy Harris, McDowell (1970, County)
Scott Harris, McDowell (2010, City)
Dan Harrison, General McLane (1971, County)
Dennis Harrison, Corry (1969, County)
Hal Hart, Wesleyville (1953, County)
Henry Hart, East (1939, East)
Pat Hart, Fairview (1985, County)
Pat Hart, East (1980, City)
Tim Hart, East (1965, City)
James Hartken, McDowell (1998, City)
Paul Hartmann, Harbor Creek (1987, County)
Jeff Harvey, Iroquois (2009, County)
Mike Harvey, Fort LeBoeuf (1985, County)
Vincent Harvey, Strong Vincent (1990, City)
Richard Hasbee, Cambridge Springs (1948, West)
Joseph Hassak, General McLane (1993, County)
Bill Hathaway, Academy (1958, City)
Steve Hathaway, East (1967, County)

Ron Haughsdahl, Strong Vincent (1980, City)
Reggie Haugsdahl, Strong Vincent (1982, City)
Ron Haugsdahl, Strong Vincent (1955, City)
Dave Haupt, Harbor Creek (1982, County)
David Hauser, Cathedral Prep (2003, City)
George Hausman, Academy (1943, East)
Randy Hawkins, Central (2000, City)
Merlin Hawley, Waterford (1948, East)
Mike Hawley, McDowell (1981, City)
Sam Hawley, Fairview (1965, County)
Matthew Hawryliw, Mercyhurst Prep (2006, City)
Ardell Hayes, Edinboro (1947, West)
Don Hayes, Edinboro (1960, County)
Jim Hayes, Strong Vincent (1967, County)
Robert Hayes, Lawrence Park (1939, East)
Ron Hayes, Fort LeBoeuf (1987, County)
Terry Hayes, Corry (1987, County)
Charles Hazen, Lawrence Park (1944, East)
Phil Hazen, Waterford (1954, County)
Sam Hazen, Fort LeBoeuf (1961, County)
Frank Hazlett, Cathedral Prep (2006, City)
Don Heald, Conneaut Valley (1953, County)
Tom Heasley, Edinboro (1960, County)
George Heath, Wesleyville (1939, East)
William Heath, Wesleyville (1939, East)
Mike Heberle, Cathedral Prep (1989, City)
John Hedberg, East (1963, City)
Herman Hedderick, Millcreek (1947, West)
James Hedderick, Academy (1962, City)
Ray Hedderick, Millcreek (1945, West)
Jim Hedlund, Harbor Creek (1975, County)
Matt Hedlund, Harbor Creek (2004, County)
Michael Hedlund, Harbor Creek (2006, County)
Chuck Heid, Mercyhurst Prep (1997, City)
Willie Heidelberg, Cathedral Prep (1984, City)
Bob Heiden, North East (1969, County)
Dick Heiden, North East (1961, County)
Ed Heidt, Cathedral Prep (1981, City)
Rob Heidt, Millcreek (1948, West)
Dan Heitzenrater, Fairview (1993, County)
Robert Heldreth, Conneautville (1948, West)
Jack Heller, Wesleyville (1963, County)
Sam Heller, Wesleyville (1960, County)
Bill Hellyer, Albion (1943, West)
Wayne Helmbreck, General McLane (1978, County)
Duane Hemphill, Strong Vincent (2005, City)
Neil Henderson North, East (1950, East)
Andre Henderson, Strong Vincent (2005, City)
Robert Henderson, East (1983, City)
Tony Henderson, Central (2006, City)
John Hendrickson, Wesleyville (1965, County)
Howard Henning, Academy (1945, East)
Carl Henry, Union City (1941, East)
David Henry, Harbor Creek (1959, County)
Doug Henry, Harbor Creek (1973, County)

Mario Henry, Strong Vincent (2005, City)
Mehnert Henry, Harbor Creek (1941, East)
Mehnert Henry, Harbor Creek (1941, East)
Paul Henry, Union City (1949, East)
Russell Henry, Iroquois (1982, County)
Zac Henry, North East (2010, County)
Dave Herbe, McDowell (2008, City)
Dave Herbe, McDowell (1977, County)
Don Herbe, McDowell (1973, County)
Don Herbe, Strong Vincent (1951, West; 1952, City)
Jay Herberg, Corry (1992, County)
Andy Herget, Iroquois (2006, County)
Chris Herman, Fort LeBoeuf (1979, County)
Daryl Herman, Academy (1989, City)
Jeff Herman, Fort LeBoeuf (1975, County)
Don Herold, Strong Vincent (1972, City)
Pat Herr, Fort LeBoeuf (1983, County)
Justin Herring, Girard (2003, County)
Sean Herron, Strong Vincent (2010, City)
John Hersch, Cathedral Prep (2003, City)
Greg Hershelman, Northwestern (1976, County)
Aaron Hertel, Cathedral Prep (1997, City)
Bill Hertel, Cathedral Prep (1964, City)
Ed Hess, Harbor Creek (1987, County)
Scott Hess, Fairview (1985, County)
Bernie Hessley, Cathedral Prep (1995, City)
Sam Hester, Strong Vincent (1959, City)
Greg Hetrick, Strong Vincent (1979, City)
Luke Hetrick, Union City (2011, County)
Todd Hetrick, Strong Vincent (1982, City)
Jesse Heubel, Seneca (2007, County)
Rob Heubel, Fairview (1992, County)
Andre Heuer, Cathedral Prep (1966, City)
Joseph Hewel, Seneca (2009, County)
Geoff Heyl, McDowell (1998, City)
Eric Hicks, Mercyhurst Prep (1994, City)
Harold Hicks, Fairview (1950, West)
Mike Higgins, Academy (1989, City)
Dave Hilbert, Academy (1956, City)
Paul Hilbert, East (1956, City)
Phil Hilbert, East (1964, City)
Tom Hilinski, Harbor Creek (1956, County)
Jack Hill, Albion (1943, West)
Jim Hill, East (1953, City)
Al Hilling, McDowell (1984, City)
Andrew Hilling, Cathedral Prep (1991, City)
Jim Hillman, Millcreek (1943, West)
Carl Hillstrom, Corry (1967, County)
Jack Hines, Strong Vincent (1940, East)
Curtis Hinkle, Fairview (1941, West)
Glenn Hinkle, Fairview (1986, County)
John Hinkle, Fairview (1948, West)
Mert Hinkle, Fairview (1942, West)
Vincent Hinkle, Fairview (1966, County)
Dennis Hinkler, Fort LeBoeuf (1996, County)

Eric Hinkler, Cathedral Prep (1997, City)
Bill Hintz, Cathedral Prep (1966, City)
Chuck Hintz, Strong Vincent (1974, City)
Matt Hintz, Cathedral Prep (2005, City)
Mickey Hintz, Strong Vincent (1976, City)
Frank Hlifka, Girard (1955, County)
Melvin Hobson, Academy (1980, City)
Blake Hockett, Fort LeBoeuf (2009, County)
Chris Hoderny, McDowell (2004, City)
Pat Hoderny, McDowell (2000, City)
Tom Hodges, Academy (1951, East)
Bud Hoffman, Wesleyville (1951, East)
Sean Hoffman, McDowell (2003, City)
Jim Hogan, Tech (1976, City)
Ralph Hogan, Tech (1940, West)
Ed Hokaj, Cathedral Prep (1954, City)
Barry Holes, Fort LeBoeuf (1978, County)
Jeff Holes, Fort LeBoeuf (1985, County)
Tori Holes, Fort LeBoeuf (2007, County)
Robert Holiday, Northwestern (1972, County)
Al Holland, Fairview (1941, West)
Brian Holland, Cathedral Prep (1990, City)
Jerry Holland, Fairview (1952, County)
Jim Holland, Academy (1963, City)
Tim Holland, Cathedral Prep (1975, City)
Tim Holland, Cathedral Prep (1954, City)
Tom Hollaran, Harbor Creek (1951, East; 1952, County)
Tony Hollingsworth, East (1984, City)
Robbie Hollis, Union City (2010, County)
Aaron Holmes, Fairview (1996, County)
Manuel Holmes, Central Tech (2011, City)
George Holowach, Edinboro (1943, West)
Steve Holowach, Cambridge Springs (1957, County)
Simon Holowack, Edinboro (1945, West)
Joe Holowich, Edinboro (1941, West)
Jeff Holt, Strong Vincent (1990, City)
Andy Holup, Edinboro (1939, West)
Ralph Hooven, Lawrence Park (1944, East)
Aaron Hoover, Seneca (1992, County)
Bob Hopkins, Girard (1942, West)
Matt Hopkins, General McLane (2000, County)
Mike Hopkins, McDowell (1993, City)
Robert Hopkins, Girard (1972, County)
Dave Horanic, McDowell (1960, County)
Bill Horihan, Tech (1962, City)
Brad Horky, McDowell (1976, County)
Brian Horn, Tech (1983, City)
Dan Horn, Strong Vincent (1976, City)
Chris Hornick, Corry (1978, County)
Aaron Horton, Mercyhurst Prep (2011, City)
Jim Horton, Strong Vincent (1975, City)
Kevin Horton, McDowell (1975, County)
Joseph Hosey, Northwestern (1985, County)
Don Hostettler, Edinboro (1946, West)
Art Hotchkiss, Corry (1964, County)

D.J. Hough, Northwestern (1994, County)
Demarcus House, East (2012, City)
Maurice House, East (1989, City)
William House, North East (1948, East)
Jeremiah Hovis, Northwestern (1996, County)
Jamie Howard, Northwestern (1993, County)
John Howard, East (1997, City)
Dan Howell, Iroquois (2005, County)
Henry Howze, Academy (1981, City)
Jack Hrinda, Girard (1956, County)
Mike Hromyak, Cathedral Prep (2001, City)
Mark Hubbart, East (1986, City)
Markel Hubbart, East (2007, City)
Frank Huber, Academy (1960, City)
Eric Hubler, Iroquois (2000, County)
David Hudson, Fairview (1985, County)
Derrick Huff, East (1995, City)
Joe Hughes, Tech (1988, City)
John Hughes, Girard (1990, County)
Tim Hughes, Cathedral Prep (1971, City)
Tony Hughes, Fairview (1976, County)
Cecil Hull, Waterford (1944, East)
John Hummell, McDowell (1982, City)
Jack Humphreys, Lawrence Park (1959, County)
Hal Hunter, Union City (1961, County)
John Hunter, Waterford (1939, East)
Marshall Huntsman, Mercyhurst Prep (2009, City)
Laverne Hurlburt, Union City (1957, County)
Charles Hutchinson, Iroquois (1990, County)
Chuck Hutchinson, Lawrence Park (1963, County)
Clarence Hutchinson, North East (1939, East)
Harold Hutchinson, North East (1940, West)
Homer Hutchison, Edinboro (1945, West)
Ted Hutchison, Edinboro (1947, West)
Fred Hyde, Girard (1972, County)

Joe Iannello, Cathedral Prep (1986, City)
Rex Ireland, Corry (1949, East)
Tom Irish, Harbor Creek (1961, County)
Jody Irwin, Cathedral Prep (1995, City)
Tom Irwin, Academy (1962, City)
Blaine Iskula, Northwestern (2010, County)
Jeff Ives, Fairview (1966, County)
Harry Izbicki, Cathedral Prep (1993, City)
Justin Izbicki, Cathedral Prep (1995, City)
Len Izbicki, Fairview (1965, County)

Mike Jack, East (1991, City)
Peter Jackson, Fairview (2010, County)
Steve Jackson, Fort LeBoeuf (2000, County)
Todd Jackson, Union City (2009, County)
Rich Jacobitz, Iroquois (1982, County)

Mark Jacobs, Fairview (1982, County)
Chuck James, North East (1958, County)
Doug James, Tech (1976, City)
Ed James, Academy (1961, City)
Ed Janek, Kanty Prep (1949, West)
Chad Jantzi, Corry (1995, County)
John Januleski, Cathedral Prep (1946, West)
Jim Jaruszewicz, Cathedral Prep (1966, City)
Joe Jaruszewicz, Cathedral Prep (1975, City)
Mike Jaruszewicz, Fairview (2001, County)
Zigmund Jasinski, Tech (1949, East)
Bill Jasper, Girard (2001, County)
Vincent Jaworek, Academy (1943, East)
James Jaycox, Tech (1957, City)
Dave Jazenski, Iroquois (2002, County)
Paul Jazenski, Iroquois (1970, County)
Pete Jazenski, Lawrence Park (1965, County)
Damian Jefferson, East (2010, City)
Dijon Jefferson, Central (2002, City)
Joe Jelinek, Mercyhurst Prep (2008, City)
Aaron Jelley, North East (1998, County)
Dietrich Jells, Tech (1991, City)
Vincent Jenco, Cathedral Prep (1947, West)
Dick Jenkins, Strong Vincent (1984, City)
Mike Jenkins, Academy (1987, City)
Mike Jenkins, Fairview (1981, County)
Richard Jenkins, East (1991, City)
Dan Jenks, Fort LeBoeuf (1974, County)
Dale Jennings, McDowell (1974, County)
Art Jensen, Academy (1957, City)
Jack Jensen, Academy (1965, City)
Mike Jensen, Tech (1974, City)
Tim Jewell, Union City (1985, County)
A.J. Jimerson, Tech (1991, City)
Adam Johnson, Iroquois (2000, County)
Albert Johnson, Lawrence Park (1942, East)
Art Johnson, Lawrence Park (1941, East)
Bill Johnson, Strong Vincent (1963, City)
Brian Johnson, Harbor Creek (1966, County)
Cameron Johnson, Northwestern (2007, County)
Chaney Johnson, Strong Vincent (1947, West)
Chaun Johnson, East (1990, City)
Chip Johnson, General McLane (1994, County)
Chris Johnson, East (1987, City)
Derrick Johnson, Girard (2006, County)
Don Johnson, Conneaut Valley (1954, County)
Eric Johnson, Harbor Creek (1972, County)
Erik Johnson, Corry (1977, County)
Harry Johnson, East (1945, East)
Jack Johnson, Lawrence Park (1955, County)
Jacob Johnson, Central Tech (2010, City)
Jared Johnson, Fort LeBoeuf (2004, County)
Jay Johnson, General McLane (1991, County)
Jeff Johnson, East (1981, City)
Jim Johnson, Harbor Creek (1974, County)

Jim Johnson, East (1951, East; 1952, City)
Jovon Johnson, Mercyhurst Prep (2002, City)
Kenneth Johnson, Fairview (1948, West)
Kyle Johnson, Harbor Creek (2008, County)
Paul Johnson, Fairview (1965, County)
Richard Johnson, Conneaut Valley (1951, West)
Scott Johnson, McDowell (1994, City)
Shane Johnson, Strong Vincent (2002, City)
Steve Johnson, Iroquois (1969, County)
Terry Johnson, Tech (1991, City)
Tim Johnson, Corry (1982, County)
Tyler Johnson, North East (2012, County)
Baron Joles, Union City (1982, County)
Albert Jones, East (1989, City)
Albert Scott Jones, East (2008, City)
Antonio Jones, Central (2002, City)
Ashton Jones, Strong Vincent (2007, City)
Curtis Jones, Mercyhurst Prep (1994, City)
Dave Jones, Mercyhurst Prep (1999, City)
Denzel Jones, Strong Vincent (2012, City)
Dick Jones, Edinboro (1943, West)
Harry Jones, Girard (1980, County)
Hunter Jones, Girard (2012, County)
Jimmy Jones, Academy (1972, City)
Ken Jones, Cathedral Prep (1967, County)
Leonard Jones, Academy (1963, City)
Mike Jones, Central (2000, City)
Quincy Jones, Strong Vincent (1996, City)
Roa Jones, Cambridge Springs (1950, West)
Robert Jones Jr., Strong Vincent (2012, City)
Ron Jones, Cathedral Prep (1964, City)
Ron Jones, Waterford (1955, County)
Tom Jones, Cathedral Prep (1969, City)
Wayne Jones, Academy (1969, City)
William Jones, Albion (1943, West)
Roger Jordan, Iroquois (1972, County)
Willie Jordan, Strong Vincent (2003, City)
Daryl Joyce, East (2002, City)
Robert Joyce, Strong Vincent (2009, City)
Joe Julian, Northwestern (2000, County)
Jake Jurkiewicz, Strong Vincent (2006, City)
Ray Justka, East (1939, East)

Bob Kaczenski, Cathedral Prep (1962, City)
Bob Kaczenski, Cathedral Prep (1986, City)
Sean Kaday, McDowell (1995, City)
Jamie Kaiser, Mercyhurst Prep (1996, City)
Pete Kaiser, Tech (1979, City)
Rob Kaiser, Mercyhurst Prep (2010, City)
V.J. Kaiser, Cathedral Prep (1981, City)
Vitus Kaiser, Cathedral Prep (1947, West)
Vic Kalicky, Fairview (1962, County)
Steve Kalista, Cathedral Prep (1966, City)
Tom Kaliszewski, Iroquois (1996, County)

Bob Kalivoda, Tech (1978, City)
Jim Kamandulis, Cathedral Prep (1969, City)
John Kaminski, Harbor Creek (1945, East)
Alan Kantorowski, Strong Vincent (2001, City)
John Kanuk, Girard (1943, West)
Alex Kapetan, North East (1947, East)
Pete Kapetan, North East (1941, East)
Joe Kardosh, Conneaut Valley (1954, County)
Gene Karnes, East (1977, City)
Jonathan Karsh, North East (1983, County)
Rich Karsh, Academy (1981, City)
Chris Karsznia, Harbor Creek (1996, County)
Jerry Karsznia, Academy (1965, City)
Mark Karuba, East (1968, City)
Pete Karuba, East (1974, City)
Pete Karuba, Tech (1946, West)
Jared Kaufmann, Cathedral Prep (2007, City)
Ray Kavelish, General McLane (1995, County)
Ray Kazebee, Conneautville (1946, West)
Dana Keeler, Corry (1997, County)
Jamie Keeney, General McLane (1996, County)
Richard Kehl, Academy (1947, East)
Dan Keil, Iroquois (1968, County)
Jeremy Keith, Northwestern (1998, County)
Bob Kelleher, East (1942, East)
Bill Keller, East (1959, City)
Mike Keller, Strong Vincent (2008, City)
Alan Kelley, Central (1999, City)
Howard Kelley, East (1964, City)
Chris Kelly, North East (2002, County)
Geoffrey Kelly, Fort LeBoeuf (1997, County)
Jerry Kelly, Fort LeBoeuf (1966, County)
Marty Kelly, Tech (1960, City)
Paul Kelly, Academy (1942, West)
Paul Kelvington, Cathedral Prep (1986, City)
Scott Kemling, Northwestern (1990, County)
Paul Kemper, McDowell (2012, City)
Chet Kempinski, Fairview (1984, County)
Gary Kempinski, Fairview (1986, County)
Eric Kempisty, Central (1994, City)
Lloyd Kendrick, General McLane (1970, County)
Shawn Kendrick, Cathedral Prep (1993, City)
Pat Kennedy, Union City (1983, County)
Rich Kennedy, Fairview (1978, County)
Shaun Kennedy, Fairview (1982, County)
Misael Kercado, East (1995, City)
James Kerns, Union City (1998, County)
Andrew Kerr, General McLane (1990, County)
Larry Kerr, General McLane (1995, County)
Richard Kestle, Waterford (1946, East)
Gordon Ketchel, Tech (1955, City)
Rich Ketchel, Academy (1942, West)
Markel Keys, Cathedral Prep (2011, City)
Blaine Kibler, Girard (1972, County)
Charles Kibler, Girard (1948, West)

Dave Kibler, Girard (1958, County)
Gordon Kidder, Wesleyville (1949, East)
Robert Kidon, Fairview (1958, County)
Larry Kielak, Tech (1967, County)
Dick Kierstan, North East (1958, County)
Bob Kierzek, Cathedral Prep (1951, West)
Bryant Kimball, McDowell (2008, City)
Colin Kimball, McDowell (2011, City)
Joseph Kimmel, Wesleyville (1944, East)
Don Kimmelman, Strong Vincent (1953, City)
Andrew Kimmy, North East (2005, County)
Chris King, Harbor Creek (1994, County)
Dale King, Northwestern (1970, County)
Ed King, Academy (1958, City)
Justin King, Fairview (1996, County)
Wade King, McDowell (1986, City)
Walter King, Edinboro (1942, West)
Brad Kingston, Strong Vincent (1964, City)
Corey Kinnard, Central (1998, City)
Ramown Kinnard, Central (1996, City)
Willie Kinnard, Tech (1963, City)
Sam Kinnear, Mercyhurst Prep (2007, City)
Todd Kinnear, Mercyhurst Prep (2005, City)
Tom Kirdahy, General McLane (1999, County)
Mark Kirkland, Cathedral Prep (1967, County)
Bryan Kirsch, North East (2008, County)
Glenn Kirsch, North East (1980, County)
Ken Kirsch, North East (1979, County)
Jack Kirsh, Cathedral Prep (1943, West)
Andy Kish, McDowell (1994, City)
Norman Kleckner, Millcreek (1944, West)
Joe Kleiner, Cathedral Prep (1983, City)
Kevin Klemm, Central (1994, City)
Bill Klenz, North East (1984, County)
Bill Klenz, North East (1959, County)
Josh Klenz, North East (2011, County)
Jason Kleps, Strong Vincent (1993, City)
Ed Klimow, East (1942, East)
Scott Klimow, Academy (1977, City)
Al Kline, Academy (1943, East)
Jim Kline, Fort LeBoeuf (1963, County)
Kevin Klino, East (2001, City)
Brad Klomp, Harbor Creek (1984, County)
John Klomp, Wesleyville (1956, County)
Tom Klomp, Wesleyville (1959, County)
Joe Kloos, Strong Vincent (1967, County)
Lewis Klus, Union City (1944, East)
Rob Klus, Union City (2002, County)
Keith Kmecik, Girard (1981, County)
J Knablein, Fort LeBoeuf (1986, County)
Keith Knauff, Union City (1995, County)
Richard Knepper, Academy (1939, West)
George Knight, Lawrence Park (1949, East)
Joel Knight, Fort LeBoeuf (1998, County)
Mark Knight, Tech (1986, City)

Marquelle Knight, Cathedral Prep (2004, City)
Marquis Knight, Strong Vincent (2008, City)
Max Knight, North East (2012, County)
Joe Kobylinski, Harbor Creek (1964, County)
Jim Koch, Cathedral Prep (1963, City)
Joe Koech, Girard (2004, County)
Bob Koegal, Union City (1950, East)
Greg Koester, McDowell (2010, City)
John Koester, McDowell (2006, City)
Kyle Koeth, Girard (2007, County)
Chris Kohler, North East (1979, County)
John Kohut, Albion (1960, County)
Matt Koket, McDowell (1990, City)
Eric Komar, Mercyhurst Prep (2006, City)
Brian Komisarski, Seneca (1994, County)
Steve Konieczki, Tech (1967, County)
Milton Konieczko, Tech (1939, East)
Chris Konieczny, Fairview (1989, County)
Eric Konieczny, McDowell (1989, City)
Edward Konkol, Tech (1944, West)
Jack Konkol, Cathedral Prep (1949, West)
Nick Konzel, Harbor Creek (1977, County)
Jordan Koper, McDowell (2009, City)
Scott Korb, Girard (1980, County)
Steve Korb, Girard (1982, County)
Bill Korell, General McLane (1968, County)
Dan Kosiorek, Wattsburg (1972, County)
John Kosiorek, Wattsburg (1967, County)
Don Kosobucki, Kanty Prep (1976, City)
Sean Kostef, Cathedral Prep (1995, City)
Pete Kosterman, Harbor Creek (1942, East)
George Kostrubanic, Fairview (1961, County)
Marcus Kouczynski, McDowell (2007, City)
Ray Kovalesky, McDowell (1983, City)
Robert Kowalewski, East (1962, City)
Bernard Kowalski, Tech (1955, City)
Ed Kowalski, Cathedral Prep (1998, City)
Ken Kowalski, Academy (1961, City)
Mike Kowalski, Academy (1966, City)
Joe Kowle, North East (2003, County)
Matthew Kowle, Fort LeBoeuf (2010, County)
Matt Kozer, McDowell (2005, City)
Joe Kozik, Wattsburg (1968, County)
Chris Kozlowski, McDowell (1991, City)
Dave Kozlowski, Tech (1963, City)
Jim Kozlowski, Tech (1970, City)
Adam Krahe, Iroquois (2009, County)
Don Krahe, Tech (1941, East)
Jack Krahe, Cathedral Prep (1948, West)
Mike Krahe, Cathedral Prep (2000, City)
Bill Kramer, Academy (1940, East)
Robert Kramer, Wesleyville (1944, East)
Dave Kranking, Fort LeBoeuf (1974, County)
David Kranz, Fairview (1993, County)
Edward Kranz, Cathedral Prep (1947, West)

Tom Kranz, Fairview (1991, County)
Ronald Krape, Academy (1946, East)
Nick Krasa, Corry (2001, County)
Richard Kraus, Strong Vincent (1971, City)
Rick Kraus, McDowell (1999, City)
Roger Kravitz, Fairview (1982, County)
Walter Kreide, Wesleyville (1955, County)
LeRoy Kreider, Northwestern (1969, County)
Kevin Kreidinger, Tech (1982, City)
Pete Krivonak, Academy (1940, East)
Willie Krivonak, Academy (1940, East)
Adam Krizanik, McDowell (2005, City)
Brett Krizanik, McDowell (2003, City)
Doug Krugger, Tech (1975, City)
Bill Kruse, McDowell (1974, County)
E.J. Kruse, Fairview (2008, County)
Kevin Kruszewski, Harbor Creek (1988, County)
Jim Kubaney, Cathedral Prep (1961, City)
Dan Kubiak, General McLane (2002, County)
Dana Kubiak, Cathedral Prep (1984, City)
Dennis Kubiak, Corry (1973, County)
Doug Kubiak, Fort LeBoeuf (1987, County)
Ed Kubiak, Tech (1941, East)
Len Kubiak, Tech (1946, West)
Robert Kubiak, Cathedral Prep (1943, West)
Jack Kuchcinski, North East (1995, County)
Ben Kuchta, North East (2002, County)
Zach Kuchta, North East (2005, County)
Scott Kucinski, Cathedral Prep (2000, City)
Chad Kuffer, General McLane (1991, County)
Luke Kuffer, General McLane (1995, County)
Shawn Kuffer, General McLane (1989, County)
Jim Kuhl, Seneca (1999, County)
Chris Kuhn, McDowell (2001, City)
Craig Kuhn, Fort LeBoeuf (1988, County)
Eric Kuhn, Strong Vincent (1990, City)
James Kuhn, McDowell (1999, City)
Jim Kujan, Harbor Creek (1976, County)
Jim Kujan, East (1949, East)
Mike Kujan, Harbor Creek (1989, County)
Greg Kujawa, Cathedral Prep (2000, City)
Jeff Kujawinski, Tech (1986, City)
Ron Kujawinski, Cathedral Prep (1957, City)
Tim Kujawinski, Tech (1989, City)
Dennis Kukola, Seneca (1987, County)
Joe Kula, Fort LeBoeuf (1968, County)
Craig Kulesza, Cathedral Prep (1995, City)
Randy Kulesza, Cathedral Prep (1991, City)
Chad Kulka, General McLane (2012, County)
Kevin Kulka, General McLane (2010, County)
Andy Kunic, Mercyhurst Prep (2007, City)
Eugene Kurt, Cathedral Prep (1962, City)
Rick Kurt, Iroquois (1973, County)
Patrick Kurtz, Fort LeBoeuf (2003, County)
Joe Kurung, Fairview (1976, County)

Chris Kurzik, Mercyhurst Prep (2011, City)
Jonathan Kutterna, North East (2003, County)
John Kutz, General McLane (1966, County)
Mike Kuzilla, Harbor Creek (1981, County)
Andy Kuzma, Corry (2002, County)
Gregg Kuzma, Cathedral Prep (1994, City)
Kip Kuzmin, Northwestern (1989, County)
Bob Kwiatkowski, East (1969, City)
Don Kwiatkowski, East (1960, City)

Rob LaBar, McDowell (1988, City)
Pete Laboda, Iroquois (1976, County)
John Laboski, Harbor Creek (2000, County)
Angelo LaFuria, Strong Vincent (1948, West)
Lou LaFuria, North East (1987, County)
Russ LaFuria, North East (1968, County)
Scott Lafuria, North East (1996, County)
Brian Laird, Union City (1983, County)
Tom Laird, Cathedral Prep (1995, City)
Steve Lakari, Strong Vincent (1987, City)
Tim Lakari, Strong Vincent (1981, City)
Jack Lally, Cathedral Prep (1940, East)
Jim Lamb, Lawrence Park (1959, County)
Roger Lamb, Cathedral Prep (1940, East)
Cory Lamison, Fort LeBoeuf (2004, County)
Ernie Lamphere, Corry (1953, County)
David Lanagan, Iroquois (1998, County)
Chad Lander, North East (2005, County)
Frank Landi, Strong Vincent (1944, West)
Richard Landis, Union City (1948, East)
Dylan Lane, McDowell (2009, City)
Greg Lane, Fairview (2006, County)
Kevin Lane, Fairview (1984, County)
Mark Lane, Fairview (1982, County)
Mike Lane, McDowell (1973, County
Scott Lane, Fairview (1987, County)
Steve Lane, McDowell (1973, County
Tom Lane, McDowell (1972, County)
Carl Langer, Harbor Creek (1940, West)
Dick Langer, Harbor Creek (1941, East)
John Langer, Fairview (1990, County)
John Langer, Harbor Creek (1946, East)
Jim Langley, Wesleyville (1965, County)
Matt Laniewicz, Iroquois (1992, County)
Dennis Lantzy, Strong Vincent (1966, City)
Jason Lantzy, Fort LeBoeuf (2000, County)
Jack Laraway, Academy (1954, City)
Jason Larson, Cathedral Prep (1996, City)
Lee Larson, Academy (1963, City)
Matt Lascak, Northwestern (1976, County)
Tim Lascek, Northwestern (1977, County)
Norm Lasher, Union City (1965, County)
Russ Lasher, Albion (1950, West)
Joe Laska, McDowell (1991, City)

Mark Laska, McDowell (2000, City)

Tom Laska, McDowell (1989, City)

Rob Laskey, General McLane (1984, County)

Mel Laskoff, East (1954, City)

Joe Lasky, General McLane (1983, County)

Tom Lathrop, Corry (1984, County)

Bob Latimer, Academy (1973, City)

Myron Latimer, Millcreek (1957, County)

Keith Latzo, East (1981, City)

Kyle Latzo, Cathedral Prep (2006, City)

Edward Lavange, Harbor Creek (1943, East)

Scott LaVange, Academy (1968, City)

William Law, Wesleyville (1939, East)

Craig Lawrence, Fairview (2005, County)

Robert Lawrence, Albion (1944, West)

T.J. Lawrence, Fairview (2010, County)

Wayne Lawrence, Fairview (1963, County)

William Lawrence, East (1946, East)

Roy Laws, McDowell (1974, County)

Floyd Lawson, Academy (1939, West)

Bob Lawton, Lawrence Park (1945, East)

Mike Lazzara, North East (1989, County)

Lou Lazzera, North East (1983, County)

Corey Lear, Northwestern (2001, County)

Jeremy Lear, Northwestern (1995, County)

Mike Learn, Harbor Creek (1983, County)

Ryan Learn, Harbor Creek (2003, County)

Jim Leasure, Kanty Prep (1980, County)

Anthony Lecce, McDowell (2012, City)

Mike LeCorchick, Cathedral Prep (1960, City)

Joe Ledford, Union City (1982, County)

Bob Lee, Strong Vincent (1990, City)

Bob Lee, Tech (1975, City)

Jack Lee, Fort LeBoeuf (1977, County)

Scott Lee, Fairview (1979, County)

Tom Lee, Strong Vincent (1941, West)

Tony Lee, East (1979, City)

John Leech, Fort LeBoeuf (1959, County)

Ron Leeds, Fairview (1993, County)

Shawn Leehan, Northwestern (2002, County)

Daniel LeFaiver, Mercyhurst Prep (2006, City)

Bill LeFevre, Strong Vincent (1945, West)

Gerald Legenzoff, Academy (1961, City)

Ken Legenzoff, East (1954, City)

Doug Leicht, Northwestern (1987, County)

Pat Leighton, East (1948, East)

Daryl Leopold, Fairview (1967, County)

Jim Leopold, Fairview (1970, County)

Tom Leopold, Fairview (1959, County)

Mike Lerch, Wattsburg (1968, County)

David Leri, Harbor Creek (1992, County)

Allyn Lesko, Strong Vincent (1956, City)

Ted Lesko, Girard (1950, West)

Mike Lesniewski, Cathedral Prep (1979, City)

Tom Lesniewski, Cathedral Prep (1975, City)

Jim Letcher, Academy (1954, City)

Chris Letkiewicz, Tech (1983, City)

Matt Leubin, McDowell (1989, City)

Ken Leuschen, Millcreek (1957, County)

Ron Leuschen, McDowell (1977, County)

Pat Levonduskie, Harbor Creek (1984, County)

Ed Lewicki, Tech (1977, City)

Bill Lewis, North East (1956, County)

Dick Lewis, East (1951, East)

Fred Lewis, Northwestern (1963, County)

Geoff Lewis, Fairview (1999, County)

Greg Lewis, McDowell (1985, City)

Matthew Lewis, Strong Vincent (2006, City)

Mike Lewis, Cambridge Springs (1961, County)

Robert Lewis, Albion (1949, West)

Frank Lichtenwalter, Tech (1942, East)

Joe Lichtinger, Fort LeBoeuf (1989, County)

Jerry Liebel, Harbor Creek (1968, County)

Mike Liebel, Cathedral Prep (1993, City)

Ray Liebel, Fairview (1981, County)

Frank Liebert, Cathedral Prep (1948, West)

Jake Lightner, Fairview (2008, County)

Jeremy Lightner, Fairview (2003, County)

Chris Lilley, East (2000, City)

Gary Lillis, Cathedral Prep (1966, City)

Marc Limano, Cathedral Prep (1998, City)

Gary Lindberg, Fort LeBoeuf (1969, County)

Tom Lindemuth, Fairview (1977, County)

Dan Lindquist, Corry (1985, County)

Merle Lindsay, Academy (1949, East)

Antre Lindsey, Strong Vincent (2009, City)

Desuan Lindsey, Cathedral Prep (2004, City)

Eric Lindsey, Central (1993, City)

Brooks Linkoski, Fairview (2009, County)

Chad Lino, Cathedral Prep (2000, City)

Joe Lisek, Northwestern (1965, County)

Kevin Litz, Tech (1979, City)

Travis Litz, Central (2006, City)

Walt Litz, Tech (1958, City)

Ted Loader, East (1953, City)

Paul Lobaugh, Iroquois (1970, County)

Len LoCastro, Academy (1968, City)

Jason Locke, North East (1994, County)

Tom Locke, Academy (1970, City)

Shawn LoDovico, Corry (1995, County)

John Loeb, Strong Vincent (1964, City)

Kevin Loftus, Iroquois (2000, County)

George Logan, Conneautville (1957, County)

Peter Logan, Harbor Creek (1979, County)

Joe Lohse, Wesleyville (1945, East)

Wilfred Lohse, Cathedral Prep (1939, West)

Dave Lojewski, Tech (1971, City)

Joe Lomax, East (1974, City)

Ron Lomax, East (1983, City)

Nick Lombardo, General McLane (2010, County)

Bill Long, Union City (1988, County)
Dan Long, Northwestern (1995, County)
Robert Long, Corry (1948, East)
Frank Longo, Iroquois (1996, County)
Chris Loomis, Cathedral Prep (1997, City)
Greg Loomis, Tech (1976, City)
Kirk Loomis, Tech (1977, City)
Larry Loper, Fairview (1975, County)
Jerry Lorei, Seneca (1975, County)
Philip Lorenz, McDowell (1975, County)
Jim Lorigo, Tech (1965, City)
Bill Lossie, Millcreek (1941, West)
Calvin Love, Millcreek (1941, West)
Dan Lovett, Girard (1995, County)
John Lowery, Albion (1951, West)
Nick Lubahn, McDowell (2002, City)
William Lubahn, Cathedral Prep (2010, City)
Mike Lubak, East (1985, City)
Al Lubiejewski, Cathedral Prep (1962, City)
Al Lubowicki, Tech (1939, East)
Zach Lucas, General McLane (2011, County)
Felix Lucero, Fairview (1973, County
John Luchs, North East (1964, County)
Bob Lugo, Cathedral Prep (1957, City)
Jorge Luiggi, Central Tech (2011, City)
Joe Lukac, Corry (1996, County)
Paul Luke, North East (1989, County)
Chris Luker, Northwestern (1997, County)
Walter Lundstrom, East (1940, West)
Steve Lunger, McDowell (1991, City)
George Luninger, Fairview (1939, West)
Pat Lupo, Cathedral Prep (1964, City)
Phil Lupo, Cathedral Prep (2002, City)
Josh Lustig, Cathedral Prep (2001, City)
Justin Lustig, Cathedral Prep (1996, City)
Tyler Lutton, Corry (2009, County)
John Lutz, Wesleyville (1942, East)
Gary Lydic, Fort LeBoeuf (1972, County)
Dave Lynch, Harbor Creek (1981, County)
Jake Lynch, Cathedral Prep (2000, City)
Jim Lynch, Cathedral Prep (1953, City)
Marty Lynch, McDowell (1985, City)
Eric Lynde, Central (1997, City)
Thomas Lynde, Academy (1986, City)
Brady Lynn, North East (2012, County)
Bill Lyons, Academy (1992, City)
David Lyons, Waterford (1940, West)
Kevin Lyons, Seneca (2000, County)
Jim Lytle, Millcreek (1946, West)

M

Gus Maas, North East (1975, County)
Rick Maas, North East (1977, County)
Mike MacDonald, North East (1994, County)
Scott MacEwen, Girard (1981, County)

Don MacGregor, Strong Vincent (1963, City)
B.J. MacIntosh, Fort LeBoeuf (1972, County)
Tom Maciulewicz, McDowell (1988, City)
John Mackanos, Girard (1990, County)
Scott MacKelvey, Fairview (1978, County)
Frank Macko, Academy (1968, City)
Dave Mackowski, Millcreek (1957, County)
Jason MacQuarrie, Harbor Creek (1989, County)
Alex Macrino, Mercyhurst Prep (2008, City)
Mike Madalena, McDowell (1979, City)
Dan Madden, Northwestern (1999, County)
Paul Madden, Albion (1948, West)
Russ Madonia, Cathedral Prep (1975, City)
Sean Madura, Tech (1990, City)
Christian Magee, Central Tech (2009, City)
Jack Magee, Union City (1957, County)
Joel Magee, Harbor Creek (1966, County)
Mike Magee, Union City (1984, County)
Gary Magorien, McDowell (2002, City)
Joe Magorien, McDowell (1996, City)
Denny Maguire, Harbor Creek (1984, County)
Matt Magyar, Cathedral Prep (2002, City)
Edwin Magzai, Kanty Prep (1950, West)
Josh Maher, Girard (2001, County)
Jerry Mahle, Fort LeBoeuf (1963, County)
Walley Mahle, Fort LeBoeuf (1961, County)
Bob Mahon, East (1942, East)
Eugene Mahon, East (1946, East)
Jim Mahon, East (1940, West)
John Mahon, East (1956, City)
Bob Mahoney, Cathedral Prep (2009, City)
D.J. Mahoney, Mercyhurst Prep (2012, City)
Jim Mahoney, Cathedral Prep (1944, West)
Tim Mahoney, Cathedral Prep (1979, City)
Frank Maille, Wesleyville (1945, East)
Kyle Maio, Northwestern (2009, County)
Matt Maisner, Fort LeBoeuf (2002, County)
Kyle Majewski, General McLane (2009, County)
Tony Major, Iroquois (1967, County)
Ron Malek, Tech (1953, City)
Scott Malesiewski, North East (1995, County)
T.J. Malesiewski, North East (1991, County)
Tim Malesiewski, North East (1993, County)
Chad Maleski, Union City (1996, County)
Ted Maleski, East (1964, City)
John Malinowski, Tech (1948, East)
Matt Malinowski, Kanty Prep (1976, City)
Tim Malinowski, Strong Vincent (1987, City)
Donny Mallin, Cathedral Prep (2009, City)
Royce Mallory, Edinboro (1950, West)
James Malone, Cathedral Prep (2012, City)
John Maloney, Corry (1979, County)
Mickey Maloney, Harbor Creek (1950, East)
Sean Maloney, Corry (1981, County)
John Mancini, Cathedral Prep (1945, West)

Save-An-Eye Game Players

Mike Mangel, Union City (2001, County)
George Mangol, Cathedral Prep (1955, City)
John Mangol, Union City (2007, County)
Rick Mangold, Cathedral Prep (1971, City)
Bill Maniece, East (1973, City)
Mark Manna, Academy (1981, City)
Bob Manners, Edinboro (1954, County)
Mike Manning, Harbor Creek (1993, County)
Norm Manross, Academy (1940, East)
Mike Marcinko, General McLane (1982, County)
Tom Marcinko, General McLane (1980, County)
Marty Mariani, General McLane (1999, County)
Mike Mariani, General McLane (1991, County)
Bill Marinelli, Lawrence Park (1941, East)
Don Marinelli, Tech (1945, West)
Anthony Marino, Northwestern (1995, County)
Dennis Markham, Academy (1962, City)
Howard Markham, Waterford (1955, County)
Bill Markle, Seneca (1984, County)
Larry Marlett, Corry (1964, County)
Brandon Marlow, Strong Vincent (2009, City)
Jim Marnella, Cathedral Prep (1963, City)
Ryan Marovich, McDowell (2003, City)
Joshua Marques, Strong Vincent (2011, City)
Jay Marquis, McDowell (2005, City)
Dick Marr, Wesleyville (1950, East)
Gilbert Marsh, East (1981, City)
Gunther Martena, Waterford (1944, East)
Carl Marthaler, Cathedral Prep (1944, West)
Alan Marthesen, Academy (1957, City)
Craig Marti, Corry (2010, County)
Bob Martin, Academy (1966, City)
George Martin, Wesleyville (1944, East)
Malik Martin, Strong Vincent (1992, City)
Mike Martin, Fairview (1989, County)
Robert Martin, Harbor Creek (1947, East)
Scott Martin, East (1980, City)
Zac Martin, McDowell (1998, City)
Sam Martina, North East (1945, East)
Jerry Marzka, Tech (1968, City)
John Marzka, Academy (1987, City)
Randy Marzka, Academy (1976, City)
Tom Masi, Tech (1974, City)
Tony Masi, Academy (1952, City)
Nicholas Maskrey, Northwestern (2010, County)
Stephen Maskrey, Northwestern (2012, County)
Dale Massing, Strong Vincent (1962, City)
David Massing, Strong Vincent (1995, City)
Barry Masterson, Cathedral Prep (1966, City)
Pat Masterson, Cathedral Prep (1976, City)
Mike Mastrog, McDowell (1983, City)
John Matcham, Iroquois (1972, County)
Jim Mathers, North East (2007, County)
Mike Mathis, East (2008, City)
Mike Matos, East (1983, City)

Louis Matosian, Lawrence Park (1948, East)
Travis Matson, Mercyhurst Prep (2003, City)
Chic Matthews, Academy (1968, City)
Rob Mattis, McDowell (2005, City)
John Matts, Tech (1970, City)
Steve Maxumczyk, East (1940, West)
Mike May, Cathedral Prep (1979, City)
Richard May, Academy (1949, East)
Tom May, Harbor Creek (1981, County)
Dave Mayer, General McLane (1992, County)
Bernard Maynard, Wesleyville (1952, County)
Ron Mayott, Union City (1952, County)
Zach Mayr, McDowell (2011, City)
Dana Mays, Girard (1972, County)
Garrett Mays, Cathedral Prep (2000, City)
Mike Mazanowski, East (1972, City)
Arsenio McAdory, East (2002, City)
Rashad McAdory, East (2005, City)
Jim McAndrew, General McLane (1991, County)
Joe McAndrew, Tech (1974, City)
Pat McAndrew, Tech (1980, City)
Tim McAndrew, Harbor Creek (2008, County)
Josh McAnulty, Harbor Creek (2008, County)
Joe McCafferty, Cathedral Prep (1940, East)
Glenn McCall, North East (1991, County)
Marshall McCall, Wattsburg (1949, East)
Ron McCall, Waterford (1951, East; 1952, County)
Bill McCamey, Millcreek (1941, West)
Bob McCammon, Harbor Creek (1960, County)
Jack McCann, Fairview (2007, County)
Jim McCarthy, Strong Vincent (1940, East)
Rick McCauley, General McLane (1969, County)
Gene McChesney, Corry (1967, County)
Ken McChesney, Corry (1966, County)
Shane McChesney, Corry (1996, County)
Bud McClain, Cathedral Prep (1941, West)
Joe McClaran, Lawrence Park (1949, East)
Bob McClean, Harbor Creek (1942, East)
John McClellan, Waterford (1958, County)
Scott McClellan, Corry (1989, County)
Ron McClelland, Harbor Creek (1976, County)
Dick McClure, Girard (1962, County)
Eric McCommons, Northwestern (1998, County)
Chuck McConnell, Girard (1976, County)
Neil McCord, North East (2009, County)
Jerry McCormick, Kanty Prep (1979, City)
Matt McCormick, Strong Vincent (1983, City)
Chawn McCowien, Mercyhurst Prep (2009, City)
Mike McCoy, Cathedral Prep (1966, City)
Ron McCoy, Girard (1939, West)
Keith McCracken, Union City (1991, County)
Eric McCray, Corry (1992, County)
Gerald McCray, Fairview (1947, West)
William McCray, Corry (2006, County)
Greg McCreary, General McLane (1969, County)

Save-An-Eye Game Players

Dick McCrillis, Academy (1954, City)
Brian McCullough, Strong Vincent (2003, City)
Tony McCullum, Academy (1983, City)
David McDonald, General McLane (1988, County)
Dennis McDonald, Girard (1983, County)
Randy McDonald, Fairview (1978, County)
Kevin McEldowney, Corry (1985, County)
Steve McEldowney, Corry (1980, County)
Joe McFadden, Mercyhurst Prep (2000, City)
Shawn McFadden, General McLane (2008, County)
Bob McGahen, Fort LeBoeuf (1975, County)
Rob McGahen, Harbor Creek (2001, County)
Ron McGahen, Fort LeBoeuf (1986, County)
Winfield McGahen, Waterford (1945, East)
Greg McGill, North East (1968, County)
Brian McGowan, Fort LeBoeuf (1987, County)
T.J. McGraw, McDowell (2005, City)
Steve McGregor, McDowell (1980, City)
Mike McGuigan, North East (1998, County)
Jack McIntire, Fort LeBoeuf (2000, County)
Joe McIntire, Fort LeBoeuf (2009, County)
Mike McIntire, Strong Vincent (1995, City)
Terry McIntosh, North East (1963, County)
William McIntyre, Strong Vincent (1943, West)
Bob McKay, Girard (1961, County)
Elmer McKay, Lawrence Park (1942, East)
Ralph McKay, Girard (1957, County)
Pat McKenrick, Strong Vincent (1974, City)
Matt McKinley, Fairview (1984, County)
Matt McKinney, Union City (2000, County)
Mike McKinney, Union City (1998, County)
Randy McKinney, Fairview (1979, County)
Terrance McLaren, Mercyhurst Prep (2006, City)
Mike McLaughlin, Fairview (1979, County)
Tom McLaughlin, Fairview (1978, County)
Brandon McLaurin, Strong Vincent (2005, City)
Nathan McLaurin, Cathedral Prep (2012, City)
Lynn McLean, Harbor Creek (1941, East)
John McMahon, Cathedral Prep (1939, West)
Bill McManus, Academy (1971, City)
Bill McManus, Strong Vincent (1941, West)
Mark McManus, Fairview (1996, County)
Matt McMaster, General McLane (1999, County)
Dennis McNally, Girard (1963, County)
Barry McNerney, Tech (1968, City)
Jack McNulty, Cathedral Prep (1949, West)
Dave McQuiston, Harbor Creek (2000, County)
George McQuiston, Union City (1939, East)
Jeff McShane, Iroquois (1981, County)
Matt McShane, Iroquois (2004, County)
Tom McShane, Iroquois (1974, County)
Jim McVay, Academy (1942, West)
Corey McWilliams, Fort LeBoeuf (2010, County)
Lamont McWilliams, Strong Vincent (2007, City)
Jamie Mead, Fairview (1976, County)

Press Mead, Strong Vincent (1941, West)
Jesse Meade, McDowell (2005, City)
Josh Meade, McDowell (2012, City)
Jack Meeder, Millcreek (1952, County)
Richard Meeder, Girard (1951, West)
Zach Meeder, Fairview (2001, County)
Dave Meehl, North East (1968, County)
James Meehl, North East (1943, East)
Nick Mehall, McDowell (1998, City)
Ron Meigaard, Millcreek (1950, West)
Dan Mellow, Academy (1966, City)
Augie Mennen, Corry (1993, County)
Steve Menosky, Academy (1987, City)
Doug Mercier, McDowell (1979, City)
Dave Merritt, Northwestern (1997, County)
Harold Merritt, Northwestern (1975, County)
Mike Merritt, Harbor Creek (1976, County)
Scott Merritt, Northwestern (1987, County)
Steve Merritt, Harbor Creek (1973, County
Jim Mershon, Girard (1982, County)
Chris Merski, Cathedral Prep (1991, City)
Matt Messmer, Kanty Prep (1975, County)
Skip Metcalf, Fairview (1986, County)
Gary Metzgar, Cathedral Prep (1979, City)
Ed Metzger, Wesleyville (1943, East)
Bill Metzler, Girard (1971, County)
Brent Meyer, McDowell (1998, City)
Josh Mezzacapo, Cathedral Prep (2004, City)
Norbert Miazga, Tech (1947, West)
Bill Michael, Fairview (1974, County)
Dave Michael, General McLane (1984, County)
Don Michael, Tech (1984, City)
Matt Michael, Fairview (2007, County)
Pat Michael, Fairview (2008, County)
Ray Michael, Fairview (1976, County)
Rich Michael, Tech (1981, City)
Dave Michaels, Academy (1970, City)
Jim Michaels, McDowell (1967, County)
Bruce Mick, Corry (1972, County)
Mike Miczo, Northwestern (1986, County)
Fran Mifsud, Cathedral Prep (1977, City)
Jerry Mifsud, Cathedral Prep (1968, City)
Kevin Mihalik, Northwestern (1986, County)
Bob Mikolajczyk, Cathedral Prep (1965, City)
Eric Mikovch, Northwestern (1987, County)
Gerry Mikovich, Girard (1966, County)
John Mikovich, Girard (1964, County)
John Miles, Fairview (1967, County)
Rick Miles, North East (1992, County)
Dan Milhisler, Cathedral Prep (2002, City)
Art Miller, East (1962, City)
Bob Miller, East (1975, City)
Brandon Miller, Corry (2010, County)
Charles Miller, Strong Vincent (1939, West)
James Miller, Fort LeBoeuf (1999, County)

Jeff Miller, Seneca (1976, County)
Jim Miller, Academy (1960, City)
Joe Miller, Northwestern (1975, County)
John Miller, East (1956, City)
Josh Miller, Girard (1999, County)
Josh Miller, Fort LeBoeuf (1998, County)
Justin Miller, Corry (2011, County)
Mark Miller, McDowell (1993, City)
Mark Miller, Corry (1981, County)
Mark Miller, Tech (1973, City)
Nick Miller, North East (1998, County)
Pat Miller, Corry (1950, East)
Paul Miller, East (1971, City)
Ryan Miller, McDowell (2001, City)
Ryan Miller, Corry (2000, County)
Steve Miller, Union City (1978, County)
Ted Miller, Edinboro (1957, County)
Terry Miller, Fairview (1963, County)
Tom Miller, Iroquois (1968, County)
Walt Miller, Wattsburg (1971, County)
Kyle Millet, Iroquois (1997, County)
Scott Millhouse, McDowell (1972, County)
Marvin Millspaw, Edinboro (1940, East)
Pat Millspaw, General McLane (1967, County)
Brian Milne, Fort LeBoeuf (1991, County)
Kaylon Mims, Central Tech (2009, City)
Robert Miniger, East (1944, East)
John Minnich, Conneaut Valley (1953, County)
Todd Minor, General McLane (1997, County)
Jim Minton, Cathedral Prep (1945, West)
Mike Minton, Strong Vincent (1973, City)
Mike Miodus, Strong Vincent (1996, City)
Dennis Misko, Cathedral Prep (1986, City)
Jim Mitchel, East (1985, City)
Amos Mitchell, East (1961, City)
Brad Mitchell, Corry (1995, County)
Craig Mitchell, Fort LeBoeuf (1963, County)
Doug Mitchell, Corry (1997, County)
Fred Mitchell, Corry (1945, East)
Greg Mitchell, Harbor Creek (1984, County)
Jake Mitchell, Strong Vincent (1952, City)
Keith Mitchell, Harbor Creek (1986, County)
Keith Mitchell, Corry (1981, County)
Kenny Mitchell, East (1995, City)
Nick Mitchell, Corry (1992, County)
Shawn Mitchell, Corry (1997, County)
Tom Mitchell, Millcreek (1954, County)
William Mitchell, Corry (1957, County)
Alex Mobilia, North East (2011, County)
Prince Mobley, Academy (1975, City)
Demon Moffett, East (1993, City)
Mike Monahan, Academy (1983, City)
Scott Moneta, Harbor Creek (1992, County)
Ryan Mong, McDowell (2011, City)
Brad Mongera, Fort LeBoeuf (1996, County)

Matt Mongera, Seneca (2012, County)
Steve Mongera, Seneca (1976, County)
Joe Monocello, Cathedral Prep (1976, City)
Caesar Montevecchio, Cathedral Prep (1951, West; 1952, City)
Gary Moore, Academy (1984, City)
Jack Moore, Strong Vincent (1960, City)
Robert Moore, Northwestern (2007, County)
Skip Moore, Corry (1951, East)
Fred Moorehead, Harbor Creek (1943, East)
Jim Moorehead, Lawrence Park (1962, County)
Steve Moorhead, Harbor Creek (1958, County)
Paul Morabito, Tech (1944, West)
Vince Moran, Millcreek (1958, County)
Tom Morano, Harbor Creek (1973, County)
Ted Morasky, Cathedral Prep (1941, West)
Jeff Morey, Seneca (1986, County)
Bob Morgan, Academy (1945, East)
Dwight Morgan, East (1996, City)
Greg Morgan, Mercyhurst Prep (1996, City)
Tom Morgan, Cathedral Prep (2000, City)
Tom Morgan, East (1968, City)
Aaron Morley, Northwestern (2012, County)
William Morley, Cranesville (1957, County)
Bob Morosky, East (1959, City)
Bob Morosky, Wesleyville (1957, County)
Gabe Morretini, Tech (1958, City)
Fred Morris, East (1950, East)
Keith Morris, Corry (1984, County)
Bill Morrow, Wesleyville (1947, East)
Walter Morrow, Harbor Creek (1940, West)
Todd Morse, Northwestern (2006, County)
Lucas Morton, Harbor Creek (2012, County)
Don Mosher, Union City (1990, County)
Jim Mosher, McDowell (1964, County)
Jordan Mosher, Corry (2009, County)
Tom Moske, Cathedral Prep (1975, City)
Bob Moss, Strong Vincent (1981, City)
Hardin Moss, East (2004, City)
Tom Mowery, Fairview (1955, County)
Paul Moyak, Cathedral Prep (2012, City)
Chris Mrozowski, Tech (1980, City)
Anthony Mucciarone, Strong Vincent (1944, West)
Vern Mueller, Seneca (1975, County)
Qiydaar Muhammed, East (2009, City)
Andy Mukina, Edinboro (1942, West)
Frank Mukina, Edinboro (1948, West)
Dan Muldowney, McDowell (2007, City)
Joe Muldrew, Central (1994, City)
Jim Mullard, Strong Vincent (1946, West)
Andy Mullen, North East (2001, County)
Robert Mulligan, Fort LeBoeuf (2001, County)
Fred Munch, McDowell (1999, City)
Rob Munch, McDowell (2001, City)
John Mundy, Cathedral Prep (1987, City)
Al Murawski, East (1978, City)

Willie Murel, Central (2003, City)
Bob Murosky, Iroquois (1969, County)
Steve Murosky, McDowell (2000, City)
Dennis Murphy, Tech (1958, City)
Glenn Murphy, North East (2009, County)
John Murphy, Cathedral Prep (1957, City)
Pat Murphy, Girard (1978, County)
Ryan Murphy, Seneca (2010, County)
Bob Murray, Fairview (1992, County)
Don Murray, North East (1952, County)
Dave Murzynski, Harbor Creek (2005, County)
Mike Murzynski, McDowell (2000, City)
Mike Murzynski, Tech (1978, City)
Pat Murzynski, Iroquois (2002, County)
Zach Murzynski, Mercyhurst Prep (2011, City)
Jim Muscarella, North East (1983, County)
Frank Musiek, Union City (1964, County)
Joseph Musiek, Union City (1949, East)
Dennis Musolf, Fort LeBoeuf (1965, County)
Mike Musone, Central (2001, City)
Steve Musone, Central (1997, City)
Raymond Musser, Lawrence Park (1948, East)
Jacob Muye, Seneca (2011, County)
Brian Myers, Mercyhurst Prep (1996, City)
Chuck Myers, Academy (1959, City)
Frank Myers, General McLane (1983, County)
Gary Myers, Academy (1986, City)
Greg Myers, Academy (1967, County)
Jason Myers, Fairview (1990, County)
Ryan Myers, Union City (2011, County)

N

Larry Nagelson, North East (1969, County)
Lou Nagy, McDowell (1966, County)
Mike Nagy, East (1985, City)
Phil Nagy, McDowell (1976, County)
Fine Nai, McDowell (1998, City)
Randy Nanni, Iroquois (1968, County)
Bill Nantes, Harbor Creek (1980, County)
Louis Nardo, Wesleyville (1939, East)
Tom Narus, McDowell (1974, County)
Rick Nash, North East (1980, County)
Gene Natale, Cathedral Prep (2002, City)
George Naylor, Girard (1959, County)
Brent Neal, Fort LeBoeuf (1995, County)
Mike Neavins, Jr., Strong Vincent (2012, City)
Eric Neavins, Central (2000, City)
Ron Nece, Harbor Creek (1941, East)
Mike Nedreski, East (1986, City)
Louis Neff, North East (2010, County)
Mac Neil, North East (1969, County)
Greg Nelson, Fort LeBoeuf (1992, County)
Jim Nelson, Iroquois (1985, County)
John Nelson, Cathedral Prep (1958, City)
Matt Nelson, Girard (2004, County)

Mike Nelson, Northwestern (2000, County)
Nels Nelson, Harbor Creek (1948, East)
Bill Nemenz, Cathedral Prep (1985, City)
Bill Nemenz, Tech (1965, City)
Carl Nemenz, Academy (1943, East)
Mike Nemeyer, Iroquois (1977, County)
Paul Nenman, North East (1946, East)
David Nesselhauf, Cathedral Prep (2004, City)
Mike Nestor, Tech (1970, City)
Jamie Neuberger, General McLane (1990, County)
Joe Newara, North East (1985, County)
Joe Newara, North East (1942, East)
Louis Newara, North East (1940, West)
Sam Newara, Iroquois (1997, County)
Tim Newara, Iroquois (1992, County)
Tom Newara, Iroquois (1999, County)
Mark Newcamp, Tech (1973, City)
Craig Newell, Fort LeBoeuf (1981, County)
Eric Newhall, General McLane (1972, County)
Eric Newlin, McDowell (2003, City)
Al Nicastro, St. Gregory (1956, County)
Bob Nichols, Corry (1958, County)
Quentin Nichols, Corry (1980, County)
Tom Nichols, Corry (1985, County)
Carl Nicholson, East (1981, City)
Paul Nicholson, Northwestern (1974, County)
Wes Nicklas, Waterford (1954, County)
Jayson Nickson, Mercyhurst Prep (2007, City)
Ken Nickson, Central (1996, City)
Dom Nicolia, Academy (1948, East)
Ray Nicolia, Cathedral Prep (1985, City)
Ray Nicolia, Cathedral Prep (1956, City)
Ralph Niebauer, Fairview (1957, County)
Brett Niemeic, Cathedral Prep (2006, City)
Al Niemi, East (1971, City)
Bob Nies, Cathedral Prep (1981, City)
Paul Nies, Seneca (2003, County)
Ron Nietupski, Tech (1969, City)
Ryan Nietupski, Cathedral Prep (1998, City)
Richard Nikolishen, Tech (1962, City)
Tom Niland, Cathedral Prep (1964, City)
Mark Nipper, Fairview (1999, County)
Bill Nirmaier, Union City (1985, County)
Darryl Nirmaier, Union City (1981, County)
Brandon Nishnick, Fort LeBoeuf (1997, County)
Dave Nishnick, Fort LeBoeuf (1961, County)
Steve Nishnick, Fort LeBoeuf (1964, County)
Josh Niswonger, General McLane (2011, County)
Mike Noble, Strong Vincent (2007, City)
Chad Noce, McDowell (2007, City)
Jon Nolan, Tech (1988, City)
Mike Nolan, Strong Vincent (1987, City)
Steve Nolan, General McLane (1971, County)
Joe Noonan, Tech (1973, City)
John Noonan, Tech (1968, City)

Steve Noonan, Cathedral Prep (1999, City)
Jeff Norris, McDowell (1979, City)
Wayne Norris, McKean (1939, West)
Mark Northrup, North East (1979, County)
Dave Norton, Corry (1972, County)
Doug Norton, Tech (1969, City)
Jason Norton, Northwestern (1998, County)
Tadas Norvaisa, North East (1986, County)
Dan Nowacinski, Tech (1969, City)
Chris Nowak, Prep (1978, City)
John Nowak, Conneaut Valley (1962, County)
Jerry Nowakowski, Harbor Creek (1970, County)
Jim Nowakowski, Harbor Creek (1974, County)
Dave Noziglia, Strong Vincent (1978, City)
Mike Nuara, Strong Vincent (1965, City)
Mike Nulph, Northwestern (1973, County)
Jim Nunes, Tech (1960, City)
Tim Nunes, Academy (1969, City)
Tom Nunes, Cathedral Prep (1985, City)
Tony Nunes, Tech (1956, City)
Sean Nutter, Cathedral Prep (2005, City)
Chip Nuzzo, Corry (1983, County)
Chet Nyberg, Strong Vincent (1942, West)
Randy Nyberg, McDowell (1972, County)
Harry Nye, Waterford (1941, East)
Kenneth Nye, Albion (1946, West)

Mel Oakes, Wesleyville (1954, County)
Bob Oatman, East (1952, City)
Paul Oberacker, Strong Vincent (1939, West)
Bob Obert, Cathedral Prep (1950, West)
Bill O'Brien, Northwestern (1988, County)
Kenan O'Brien, Edinboro (1949, West)
Bill Ochalek, Northwestern (1977, County)
Phil Ochalek, McDowell (1983, City)
Mike O'Connor, Harbor Creek (1992, County)
Terry O'Connor, Harbor Creek (1988, County)
Mark Odom, Tech (1989, City)
Joe Oduho, Cathedral Prep (2012, City)
Martin Oduho, McDowell (2011, City)
John Offner, Edinboro (1946, West)
Brian O'Hara, Strong Vincent (1992, City)
Jeff Ohrn, McDowell (1997, City)
Charles Oldach, East (1947, East)
Greg Oldach, Strong Vincent (1972, City)
John Oldach, Harbor Creek (1985, County)
Ray Oldach, Cathedral Prep (1944, West)
Bob O'Leary, St. Gregory (1955, County)
Buddy O'Leary, Mercyhurst Prep (2007, City)
Mark Olesky, McDowell (1984, City)
Jeff Oleson, Fort LeBoeuf (1970, County)
Dan Olson, Strong Vincent (1992, City)
Jerry Olson, Lawrence Park (1958, County)
Jim Olszewski, Cathedral Prep (1965, City)

Paul Onachila, Albion (1944, West)
Ed Onachilla, Albion (1939, West)
Carl Onda, Cathedral Prep (1943, West)
George O'Neil, Lawrence Park (1939, East)
Kellen O'Neill, General McLane (2009, County)
Dave Onorato, McDowell (1987, City)
Ed Onorato, Tech (1958, City)
Paul Onorato, Strong Vincent (1970, City)
Tony Onorato, McDowell (1984, City)
George Orbanek, Cathedral Prep (1967, County)
David Orlando, Cathedral Prep (2007, City)
Bob Orlando, Strong Vincent (1939, West)
Brad Orlando, McDowell (1996, City)
Joe Orlando, Strong Vincent (1990, City)
Phil Orlando, Tech (1966, City)
Quentin Orlando, Strong Vincent (1992, City)
Gabe Oros, Fairview (1990, County)
Kris Oros, Fairview (2000, County)
Gary Orr, Cathedral Prep (1946, West)
Adam Orsefskie, Iroquois (1998, County)
Kyle Orth, McDowell (2001, City)
Doug Osborn, Fort LeBoeuf (2004, County)
Joe Osiecki, Tech (1943, West)
Keith Osinski, Fairview (1980, County)
Brian Ostrum, Mercyhurst Prep (1994, City)
Dave Ostrum, Wattsburg (1970, County)
Chris Oswalt, Iroquois (1991, County)
Dave Ott, Cathedral Prep (1986, City)
Joe Ott, Cathedral Prep (1960, City)
Leon Ott, Academy (1958, City)
Pat Ott, Cathedral Prep (1988, City)
Pat Otteni, General McLane (1978, County)
Scott Otteni, General McLane (1982, County)
Jack Overocker, Wesleyville (1947, East)
Andre Overton, Academy (1983, City)
Nate Overton, Tech (1986, City)
Jesse Owens, Central (2001, City)
Cory Owens, Corry (2011, County)
Lee Owens, Fairview (1993, County)
Les Owens, Waterford (1953, County)
Larry Ozimek, Cathedral Prep (1964, City)

Casey Pace, Fort LeBoeuf (2011, County)
Tajh Pacley, East (2008, City)
Archie Page, Academy (1975, City)
Daryhl Page, Academy (1985, City)
Derick Page, Central (2002, City)
Gary Page, Academy (1979, City)
Greg Page, Academy (1984, City)
Maurice Page, Strong Vincent (1999, City)
Don Palermo, Tech (1980, City)
Kevin Palermo, Kanty Prep (1980, County)
Matt Palermo, McDowell (2000, City)
Ed Palkovic, Tech (1946, West)

Jim Palkovic, Cathedral Prep (1973, City)
John Palkovic, Cathedral Prep (1970, City)
Mike Palkovic, Cathedral Prep (1973, City)
Tom Palmer, McDowell (1996, City)
Dan Palmer, Northwestern (2003, County)
Doug Palmer, Tech (1960, City)
George Palmer, Cathedral Prep (1950, West)
Mike Palmer, McDowell (1994, City)
Mike Palmer, Fairview (1983, County)
Mike Palmer, McDowell (1971, County)
Ronald Palmer, Central (2005, City)
Zach Palmer, Mercyhurst Prep (2011, City)
Brian Palotas, Cathedral Prep (1992, City)
Pete Panetta, Strong Vincent (1946, West)
Mike Panighetti, McDowell (2001, City)
Mike Panighetti, Tech (1972, City)
Patrick Papale, North East (2010, County)
Frank Papparazzo, North East (1951, East; 1952, County)
Cyril Papson, Fairview (1940, East)
Josh Paradise, Northwestern (2011, County)
Marcus Paradise, Northwestern (2008, County)
Mark Paradise, Harbor Creek (1980, County)
Dave Paris, Cathedral Prep (1961, City)
Mike Paris, McDowell (1975, County)
Ray Paris, McDowell (1980, City)
Sonny Paris, Iroquois (1988, County)
Harry Parker, Lawrence Park (1941, East)
Matthew Parker, McDowell (2002, City)
Richard Parks, Corry (1977, County)
Dave Parmeter, Tech (1958, City)
Pat Parra, Strong Vincent (1987, City)
Andy Parshall, McDowell (2005, City)
Graham Parsons, Academy (1955, City)
Matt Parsons, Cathedral Prep (2001, City)
Mike Parsons, Cathedral Prep (2008, City)
Ron Pasarelli, Strong Vincent (1957, City)
Ernie Pascarella, East (1961, City)
Jeff Pasinski, McDowell (1988, City)
Ed Pasko, Tech (1966, City)
Ed Pasky, Academy (1944, East)
Rich Pasquale, Tech (1954, City)
Bill Passerotti, Strong Vincent (1945, West)
Dick Passerotti, East (1950, East)
Rich Passerotti, Harbor Creek (1978, County)
Tracy Passerotti, Harbor Creek (1966, County)
Ryan Paszkowski, Mercyhurst Prep (1998, City)
Joe Patalita, Tech (1941, East)
Richard Paterniti, East (1949, East)
Les Patmore, Lawrence Park (1942, East)
Mark Patmore, Harbor Creek (1992, County)
Dennis Patora, Tech (1964, City)
Gus Patsy, Academy (1954, City)
Art Patterson, Millcreek (1946, West)
Carl Patterson, General McLane (1997, County)
Floyd Patterson, Albion (1951, West)

Jason Patterson, Corry (1994, County)
Casey Patton, Fairview (2008, County)
Bill Pavkov, Waterford (1946, East)
Bob Pavolko, Albion (1955, County)
Mike Pavolko, Northwestern (1985, County)
Richard Pavolko, Albion (1957, County)
Dave Pawlukovich, Wattsburg (1963, County)
Phil Pawlukovich, Wattsburg (1963, County)
Dick Payne, Girard (1961, County)
Doug Payne, Fairview (1961, County)
Vernon Payne, Strong Vincent (1976, City)
Joe Peagler, McDowell (1971, County)
Jarryd Pearson, Iroquois (2006, County)
John Pearson, Lawrence Park (1940, West)
Ed Peck, Tech (1949, East)
Gus Pede, Harbor Creek (1950, East)
Ted Peggy, Tech (1960, City)
Kyle Peirson, Northwestern (2009, County)
Carl Pekala, Lawrence Park (1955, County)
Walter Pelkowski, Strong Vincent (1955, City)
Cosimo Pellican, Academy (1946, East)
William Pellow, Girard (1943, West)
Nick Pelusi, General McLane (1978, County)
Dave Penman, McDowell (1970, County)
Andy Penna, Cathedral Prep (1979, City)
Lewis Penna, East (1947, East)
Larry Pennica, Girard (1946, West)
Joe Peplinski, Cathedral Prep (1951, West; 1952, City)
Ranfis Perez, Cathedral Prep (1992, City)
Richard Perfetto, Strong Vincent (1957, City)
Frank "Butch" Perino, St. Gregory (1956, County)
Jeff Perino, North East (1980, County)
Garrick Perkins, Cathedral Prep (1992, City)
Dave Pernice, McDowell (2003, City)
George Perry, East (1980, City)
Ty Perry, Fairview (2006, County)
Sean Perseo, Tech (1989, City)
Chris Pesch, McDowell (1985, City)
Dave Petak, East (1970, City)
Dick Peterman, Harbor Creek (1952, County)
Brian Peters, Iroquois (1999, County)
Mark Peters, Tech (1971, City)
Tom Peters, Fairview (1976, County)
Chris Peterson, Fort LeBoeuf (1980, County)
Chuck Peterson, Wattsburg (1970, County)
David Peterson, McDowell (1991, City)
Jamie Peterson, McDowell (1993, City)
Rollie Peterson, Wattsburg (1968, County)
Vernon Peterson, Cathedral Prep (1973, City)
Shamus Petrucelli, Cathedral Prep (1990, City)
Dennis Petrunger, General McLane (1969, County)
Jim Petrunger, General McLane (1977, County)
Dan Petrush, Northwestern (1974, County)
Mark Petruso, Academy (1977, City)
Paul Petruso, McDowell (2004, City)

Save-An-Eye Game Players

Joe Pettinato, Tech (1949, East)
Jack Pettis, Northwestern (1984, County)
Joe Pfadt, Fort LeBoeuf (1979, County)
Matt Pfadt, Harbor Creek (2006, County)
Terry Pfeffer, Strong Vincent (1959, City)
Ed Pfeiffer, Seneca (2002, County)
Joe Pfeiffer, Wattsburg (1973, County
Dave Pfeil, Girard (1954, County)
Harold Pfister, Cathedral Prep (1939, West)
Mike Pfister, Tech (1939, East)
Aaron Phanco, North East (1993, County)
Dave Phenneger, Fairview (1964, County)
Milt Phenneger, Fairview (1960, County)
Tyler Phenneger, Cathedral Prep (1995, City)
Brandon Phillips, Harbor Creek (2012, County)
Doug Phillips, Strong Vincent (1982, City)
Emmett Phillips, Millcreek (1943, West)
Jim Phillips, Strong Vincent (1940, East)
Jeff Piaza, Tech (1987, City)
Joe Piazza, Seneca (2002, County)
Gary Picheco, Northwestern (1988, County)
Neil Pickens, Northwestern (1989, County)
Jim Piekanski, Strong Vincent (1969, City)
Bruce Pieper, Union City (1951, East; 1952, County)
Harry Pier, Girard (1964, County)
Anthony Pierce, Strong Vincent (1983, City)
Doug Pierce, East (1976, City)
Matt Pierce, McDowell (1995, City)
Phil Pieri, McDowell (1978, County)
David Pifer, Union City (1959, County)
Jack Pikiewicz, Cathedral Prep (1963, City)
Ron Pilarski, Cathedral Prep (1994, City)
Dan Pilewski, Cathedral Prep (1974, City)
Mike Piotrowski, Cathedral Prep (1977, City)
Rick Pire, McDowell (1966, County)
Mike Pistone, McDowell (2004, City)
Art Pitts, Corry (1949, East)
Chuck Pituch, Union City (1966, County)
Bob Pivetta, McDowell (1981, City)
Ben Pizzo, Strong Vincent (1949, West)
Frank Pizzo, Tech (1982, City)
Sam Pizzo, Strong Vincent (1948, West)
Emil Plalet, Harbor Creek (1963, County)
Dean Platz, Fairview (1987, County)
Dick Platz, East (1952, City)
Justin Platz, Girard (2000, County)
Tim Platz, Fairview (1953, County)
Don Ploss, General McLane (1965, County)
Greg Pochatko, Tech (1973, City)
Bill Podoll, Albion (1947, West)
Pat Podoll, Albion (1958, County)
Mike Podskalny, Harbor Creek (2008, County)
Adam Podufal, Girard (2001, County)
Dick Pohl, East (1950, East)
Jonathan Pohl, McDowell (2010, City)

Tippy Pohl, East (1963, City)
Tony Pol, Tech (1947, West)
Tony Pol, Cathedral Prep (1974, City)
Mike Polakowski, General McLane (1995, County)
Brian Polk, Girard (1996, County)
Dave Polk, Fairview (1984, County)
Erik Pollard, Fairview (2006, County)
Jeff Pollard, Fairview (2008, County)
Matt Pollock, Strong Vincent (1991, City)
Robert Pollok, Girard (1944, West)
Joe Pomorski, East (1944, East)
Ray Pomorski, East (1941, East)
Josh Ponsoll, General McLane (2012, County)
Kelly Ponsoll, General McLane (2007, County)
Kyle Ponsoll, General McLane (2010, County)
Patsy Pontillo, Strong Vincent (1977, City)
Joe Pontoriero, Cathedral Prep (1953, City)
George Popa, McDowell (1965, County)
John Popoff, East (1979, City)
Gabriel Popp, Cathedral Prep (1939, West)
Doug Porath, East (1966, City)
Kevin Porath, General McLane (2002, County)
John Porreca, Tech (1947, West)
Jerry Port, Fort LeBoeuf (1983, County)
Doug Porte, McDowell (1966, County)
J.R. Porter, North East (2007, County)
Jeff Porter, East (1986, City)
Ronnie Porter, East (1982, City)
Al Post, Wattsburg (1964, County)
Geno Posterti, Academy (1941, West)
Bernard Postewka, Tech (1943, West)
Bob Potocki, Corry (1965, County)
Ron Potocki, Cathedral Prep (1953, City)
Ron Potocki, Cathedral Prep (1978, City)
Jamie Potosnak, Strong Vincent (1993, City)
Don Potter, Lawrence Park (1959, County)
Steve Potter, Fairview (1976, County)
Don Potts, East (2000, City)
Zach Poulson, Iroquois (2009, County)
Darrel Pound, Seneca (1989, County)
Alan Powell, Strong Vincent (1976, City)
Bob Powell, Strong Vincent (1970, City)
Rausaan Powell, Cathedral Prep (1996, City)
Ronald Powell, Cambridge Springs (1948, West)
Jeremy Powers, Fort LeBoeuf (2012, County)
Ben Pratt, McDowell (1959, County)
Dave Pratt, Girard (1979, County)
John Preister, East (1953, City)
Jim Presley, General McLane (1998, County)
Kyle Presogna, Cathedral Prep (1999, City)
Milt Preston, Girard (1978, County)
Fred Price, Fairview (1995, County)
Nick Price, Iroquois (1993, County)
Ron Price, Academy (1952, City)
Roosevelt Price, East (1984, City)

Scott Price, Northwestern (1988, County)
Ravaire Prince, Central (1999, City)
Lloyd Prindle, Girard (1972, County)
Tim Prior, Central (1998, City)
Josh Prischak, Cathedral Prep (2008, City)
Howard Proctor, Waterford (1940, West)
Mike Proctor, Fort LeBoeuf (2005, County)
Ray Proctor, Waterford (1942, East)
Kyle Protho, Central Tech (2008, City)
Jim Pruckner, McDowell (1978, County)
Mike Pruveadenti, General McLane (2003, County)
Mike Pry, Tech (1971, City)
Paul Przepierski, Academy (1980, City)
Rich Przybylski, Wattsburg (1970, County)
Walt Ptaskiewicz, Wesleyville (1954, County)
Doug Puckly, McDowell (1982, City)
Gene Puingley, Edinboro (1950, West)
George Pulakos, Millcreek (1940, East)
Dick Pulling, North East (1950, East)
Doug Pulling, Fairview (1986, County)
Markese Pullium, Strong Vincent (2010, City)
Shyquawn Pullium, Cathedral Prep (2010, City)
Tyler Pullium, Mercyhurst Prep (2011, City)
Ron Pushinsky, Fairview (1975, County)
Matt Puskar, Seneca (1999, County)
Steve Puskar, Seneca (2004, County)
John Puzarowski, Harbor Creek (1957, County)
Ray Puzarowski, Harbor Creek (1988, County)

Dave Quadri, Cathedral Prep (1959, City)
Dick Quadri, Cathedral Prep (1951, West; 1952, City)
Richard Quadri, Cathedral Prep (1977, City)
Bill Quay, Northwestern (1994, County)
George Quick, Cathedral Prep (1974, City)
Jack Quinn, Cathedral Prep (1941, West)
Jonathan Quinn, East (2004, City)
Kevin Quinn, East (1951, East; 1952, City)
Richard Quinn, Academy (1963, City)
Tony Quinn, Strong Vincent (1988, City)
Blake Quirk, Strong Vincent (2012, City)
Brian Quirk, Corry (1986, County)

Gene Rachocki, East (1952, City)
Geoff Radziszewski, Central (1997, City)
Al Rafalowski, Tech (1968, City)
Mark Rafalowski, Academy (1974, City)
Larry Raimondi, Cathedral Prep (1986, City)
Ron Raimondi, Cathedral Prep (1986, City)
Tom Raleigh, Academy (1959, City)
Norm Ralph, Harbor Creek (1966, County)
Dave Ramsdell, Seneca (1981, County)
Harry Ramsey, Academy (1940, East)

Max Randall, Lawrence Park (1947, East)
Mike Randall, Iroquois (1975, County)
Seth Randall, North East (2002, County)
Jake Randolph, Iroquois (2007, County)
John Randolph, Harbor Creek (1971, County)
Paul Randolph, Iroquois (1977, County)
Rick Randolph, Harbor Creek (1969, County)
Ryan Randolph, Harbor Creek (1997, County)
Gerald Rankin, Academy (1972, City)
Ed Ranowiecki, Academy (1966, City)
Matthew Rapp, McDowell (2003, City)
Vincent Rapp, Strong Vincent (1962, City)
Chip Rappe, Fairview (1979, County)
Brian Ras, McDowell (2006, City)
Len Rastatter, Academy (1941, West)
Roger Ratcliff, Strong Vincent (1977, City)
Tom Ratkowski, Academy (1968, City)
Corey Ratliff, East (2009, City)
Anthony Raucci, McDowell (2012, City)
Matt Raun, Cathedral Prep (2004, City)
Bill Rausch, Girard (1944, West)
Larry Rausch, Girard (1970, County)
Matt Rausch, Albion (1939, West)
Larry Raymond, Strong Vincent (1950, West)
Walt Razanauskas, Tech (1941, East)
Ray Reade, McDowell (1968, County)
John Reagan, Albion (1960, County)
Bob Rebar, Tech (1973, City)
Mark Rebar, Tech (1975, City)
Steve Rebro, Harbor Creek (1961, County)
Jim Reddinger, McDowell (1989, City)
Harold Redinger, Strong Vincent (1957, City)
Mike Redinger, McDowell (1980, City)
Scott Redinger, Fairview (1983, County)
Gary Reed, East (1998, City)
Paul Reed, Fort LeBoeuf (1965, County)
William Rees, East (1949, East)
Dan Reese, North East (1967, County)
William Regelman, Tech (1939, East)
Bob Rehberg, McDowell (1990, City)
Tom Rehberg, Cathedral Prep (1960, City)
Scott Reichard, Mercyhurst Prep (1998, City)
Sean Reichard, Tech (1990, City)
Edwin Rcid, Academy (1962, City)
Tim Reid, Lawrence Park (1962, County)
Al Reidel, East (1945, East)
Greg Reinke, Union City (2011, County)
Robert Reinwald, Academy (1944, East)
Jim Reiser, Tech (1982, City)
Matt Reiser, Academy (1990, City)
Gary Renaud, McDowell (1966, County)
Dan Renick, General McLane (1987, County)
Greg Renker, Harbor Creek (2002, County)
Al Renshaw, Lawrence Park (1960, County)
Allan Repine, Lawrence Park (1958, County)

Andy Resinger, Harbor Creek (1999, County)
Alex Retcofsky, Fairview (2006, County)
Doug Rettman, Wesleyville (1965, County)
Dick Reusch, Cathedral Prep (1951, West; 1952, City)
Len Reuss, Iroquois (1971, County)
Aaron Reynolds, Union City (1986, County)
Keith Reynolds, Harbor Creek (1969, County)
Robert Reynolds, Iroquois (1983, County)
Ryan Rezzelle, McDowell (1994, City)
Owen Rhodes, Central (2000, City)
Pat Ricart, Strong Vincent (1949, West)
Matt Riccomini, General McLane (2000, County)
John Rice, Union City (1964, County)
John Richardson, Fairview (1971, County)
Vance Richmond, Iroquois (1974, County)
Bill Rickard, Albion (1939, West)
Ron Rickards, Albion (1956, County)
Marvin Ridgeway, Academy (1984, City)
Jerry Rife, McDowell (1964, County)
David Riggs, Union City (1955, County)
Ernie Riley, Academy (1956, City)
Greg Riley, Tech (1979, City)
Rich Riley, Cathedral Prep (1989, City)
Jody Rindfuss, Fort LeBoeuf (1993, County)
Kevin Rinn, Tech (1971, City)
James Ritchie, Fairview (1944, West)
Mike Rittenhouse, Corry (1990, County)
Brian Rizzo, North East (1986, County)
Joe Rizzo, North East (1985, County)
Joe Rizzo, North East (2007, County)
Nate Rizzo, North East (1998, County)
Tom Rizzo, North East (1942, East)
Bill Roach, Academy (1944, East)
Dave Roach, Cathedral Prep (2007, City)
Jack Roach, Strong Vincent (1940, East)
Jarad Roach, General McLane (2003, County)
Mike Roach, Girard (2001, County)
Ed Robasky, Cathedral Prep (1963, City)
Joe Robasky, Academy (1941, West)
Bill Roberts, Tech (1963, City)
Clint Roberts, Tech (1971, City)
Gerald Roberts, Waterford (1953, County)
Jerry Roberts, Tech (1992, City)
Terry Roberts, Tech (1992, City)
Bryan Robie, Cathedral Prep (1993, City)
Tom Robie, Strong Vincent (1967, County)
Tony Robie, Strong Vincent (1992, City)
David Robinson, North East (2011, County)
Thomas Robishaw, Cathedral Prep (2010, City)
Robert Robison, Strong Vincent (2002, City)
Joe Robson, McDowell (1968, County)
Keith Rocca, General McLane (1996, County)
Armand Rocco, Strong Vincent (1988, City)
Mike Rocco, Academy (1953, City)
Thomas Rodak, Edinboro (1944, West)

Mike Rodeno, Fairview (1969, County)
Brian Roderick, Strong Vincent (1978, City)
Perry Rodland, Harbor Creek (1973, County)
John Roehl, Academy (1939, West)
Jim Roesch, Strong Vincent (1940, East)
Dick Rogers, Kanty Prep (1948, West)
Galen Rogers, Seneca (1975, County)
Norman Rogers, Fairview (1949, West)
Ron Rogers, Tech (1953, City)
Tom Rogers, Academy (1949, East)
Luke Rohler, Girard (2001, County)
Jim Romanski, Cathedral Prep (1991, City)
Tim Romanski, Strong Vincent (1992, City)
Art Romecki, Wesleyville (1939, East)
Bull Romecki, Wesleyville (1941, East)
Joe Romeo, Strong Vincent (1954, City)
John Root, Fairview (1985, County)
Nick Roseberry, General McLane (2003, County)
Max Rosenberg, Fairview (1939, West)
Jared Rosendahl, Fairview (1996, County)
Stan Rosikowski, Kanty Prep (1948, West)
Jim Ross, East (1954, City)
Larry Ross, Strong Vincent (1966, City)
Robert Ross, Wesleyville (1957, County)
Wirt Ross, Harbor Creek (1949, East)
Dave Rossell, Fort LeBoeuf (1966, County)
Dan Rossman, Tech (1982, City)
Ed Rossman, Tech (1972, City)
Frank Rossman, Tech (1974, City)
Jeff Rosthauser, Seneca (1975, County)
Mike Roszkowski, Tech(1940, West)
Seth Rotko, Northwestern (2003, County)
Dywon Rowan, Mercyhurst Prep (2002, City)
Javon Rowan, Cathedral Prep (2006, City)
Lavonne Rowan, Academy (1981, City)
Buddy Rowell, Academy (1950, East)
Shawn Roy, East (1975, City)
Tom Rozantz, Fairview (1975, County)
William Roznek, Tech (1961, City)
Bob Rudd, East (1964, City)
Richard Rudenski, East (1971, City)
Derek Rudler, McDowell (2001, City)
Ron Rugare, Academy (1975, City)
Dave Ruggerio, Strong Vincent (1963, City)
Jay Ruggerio, Strong Vincent (1976, City)
Jim Ruggiero, Tech (1948, East)
Bill Ruhl, General McLane (1973, County)
Noel Ruiz, Central Tech (2012, City)
John Rumbaugh, McDowell (1990, City)
Joe Rumberger, Cathedral Prep (2008, City)
Gene Rumsey, Conneautville (1949, West)
Carl Rundquist, Tech (1957, City)
Tom Rupczewski, Tech (1983, City)
Bill Rusch, Strong Vincent (1941, West)
Cory Rush, Mercyhurst Prep (1999, City)

Tony Rushin, Corry (1979, County)
Norm Rushton, Lawrence Park (1951, East)
Jason Russell, McDowell (1999, City)
Todd Russell, Central (2007, City)
Glen Rust, Cambridge Springs (1954, County)
Jack Rust, Cambridge Springs (1951, West)
Barney Rutkowski, Wesleyville (1958, County)
Brian Rutkowski, Cathedral Prep (1988, City)
David Rutledge, North East (1982, County)
Eric Ryan, General McLane (1977, County)
Tom Rys, Cathedral Prep (1961, City)
Bob Rzepecki, East (1959, City)
Dan Rzepecki, Cathedral Prep (1995, City)
Joshua Rzepecki, Harbor Creek (2010, County)
Len Rzepecki, Tech (1950, East)
Ron Rzepecki, East (1959, City)

S

Kevin Sabol, Northwestern (1998, County)
Bill Saborsky, Corry (1986, County)
Mike Saccamozzone, St. Gregory (1958, County)
George Sachrison, East (1950, East)
Jack Sadler, Strong Vincent (1941, West)
Jason Sadowski, Union City (2004, County)
Kevin Sakuta, Girard (1977, County)
Bill Salchak, Fort LeBoeuf (1963, County)
Stan Salen, North East (1941, East)
Ray Salmon, McDowell (1994, City)
Vincent Salmon, Waterford (1945, East)
Mike Salter, East (1982, City)
Tywan Salter, Strong Vincent (2008, City)
Ernie Salzer, Millcreek (1940, East)
Steve Samol, McDowell (1960, County)
Pedro Sampani, Tech (1956, City)
Duffy Sample, Fairview (1971, County)
Jim Sampson, Academy (1980, City)
Andy Samsel, Lawrence Park (1945, East)
Joe San Pietro, Academy (1946, East)
Craig Sanders, Fort LeBoeuf (1981, County)
Mario Sanders, Cathedral Prep (2011, City)
Maynard Sanders, Girard (1947, West)
Walter Sanders, Corry (1955, County)
Bill Sandusky, Strong Vincent (1980, City)
Anthony Sanfilippo, Harbor Creek (1994, County)
Donald Sanfilippo, North East (2009, County)
Tony Sanfilippo, North East (1956, County)
Derek Sanford, McDowell (1989, City)
Don Sangston, Wesleyville (1942, East)
Gene Sanner, Academy (1965, City)
Nick Sansone, Strong Vincent (1965, City)
Tony Sansone, Strong Vincent (1971, City)
Bob Sargent, Northwestern (2003, County)
Nick Sargent, Fort LeBoeuf (1997, County)
Rod Sargent, Fort LeBoeuf (1968, County)
Tyler Sargent, Fairview (2008, County)

Al Sarti, East (1942, East)
Jay Sarvis, Harbor Creek (1992, County)
Abe Satterfield, Cathedral Prep (2007, City)
Akeem Satterfield, Cathedral Prep (2008, City)
Aaron Satyshur, McDowell (1989, City)
Denny Satyshur, East (1968, City)
Gary Satyshur, East (1975, City)
Jeff Satyshur, East (1972, City)
Craig Sauers, Central (1999, City)
Jim Sauers, Fort LeBoeuf (1964, County)
John Sauers, General McLane (1969, County)
Mark Saunders, Academy (1978, City)
Mike Savelli, Cathedral Prep (2004, City)
Dave Sawtelle, Harbor Creek (1981, County)
Mike Sawtelle, Fairview (1980, County)
John Saxon, Seneca (1985, County)
Jon Sayles, Central (2007, City)
Mark Scarpino, Harbor Creek (1978, County)
Jim Schaaf, Cathedral Prep (1955, City)
Paul Schaaf, Cathedral Prep (1992, City)
Nick Schafer, Northwestern (2005, County)
Zack Schafer, Northwestern (2003, County)
T.J. Schaffner, Fairview (1998, County)
Bob Scharrer, Tech (1977, City)
Dick Schau, McDowell (1961, County)
Mitchell Schauble, Harbor Creek (2012, County)
Dick Scheffner, Cathedral Prep (1944, West)
John Scheffner, Academy (1956, City)
Tom Schelhammer, McDowell (1989, City)
Steve Scheloske, Strong Vincent (1997, City)
Dick Scheppner, Cathedral Prep (1962, City)
Matt Scheuer, Girard (2006, County)
Austin Schied, North East (2011, County)
Jim Schiefferle, Fairview (1985, County)
Matt Schiefferle, Fairview (1989, County)
Mark Schinke, Girard (2005, County)
Howard Schirmer, Cambridge Springs (1946, East)
Larry Schirmer, Edinboro (1949, West)
Lee Schlecht, Cathedral Prep (1950, West)
Don Schlindwein, Harbor Creek (1953, County)
Carl Schlipf, Wesleyville (1955, County)
Dan Schloss, McDowell (1979, City)
Tim Schloss, Tech (1972, City)
Joe Schlossle, Cathedral Prep (1956, City)
Richard Schmeider, Wesleyville (1955, County)
Chet Schmelter, Girard (1943, West)
Bill Schmid, Wesleyville (1951, East)
Scott Schnars, Iroquois (1993, County)
George Schneider, Academy (1953, City)
Jim Schneider, Strong Vincent (1950, West)
Josh Schneider, Harbor Creek (2007, County)
Nick Schneider, Harbor Creek (1999, County)
Ralph Schneider, Academy (1948, East)
Todd Schneider, Seneca (1988, County)
Tom Schneider, Cathedral Prep (1963, City)

Save-An-Eye Game Players

Josh Schneidmiller, Cathedral Prep (1991, City)
Brad Schnell, Strong Vincent (1986, City)
Tom Schoenfeld, Iroquois (1967, County)
Bill Scholz, Cathedral Prep (1972, City)
Jack Schrecengost, Academy (1943, East)
Joel Schreiber, Seneca (1999, County)
Eric Schrimper, Fort LeBoeuf (1990, County)
Paul Schrock, Tech (1950, East)
Austin Schroder, North East (2006, County)
Fred Schroeck, Cathedral Prep (1946, West)
Mike Schroeder, North East (1998, County)
Chris Schroyer, Academy (1991, City)
Martin Schuller, General McLane (1962, County)
Cale Schultz, North East (1997, County)
Derek Schultz, General McLane (2011, County)
Ronald Schultz, Tech (1943, West)
Ryan Schulz, Fort LeBoeuf (2005, County)
Jim Schumacker, Cathedral Prep (1954, City)
Dave Schuster, Northwestern (1987, County)
Bill Schwab, Fort LeBoeuf (1987, County)
Edward Schwarz, Strong Vincent (1943, West)
Joe Schweigert, Academy (1965, City)
Jeff Schweitzer, Harbor Creek (1966, County)
Jerry Schwenk, McDowell (1993, City)
Timothy Schwenk, Harbor Creek (2011, County)
Arthur Schwindt, Academy (1943, East)
George Scieford, North East (1953, County)
Rich Scolio, Cathedral Prep (1960, City)
Dick Scott, Harbor Creek (1956, County)
Joe Scott, Fort LeBoeuf (2001, County)
Sam Scott, Girard (1973, County)
Jeff Scully, Academy (1990, City)
Joe Scully, Cathedral Prep (1960, City)
Ernie Scutella, Strong Vincent (1972, City)
Gary Scutella, Seneca (1995, County)
Steve Scutella, Strong Vincent (1974, City)
John Scypinski, Cathedral Prep (1971, City)
Bryan Sechrist, Cathedral Prep (2004, City)
Bud Sedler, Girard (1942, West)
Don Sedler, Girard (1950, West)
Roy Sedler, Girard (1940, East)
Karl Sedmina, Union City (1953, County)
Eric Seggi, Academy (1985, City)
Dave Seifert, Fort LeBoeuf (1978, County)
Harold Seifert, Harbor Creek (1955, County)
Gene Seip, Tech (1974, City)
Larry Sekula, East (1966, City)
Derek Selby, Strong Vincent (2005, City)
Jermaine Selby, Strong Vincent (2003, City)
Frank Semelko, North East (1986, County)
Art Sementelli, Tech (1945, West)
Dom Sementelli, Strong Vincent (1939, West)
Richard Sementilli, Strong Vincent (1957, City)
Jason Senita, Cathedral Prep (2003, City)
Justin Senita, Cathedral Prep (2003, City)

Vince Senita, McDowell (2004, City)
Mike Sequite, McDowell (1971, County)
Chris Serafini, Cathedral Prep (1993, City)
Chuck Serafini, Strong Vincent (1967, County)
Ed Serafini, Cathedral Prep (1996, City)
Joe Serbati, Cathedral Prep (1980, City)
Jim Servidio, Strong Vincent (1967, County)
Brent Sesler, McDowell (1982, City)
Doug Sesler, Academy (1980, City)
John Sestak, East (1975, City)
James Seth, Cathedral Prep (1944, West)
Jerome Seth, Cathedral Prep (1939, West)
Matt Seth, General McLane (1977, County)
Matt Seth, General McLane (2003, County)
Doug Seus, McDowell (1961, County)
Dave Seyboldt, Cathedral Prep (1991, City)
Branden Seyler, Cathedral Prep (2008, City)
Dan Shade, Cathedral Prep (1960, City)
John Shade, Northwestern (1984, County)
Tom Shade, Cathedral Prep (1989, City)
Denny Shafer, General McLane (1966, County)
Andy Shaffer, McDowell (2008, City)
Tim Shaloiko, Mercyhurst Prep (2009, City)
Joe Shannon, East (1941, East)
Eric Sharie, Seneca (1997, County)
James Shaver, Corry (1955, County)
Jeff Shaw, Tech (1973, City)
Robert Shaw, Strong Vincent (1949, West)
Gordy Shay, Academy (1953, City)
William Shay, Wesleyville (1948, East)
Chad Sheehan, Iroquois (1999, County)
Garrett Sheely, General McLane (2009, County)
Eddie Sheldon, North East (2012, County)
Jeff Sheldon, Iroquois (1990, County)
Wilbur Shenk, Fairview (1959, County)
Robert Shepard, Union City (1939, East)
Mike Sherbin, Tech (1973, City)
Ryan Sheridan, Harbor Creek (2008, County)
Dan Sheridan, Harbor Creek (2004, County)
James Sheridan, Millcreek (1944, West)
Matt Sheridan, North East (1982, County)
Sean Sherman, Northwestern (1992, County)
Tim Sherrange, McDowell (1973, County)
Scott Sherretts, Albion (1946, West)
James Sherrod, Cathedral Prep (1981, City)
Norm Sherrod, Union City (1946, East)
Bill Sherwood, Waterford (1951, East; 1952, County)
Louie Sherwood, Corry (1946, East)
Ryan Sherwood-Ericsson, McDowell (2002, City)
Matt Shesman, General McLane (1977, County)
Albert Shields, Waterford (1948, East)
Brad Shields, Fort LeBoeuf (1974, County)
Dan Shields, Fort LeBoeuf (2001, County)
Dell Shields, Waterford (1954, County)
Jordan Shields, Union City (2008, County)

Matt Shields, East (2004, City)
Robert Shields, Academy (1947, East)
Ronnie Shields, Waterford (1941, East)
Ron Shilling, Girard (1960, County)
Kyle Shinn, General McLane (2011, County)
Vincent Shioleno, North East (1944, East)
Bob Shollenberger, Girard (1939, West)
Paul Shopene, East (1955, City)
Chet Shorts, Fort LeBoeuf (1963, County)
Bob Shreve, Cathedral Prep (1967, County)
Brian Shreve, McDowell (2004, City)
Joe Shugart, Strong Vincent (1943, West)
Andy Shupala, Fairview (1979, County)
Craig Shupenko, Cathedral Prep (1992, City)
Jason Sibley, Mercyhurst Prep (2002, City)
Greg Sidun, Harbor Creek (1982, County)
George Siegel, McDowell (1998, City)
Scott Siergio, Harbor Creek (1986, County)
Paul Siever, Tech (1943, West)
Sean Siggins, Harbor Creek (1991, County)
George Silay, East (1989, City)
Russell Silverthorn, Millcreek (1943, West)
Butch Silverthorne, Girard (1947, West)
Arnold Simmons, Harbor Creek (1948, East)
Bill Simmons, Harbor Creek (1950, East)
Bill Simon, McDowell (1962, County)
Steve Simon, East (1947, East)
Ara Simonian, Strong Vincent (1963, City)
Joe Sinecki, Tech (1950, East)
Richard Sins, Academy (1957, City)
Dan Sipple, Wattsburg (1967, County)
Tim Sisinni, Cathedral Prep (1978, City)
Mendel Sisley, Girard (1940, East)
Darrel Sisson, Girard (1973, County)
Dan Sitter, Tech (1975, City)
Jim Sitter, Cathedral Prep (1992, City)
Jonathan Sitter, Cathedral Prep (2000, City)
Eric Sittinger, Iroquois (1992, County)
Greg Sivik, Central (1994, City)
Ebbo Skadhague, Cathedral Prep (2002, City)
John Skalos, Seneca (1990, County)
Ted Skarupski, Tech (1959, City)
Ted Skarupski, Tech (1960, City)
Tim Skarupski, Fairview (1982, County)
Tim Skarupski, Tech (1956, City)
Francis Skeabeck, East (1943, East)
Larry Skeel, Northwestern (2002, County)
Alton Skelly, Fairview (1964, County)
David Skelly, Fairview (1989, County)
Ben Skelton, Edinboro (1942, West)
Brad Skelton, Fort LeBoeuf (2002, County)
Chuck Skelton, Edinboro (1941, West)
Dan Skelton, General McLane (2007, County)
Dennis Skelton, General McLane (1971, County)
Fred Skelton, Edinboro (1948, West)

Ryan Skelton, General McLane (2008, County)
Garrett Skindell, Cathedral Prep (1988, City)
Jim Skindell, Strong Vincent (1965, City)
Rich Skinner, Academy (1963, City)
Rick Skonieczka, Academy (1981, City)
Doug Slater, North East (1989, County)
Chris Slawson, McDowell (1993, City)
Kyle Sliker, McDowell (2007, City)
Aaron Slocum, McDowell (1998, City)
Joe Slomski, East (2001, City)
Wes Smeltzer, McDowell (1970, County)
Gary Smialek, Girard (1983, County)
Greg Smialek, Girard (2002, County)
Austin Smith, Cathedral Prep (2009, City)
Butch Smith, Girard (1967, County)
Byron Smith, Tech (1958, City)
Chad Smith, Girard (1999, County)
Chris Smith, Fort LeBoeuf (1999, County)
Chris Smith, General McLane (1995, County)
Cliff Smith, East (1971, City)
Dan Smith, General McLane (1991, County)
Don Smith, McDowell (1979, City)
Elmer Smith, Strong Vincent (1964, City)
Eugene Smith, Tech (1944, West)
Gary Smith, Seneca (1983, County)
George Smith, East (1955, City)
Harvey Smith, Fort LeBoeuf (1966, County)
Jeffrey Smith, Fort LeBoeuf (1998, County)
Jerahmy Smith, Iroquois (2005, County)
Jerry Smith, Tech (1941, East)
Jim Smith, Conneautville (1945, West)
Jim Smith, Lawrence Park (1965, County)
Jim Smith, North East (1954, County)
Jim Smith, Wesleyville (1956, County)
John Smith, Cathedral Prep (1989, City)
Kimani Smith, Cathedral Prep (2012, City)
Kory Smith, Cathedral Prep (2003, City)
Kyle Smith, Harbor Creek (2003, County)
Louis Smith, North East (1943, East)
Mike Smith, Strong Vincent (1985, City)
Mike Smith, Tech (1979, City)
Ray Smith, Iroquois (1975, County)
Rich Smith, Northwestern (1976, County)
Russ Smith, Mercyhurst Prep (1994, City)
Shawne Smith, Union City (1989, County)
Terry Smith, Girard (2000, County)
Wain Smith, Strong Vincent (1967, County)
Bob Smock, Cambridge Springs (1961, County)
Dean Smock, Conneautville (1950, West)
Chester Smogorzewski, Tech (1942, East)
Tom Smogorzewski, Cathedral Prep (1977, City)
Joe Smollek, Union City (1947, East)
Pat Smrekar, Cathedral Prep (1980, City)
Mike Smyklo, Iroquois (1996, County)
Matt Snippert, Central (1999, City)

Save-An-Eye Game Players

Don Snodgrass, Strong Vincent (1945, West)
Kyle Snoke, Cathedral Prep (2003, City)
Arlyn Snyder, Lawrence Park (1960, County)
Bruce Snyder, Tech (1973, City)
Chris Snyder, Seneca (1991, County)
Jim Snyder, Edinboro (1951, West; 1952, County)
Frank Sobieski, Conneautville (1945, West)
Mark Soboleski, McDowell (1987, City)
Bill Sobucki, Girard (2010, County)
Joe Sobucki, Girard (2011, County)
Dan Sockett, McDowell (2004, City)
Jason Sokol, Harbor Creek (1995, County)
Don Sokoloff, East (1957, City)
Vic Sokoloski, Kanty Prep (1951, West; 1952, County)
Goral Soldo, Central (2002, City)
Kevin Soles, Iroquois (1986, County)
Don Soliday, Wesleyville (1946, East)
Tom Solvedt, Strong Vincent (1949, West)
Dave Soltis, Northwestern (1968, County)
Mike Soltis, Northwestern (2000, County)
Mick Solymosi, Fairview (2001, County)
Tibor Solymosi, Cathedral Prep (1973, City)
Bob Songer, Northwestern (1971, County)
Eric Sonnenberg, Tech (1974, City)
Pat Sorek, East (1977, City)
Dale Sorensen, East (1957, City)
Phil Sorensen, Cathedral Prep (1984, City)
Dick Sorenson, Corry (1955, County)
Jeff Sorenson, Fort LeBoeuf (1988, County)
Chuck Sorger, Strong Vincent (1946, West)
Lyman Sornberger, Fairview (1956, County)
Mike Sornberger, Fairview (1981, County)
Ty Sornberger, Fairview (1984, County)
Joe Sosnowski, North East (1957, County)
Roger Soth, Academy (1939, West)
Dick Soudan, Lawrence Park (1963, County)
Dusty Soudan, Girard (2000, County)
Mike Sowers, Girard (2001, County)
Stanley Sowry, Conneautville (1947, West)
Andrew Space, Strong Vincent (1982, City)
Merle Spacht, North East (1956, County)
Anthony Spada, North East (1961, County)
Dave Spada, North East (1968, County)
Dante Spain, Central (2000, City)
Pedro Spampani, Tech (1956, City)
Dale Sparber, Girard (1966, County)
David Spate, Millcreek (1949, West)
Scott Spaulding, Northwestern (1988, County)
Bob Spearman, Academy (1970, City)
Lonnie Spearman, Strong Vincent (2005, City)
Steve Spearman, Academy (1987, City)
Don Spears, Lawrence Park (1950, East)
Richard Speicher, North East (1971, County)
Dick Speros, Strong Vincent (1953, City)
Mike Speros, East (1973, City)

Steve Spiegel, Iroquois (1973, County)
Greg Spilko, Fort LeBoeuf (1973, County)
Bob Spinelli, Academy (1951, East)
Jeff Spires, General McLane (1996, County)
Ben Spitzer, Girard (1981, County)
Brian Sprague, General McLane (1976, County)
Brett Sproveri, Corry (1994, County)
David Squeglia, Cathedral Prep (1956, City)
Joe St. George, Cathedral Prep (1961, City)
Terry St. John, Academy (1959, City)
Bob Staab, Tech (1973, City)
Donnie Staaf, Mercyhurst Prep (1999, City)
Brian Stablein, McDowell (1988, City)
Chris Stablein, McDowell (1986, City)
Dan Stablein, Fort LeBoeuf (1995, County)
Mike Stablein, Fort LeBoeuf (1997, County)
Scott Stablein, McDowell (1988, City)
Mike Stadtmiller, Cathedral Prep (1984, City)
Tim Stafford, General McLane (2000, County)
Rodney Stage, North East (1971, County)
Joe Stahon, Iroquois (1975, County)
Ray Stahon, Academy (1957, City)
Steve Stahon, Iroquois (1980, County)
Jim Stalford, Seneca (2008, County)
Ben Stanback, East (1986, City)
Gary Stanbro, Strong Vincent (1997, City)
Mike Stanbro, Strong Vincent (2000, City)
Mike Stanford, North East (1978, County)
Roy Stanford, North East (1983, County)
George Stanley, Harbor Creek (1943, East)
Zack Stano, McDowell (2009, City)
Ron Starkey, Kanty Prep (1949, West)
Tony Starocci, Tech (1948, East)
Tom Staszewski, Academy (1970, City)
B.J. States, Iroquois (2010, County)
Rick States, Seneca (1985, County)
Dennis Stauffer, Harbor Creek (1994, County)
Branden Stearns, General McLane (2005, County)
Curly Stearns, Girard (1941, West)
Dan Stearns, Girard (1974, County)
Bill Stebinski, Albion (1940, East)
Ron Steele, Strong Vincent (1972, City)
Gerry Steenberge, Cathedral Prep (1971, City)
Pat Steenberge, Cathedral Prep (1969, City)
Don Stefano, Lawrence Park (1961, County)
Scott Steffey, Academy (1976, City)
John Steger, North East (1988, County)
Mike Steigerwald, Fort LeBoeuf (1999, County)
Robert Steinmetz, Strong Vincent (1947, West)
Troy Stenger, Iroquois (1992, County)
Frank Stepchnek, Conneautville (1946, West)
Bill Stephenson, Harbor Creek (1942, East)
Kevin Stephenson, Fairview (2006, County)
Ryan Stephenson, Fairview (2004, County)
Marty Stepnoski, Tech (1961, City)

Mick Stepnoski, Tech (1981, City)
Mike Stetson, North East (1994, County)
Demetris Stevenson, Central Tech (2009, City)
Bashan Stewart, Central (1995, City)
Dajour Stewart, East (2008, City)
Doug Stewart, Academy (1982, City)
Maolo Stewart, Tech (1992, City)
Craig Stocker, Girard (1993, County)
Gil Stoddard, Academy (1962, City)
Garrett Stolz, Fairview (2009, County)
Frank Storacci, Millcreek (1951, West)
Bob Stovall, Tech (1971, City)
Davon Stovall, Central Tech (2010, City)
Fred Stover, East (1961, City)
Mark Strain, Tech (1984, City)
J.C. Strait, Northwestern (1995, County)
Jeffrey Strait, Northwestern (1994, County)
Doug Stratton, North East (1974, County)
Lou Strelecki, McDowell (1995, City)
Lou Strelecki, Strong Vincent (1969, City)
Andy Stritzinger, Harbor Creek (1998, County)
Ethan Strobel, General McLane (2012, County)
David Stromenger, McDowell (2009, City)
Len Strong, Tech (1952, City)
Jack Strubel, Fairview (1954, County)
Ed Strucheon, Girard (1941, West)
John Strucher, Strong Vincent (1945, West)
Anthony Stuart, Girard (2011, County)
Phil Stuczynski, Girard (2005, County)
Brian Stull, Fort LeBoeuf (1977, County)
Wes Stull, Fort LeBoeuf (1975, County)
Tim Stumpf, McDowell (1995, City)
Jim Sturm, Cathedral Prep (1981, City)
John Styborski, Cambridge Springs (1952, County)
Stan Styborski, Cambridge Springs (1954, County)
Joe Sullivan, East (1973, City)
Ken Sullivan, Academy (1955, City)
Kevin Sullivan, Cathedral Prep (1967, County)
Ray Sullivan, Cathedral Prep (1945, West)
Charles Sult, Strong Vincent (1943, West)
Brian Suminski, General McLane (2012, County)
Joe Suminski, Tech (1948, East)
John Suminski, Cathedral Prep (1980, City)
William Suminski, East (1944, East)
Jack Summerville, Albion (1940, East)
Eugene Sunberg, Academy (1947, East)
Dave Sundberg, Fairview (2001, County)
Matt Sundberg, Fairview (2008, County)
Glenn Surrena, Fort LeBoeuf (1991, County)
Jody Sutton, Harbor Creek (1993, County)
Alex Svetz, North East (2012, County)
John Swanseger, East (1942, East)
Bob Swanson, East (1945, East)
Don Swanson, Millcreek (1945, West)
Eric Swanson, Seneca (1982, County)

Walter Swanson, East (1939, East)
Jon Swart, Corry (1990, County)
Keith Swart, Corry (1978, County)
Don Swartwood, Harbor Creek (1954, County)
Jeremy Swartzfager, Fairview (1994, County)
Dustin Lee Sweet, North East (2012, County)
Andy Swift, General McLane (2005, County)
Bill Swift, Academy (1961, City)
Brian Swift, Northwestern (1998, County)
Michael Swift, McDowell (1988, City)
Jim Sykes, Fairview (1984, County)
Tony Szabo, Tech (1988, City)
Jerry Szorek, East (1953, City)
Jake Szoszorek, Iroquois (2010, County)
Jim Szymanowski, East (1969, City)
Mike Szymanski, East (1989, City)
Bill Szympruch, Girard (1994, County)
James "E." Szympruch, Tech (1970, City)

T

John Tabaka, Tech (1970, City)
Andrew Tamilin, Strong Vincent (1996, City)
Donnell Tangle, Central (2003, City)
Greg Tarbell, McDowell (1998, City)
Ben Tarcson, Mercyhurst Prep (2012, City)
Jim Tarkowski, Cathedral Prep (1978, City)
Amos Tate, Tech (1980, City)
Andrew Tate, Academy (1979, City)
David Tate, Strong Vincent (2007, City)
Jerry Tate, East (1973, City)
Tony Tate, Mercyhurst Prep (1993, City)
Donnie Tatum, Strong Vincent (1995, City)
Harley Tau, Cambridge Springs (1947, East)
Brendan Taylor, Girard (2006, County)
Chad Taylor, North East (1990, County)
Charles Taylor, Fairview (1944, West)
Dan Taylor, Corry (1970, County)
Dennis Taylor, Fort LeBoeuf (1965, County)
Duane Taylor, Albion (1958, County)
Ron Taylor, Fort LeBoeuf (1968, County)
Steve Taylor, Corry (1994, County)
Tim Taylor, Cathedral Prep (2004, City)
Tywonn Taylor, East (2012, City)
Walter Taylor, Millcreek (1942, West)
Brian Tech, Seneca (1999, County)
Jaime Tecza, General McLane (1995, County)
Randy Tecza, Cathedral Prep (1994, City)
Dennis Teed, Northwestern (1977, County)
Gerald Teed, Albion (1945, West)
Vince Teed, Cathedral Prep (1959, City)
John Teel, Academy (1992, City)
Randy Terizzi, Cathedral Prep (1993, City)
Bob Terrill, Fort LeBoeuf (1960, County)
Jason Terry, Strong Vincent (2001, City)
Chris Testrake, Strong Vincent (1999, City)

Matt Testrake, Strong Vincent (1999, City)
Pat Testrake, Strong Vincent (1996, City)
Bill Thaler, General McLane (1964, County)
William Thames, East (2006, City)
Richard Thayer, Conneautville (1948, West)
Eddie Theiss, Cathedral Prep (2011, City)
Art Thomas, East (1940, West)
Bob Thomas, Tech (1969, City)
Charles Thomas, East (1939, East)
Dick Thomas, Cambridge Springs (1946, East)
Harry Thomas, Fort LeBoeuf (1959, County)
Jeff Thomas, Tech (1968, City)
Phil Thomas, Iroquois (2008, County)
Roland Thomas, Union City (1956, County)
Ron Thomas, Strong Vincent (1955, City)
Sheldon Thomas, Cathedral Prep (1993, City)
Steve Thomas, Central (2002, City)
Steve Thomas, Tech (1984, City)
Tim Thomas, McDowell (1985, City)
Brent Thompson, Cathedral Prep (2007, City)
Gary Thompson, Wattsburg (1974, County)
Jeff Thompson, Tech (1978, City)
Jeremy Thompson, Northwestern (1999, County)
Larry Thompson, Northwestern (1961, County)
Rickie Thompson, North East (2004, County)
Shawn Thompson, Seneca (1996, County)
Woody Thompson, East (1971, City)
Scott Thomson, North East (1971, County)
Jermaine Thornton, East (2011, City)
Richard Thornton, East (1994, City)
ReSean Thrower, Cathedral Prep (2010, City)
Mike Tighe, Cathedral Prep (1978, City)
Pat Tighe, Cathedral Prep (1990, City)
Terry Tighe, Cathedral Prep (1982, City)
Joe Timmons, Fairview (1953, County)
Joe Tinko, Strong Vincent (1967, County)
James Tobin, Cambridge Springs (1955, County)
Jake Tobolewski, Girard (2000, County)
Marlowe Tolbert, Strong Vincent (1951, West)
Kevin Tolon, Harbor Creek (2005, County)
Ray Tomb, Academy (1964, City)
Tom Tomb, Strong Vincent (1955, City)
Dana Tomczak, Cathedral Prep (1954, City)
Eugene Tomczak, Cathedral Prep (1957, City)
Len Tomczak, Cathedral Prep (1951, West; 1952, City)
Pat Tomczak, Cathedral Prep (1960, City)
Dan Tome, Girard (1971, County)
Mike Tome, Girard (1977, County)
Sam Tome, Girard (1972, County)
Paul Tomlin, East (1964, City)
Ron Tomlin, Harbor Creek (1963, County)
Kelly Tompkins, Strong Vincent (1974, City)
Jim Toohey, Cathedral Prep (1988, City)
Anthony Topolski, Kanty Prep (1951, West; 1952, County)
John Toran, Academy (1977, City)

Maleek Toran, Central Tech (2008, City)
Tom Torok, Academy (1969, City)
John Torrelli, Academy (1955, City)
Mike Torrelli, Cathedral Prep (1950, West)
David Torres, Academy (1985, City)
Norman Tousey, Millcreek (1942, West)
Doug Tracy, Fort LeBoeuf (1993, County)
Rusty Tracy, Cathedral Prep (1970, City)
Tom Tracy, Fort LeBoeuf (1989, County)
Ishmael Trainor, Mercyhurst Prep (2000, City)
V.J. Trapolsi, Cathedral Prep (1990, City)
George Traut, Fairview (1951, West)
Ken Traut, Fairview (1954, County)
Walter Traut, Academy (1940, East)
Phil Trejchel, Tech (1952, City)
Steve Trejchel, Cathedral Prep (1987, City)
Matt Tressler, Strong Vincent (1991, City)
Dick Triana, St. Gregory (1955, County)
Donald Triana, North East (1944, East)
Jim Triana, North East (1987, County)
Matt Triana, North East (1995, County)
Nick Triana, North East (1940, West)
Nick Triana, North East (1955, County)
Shawn Triana, Iroquois (1990, County)
Steve Triana, North East (1970, County)
Mike Tripp, Girard (2004, County)
Jerry Trocha, Tech (1965, City)
Don Trohoske, Millcreek (1958, County)
Bruce Trojan, East (1969, City)
Travis Trojan, Harbor Creek (2007, County)
Jeff Trombacco, Cathedral Prep (1968, City)
Ato Troop, Central (1996, City)
Jerry Troop, Central (1998, City)
Mo Troop, Central (1994, City)
Fred Trott, Academy (1955, City)
James Trott, Academy (1951, East)
Lance Trott, Cathedral Prep (1981, City)
Norm Troyer, Union City (1954, County)
Ron Troyer, Fort LeBoeuf (1971, County)
Dan Truitt, East (1975, City)
Louis Truitt, Academy (1943, East)
Tim Truitt, East (1972, City)
Tony Truitt, East (1966, City)
Loel Tubbs, McDowell (1976, County)
Dave Tullio, Cathedral Prep (1960, City)
Don Turberson, Wesleyville (1963, County)
Rick Turiczek, North East (1982, County)
Dan Turley, Cathedral Prep (1993, City)
Bryan Turnbull, Fort LeBoeuf (1994, County)
Bill Turner, Fairview (1982, County)
Scott Turner, Fairview (1987, County)
Steven Turner, Fairview (2011, County)
Dan Tuschak, Girard (1952, County)
Tony Twillie, Strong Vincent (2011, City)
Clark Tysinski, East (1939, East)

Tim Tyzinski, Cathedral Prep (1975, City)

U

Dave Uglow, Harbor Creek (1979, County)
Tim Uglow, Harbor Creek (1975, County)
Bob Uhlman, Cathedral Prep (1982, City)
Brian Ulrich, Strong Vincent (1995, City)
Lud Ulrich, Academy (1941, West)
Steve Ulrich, Strong Vincent (1993, City)
Butch Unger, Fort LeBoeuf (1967, County)
Dave Urban, General McLane (1981, County)
Les Utegg, Corry (1986, County)

V

David Vactor, East (1971, City)
George Vadmer, Edinboro (1944, West)
Rich Valahovic, Tech (1959, City)
Tom Valahovic, Tech (1953, City)
Kary Valentine, Northwestern (1986, County)
Larry Valentine, Northwestern (1961, County)
Gary Valerio, Strong Vincent (1958, City)
Tom Valerio, Academy (1987, City)
Chris Valimont, Mercyhurst Prep (1993, City)
Jack Van Honk, Millcreek (1951, West; 1952, County)
Jeff Van Volkenburg, Cathedral Prep (1997, City)
Jon Van Cise, Girard (1951, West)
Lucas Vance, Corry (2003, County)
Adam VanHooser, Iroquois (2006, County)
Don VanKeuren, Corry (1959, County)
Dave Vannoy, Corry (1958, County)
Craig VanTassel, Strong Vincent (2005, City)
Dana VanTassel, Girard (1984, County)
Mike Varchola, East (1941, East)
Jerry Varich, McDowell (1993, City)
Dan Vasil, McDowell (2008, City)
Bob Vaughan, General McLane (1984, County)
Mike Vaughan, General McLane (1987, County)
Jim Vaughn, Iroquois (2000, County)
Jesse Vazquez, Union City (2010, County)
Jay Veith, Girard (1975, County)
Norm Veith, Fairview (1950, West)
Jerry Verga, Cathedral Prep (1968, City)
Tony Verga, Strong Vincent (1970, City)
Craig Vergotz, Fort LeBoeuf (1988, County)
Frank Vicary, North East (2007, County)
Frank Vicary, Academy (1985, City)
Rich Vicary, Strong Vincent (1976, City)
Dick Vidic, Wesleyville (1956, County)
Anthony Viglione, Cathedral Prep (1982, City)
Luca Viglione, Cathedral Prep (2007, City)
Nick Viglione, Cathedral Prep (1989, City)
V.J. Viglione, Cathedral Prep (2010, City)
Chuck Villa, North East (1957, County)
Craig Villa, General McLane (1991, County)
Jim Villa, North East (1951, East; 1952, County)

Jim Vincent, Strong Vincent (1942, West)
Don Virosko, Millcreek (1949, West)
Joshua Voelker, Harbor Creek (2006, County)
Tom Voelker, Iroquois (2005, County)
John Vogel, Girard (2011, County)
John Vogel, Tech (1982, City)
Josh Vogel, Harbor Creek (2002, County)
Casey Vogt, Harbor Creek (1995, County)
Chad Vogt, Harbor Creek (1992, County)
Dave Vogt, Fort LeBoeuf (1968, County)
Dick Vogt, Fort LeBoeuf (1960, County)
Gene Vogt, Wattsburg (1967, County)
Jim Vogt, Fort LeBoeuf (1967, County)
Mike Vogt, Fort LeBoeuf (1985, County)
Bob Vomero, East (1954, City)
Dean Vomero, McDowell (1985, City)
Ron Vomero, Cathedral Prep (1960, City)
Mark Vommaro, Mercyhurst Prep (2001, City)
Rich Vommero, Millcreek (1950, West)
Pat Vona, Academy (1989, City)
Bill Vorsheck, Lawrence Park (1953, County)
Frank Voytek, East (1939, East)
Dave Vrenna, Iroquois (2002, County)
Doug Vroman, Tech (1984, City)

W

Bob Wachter, Academy (1946, East)
Jim Wade, Fort LeBoeuf (1989, County)
Bill Wagner, Northwestern (1972, County)
Jeff Wagner, Academy (1984, City)
Jim Wagner, Harbor Creek (1957, County)
Pat Wagner, Strong Vincent (1973, City)
Steve Wagner, Strong Vincent (1971, City)
Dan Waisley, General McLane (1998, County)
Vic Waisley, Fairview (1957, County)
Rich Walach, East (1959, City)
Ron Walcheck, Northwestern (1974, County)
Andy Walczyk, Fort LeBoeuf (2005, County)
Bob Walker, Academy (1953, City)
Dave Walker, Fairview (1987, County)
Dick Walker, Fairview (1945, West)
John Walker, Fairview (1947, West)
Ken Walker, General McLane (1966, County)
Kevin Walker, General McLane (2004, County)
Matt Walker, General McLane (1990, County)
Mickey Walker, General McLane (1963, County)
Shawn Walker, General McLane (2008, County)
William Walker, Fairview (1943, West)
Stan Walkiewicz, East (1976, City)
Tom Walkiewicz, Cathedral Prep (1958, City)
Bob Wall, Strong Vincent (1951, West; 1952, City)
Steve Wall, Harbor Creek (1979, County)
Dupre Wallace, Central (2005, City)
Tom Wallace, Central (2003, City)
Andy Wallen, Iroquois (2008, County)

Clancy Walsh, Corry (1967, County)
Darby Walsh, Corry (1991, County)
John Walter, Academy (1946, East)
Mike Wander, McDowell (1955, County)
Greg Waples, Fairview (2006, County)
Jamie Ward, Girard (1991, County)
Robert Ward, McDowell (2008, City)
Bill Warner, Northwestern (2003, County)
Eric Warner, Girard (1982, County)
Parris Warner, Harbor Creek (2012, County)
Josh Warren, Harbor Creek (2005, County)
Tate Warren, Seneca (2002, County)
John Wasiliewski, East (1951, East)
Joseph Wasiulewski, Tech (1962, City)
Don Waskiewicz, Tech (1964, City)
Harry Watkins, East (1996, City)
Walt Watral, East (1954, City)
Eric Watters, Girard (1990, County)
Jesse Wattle, Strong Vincent (2008, City)
Ashley Watts, Strong Vincent (2002, City)
Rich Way, North East (1974, County)
Mike Wayne, Tech (1984, City)
Anthony Weaver, McDowell (2006, City)
Arthur Weaver, Strong Vincent (1943, West)
Dan Weaver, Corry (1970, County)
Howie Weaver, McKean (1941, West)
Lewis Weaver, Albion (1948, West)
Darren Weber, McDowell (1987, City)
Don Weber, Academy (1979, City)
Eric Weber, McDowell (2001, City)
Joe Weber, Harbor Creek (1993, County)
Michael Weber, Mercyhurst Prep (2012, City)
Ron Weber, Tech (1974, City)
Tom Weber, Academy (1973, City)
Phil Wedzik, East (1953, City)
Ken Weed, Millcreek (1954, County)
Pete Wegley, Iroquois (1987, County)
Dick Weidler, Girard (1940, East)
Eric Weidler, Girard (2002, County)
Eugene Weidler, Albion (1942, West)
Mike Weidler, Northwestern (1975, County)
Dennis Weigle, Academy (1965, City)
Dick Weigle, Fairview (1940, East)
Rob Weis, Corry (1989, County)
Greg Weislogel, Fairview (1965, County)
Randy Weislogel, Fairview (1967, County)
William Weislogel, Fairview (1946, West)
Mike Weissinger, McDowell (2011, City)
Paul Weldon, Northwestern (1964, County)
Durfey Wells Jr., Strong Vincent (2007, City)
Dan Wells, Seneca (1975, County)
Emmanuel Wells, Strong Vincent (2010, City)
Matt Wells, Cathedral Prep (1993, City)
Thomas Wells, Millcreek (1944, West)
Joe Welton, Central (2005, City)

Tom Weltzel, Union City (1949, East)
Dan Wenner, Strong Vincent (1976, City)
Dan Wenrick, Tech (1962, City)
Dave Wenrick, Cathedral Prep (1965, City)
Bill Wentling, McDowell (1963, County)
Jonathan Wentz, Cathedral Prep (2006, City)
Brad Wernicki, Cathedral Prep (2001, City)
Joe Weschler, Cathedral Prep (1942, West)
Jeff West, Northwestern (1997, County)
Norm West, General McLane (1966, County)
Benjie Westfall, Northwestern (1988, County)
Braidy Westfall, Corry (2010, County)
Nick Weston, Seneca (1999, County)
Dave Wethli, Fort LeBoeuf (1998, County)
Ron Wetmore, Union City (1965, County)
Oliver Whaley, Harbor Creek (1952, County)
Chris Wheeler, General McLane (2004, County)
Don Wheeler, Strong Vincent (1976, City)
Forest Wheeler, Wesleyville (1965, County)
Don Whipple, Lawrence Park (1953, County)
Ronnie Whipple, Lawrence Park (1943, East)
Kent Whitaker, Fairview (1982, County)
Bill White Lawrence, Park (1943, East)
DeMoyne White, Academy (1990, City)
Harry White, Northwestern (1968, County)
Jayson White, McDowell (2005, City)
John White, East (1991, City)
John White, Strong Vincent (1989, City)
Scott White, Academy (1992, City)
Vinny White, Fort LeBoeuf (1987, County)
Bill Whitford, Cathedral Prep (1959, City)
Randy Whittelsey, Fort LeBoeuf (1970, County)
Matt Widdowson, Harbor Creek (2002, County)
Rich Widdowson, Seneca (2008, County)
Rich Widdowson, Wattsburg (1968, County)
Jerry Widmann, Cathedral Prep (1948, West)
Rob Wierbinski, Strong Vincent (1981, City)
Dave Wierzchowski, Wesleyville (1965, County)
Chris Wiesner, McDowell (1988, City)
Douglas Wilbur, Fairview (1985, County)
Blaine Wilcox, Waterford (1943, East)
Scott Wilcox, East (2004, City)
Craig Wilczynski, Cathedral Prep (1998, City)
John Wiley, Academy (1942, West)
Craig Wilfong, East (1994, City)
Tim Wilkins, Fairview (1980, County)
Howard Wilkinson, Harbor Creek (1944, East)
Roy Wilkinson, Corry (1956, County)
Eric Wilkosz, Cathedral Prep (1996, City)
Brent Willey, General McLane (1971, County)
Bob Williams, Lawrence Park (1962, County)
Cliff Williams, East (1964, City)
Corey Williams, Union City (1997, County)
Dale Williams, Cathedral Prep (2001, City)
Dearis Williams, Cathedral Prep (2011, City)

Fred Williams, East (1970, City)
Gary Williams, Strong Vincent (2006, City)
Jason Williams, Central (1994, City)
Jerry Williams, Corry (1962, County)
Joe Williams, Lawrence Park (1963, County)
Josh Williams, Fort LeBoeuf (2008, County)
Joshua Williams, Girard (2010, County)
Jovan Williams, Strong Vincent (2003, City)
Lee Williams, Corry (1958, County)
Mark Williams, East (1982, City)
Matt Williams, McDowell (1985, City)
Mike Williams, North East (2005, County)
Mike Williams, Fairview (1996, County)
Pete Williams, McDowell (1985, City)
Roger Williams, Fort LeBoeuf (1984, County)
Ron Williams, Academy (1956, City)
Bob Williamson, Academy (1971, City)
Buddy Williamson, General McLane (1996, County)
Pat Williamson, Cathedral Prep (1990, City)
Andy Willis, Mercyhurst Prep (2002, City)
Ted Willis, Girard (1971, County)
Eric Willow, Fairview (1987, County)
Loren Wilshire, Corry (1986, County)
Fred Wilson, Fairview (1973, County
Gary Wilson, Girard (1978, County)
Greg Wilson, Corry (1993, County)
Jack Wilson, North East (1946, East)
Paul Wilson, Strong Vincent (1951, West; 1952, City)
Mark Wilwohl, Cathedral Prep (1976, City)
Dan Wingerter, Fairview (1980, County)
Frank Wingerter, Cathedral Prep (1968, City)
Eric Wingrove, Iroquois (1984, County)
Tyler Wingrove, McDowell (2009, City)
Jeremiah Winnie, Fairview (1999, County)
Ben Winslow, Harbor Creek (1940, West)
Ray Winslow, Millcreek (1942, West)
Richard Winslow, Millcreek (1948, West)
Jerry Winters, Academy (1955, City)
Ed Wise, Albion (1953, County)
Peter Wishnok, McDowell (2002, City)
Rich Wisinski, Tech (1942, East)
Dan Wisniewski, East (1953, City)
Matt Wisniewski, East (1948, East)
Pete Wisniewski, Northwestern (1993, County)
Ray "Jambers" Wisniewski, Tech (1940, West)
Richard Wisniewski, Tech (1944, West)
Ted Wisniewski, Fort LeBoeuf (1992, County)
Dave Witherow, Harbor Creek (1945, East)
Dan Woitovich, Girard (1957, County)
Steve Woitovich, Girard (1953, County)
Ted Woitovich, Girard (1955, County)
Dave Wojtecki, Union City (1997, County)
Fred Wolchik, Albion (1943, West)
Dan Wolf, Tech (1989, City)
Don Wolf, Cathedral Prep (1951, West; 1952, City)

Jim Wolf, Academy (1975, City)
John Wolf, Seneca (1988, County)
Kiel Wolf, Corry (2005, County)
Tom Wolf, Tech (1990, City)
Bill Wolfe, Fort LeBoeuf (1991, County)
Donald Wolfe, Albion (1944, West)
Carl Wolfrom, Fort LeBoeuf (1983, County)
Carl Wolfrom, Waterford (1958, County)
Sean Wolfrom, Fort LeBoeuf (1989, County)
Francis Wontenay, Union City (1944, East)
Albert Wood, Wattsburg (1965, County)
Dick Wood, East (1956, City)
Frank Wood, Albion (1942, West)
William Wood, Albion (1943, West)
Chris Woodard, Strong Vincent (2001, City)
Craig Woodard, Mercyhurst Prep (1992, City)
Dwaon Woodard, Central (2001, City)
Eddie Woodard, East (1970, City)
Elmer Woodard, Academy (1960, City)
Errick Woodard, Fort LeBoeuf (1997, County)
Herman Woodard, East (1963, City)
Jim Woodard, Strong Vincent (1970, City)
Tommy Woodard, East (1979, City)
Tom Woodring, Cambridge Springs (1960, County)
Mark Woodrow, General McLane (1984, County)
Bob Woods, East (1966, City)
Orrin Woods, Fairview (1964, County)
Steven Woods, General McLane (2006, County)
Thomas Woods, Fairview (1983, County)
Pat Worley, Fort LeBoeuf (1990, County)
Logan Woznicki, Mercyhurst Prep (2010, City)
Clark Wren, Fairview (1979, County)
Bob Wright, Tech (1970, City)
Bud Wright, Waterford (1943, East)
Dick Wright, Strong Vincent (1956, City)
Josh Wright, Strong Vincent (1993, City)
Mike Wright, Girard (2007, County)
Rick Wright, Seneca (1976, County)
Jonathan Wroblewski, Seneca (2006, County)
Mark Wroblewski, Seneca (1976, County)
Dick Wronek, Strong Vincent (1946, West)
Lane Wroth, Strong Vincent (1943, West)
Kyle Wunz, Northwestern (2005, County)
George Wurst, Academy (1958, City)
P.J. Wycech, Mercyhurst Prep (2012, City)
Michael Wydro, North East (2012, County)
Ron Wygant, Girard (1989, County)
Bill Wykoff, Harbor Creek (1976, County)
Cliff Wynkoop, Seneca (1995, County)

Y

Tom Yacobozzi, Strong Vincent (1957, City)
Jeff Yahn, McDowell (1972, County)
Bob Yamma, McDowell (1971, County)

Jim Yamma, Tech (1967, County)
Ed Yarrington, Fairview (1945, West)
John Yatzor, Edinboro (1952, County)
Gregg Yeager, Fairview (1974, County)
Peter Yeaney, Cathedral Prep (2004, City)
Ed Yezzi, Tech (1941, East)
Paul Yoculan, Iroquois (1967, County)
Dennis York, Harbor Creek (1991, County)
Denny York, Iroquois (1966, County)
Larry Yost, Harbor Creek (1968, County)
Glen Yosten, Lawrence Park (1943, East)
Jim Yosten, Seneca (1979, County)
Tanner Youkers, Strong Vincent (1997, City)
Aaron Young, McDowell (1987, City)
Andrew Young, Central (1997, City)
David Young, Union City (1948, East)
DeJon Young, McDowell (2010, City)
Jeffrey Young, Academy (1979, City)
Jeremy Young, Harbor Creek (1998, County)
Josh Young, Northwestern (2010, County)
Marshall Young, Union City (1945, East)
Rob Young, Strong Vincent (1984, City)
Dan Youngs, North East (1948, East)
Jack Yount, Lawrence Park (1954, County)
Joe Yuhas, Girard (2002, County)
Charles Yunker, Waterford (1943, East)
William Yunker, Waterford (1947, East)
Steve Yurkiewicz, Tech (1951, East; 1952, City)
Dan Yurkovic, Tech (1951, East; 1952, City)

John Zack, Cathedral Prep (1958, City)
Jim Zahner, North East (1973, County
John Zambroski, Cathedral Prep (1971, City)
Tony Zambroski, Cathedral Prep (1947, West)
Gary Zamieroski, Cathedral Prep (1980, City)
Paul Zampino, Northwestern (1981, County)
Nick Zappia, Strong Vincent (1997, City)
Craig Zarzeczny, Harbor Creek (1988, County)
Al Zenner, Cathedral Prep (1984, City)
Bill Ziegler, Academy (1960, City)
Craig Ziegler, Tech (1980, City)
Bill Ziemer, Academy (1961, City)
Corey Zieziula, Cathedral Pre (1991, City)p
Ed Zimmer, McKean (1941, West)
Jerry Zimmer, Iroquois (1966, County)
Mark Zimmer, Cathedral Prep (1969, City)
Adam Zimmerman, Corry (2011, County)
Carl Zimmerman, Strong Vincent (1951, West; 1952, City)
Charles Zimmerman, Strong Vincent (1939, West)
Henry Zimmerman, Strong Vincent (1947, West)
Mark Zimmerman, Northwestern (1973, County
Doug Zirkle, McDowell (1962, County)
Harry Zmijewski, Academy (1969, City)
Jim Zoldach, Cathedral Prep (1967, County)

John Zolikoff, East (1957, City)
Michael Zona, Cathedral Prep (1997, City)
Don Zonna, Strong Vincent (1947, West)
Angelo Zonno, Strong Vincent (1955, City)
Mark Zonno, Cathedral Prep (1973, City)
John Zuck, Tech (1954, City)
Ron Zuck, Harbor Creek (1961, County)
Jeff Zuravleff, Iroquois (1974, County)
Joe Zuravleff, Tech (1945, West)
Bart Zurn, Strong Vincent (1956, City)
David Zurn, Strong Vincent (1981, City)
Norm Zymslinski, Cathedral Prep (1951, West)

NOTE: Players names were obtained from game programs and newspaper reports.

Save-An-Eye Players in the NFL

PLAYER	YEAR	HIGH SCHOOL	COLLEGE	NFL TEAM (YEAR)
Art Baker	1957	Academy	Syracuse	Buffalo (1961–1962)
Charlie Baumann	1985	Cathedral Prep	West Virginia	Miami (1991) New England (1991–1992)
Cliff Crosby	1994	East	Maryland	St. Louis (1999) Indianapolis (2001–2003)
Eric Hicks	1994	Mercyhurst Prep	Maryland	Kansas City (1998–2006) New York Jets (2007)
Dietrich Jells	1991	Tech	Pittsburgh	New England (1996–1997) Philadelphia (1998–1999)
Jovon Johnson	2002	Mercyhurst Prep	Iowa	Pittsburgh (2008)
Jack Laraway	1954	Academy	Purdue	Buffalo (1960) Houston (1961)
Mike McCoy	1966	Cathedral Prep	Notre Dame	Green Bay (1970–1976) Oakland (1977–1978) New York Giants (1979–1980) Detroit Lions (1980)
Brian Milne	1991	Fort LeBoeuf	Penn State	Cincinnati (1996–1999) Seattle (1999) New Orleans (2000)
Chip Nuzzo	1983	Corry	Princeton	Buffalo (1987)
Steve Potter	1976	Fairview	Virginia	Miami (1981–1982) Kansas City (1983) Buffalo (1984)
Brian Stablein	1988	McDowell	Ohio State	Indianapolis (1995–1997) Detroit (1998–2000)
Woody Thompson	1971	East	Miami	Atlanta (1975–1977)

A

Ryan Abbott (2001, City; 2006, City)

Eddie Abramoski (1939, East; 1940, East; 1941, East; 1942, East; 1945, West; 1947, West)

Don Adams (1986, County; 1989, County)

Mike Alexa (1989, City)

Dana Anderson (2002, County)

Gus Anderson (1939, West; 1940, West; 1947, West)

Hienie Anderson (1939, East; 1940, East; 1947, East)

Mike Anthony (1997, County)

Bob Arrowsmith (1939, West)

B

John Ballard (1979, County; 1995, County; 2006, County)

Drew Barelho (2012, City)

Mike Baniszewski (2006, City)

Glenn Barthelson (1968, City; 1972, City; 1976, City)

Malcolm Beall (2008, County)

John Beaumont (1995, County)

Jason Beer (2004, County; 2009, City)

Roosevelt Benjamin (2002, City)

Lou Benko (1991, County; 1999, County)

John Berchtold (1986, City)

Jack Bestwick (1976, County; 1993, County)

Tom Blose (1979, County; 2006, County)

Aaron Bluey (2008, County)

Rick Boesch (1999, City)

Scott Bolheimer (2012, County)

Jeff Bomba (2010, City)

Carm Bonito (1953, County; 1958, County; 1963, County; 1999, County)

Drew Botehlo (2006, City)

Steve Boucher (2004, City)

Jim Bowen (1962, County)

Mike Bowers (2003, City)

Terry Bowersox (1986, County; 1989, County)

Kevin Boxer (2005, City)

Roman Boykin (2010, County)

Bill Brabender (1964, City; 1971, City; 1974, City)

Russell Brant (1955, County)

Ken Brasington (1994, City)

Andre Bridgett (2002, City; 2008, City; 2011, City)

Jim Brinling (2008, County)

Mark Brooks (2006, County)

Jim Brown (1998, County)

Jeff Brzezinski (2003, City)

Doug Bubna (1995, City; 1999, City)

Dan Budziszewski (1979, County; 1992, County; 2006, County)

Joe Bufalino (1977, City; 1978, City; 1992, City; 2003, City)

Mike Burke (1998, City)

Dave Buzard (2002, County)

C

Jon Cacchione (2003, City)

Tim Cacchione (1985, City; 1998, City)

Tom Cacchione (2000, City; 2005, City)

Al Calabrese (1956, City)

Ralph Calabrese (1962, City)

Tom Calabrese (1979, City)

Chris Caldwell (2003, City; 2011, City)

Pat Callahan (2010, County)

John Campbell (2004, County)

Travis Carey (2009, County)

Chris Carpin (2006, County)

Jerry Carr (2002, City)

Kareem Carson (2011, City)

Joe Chevalier (2006, City)

Don Chludzinski (2003, County)

Mark Chludzinski (2003, City; 2009, County)

Jon Christensen (1972, County; 1975, City; 1983, City)

Jamie Cipalla (2001, County; 2007, County)

Dan Clark (1994, County)

Pat Comer (1989, County)

Jim Concilla (1968, County; 1973, County)

Darwin Cook (1958, County)

Don Costa (1986, County; 1989, County)

Jack Costello (1982, City)

Ron Costello (1969, City; 1980, City; 1987, City)

James Cowles (2012, City)

John M. Csir (2001, City)

John P. Csir (2010, City)

Bill Cummins (1939, East; 1940, East)

Bill Cutcher (1973, City)

Michael Cutter (2008, City)

Pat Czytuck (1986, City; 1989, City; 2001, City; 2010, City)

D

Jeff Dahlstrand (2000, City; 2004, City)

Joe Dahlstrand (1995, City; 2004, City)

John Dahlstrand (1995, City)

Marty Dale (2006, County)

Ed Dalton (1985, City)

Mike Daniels (1997, County)

Terry Darcangelo (1954, County)

Brad Darrow (1997, City)

Terry Dawley (2002, County)

Bruce Decker (1978, City)

Homer DeLattre (2009, County)

Frank Dennis (1966, County)

Frank Dennison (1947, East)

Dick Detzel (1959, City; 1965, City)

Duke Detzel (1951, East; 1958, City; 1964, City; 1967, City)

Tracy Dinger (2011, County)

Pat DiPaolo (2002, City)

Dan DiTullio (1981, City; 1990, City; 2006, City)

Ray Dombrowski (1957, City; 1965, City)

Pete Donatucci (1985, City)

Gerry Drabina (1976, City; 1996, County)

Ryan Drabina (2010, City)

Lowell Drake (1939, West; 1940, West; 1941, West; 1942, West; 1943, East; 1944, East)

Jerry Drozdowski (2000, County; 2010, County)

Tom Duff (1961, City)

Doug England (2002, City)

Tom Erdman (1983, County; 2006, County; 2011, County)

John Fails (1956, County)

John Falk (2000, County)

Mike Ferrare (1955, City)

John Ferrare (2005, City)

Tony Ferrari (1976, County)

Kyle Ferrick (1996, City)

Bernie Fitch (2000, County)

Jim Foti (1939, West; 1940, West)

Bill Frick (2012, County)

Jeremy Friel (1996, County)

Jim Funk (2011, County)

Tom Gage (1998, County)

Steve Galich (1994, City)

Darren Galkowski (2002, County)

Chris Gaub (2002, City)

Mina George (1986, City; 1989, City; 1996, City; 2001, County)

Jeff Gibbens (2000, City; 2005, City; 2009, City)

Paul Gibson (1947, West)

John Gillette (1975, County; 1978, County)

Phil Glass (2000, County)

Rob Glus (1998, County)

Paul Goll (1951, West; 1952, County; 1956, County; 1961, County)

Rich Goodenow (1999, County; 2005, County)

Jeff Goodwill (2009, County)

Scott Gorring (2012, City)

Dave Grack (2003, City)

John Graeb (2012, City)

Luke Graham (2003, County; 2012, County)

Rick Graziani (1996, County)

Rob Grygier (2002, County)

Chris Grychowski (2001, City)

Rick Grychowski (1989, City; 2001, City)

Ed Gumbert (1947, West)

Randy Gunther (2002, County)

Nate Hain (2006, City)

James Hall (1947, East)

Bob Hammer (2004, County; 2009, City)

Lou Hanna (1955, County)

Dave Hannah (1969, County; 1970, County)

John Hardy (1996, County)

Bernard Harkins (1940, West)

Al Harper (1939, West; 1940, West)

Ron Hayes (2008, City)

Nate Hein (2012, City)

Ed Heidt (2001, County)

Gary Hess (1994, City; 2004, City)

Stephen Hiegel (2010, City)

Bill Hoffman (2002, County)

Bob Hoffman (1994, City; 2003, City; 2004, County)

Brian Holland (1994, City; 2005, City)

Tim Holland (1994, City; 2004, County)

Tony Hollingsworth (2005, City)

Kevin Horton (2004, City)

D.J. Hough (2007, County)

Blair Hrovat (1986, County)

Chris Hudnol (2004, County)
Dave Hudson (2008, County)
Shawn Humes (2005, County)
Vern Hurlburt (1966, County)
Jim Hyde (1939, East; 1945, East; 1946, East; 1948, East; 1950, East)

Cy James (1947, West)
Bob Jamison (1960, County; 1965, County; 1969, County; 1974, County)
Tony Jenco (1996, City)
Scott Jenco (2003, County)
Jason Johnson (2011, County)
Jeff Joint (1996, City; 2001, County)
Ron Jones (1971, County)

K
Carl Karsh (1982, County, 1983, County)
Jeff Kerns (2009, County)
Tony Kitchen (1998, County)
Joe Kleiner (1970, City; 1973, City; 1979, City)
Kevin Klemm (2008, City)
J Knablein (2002, County)
Mark Knight (1999, City; 2001, City)
Jack Komora (1953, City, 1959, City)
John Kordich (1979, City)
Phil Koval (1982, City; 1984, City; 1995, City)
Rich Krafty (2006, City; 2012, City)
Sam Kramer (1939, West; 1940, West; 1943, West; 1944, West; 1947, West; 1950, West; 1952, City)
John Krkoska (1957, City)
Chubby Kuhl (1956, City)
Bob Kwiatkowski (1995, City; 1999, City)

Tom Laird (2002, City)
Rob Lange (2003, County)
Elliott LaPlaca (2012, County)
Jack Laraway (1967, City)
Lee Larsen (1975, City, 1983, City)
Tom Laska (1996, County)
Tiger LaVerde (2004, City)
Tom Lenox (2004, City)

Joe Leson (1939, West; 1940, West)
Dale Lewis (1996, County; 1999, City)
Mike Liebel (1996, City; 2001, County)
Jerry Lightner (2008, County)
Tracy Lindsey (2005, City)
Joe Lisek (1947, West)
Joe Lukac (1997, County)
Robert Lytle (1947, East)

M
Mike MacDonald (1995, County)
Craig MacKelvey (1996, County; 1998, City)
Gary Magorian (2007, City; 2011 City)
Walley Mahle (1999, County; 2005, County)
Jim Mahoney (1961, City)
Jim Manafo (1939, East; 1940, East; 1947, East; 1951, East; 1959, County)
Ed Margie (1994, County)
Jim Marnella (1971, City; 1977, City; 1980, City)
Jerry Mathis (1968, County)
Dave McDonald (2001, City)
D.K. McDonald (2003, County)
J.J. McGahen (1939, East; 1940, East)
Jim McGowan (1971, County; 1975, County; 1978 County)
Ed McMahan (2009, County)
Bill McNally (2011, County)
Jim McQuaide (1972, City)
Jeff McShane (2010, County)
Matt Melle (2010, City)
Dave Merritt (1998, County)
Harold Merritt (1998, County)
Carney Metzgar (1960, City; 1966, City; 1974, City)
Jerry Mifsud (1977, City)
Pat Mifsud (2003, City)
Eric Mikovch (1989, County; 1998, County)
Mike Mischler (2001, City; 2010, City)
Brian Moles (2000, City)
Paul Moneta (1979, County)
George Mooney (1939, West; 1940, West)
Joe Moore (1967, County)
John Moore (2001, City)
Bob Morgan (1969, City)
Matt Morgan (2000, City; 2006, City; 2012, City)
Thomas Muriel (2009, City)
William Muriel (2009, City)

Dave Murosky (2002, County)

Steve Musone (2009, City; 2011, City)

N

Bill Naughton (1991, County; 1999, County)

Tim Neal (2007, County)

Eric Neavins (2008, City)

Jeff Nichols (1991, County; 1997, City; 2008, County)

Jayson Nickson (2012, City)

Ken Nickson (2002, City)

Steve Nishnick (1991, County; 1999, County)

Tony Nunes (1984, County; 1985, County; 1991, City)

O

George Ogeka (1995, City; 1999, City)

Dan Olson (2000, City; 2005, City)

Brad Orlando (2003, City; 2010, City)

Ed Orris (1991, County; 1999, County; 2005, County)

P

Zack Palmer (2012, City)

Kim Parker (2007, City; 2011, City)

Mike Parmeter (1997, City; 2008, County)

Brian Patten (2009, County)

Jim Paul (1974, County)

Ray Pegg (1984, County; 1985, County; 1991, City)

Paul Pennington (2005, County)

Jeff Perino (1982, County; 1983, County)

Paul Petriani (1991, City)

Jack Pettis (1985, County)

Gary Picheco (1989, County)

Jim Piekanski (1981, City)

Ron Platz (2011, County)

Ed Poly (1947, East; 1954, County; 1959, County; 1964, County; 1970, County; 1977, County)

Ron Pontorierro (1991, City)

Fred Pusch (1939, East; 1940, East)

R

Stan Ralston (1940, East)

Dave Reichard (1997, City)

Keith Reynolds (1995, County)

John Rimmy (1957, County)

Marty Rimpa (1997, County; 1999, County)

Ted Robb (1949, East; 1952, City; 1954, City)

Joe Robie (1954, City)

Armand Rocco (2000, City)

Alex Rohde (1947, West)

Bill Ross (1994, County; 1997, County; 2009, County)

Ron Rudler (1993, City; 1998, City; 2007, City)

S

Dick Sabo (1962, County)

Tony Sanfilippo (1973, County)

Joe Sanford (1981, County; 1988, City)

Jim Schoonover (2004, County; 2009, City)

Ed Schneider (1983, County)

Doug Schreiber (1997, City)

Bill Schroth (1999, City)

Bob Sensor (1991, County; 1999, County; 2005, County)

Dan Senyo (2001, County)

Jim Senyo (2001, County)

Joe Setcavage (1952, County; 1956, County)

Tom Shade (2004, County)

Eric Sharie (2002, County)

Jeff Shaw (1982, City)

Jim Sheldon (2002, County)

Joe Shesman (1986, County; 1991, County; 1999, County; 2005, County)

Matt Shesman (2000, County; 2005, County)

Bill Shotta (1995, City)

Arnold "Rip" Simmons (1961, County; 1980, County; 1982, County; 1983, County)

Jim Sisson (1972, County)

Joe Sivak (1947, East)

Dan Skelton (2012, County)

Jim Skindell (2001, City; 2010, City)

Aaron Slocum (2010, City)

Tom Slomski (1999, City)

John Smilo (1964, County)

Mark Soboleski (1998, City; 2003, City; 2007, City; 2011, City)

Ted Sowle (1946, West)

Chris Spooner (2011, City; 2005, City)

Mark Srnka (2010, County)

Chris Starocci (2005, City)

Bobbie Stauffer (2012, County)

Todd Strasenburgh (2007, City; 2011, City)

Walt Strosser (1948, West; 1949, West; 1951, West; 1955, City; 1963, City)

Jake Szoszorek (2012, City)

Pete Szoszorek (2000, County; 2010, County; 2012, City)

T

Regan Tanner (1995, County)

Joe Tarasovitch (1994, City; 2004, County; 2009, City)

Tywonn Taylor (2008, City)

Dennis Teed (1998, County)

Ed "Pee Wee" Thomas (1946, East; 1947, East)

Gus Thomas (1967, City)

J.B. "Joe" Timmons (1947, West; 1953, County)

Jim Tonks (1977, County)

Tom Torok (1991, City)

Maurice "Mo" Troop (1999, City; 2008, City)

Lou Tullio (1960, City)

U

Tom Uglow (1979, County)

V

Ralph Van Stone (1939, East)

Bob Vasic (2001, County)

D.J. Vendetti (2001, County)

Tony Verga (1962, City)

Craig Villa (2007, City)

Jim Vogt (1988, County; 2000, County; 2010, County)

Bill Vorsheck (1965, County; 1967, County)

W

Ken Walker (1990, County)

Steven Wall (1995, County)

Adam Walstrom (2009, County)

Joe Wanson (2011, City)

Orr Weislogel (1996, County)

Jim Wells (2003, County; 2012, County)

Ken Westlake (1939, West; 1940, West)

Brad Wheeler (2012, County)

Scott White (2000, City; 2005, City)

Brad Whitman (2011, City)

Mike Whitney (2010, County)

Ed Williams (2008, City)

John Wilson (1981, County; 1994, County; 1997, County)

Paul Wilson (1960, County)

Sean Wolfrom (1999, County)

Lonnie Wright (2005, City)

Y

Paul Yoculan (1998, City; 2002, County)

Russell Yost (1947, East)

Bill Young (1963, County)

Z

Tony Zambroski (1958, City; 1963, City; 1968, City)

Dave Zewe (1982, City)

Mike Zona (2011, County)

Don Zonno (1966, City; 1970, City)

NOTE: Coaches names were obtained from game programs and newspaper reports. Assistant coaches were not always listed.

Save-An-Eye Game Referees

A
Dave Arneman (1990–2001, 2010)

B
Ed Betza (2008, 2009, 2011)
John Bradford (1939–1980)

C
Bruce Campbell (2004)
Marty Carroll (1990–1995)
Gerry Cassidy (2003, 2005, 2007)
Mark Chludzinski (2009)
Shad Connelly (2002, 2006, 2007)
Dale Cook (2010)

D
Greg Deemer (2005)
Chubbles DeFazio (1964–1967)
Darren DeFranco (2012)
Gerry DeLuca (2005, 2007–2009, 2011)
John DeLuca (2005, 2007–2009, 2011)
Bob DeMarco (1973–2000)

E
Scott Earl (2011)
Don Eisaman (2003, 2010)
Len Ekimoff (1974, 1977)
John Edler (1969–1971, 1978–1996)

F
Bob Finnecy (2002)
Pete Freed (2004, 2006, 2007)
Tom Fuhrman (1960–1971, 1973–1976)

G
Hank Galla (1939–1967)
Joe Gausman (1997–2000, 2009)
Jim Getty (2005)

H
Jerry Harkness (2004, 2006)
Bill Hale (1984–1988, 1996–2001)
Darin Hayes (1992–1998, 2002–2003, 2012)

J
Rick Johannesmeyer (2005, 2008)

K
Dan Kelly (2005)
Larry Kinter (2001, 2007)
Jim Klemm (2007)

L
Jeff Lane (1996, 2001, 2010)

Joe LeCorchick (1949–1972)
Huck Lininger (1980–1985)

M
Frank Macko (2006)
Vinnie Marchant (1960–1973, 1975–1985)
Dick McCrillis (1984–1998)
Chris McNally (2002)
Jim Mullaney (2001, 2009, 2011, 2012)
Dick Murray (1978)

N
Lou Nardo (1964–1969)

P
Ed Peck (2002)
Elmer Petrucelli (1988–2001, 2003)
Chuck Piano (2000)
Paul Pilatowski (2008, 2011)
Lou Presta (1981–1983, 1988)
George Puskar (1996–2001, 2006, 2010, 2011)

R
Frank Ropelewski (1948–1972)
Don Roth (1978–1980)
Lew Rundell (2004)

S
Michael Schreifer (1977)
Paul Schultz (2011)
Barry Shapiro (2002, 2010, 2012)
Joe Sivak (1963–1977, 1979, 1981)
Lorn Smith (2000)
Bob Stazer (2008)
Scott Steffy (1992–1998)
Don Stolz (1965–2001, 2003)
Dick Szocki (2012)

T
Rob Thompson (2006)
Jacob Tobolewski (2012)
Fred Trott (1972–1983)

U
Steve Utegg (2002, 2004, 2012)

W
Jim Wassink (1996–2000, 2002, 2004)
Joe Weidenboerner (2001–2002, 2008, 2009)
Chris Whitling (2002)
Dave Wiley (1982–1990, 2001)
Jim Wolf (2006)
Doug Wright (2004, 2010)
Bill Wykoff (1999–2000, 2003)

Frank Musiek, 1964 County

Tim Tyzinski, 1975 City, with his father
Chuck Tysinski's 1939 East jersey

Joseph Musiek, 1949 East

Dave Ostrum, 1970;
Gene Vogt, 1967;
Art Eller with 1972
County jersey;
Mark Eller, 1972; and
Dan Kosiorek, 1972.

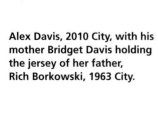

Alex Davis, 2010 City, with his
mother Bridget Davis holding
the jersey of her father,
Rich Borkowski, 1963 City.

Patrick Papale, 2010 County.
(Less than two months after
the 2010 game he died in
an automobile accident.)